THE

PRINCIPLES

OF

METAPHYSICAL AND ETHICAL SCIENCE

APPLIED TO THE

EVIDENCES OF RELIGION.

A NEW EDITION,

REVISED AND ANNOTATED, FOR THE USE OF COLLEGES.

By FRANCIS BOWEN, A.M.

ALFORD PROFESSOR OF NATURAL RELIGION, MORAL PHILOSOPHY, AND CIVIL POLITY IN HARVARD COLLEGE.

BOSTON:
BREWER AND TILESTON.
CLEVELAND: INGHAM AND BRAGG.

PREFACE.

THE substance of this work was delivered in two courses of lectures before the Lowell Institute in Boston, in the winters of 1848–9. These lectures were afterwards published, but the edition of them is now exhausted. Having had occasion to use the work as a text-book of instruction, for the students of Harvard College, in the leading doctrines of Metaphysical and Ethical Philosophy, considered as bearing upon the Evidences of Religion, I have endeavored to recast the materials in this edition, so as to render it more available for such a purpose. A few abridgments have made room for considerable additions, mostly in the form of notes, which are principally designed to elucidate and criticize at greater length those doctrines and theories on philosophy and science which were but briefly noticed in the lectures. In its present form, the work is designed to be a compend of the principles of Ethics and Metaphysics, so far as these affect the foundations of our religious belief. Some of the notes are merely explanatory, while others are intended, by citations from different writers, to support the positions maintained in the text. I have made free use, for this purpose, of the writings of Isaac Taylor, John S. Mill, Dr. Whewell, and Sir William Hamilton. In its present form, the work may be regarded as an imperfect supplement to the invaluable treatises of Dr. Butler and Dr. Paley, the principal object being to consider those objections and difficulties in the way of the believer which are of recent origin, or have grown out of recent discoveries and speculations in science and philosophy, as well as the important additions to the Evidences of Religion which have been derived from the same source.

In the Preface to the first edition, it was remarked, that though so many volumes have been written upon the Evidences of Religion, it does not appear that the subject is exhausted, or that the productions of a former age are, in every respect, suited to the exigencies of our own times. There are peculiar forms of infidelity, or peculiar causes of latitudinarian opinions in religion, which are more prevalent in one age than another. I have endeavored in this work to meet those objections and difficulties which are most current in our own day; to meet them with that course of argument and illustration which has seemed most satisfactory to my own mind, and without fear of incurring the charge of a want of originality on the one hand, or of a fondness for novel and abstruse speculations on the other. I have not been afraid, either to follow in the footsteps of others, if their arguments happened to be best adapted to my purpose, or to strike off into a new path, if I might thereby more surely and safely attain the great object in view. Those who find little that is new in this book, may be assured that it was not written for them, but for a class of readers who are less adequately informed upon the subject. Those who dislike abstract speculations, may pass it over for a similar reason; if they have never been entangled in a web of metaphysical subtilties, a clew to the labyrinth will be of no service to them.

Some repetitions may be found in these pages, as I have been more willing to incur the charge of prolixity and a frequent recurrence to the same line of remark and argument, than of obscurity or an affected abstruseness. The nature of the objections considered has unavoidably led me into some of the dark corners of speculation; but I have honestly tried to dissipate rather than increase the obscurity, and for this purpose, have often held up the same subject in many different lights, and looked at it from various points of view. Though the recapitulation, at the beginning of one chapter, of the argument in the preceding one, is not so useful for the reader as the hearer, I have allowed it to remain as it was written, because, when an argument has been once explained at length and with some minuteness, a brief summary of it often makes the connection of its parts more obvious, and the reasoning itself more clear and convincing.

In alluding to some of the novel opinions and theories in science and philosophy, which have gained a little popularity of late both in England and America, though their place of origin must be sought elsewhere, it has not been my wish to provoke controversy. Opinions may be freely discussed without causing offence; I have never referred to the individuals or sects who entertain and defend them. Some of these opinions, I am well aware, are held by many persons who unite with them a lively and steadfast faith, a devotional spirit, and a religious life; but they have been stumbling-blocks to others, for whom alone I have endeavored to surmount or remove them. The discussion of them has sometimes led me further into the territory of the natural sciences than it was perhaps prudent for one to venture who has only a general acquaintance with these subjects, and has never made them objects of special pursuit. But in these days, when knowledge is so widely diffused that the latest theories and discoveries in science are familiarly discussed in the newspapers, the bearing of these theories upon the religious belief of the multitude cannot be safely neglected. I have no fears of any conflict between the truths of real science and those either of Natural or Revealed Religion. The voice of nature, when rightly interpreted, never contradicts itself, and the truth that is fully comprehended is always sufficient for its own defence. But when sciolism is almost universal, speculations which usurp the name and garb of science may often give a rude shock to the convictions of a large class who are not well instructed enough to be able to separate hypotheses from established facts, and who can be dazzled by the fluent use of scientific phraseology. Such speculations are easily exposed in their true character, even by those whose studies have not gone beyond the limit which every educated person at the present day is supposed to have reached.

The business of a writer upon the Evidences is to reason, and not to preach. I have endeavored to show, that the fundamental doctrines of religion rest upon the same basis which supports all science, and that they cannot be denied without rejecting also the familiar truths which we adopt almost unconsciously, and upon which we depend for the conduct of life and the regulation of our ordinary concerns. The application of these doctrines to the heart and the life, is the business of the professed teachers of Christianity, into whose province I have not felt competent to intrude. Some may think that I have been too cautious in this respect, and have placed too little stress upon sentiment, and too much upon argument, as if religion were less an affair of the heart than of the intellect. To this objection it may be answered, that belief is one thing, and the regulation of conduct according to that belief is another. A cold and passive assent to the doctrines of Christianity, is not enough to constitute a religious life; but no one will maintain, that a Christian life is compatible with a denial of those doctrines, or with indifference upon the question whether they are true or false. Emotion which is not directed towards any object, nor excited by the contemplation of any truth, may spring from a source as low as mere physical stimulus; it is then animal rather than spiritual in its nature. Religious emotions must rest upon religious ideas and convictions, or they will be as transitory as they are vehement. The heart and the intellect must move together and in concert, for nothing can be more barren than their separate action, or more pitiable than a conflict between them. If there are any whose enjoyment of spiritual truth is never darkened or perplexed by doubts and questionings, they are those who have first acquired clear and distinct conceptions of what that truth is, and have then satisfied themselves, by study and experience, that it is founded upon a rock. It is doing no honor to our religious faith to p.ace it upon the footing of a necessary prejudice.

But as this subject is considered at length in some of the following chapters, there is no occasion to pursue it here. I wished only to express my earnest dissent from the doctrine which is now not infrequently avowed, even from the pulpit, that any study of the Evidences of Religion is unprofitable and vain. On the contrary, I believe that there has seldom been a time when such study has been more necessary than it is at the present day. Religious fanaticism has given way to religious indifference; the strife of sects with each other has somewhat cooled, but the strife of opinions upon all the great subjects that are interesting to humanity is more active and universal than ever. The thirst for innovation has greatly increased, and all restraint upon speculation in science, philosophy, politics, and social economy is taken away. In France and Germany, at this hour, [1849,] we see the mournful consequences of this chaotic state of public opinion, this upheaval of the foundations of belief. The best minds of the former country are even now engaged in an attempt to undo their own work, and to resettle the belief of the people upon those subjects in relation to which they had formerly conspired to shake it. The philosophical party in the French Institute, after being at open war with the clergy for a century, are now zealously coöperating with them in the endeavor to teach the fundamental truths of religion to a deluded and exasperated people. If society in our own country is not to experience a similar crisis, it must be through the efforts of the educated laity, working in concert with the clergy, to erect a barrier against the licentious and infidel speculations which are pouring in upon us from Europe like a flood. The time seems to have arrived for a more practical and immediate verification than the world has ever yet witnessed of the great truth, that the civilization which is not based upon Christianity is big with the elements of its own destruction.

CAMBRIDGE, January 10, 1855.

CONTENTS.

FIRST PART.

CHAPTER I.

CHAPTER II.

CHAPTER III.

CHAPTER IV.

CHAPTER V.

CHAPTER VI.

CHAPTER VII.

CHAPTER VIII.

CHAPTER IX.

SECOND PART.

CHAPTER I.

CHAPTER II.

CHAPTER III.

CHAPTER IV.

CHAPTER V.

CHAPTER VI.

CHAPTER VII.

CHAPTER VIII.

CHAPTER IX.

CHAPTER X.

CHAPTER XI.

FIRST PART.

CHAPTER I.

THE DISTINCTION BETWEEN PHYSICAL AND METAPHYSICAL SCIENCE.

Supposed conflicting claims of Philosophy and Religion. — According to a common opinion, Philosophy and Theology are sister sciences, so closely allied that it is often difficult to make a distinction between them. Every person must hold some opinions relative to each; and these opinions form two mutually dependent creeds, which may be, in a greater or less degree, peculiar to himself, and of which the action and reaction are so nearly equal, that it is often difficult to determine which is the parent of the other. Every theory respecting the origin and first principles of human knowledge must bear a close relation to that subject in regard to which knowledge is of the highest value, — the doctrine of God, duty, and immortality. The religion of the Greeks and Romans, so far as it existed in a definite and consistent form, — that is, as it was conceived by enlightened and thinking men among them, — was wholly drawn from their philosophical tenets, or, more properly speaking, it was identical with those tenets. And so it has been in modern times. Skepticism in philosophy and skepticism in religion, if not the same thing, at least usually go together

This, I say, is the common view of the subject; and we might therefore well expect, what often happens, that the claims of the two sciences, so called, should seriously conflict. Men are drawn different ways by opposite fears, — by their dread, on the one hand, of an *irreligious philosophy*, and on the other, of an *unphilosophical religion.* Loyalty to truth, which is the highest claim that can be made upon human reason, is drawn into open hostility with our sense of duty to God, which is the most awful and imperative of all obligations. The course of the student of science, the honest and sincere inquirer after knowledge, often appears adverse or injurious to the feelings or the faith — the prejudices, if you like — of the religious believer, the devout worshipper of an Omnipotent Father and Friend. And even where direct opposition is avoided, a disputed claim to precedence is set up, and sometimes brings with it an intolerable burden of anxiety and doubt. On the one hand, it is maintained that every religious creed must be tried at the bar of human science, and its doctrines accepted or rejected according to their agreement with the speculative dogmas which the unaided reason has evolved as the limits and criteria of truth; on the other, the sacredness of the subject is unwarily held up to shield theology from all investigation, and, not infrequently, discoveries in science and theories in philosophy are denounced, if they are at variance with the supposed dictates of revelation. If metaphysics are made a test of the truth of Christianity, it seems but equal justice to make Christianity a test of the correctness of metaphysics. Sometimes a compromise is proposed, which is no less shocking to the feelings of the believer than a contumelious rejection of his faith. Philosophy is represented as candid and liberal; as superseding religion, it is true, in the minds of the cultivated and reflecting classes, but continuing to respect it, as an imperfect likeness of itself, in the bulk of mankind. According to this theory, there are many stages of progress for the human intellect, and men pass on from religion to philosophy, as they do from barbarism to civilization.

Now, before conflicting claims like these can be reconciled, it is necessary to get clearer ideas of the subjects of dispute, to determine their respective boundaries, to see how far, if at all, they encroach upon each other, and, if possible, to settle the logic of the inquiry. Perhaps it will be found, after all, that the provinces of Philosophy and Theology are entirely distinct, so that there is no proper interference, and no cause for controversy between them. To establish this point is the object of the present chapter. We must begin with definitions, and if these appear somewhat abstruse at first, I hope they will become clearer as we go on.

Classification of the objects of Knowledge. — The simplest, as well as the most comprehensive, classification of all objects of knowledge, is that which separates them into relations of ideas and matters of fact. I borrow the language of him who was at once the most subtile logician and the most consistent skeptic of modern times: "All the objects of human reason or inquiry," says Hume, "may naturally be divided into two kinds, to wit, *Relations of Ideas* and *Matters of Fact*." This coincides very nearly with the familiar distinction between physics and metaphysics, except that the meaning of the latter must be so far extended as to embrace the cognate sciences of grammar, logic, and mathematics. Stating the proposition in other words, we say that all science may be reduced to two branches: — 1. The study of things physical, or those which exist distinct from our thoughts; 2. The study of things metaphysical, or those which do not exist apart from our thoughts.

No one can fail to see an essential difference between a fact and an abstraction, or a pure idea, like that of *cause, goodness, power, existence*, and the like. The former is an object of sense, something which can be seen, heard, felt, or touched, — whether we have had sensible evidence of it ourselves, or rely upon the testimony of others who have had such evidence, or infer its existence from inductive reasoning, or from the presence of its effects. The latter is a pure mental conception, which has no existence except in relation to the mind which forms it. Such conceptions are called *realities* only by a figure of speech; they are so called to mark our strong sense of the correctness with which a certain quality is attributed to a substance or an action.

Thus, *virtue* is said, figuratively, to be a *reality*, only to mark our firm belief that there are such things as virtuous actions. In this class must be ranked all the abstractions of the geometer and the algebraist. There are no such things in nature as circles and triangles; the only proper realities are circular objects and triangular objects.

Two classes of matters of fact. — But the nature of these abstractions may be most clearly apprehended by considering, in the first place, what we mean by *matters of fact.* These may be distinguished into *things which exist,* and *events which take place.* All the objects of natural history and physical science — stones, shells, plants, and animals — are ranked in the former class; all the laws, so called, of physical science, — the laws of motion, for instance, — all the habits observed by the naturalist, such as the modes of growth and reproduction of plants and animals, are comprehended in the latter. Both alike are matters of fact. It is a fact that the earth exists, or is; it is equally a fact that the earth moves. That there is a sun in the heavens is a fact of one order; that this sun illumines objects on the earth is a fact of a different order, — it is an event which takes place. We have sensible evidence of both.*

Mode of inquiry and reasoning about abstract ideas. — I am dwelling too long, perhaps, on a very familiar distinction; but it is one that is fundamental to the present inquiry, which cannot proceed without the fullest and clearest comprehension of it. These two classes, which comprehend all objects of knowledge, are distinguished from each other, not merely by the broad and obvious lines of distinction inherent in their nature, which have been already explained, but by *radical differences in the modes of inquiry and reasoning which are respectively*

* "The communication of this kind of knowledge," says Whateley, "is most usually, and most strictly, called *information.* We gain it from *observation* and from *testimony.* No *mere internal workings* of our own minds (except when the mind itself is the very object to be observed), or mere discussions in words, will make a *fact* known to us." — *Logic,* p. 268.

applicable to them. The *relations of ideas* — that is, of abstractions, or pure ideas — are made known to us by intuition or reflection; and reasoning about them proceeds by the demonstrative method, the conclusions at which we arrive being absolutely certain. According to the absolute laws of the human understanding, — I speak it reverently, — it is not within the power of Omnipotence to disprove these results, or even to render them doubtful. Their falsity would involve a contradiction; to maintain that they are untrue, is to say, that it is possible for a thing to be and not to be at one and the same moment. All the truths of pure mathematics, pure logic, and pure reason are metaphysical truths, and we can no more doubt them than we can question the accuracy of the multiplication table. Their falsity is inconceivable. This attribute of logical certainty proceeds from *the pure, abstract, and perfectly simple or uncompounded nature of the ideas which enter into such reasoning.* These ideas are pure creations of the intellect; in their uncompounded and abstract character, they are not derived from observation, and are therefore not perverted by that great source of error, the imperfection of our senses, or the limitations of our power of perception. When we entertain these ideas, or reason about them, the mind is closed to all outward impressions, and freed even from the memory of their former occurrence.* The ideas that are contemplated, then, are contemplated *in their entireness;* for, being uncompounded, *if they are apprehended at all, they must be perfectly apprehended,* and consequently the relations between them are discerned at once, or by intuition. Demonstrative reasoning proceeds by a series of such intuitions, and hence the absolute character of its results. If the chain of such reasoning be too far extended, indeed, without a system of notation, the

* "A clever man," says Sir J. Herschel, "shut up alone, and allowed all unlimited time, might reason out for himself all the truths of mathematics, by proceeding from those simple notions of space and number of which he cannot divest himself without ceasing to think; but he could never tell by any effort of reasoning, what would become of a lump of sugar if immersed in water, or what effect would be produced on his eye by mixing the colors yellow and blue."

imperfections of memory may come in, some steps may be forgotten, and mistakes will be committed. But this cause of error never affects a simple intuition, or a step in the process when taken by itself. Here the certainty is absolute.

Mode of inquiry and reasoning about matters of fact. — Now, what is the method of inquiry or procedure for the other class of objects of knowledge, — for *matters of fact?* We enter upon totally different ground here. Instead of abstractions, we have realities; instead of shutting out sensible evidence altogether, we are obliged to rely upon it exclusively; instead of intuitions, we have observations and experiments; instead of demonstration, we have induction; instead of the objects of inquiry being perfectly simple and uncompounded, they are made up of an *unknown and unknowable* number of elements and qualities; and instead of arriving at conclusions which are absolutely true, we gain those only which are morally certain. I speak now of *both kinds* of matters of fact, — both of things which exist, and of events which take place. The imperfections of the senses come in here to their full extent, as causes of possible error. *The objects of physical science must always be imperfectly known;* we never can be sure that our analysis of them is complete, or that our observation has taken in all their outward qualities. The attractive power of the loadstone was known for ages before its attribute of polarity was discovered; yet what is apparently more simple and obvious than this quality, which can be detected at once by floating a magnet on a piece of cork in a basin of water? Down to the times of Watt and Cavendish, water was supposed to be a simple element, and it figures as such in some of the most remarkable of the ancient theories of cosmogony; these chemists, about a century ago, discovered that it was compounded of two gases. But it is useless to multiply instances. The chemist will tell you that it is not impossible, that it is even probable, that every one of the sixty substances now counted as elementary will ultimately be decomposed. Of course, the vast number of compounded objects of which Natural History takes cognizance are still more imperfectly known in their qualities and relations, than those substances which, as yet, are reckoned elementary. This limited acquaintance with the subjects of investigation must lead only to qualified, and, *in the logical meaning of the term,* uncertain, conclusions respecting them.

If this is the case with things which exist, it holds still more obviously true of events which take place. Our knowledge of past events depends either on *memory,* with its acknowledged manifold defects, or on the *testimony* of others, with the multiplied causes which bring either their intelligence or their veracity into doubt. As to *future occurrences,* the field of positive science is yet more limited ; the truth of every proposition respecting them depends on the axiom, that the course of nature is uniform, and under similar circumstances we may look for similar effects. Now, in the first place, we never can be sure that the circumstances *are* perfectly similar; and, secondly, the truth of the axiom itself depends wholly on empirical evidence. It is possible, that is, it is conceivable, that the sun may not rise to-morrow ; but it is not conceivable that two and two should make five, or that a straight line should not be the shortest distance between two points. The laws of motion are instances of the highest generalization and of the most cautious and rigid induction, which the whole field of physical science can afford; but what assurance have we that these laws will hold good for one moment beyond the present time? Obviously, we can have only a moral certainty of their future operation; intuition or demonstration is here out of the question.

The two methods afford equally safe grounds of belief. — There is, then, a radical difference, or a difference *in kind,* between the two methods of investigation which are applicable respectively to physical and to metaphysical science. But so far as the truth of the conclusions, in either case, is concerned, this difference is not one *of degree ;* our conviction is just as firm in the one case as in the other. No one complains of the insufficiency of the evidence on which rest all the truths of physical science and all the facts of history. Our persuasion of the reality of our past experience, and of the truths which depend on that experience, would not be affected, certainly would not be increased in the slightest degree, by a technical demonstration of that reality or of those truths. In fact, the theorems of geometry are received, and practically applied, by multitudes who are incapable of demonstrating them. The carpenter, for instance, makes almost daily use of the forty-fifth proposition of Euclid, though he is not usually able to supply the steps of its logical proof; he knows that it is correct by the results of his application of it, and because he is told that others have demonstrated it, and that he could easily follow out the demonstration himself, if he were to give the requisite time and attention to the process. The mariner, also, steers his ship by the aid of his Practical Navigator and Nautical Almanac, though he cannot give the *rationale* of one of his own calculations. Instruct him in this respect, teach him trigonometry enough to demonstrate the rules of plain sailing, and you will enlarge the sphere of his ideas and add to his sources of intellectual enjoyment; but you will not increase by one iota the strength of his belief in the correctness of the processes.* The moral evidence

---

* Mr. Stewart remarks, that the mathematician himself is obliged to admit the evidence of *testimony* while engaged in his most abstruse investigations. "In astronomical calculations, for example, how few are the instances in which the data rest on the evidence of our own senses; and yet our confidence in the result is not, on that account, in the smallest degree weakened. On the contrary, what certainty can be more complete than that with which we look forward to an eclipse of the sun or the moon, on the faith of elements and of computations which we have never verified, and for the accuracy of which we have no ground of assurance whatever, but the scientific reputation of the writers from whom we have borrowed them. An astronomer who should affect any scepticism with respect to an event so predicted, would render himself no less an object of ridicule, than if he were disposed to cavil about the certainty of the sun's rising to-morrow.

"Even in pure mathematics, a similar regard to testimony, accompanied with a similar faith in the faculties of others, is by no means uncommon. Who would scruple, in a geometrical investigation, to adopt as a link in the chain, a theorem of Apollonius or of Archimedes, although he might not have leisure at the moment to satisfy himself, by an actual examination of their demonstrations, that they had been guilty of no paralogism, either from accident or design, in the course of their reasonings?"

on which it formerly rested in his mind was sufficient; the strength of the conviction produced by it could not be increased.

It is more pertinent to my present object to remark, that the conduct of human beings is governed exclusively by the evidence and the reasoning which are applicable to matters of fact, or, in other words, by experience. It is the only proof they have that food will nourish, fire burn, or water drown them, — that any place exists which they have never visited, or that any person lives with whom they have not conversed. These contingent truths enter into all our inferences from the past, and all our calculations for the future; man's life is guided by them, from the cradle to the grave. If it be objected to this view, that our convictions of *duty* are intuitive, and therefore absolute, I answer, that duty relates only to motives and a choice of ends; *action* is always a use of means, and the selection of means is the work of experience. The moral law, for instance, bids me cultivate honest and humane intentions towards my fellow man; how those intentions shall be most properly manifested in outward conduct, is a question for the intellect, and one that can be answered only by the lessons of experience. The sense of obligation stops short with the active intent.

The logic of physical and metaphysical inquiry. — Here, then, we rest the basis of our inquiry. *All objects of human knowledge are divided into two classes, perfectly distinguishable from each other; a distinct method of investigation, and a peculiar logic, or reasoning process, being appropriate to each. The conclusions at which we arrive in the two cases are equally well founded, equally deserving of confidence; but they differ widely in the kind or character of the conviction on which they rest, and in the nature of the process by which they were obtained.*

Evil of confounding the two methods. — My next proposition is, that these two modes of inquiry are not interchangeable, but confusion, uncertainty, and error invariably result from mistaking one for the other, or from attempting to extend the limits of either beyond its proper province. *Matters of fact cannot be demonstrated;* the attempt at a demonstration leads directly to that insane skepticism which teaches us to distrust or reject all experience. *The relations of pure ideas cannot be ascertained by the inductive method;* they can neither be proved by testimony, nor learned from experiment and observation. The trial of these inadequate media of proof tends only to deprive the soul of its highest convictions, and terminates in a mean and shallow empiricism. The history of science, from the earliest period down to the present day, affords numberless illustrations of the evil of confounding these two methods. The physical inquiries of the ancients were all fruitless, because their false notions of the dignity of science made them despise particulars and begin with general ideas, from which, by logical deduction, they hoped to obtain all special truths; that is, *from abstractions they sought to infer matters of fact,* and thus to change the labor of the inquirer from observation to reflection. *Their physics were all metaphysics.* "The early philosophers of Greece," says Dr. Whewell, "entered upon the work of physical speculation in a manner which showed the vigor and confidence of the questioning spirit, as yet untamed by labors and reverses. It was for later ages to learn, that man must acquire, slowly and patiently, letter by letter, the alphabet in which nature writes her answers to such inquiries; the first students wished to divine, at a single glance, the whole import of the book." As their first inquiry, they endeavored to discover the origin and principle of the universe. Thales maintained that it was water; according to another, it was air; while a third considered fire as the origin of all things. This last hypothesis, it may be remarked, has been revived by a popular cosmogonist * of our own day, who has found the seminal principle of all things, including the various ranks of animate being, the body, and even the soul, of man, in a primitive fiery mist. These wide and ambitious doctrines, it has been well remarked, are "better suited to the dim magnificence of poetry, than to the purpose of a philosophy which was to bear the sharp scrutiny of reason. When we speak of the *principles* of things, the term, even now,

* The author of the *Vestiges of Creation.*

is very ambiguous and indefinite in its import; but how much more was that the case in the first attempts to use such abstractions!"

Error of the Schoolmen. — The history of physical science, as it was studied by the schoolmen during the Middle Ages, is quite as unsatisfactory as the record of its treatment by the ancients. *Logic*, which I have ventured to class with the *metaphysical* sciences, because it is exclusively concerned with the relations of ideas, or with abstractions of the highest order, now claimed the chief attention in the schools. There were two reasons for giving it this preference: first, because it was held, as before, that *all knowledge might be deduced from general ideas*, so as to avoid the necessity of studying nature or observing *particulars;* and secondly, because it was believed that the ancients had already exhausted the inquiry and completed the work, so that all truth might be ascertained, and all controversies terminated, by a right interpretation of the works of Aristotle and his commentators, — this interpretation being governed, of course, by the rules of a sound logic. The scholastics held, "that all science may be obtained by the use of reasoning alone, — that by analyzing and combining the notions which common language brings before us, we may learn all that we can know." The fallacy of this, it has been well remarked, consists in mistaking the universality of the theory of language for the generalization of facts. All words, excepting proper names, denote either general conceptions or abstract ideas; and the study of the relations of words is therefore a study of the relations of ideas, and must proceed by the former of the two methods which we have been considering, — that is, by intuition and demonstration.

This method barren of results. — We might well expect that physical science, or the study of matters of fact, when pursued by this method, would produce only nugatory or profitless results. It has been stated on high authority, that not one step had really been taken in physical science down to the period of the Revival of Letters; — not a foot of ground had been gained by the labors of more than two thousand years.* This statement is perhaps too strong; for something was undoubtedly accomplished in astronomy by Hipparchus and Ptolemy, something in natural history by such observers as Aristotle, Theophrastus, and Pliny, while the medical profession, even at the present day, does not wholly repudiate the authority of Hippocrates and Galen. But how little real progress the human mind had made during this long lapse of centuries, may be correctly inferred from the round of studies pursued at the Universities; the course of seven sciences, included under the fantastic names of the *trivium* and the *quadrivium*, comprised grammar, logic, and rhetoric, together with arithmetic, geometry, music, and astronomy. Of these, only the last can be ranked among the physical sciences, as *music* was then only *an art* which had not been reduced to its *scientific* principles. The others are all *metaphysical in character*, and the only *organon*, or method of investigation, which was then in use, being appropriate to these, the success with which they were cultivated affords a striking contrast to the barrenness of physical inquiry. Logic came almost perfect from the hands of him who may be called its inventor. Sir William Hamilton, the most accomplished logician of our own day, asserts distinctly, that there has been, "in fact, no progress made in the general development of the

* "Of the criteria for guiding our judgment among so many different and discordant schools, there is none more to be relied on than that which is exhibited in their fruits; for the fruits of any speculative doctrine, or the inventions which it has really produced, are, as it were, sponsors or vouchers for the truths which it contains. Now, it is well known, that from the philosophy of the Greeks, with its numerous derivative schools, hardly one experimental discovery can be collected which has any tendency to aid or ameliorate the condition of man, or which is entitled to rank with the acknowledged principles of genuine science. Wherefore, as in religion, faith is proved by its works, so in philosophy, it were to be wished, that those theories should be accounted vain, which, when tried by their fruits, are barren; much more those which, instead of grapes and olives, have produced only thorns and thistles of controversy." —Bacon's *Nov. Org.* Aph. lxxiii

syllogism since the time of Aristotle." The case of mathematics is nearly as strong, the geometry of Euclid and Archimedes being still the boast of the science. These were the results of applying the appropriate mode of reasoning to the metaphysical sciences, or those which are concerned exclusively with the relations of ideas; while the inappropriateness of this same mode of reasoning to physical science, that is, to matters of fact, is proved by the almost total failure of all attempts in this department for more than twenty centuries.

Rapid progress of physical science after the Baconian reform. — It is not necessary to dwell here on so familiar a history as that of the sudden rise and extraordinary development of physical science at the close of the sixteenth century. The rapid succession of brilliant discoveries made by Galileo, Stevinus, and Gilbert, was in itself a proof that they had at length hit upon the true method of physical investigation, just before the illustrious Englishman — himself hardly capable of reducing any one of his own rules successfully to practice, but gifted with an intellect no less clear and penetrating than comprehensive and profound, and with a sagacity and hopefulness which unrolled before him the history of the future triumphs of science almost as distinctly as the record of its past defeats — supplied the *rationale* of this method, reduced it to a complete system, and evolved and stated with wonderful precision the rules for its successful use, in those immortal works which have gained for him the deserved title of Father of the Inductive Philosophy. To say that the inductive method was practised in some cases before the time of Bacon, is about as idle as to assert that men sometimes reasoned correctly before Aristotle wrote his Logic; though the assertion in the former case is not true to the same extent as in the latter, since the latter half of the century in which Bacon was born, though not that in which his principal works were published, witnessed the first successful application of this method to physical science. The merit of these two great men is of the same order; *each wrought out* with scientific precision and completeness *the logic of discovery and proof in one of the two great departments of human knowl-*

edge. The one taught us the theory of *reasoning syllogistically, or to a demonstration, about the relations of ideas;* the other showed us the theory of *reasoning inductively from matters of fact.*

Corruption of metaphysical science by the inductive method.— The extraordinary success of physical inquiry after Bacon's time tended naturally to the depression, and somewhat to the injury or corruption, of abstract science. The undue extension of the inductive method to the region of pure ideas produced the ethical system of Hobbes, himself a friend and disciple of the great master, but whose philosophy is now a byword from its degrading principles, and its tendencies to selfishness in morals, to materialism in philosophy, and to despotism in politics. Among his successors may be counted Mandeville, "the buffoon and sophister of the ale-house," and the English school of deists of the early part of the last century, including Bolingbroke, the friend and philosophical instructor of Pope. From him his satirical pupil learned to sneer at the metaphysicians of the older school, who, in the Universities or the Church, distrustful of the tendencies of modern physical science, and perhaps ignorant alike of its principles and its practice, still kept up their fondness for ancient and abstract learning.

A later instance of the erroneous application of the method of physical inquiry to metaphysical subjects may be found in the writings of the celebrated David Hartley, who endeavored to account for the course and association of our ideas by vibrations and vibratiuncles in the medullary substance of the brain. Of the same school was Dr. Priestley, whose just fame for his brilliant discoveries in natural science inclines one to speak tenderly of his philosophical speculations, though his habits, formed in the laboratory and other schools of experimental investigation, betrayed him into the avowed support of materialism, and of what he calls the doctrine of "*philosophical* necessity." The influence of the same cause of error may be traced in the works of the French philosophers, so called, of the last century, especially in those of Helvetius, Volney, D'Holbach, and Condillac. Helvetius, for instance, refusing to receive any other evidence than that of the senses, tracing all ideas to this source, and assuming the inductive method to be the only guide to knowledge, can find no cause for the superiority of man over the brute, except that the human hand is a more convenient instrument than the foot of a quadruped, which terminates in horn, nails, or claws. "The life of animals, in general," he observes, "being of a shorter duration than that of man, does not permit them to make so many observations, or to acquire so many ideas; and animals, being better armed and better clothed by nature than the human species, have fewer wants, and consequently fewer motives to stimulate or exercise their invention. Who can doubt, then," he triumphantly asks, "that if the wrist of a man had been terminated by the hoof of a horse, the species would still have been wandering in the forest?"

Such vagaries of speculation are not a whit more respectable than the opposite errors of the schoolmen, who sought to interpret nature by the relations of abstract ideas, or, in other words, to ascertain facts by the aid of a transcendental logic. It would be very unjust to accuse *the inductive method* of leading to these gross blunders, which have arisen solely from a misapplication of that method, *from an extension of it to a province which it was never formed to govern*, namely, the region of pure mental conceptions. We shall be likely to avoid both causes of error by keeping constantly in view the axiom, that the methods, as well as the objects, of physical and of metaphysical inquiry are radically different. We never can *demonstrate* a matter of fact; we can have no *sensible* evidence of the relations of *abstract ideas*. There is no question of dignity between the two methods; each is sovereign in its own sphere. *There is no superiority of the one kind of evidence over the other, when considered as a foundation of belief;* both lead to positive and well-founded convictions.

Confusion of the two methods in our own times. — The latest historian of the Inductive Sciences is not satisfied with this exclusion of metaphysical ideas from the domain of physical investigation; his work upon the Philosophy of these sciences, wh'ch is an elaborate attempt to enlarge the inductive method by the doctrines, and to clothe it in the terminology, of Kantian metaphysics, is a virtual restoration of the scholastic method, or the philosophy of the Middle Ages, and must be considered as "a remarkable instance of what has been aptly called the peculiar zest which the reaction against modern tendencies gives to the revival of ancient absurdities." When Dr. Whewell, in his glowing admiration of the brilliant discoveries recently made in natural science, expresses his confident hope * that the mere physical inquirer will soon pass on from a determination of the *laws of phenomena* to a knowledge of the *efficient causes* of these phenomena, and gives, as a reason for this expectation, the light that has recently been thrown upon the action of polar forces, one may be permitted to doubt whether he knows the meaning of the words he uses, or is able to distinguish *efficient* from *occasional* causes. A far more cautious thinker, Mr. John Stuart Mill, in his zeal for inductive logic, falls into an error of the opposite character, by boldly taking up the doctrine, that even the axioms of the mathematician are but generalizations from experience, that there is no distinction between necessary truths and facts of observation, and, consequently, that the reasonings of the geometer do not differ *in kind* from the inductions of the optician or the chemist. It is hardly necessary to say, that the common opinion of the scientific world lies between the extreme doctrines maintained respectively by these two theorists.

The case of the Mixed Sciences considered. — The case of the Mixed Sciences deserves consideration here, as it really corroborates the principles that have been advanced, though it may appear at first sight to conflict with them. *Pure logic* and *pure mathematics* are not so much sciences, as methods of scientific inquiry, or *organa* of investigation and proof. They are *modes of reasoning, irrespective of the subjects or facts which we reason*

---

* Nay, more; he does not merely *hope*. If language rightly conveys his meaning, he believes the thing *has been done*. He says, "Newton then discovered, *not merely a law of phenomena, but a true cause;* and *therefore* he was the greatest of discoverers!" Greatest indeed; if this assertion were **true**, he was *divine*. — *Phil. of the Inductive Sciences*, 2d ed., Vol. II. p. 32[illegible]

about, and therefore applicable to all subjects. In the syllogism, for instance, the conclusion follows with absolute certainty from the premises, the truth of the premises being presupposed; whether this truth rests upon sensible evidence, or intuition, or a previous demonstration, is of no consequence. The principles of the syllogism, then, are pure abstractions; and the letters of the alphabet, or purely arbitrary marks taken as signs of any ideas or facts whatsoever, are the most convenient notation for expressing them. If the premises are matters of fact, or contingent truth, the conclusion will also be a matter of fact, or contingent truth; only the relation between premises and conclusion is a metaphysical truth, and as such is made known by intuition.

Pure mathematics never lead to a discovery of matters of fact. — The case is precisely similar with mathematics, in which we employ a notation of the same sort. In its pure form, this science proceeds from abstraction to abstraction, the truth developed by it having no foundation in *fact,* and never being exemplified in the external world. If an event in the physical world, or a proposition founded on experience, be taken as a *datum,* or point of departure for the inquiry, however long the chain of mathematical reasoning may be which proceeds from it, the result at which we arrive is a truth of the same order with the one which formed the basis of the investigation. It has lost nothing, and it has gained nothing, in point of logical certainty, through the process to which it has been subjected.

Take, for instance, the most brilliant achievement that is recorded in the whole history of mathematical science, — the recent discovery, by Adams and Leverrier, of a new orb on the further verge of our planetary system. Its existence was long before suspected, for it was said that its influence had been felt trembling along the far-extended line of our delicate analysis. But *how* was this influence detected? It was through repeated *observations,* made by the telescope, of certain irregularities in the motion of Uranus, — observations so delicate, and irregularities so slight, that many years elapsed before it could be said with certainty that the latter were real, or before they could be measured so nicely as to afford a basis for the calculations which were to reveal the mass and the position of the body that caused them; — I say *the mass and the position*, for the general fact of *the existence* of such a body was inferred at once, by strict induction, from the mere knowledge that there were such irregularities.

A boat, moored at night by the side of a placid stream, suddenly heaves and oscillates as a few slight ripples move over the surface of the waters; and the watcher in that little boat, though he can descry nothing in the darkness, knows at once that some large object not far off is passing up or down the river, and throwing off those waves which extend obliquely from its wake. Had he instruments nice enough to measure the exact size and force of these ripples, and the aid of an empirical law, like that of Bode, to teach him that the object could move only through a certain channel at a known distance from him, he might calculate the size and exact position of the moving mass, so as to turn his night-glass directly upon it. This is precisely what was done by Adams and Leverrier. The calculation alone was mathematical; the existence of the new planet had previously been made known by induction, and the *data* used by the computers were all observed facts. And *it was not the mathematical process which afforded any new evidence*, or added to the convictions of astronomers that a hitherto unobserved planet rolled beyond the path of Uranus. *The calculations left this supposed fact precisely where it was before*, with the exact measure or kind of certainty which belongs to *a truth of induction*.* The crowning labor of the whole, the real *discovery*, which, in legal phrase, changed circumstantial to direct evidence, was made when Challis at Cambridge and Galle at Berlin turned their telescopes to the region indicated,

* "Calculation," says Dugald Stewart, "is certainly not an instrument of discovery at all analogous to experiment and observation; it can accomplish nothing in the study of nature till they have supplied the materials; and is indeed only one of the arts by which we are enabled to give a greater degree of accuracy to their results."

and actually *saw* the new orb which was causing this ripple in the heavens. In what sense, or with what color of reasoning, then, can it be said that moral evidence, the testimony of the senses, is inferior *in degree* to mathematical certainty?

Mixed character of ethical science. — It would not be difficult, in the case of any of the Mixed Sciences, to separate demonstrative from empirical truths, by simply inquiring whether the terms of the proposition express abstract or concrete ideas. Ethical science has this mixed character, quite as much so as Mechanics. Casuistry consists in the application of the general and abstract principles of ethics to particular cases; and here, from the difficulty of getting at or expressing all the facts in the case, doubt comes in. If I say, that *veracity is a duty of paramount obligation*, I affirm what no human being, in the full possession of his reason, will dare to deny, any more than to question the conclusions of the geometer. But if informed, on some express occasion, that I am bound *to tell the whole truth to a sick person, or a madman*, I demur; here is a particular case, and all the attendant circumstances must be noted; it seems necessary to inquire what are the motives for giving intelligence to such a person, and what will be the probable consequences of imparting to him the whole truth. I do not undertake to decide the point; moralists differ about it; and this difference is quite enough for my purpose, which is to show, that whenever we come down from the abstract to the concrete, doubts may reasonably and righteously be entertained. We have left the region of abstract truths, of intuition and demonstration, and come down to a practical application, to the world of realities, where a different method must be pursued; we must here observe facts, weigh probabilities, estimate consequences, and bring all the resources of the inductive logic into play. Let it not be said, that this is removing the certainty of moral obligation to a point whence it can never actually guide the conduct of men. In vastly the greater number of instances, *the light which observation and experience afford for the application of the rule is quite as clear and convincing as the boasted demonstration which supports the abstract principle;* and in the few remaining cases.

as the moral law relates exclusively to motives, there is no danger of fatal error.

Ultraism and fanaticism traced to the abuse of abstract principles. — And herein, as it seems to me, is one great cause of the abuse of general principles in morals, politics, and jurisprudence, and of the intolerable evils which are occasioned by fanaticism of belief and a reckless ultraism. It may be granted that the abstract principle, the grand object in view, is one of awful and imperative obligation, overriding all considerations of personal interest, and needing to be prosecuted with a martyr's zeal, perhaps even to a martyr's fate. But this admission does not justify me, on a particular occasion, in shutting my eyes and rushing at that object like a mad bull, careless of the injury or ruin that I may cause, or of the other duties that I may trample down in my path. *The question respecting the validity of the principle is totally distinct from that which concerns the choice of means, of the time and manner of carrying it into effect.* The former is determined by intuition, — by "the inner light," if you will, — by the candle which the Lord hath set up in every unperverted conscience, lighting him on to that clear, absolute, and immediate conviction which knows no doubt, and quails not at any personal sacrifice. The latter is to be settled by careful and anxious observation of the particular circumstances of the case, by a cautious induction of examples illustrating consequences, by examining heedfully and reverently all the other duties that may possibly be violated by our conduct. If this scrutiny be neglected, not even the glory of self sacrifice will avail to cover up the awful error, except, perhaps, in our own esteem. Omitting this, though the zealot should follow his principles even to the scaffold or the stake, his name shall not be encircled with the glory of a martyr, but it shall be said of him, that he "died as the fool dieth."

In what proportions demonstrative reasoning is applicable to the various Mixed Sciences. — Coming back for a moment to the main subject of discussion, it may be observed, that *the peculiar clearness and force of demonstrative reasoning seem to depend on that perfect knowledge* of the subjects of inquiry, which results from their *simplicity or uncompounded character.* In the science of Medicine, at least in the therapeutical branch of it, we need to know many or all of the qualities and constituents of very complex objects, — the medicinal qualities of the drugs, the peculiarities of the patient's constitution, and the circumstances of the moment, which may greatly modify the action of the former upon the latter. Obviously, this is the business of sheer empiricism, being in many instances no better than guess-work.* In Chemistry, we go a step higher, as it is necessary to attend, at most, to the qualities or elements of but one class of objects; still, we never can know that the analysis is complete, or the observation perfect, and are therefore obliged to grope our way by experiment and very limited induction, perhaps never establishing a universal principle by *a priori* evidence. In the science of Mechanics, we make a great advance, as many abstractions are employed, friction, the rigidity of materials, and the resistance of the air, being generally put aside; mathematical reasoning here comes into play, which had no application in the former sciences, and our conclusions are more abstract, more general, and *therefore less practically available.*† In Celestial Mechanics, it happens curiously, that the

---

* "The evidence on which the physician proceeds," says Dugald Stewart, "so far as it rests on experience, is weakened or destroyed by the uncertain condition of every new case to which his former results are to be applied. Without a peculiar sagacity and discrimination in marking not only the resembling, but the characteristical, feature of disorders classed under the same technical name, his practice cannot be said with propriety to be guided by any one rational principle of decision, but merely by blind and random conjecture."

† "That practical science which relates to the strength of materials," for instance, "combines the principles of several sciences. Let the problem be, to determine the necessary breadth and depth of the girder of a floor, that shall sustain a given weight, the length of the span also being given. Now, these dimensions are not to be found without having recourse, first, to the higher mathematics, or those purely *abstract* truths which are independent of all the laws of the actual world, and which would be what they are, although there were no such principle as gravitation, or no material system. In the next place, this law of gravitation

abstractions are, as it were, ready-made by nature, gravitation being the sole quality that it is necessary to take into view. Friction, the rigidity of materials, and a resisting medium — though of this last there may be some doubt — are eliminated by the nature of the case; the problem is complicated only by the gravitating effect of different bodies on each other. Our conclusions are very general, then, *but also very limited,* as they relate *exclusively to position and motion.* Astronomy, it was remarked many years ago, is a perfect science; and so it is, the theory of it, though the improvement of instruments is daily bringing to light new facts.

Thus it appears, that we approximate the sphere of metaphysical evidence and demonstrative reasoning just in proportion as we leave the world of realities and facts, and abandon the consideration of objects in their entireness, or in all their relations.*

---

must be understood, in order to find the point of the strain, as well as the true proportion between depth and breadth. And, lastly, the *peculiar properties* of the several species of timber must be precisely known, and *known by experiment;* . . . and it is not the *mathematician,* but the *naturalist,* who must inform the practical man on these points."

"Now, let it, in these cases, be supposed that the mathematician, dogmatically confident of his demonstrations, (and this is in fact the fault of the earlier mathematicians, and not seldom of Leibnitz,) to determine the problem above mentioned, *as if it were a pure abstraction;* or, if he referred loosely to certain vulgar facts concerning the strength of timber, were neither to make experiments of this physical kind, nor to swerve at all from his mathematical processes in regard to them: — in this case, all his products must be erroneous. Or, though correct *mathematically,* they would be inapplicable to the real world, and useless, or worse than useless, in practice." — Isaac Taylor's *Introduction to Edwards on the Will,* p. cxxxiii.

* Every one would wish to speak of Dr. Whewell with the respect which is required by his encyclopædic learning, his indefatigable activity of mind, and the zealous devotion of all his powers to the best interests of science and education. But it has been wittily said of him, that "his *forte* is science, and his foible is omniscience." It is to be wished that he had let metaphysics alone, and had contented himself with the glory of mastering, and doing something to improve, every one of the Inductive Sciences. His great work on these sciences contains, along with many ingenious disquisitions and a prodigious amount of learning, a great deal of bad phi-

losophy. He seriously undertakes to prove, that Astronomy and Mechanics are not Mixed, but Pure Sciences; that the data on which they rest, as well as the steps of reasoning by which they proceed, are intuitions of pure reason, independent of all experience; that *gravity*, for instance, is a necessary and inherent quality of matter, like *extension* and *figure*, — a doctrine which Newton himself emphatically disavows; and that the three primary laws of motion, in like manner, are not general *facts*, made known by induction, but are original and necessary truths, not evolved out of experience, but first revealed by careful study and reflection upon the train of our ideas. He thus binds himself to prove, (to adopt Sir J. Herschel's illustration,) that a clever man, shut up alone, might work out for himself, by dint of hard thinking, the whole Principia of Newton, without any aid from experiment and observation. These heresies have been sufficiently and sharply reproved by Sir William Hamilton, Mr. Mansel, (the author of *Prolegomena Logica*,) and, in advance, by Dugald Stewart. Hamilton argues thus: —

"Dr. Whewell asserts, 'that such propositions do not depend at all upon experience.' On the contrary, I maintain that all propositions which involve the notion of *gravitation*, *weight*, *pressure*, presuppose experience; for by experience alone do we become aware, that there is such a *quale* and *quantum* in the universe. To think it existent, there is no necessity of thought; for we can easily in thought conceive the particles of matter, (whatever these may be) indifferent to each other, — nay, endowed with a mutually *repulsive*, instead of a mutually *attractive* force. We can even, in thought, annihilate matter itself. So far, the asserted axiom is merely a derived, and that too merely an empirical, proposition. But, moreover, not only are we dependent on experience for the fact of the *existence* of gravitation, etc., we are also indebted to observation for the further facts of the *uniform* and *continuous* operation of that force; and thus, in a second (and even *third*) potence, are all such propositions dependent upon experience."

But Dr. Whewell remarks, if it be said that we cannot have the idea of pressure without the use of the senses, and this is experience, the same may be said of our ideas of relation in space; and thus Geometry, no less than Mechanics, depends upon experience in this sense.

Hamilton replies, "This is only another instance of confusion of thought and ignorance of the subject. The ideas of *relation in space* and the ideas of *pressure* differ obtrusively in this: — that we can, in thought, easily annul pressure, all the properties of matter, and even matter itself; but are wholly unable to think away from *space and its relations*. The latter are *conditions of*, the former are *educts from*, experience; and it is this difference of their object-matters, which constitutes Geometry and Arithmetic *pure* or *a priori* sciences, and Mechanics a science *empirical*, or *a posteriori*."

Mr. Stewart in animadverting upon the error into which Dr. Whewell has since fallen, has pointed out very clearly the bias of mind in which it has its origin. "As the study of the mechanical philosophy," he observes, "is, in a great measure, inaccessible to those who have not received a regular mathematical education, it commonly happens, that a taste for it is, in the first instance, grafted on a previous attachment to the researches of pure or abstract mathematics. Hence a natural and insensible transference to physical pursuits, of mathematical habits of thinking; and hence an almost unavoidable propensity to give to the former science that systematical connection in all its various conclusions which, from the nature of its first principles, is essential to the latter, but which can never belong to any science which has its foundations laid in facts collected from experience and observation."

"In pure geometry, no reference to the senses can be admitted, but in the way of illustration; and any such reference, in the most trifling step of a demonstration, vitiates the whole. But in *Natural Philosophy*, all our reasonings must be grounded on principles for which no evidence but that of sense can be obtained; and the propositions which we establish, differ from each other only as they are deduced from such principles immediately, or by the intervention of a mathematical demonstration. An experimental proof, therefore, of any particular physical truth, when it can be conveniently obtained, although it may not always be the most elegant or the most expedient way of introducing it to the knowledge of the student, is as rigorous and as satisfactory as any other; for *the intervention of a process of mathematical reasoning can never bestow on our conclusions a greater degree of certainty than our principles possessed.*

"I have been led to enlarge on these topics by that unqualified application of mathematical method to physics, which has been fashionable for many years past among foreign writers, and which seems to have originated chiefly in the commanding influence which the genius and learning of Leibnitz has so long maintained over the scientific taste of most European nations. I have [elsewhere] taken notice of some other inconveniences resulting from it, still more important than the introduction of an unsound logic into the elements of *Natural Philosophy*; in particular, of the obvious tendency which it has to withdraw the attention from that unity of design, which it is the noblest employment of philosophy to illustrate, by disguising it under the semblance of an eternal and necessary order, similar to what the mathematician delights to trace among the mutual relations of quantities and figures. The consequence has been, (in too many physical systems,) to level the study of nature, in point of moral interest, with the investigations of the algebraist; — an effect, too, which has taken place most remarkably, where, from the sublimity of the subject, it was least to be expected, — in the application of the mechanical philosophy to the phenomena of the heavens."

CHAPTER II.

THIS DISTINCTION APPLIED TO PHILOSOPHY AND THEOLOGY.

Summary of the last Chapter. — In the last chapter, I endeavored to define and distinguish the nature and scope of physical and metaphysical inquiry, — to show that the one was properly confined to matters of fact, and the other to relations of ideas. Demonstrative reasoning, I attempted to prove, belongs exclusively to the latter, and its conclusions are always abstract; the truths of physical science are obtained only by the inductive method, by observation and experiment, and by generalizations extending from individuals to a class. Yet the former method has no superiority over the latter, when considered simply as a foundation of belief. Both alike command our assent on indisputable grounds, though the media of proof are radically unlike. Sensible evidence and inductive reasoning, it is true, admit of degrees, and lead to all shades of belief, from the faintest probability up to what is called moral certainty. Demonstrative reasoning, on the other hand, has no degrees; a proposition is established by it either conclusively, or not at all. If successful, it would be contradictory and absurd to deny the conclusion, the proof being then equivalent, but not superior, to that which in the former case renders a fact morally certain. To adopt Locke's distinction between insanity and idiocy, we might say that only a madman can reject a mathematical proof after it has been once explained to him, while to be incapable of governing one's conduct by that sensible evidence which controls the actions of our fellows, is simply idiocy. Such a person is usually said to be incapable of keeping out of fire and water, because he is not able to learn from induction, or repeated experiment, that the former will burn and the latter will drown him. A very brief glance at the history of science was intended to sh.w, that most of the mistakes, retrogressions, and absurdities which have hindered the progress of it, may be traced to ignorance or forgetfulness of the distinction here pointed out, — to an attempt to deduce facts from abstract conceptions, or to draw down pure ideas to sensible observation and material tests, — to calling for demonstration in physics, or following the guidance of the senses only in metaphysical investigations. Illustrations of this error might easily be multiplied from the whole domain of science and speculation, not less numerous and apt in our own day, perhaps, than they were among the ancients or in the times of the schoolmen; but less conspicuous, affecting a smaller class of minds, and therefore less likely, we may hope, to be chronicled for the mingled amusement and pity of future generations. They are now the follies of a sect, a party, or a *clique,* — usually a small one; while in former days, they were the indications of a universal evil, proceeding from ill-formed habits of thought, and offering a far-extended and almost insuperable barrier to the progress of knowledge.

Nature and Object of Philosophy, or Metaphysical Science. — Leaving the task of mere illustration, then, I proceed to inquire how far the distinction now pointed out may be made available for one great purpose of this work, — to determine clearly the respective limits of *Religion* and *Philosophy.* It is obvious that the latter term, which is often applied very generally to the pursuit of all knowledge, must here be used in a restricted sense, and be made synonymous, in fact, with *metaphysics.* It cannot be defined more clearly, without a tedious enumeration of all the questions and problems which it comprehends. It is concerned with the origin and explication of our ideas of *cause, power, infinity, knowledge, freewill, identity, substance,* and the like, all of which are pure abstractions, so that we must reason about them demonstratively, or not at all. Philosophy, in this narrow meaning of the word, includes precisely that class of subjects which Milton assigned for contemplation to one band of the spirits fallen from heaven, who, in their place of punishment,

"apart sat on a hill retired,
In thoughts more elevate, and reasoned high
Of providence, foreknowledge, will, and fate,
Fixed fate, freewill, foreknowledge absolute,
And found no end, in wandering mazes lost."

All science proceeds from one generalization to another, and must therefore end at a point, in a science that surveys the basis of all the others, determines their proper relations, and binds the whole into one orderly system of knowledge. This seems to have been Lord Bacon's conception of the matter, when, in his general scheme of knowledge, he says, "The basis is Natural History, the stage next the basis is Physics, the stage next the vertical point is Metaphysics." To examine in turn all the questions with which metaphysical philosophy is conversant, so as to exhibit their abstract character, would be a long, and, it may be, an unprofitable undertaking. I shall not attempt it, as the fact, perhaps, is apparent enough from a mere enumeration of the subjects, and because all of them which are immediately connected with my principal theme will come up for subsequent consideration. It will be enough for the present briefly to allude to a few of them, the purely ideal character of which may perhaps be questioned by some persons.

Metaphysics distinguished from Psychology.—And here a distinction is to be made, as one portion of what is usually called the Philosophy of Mind is certainly occupied with matters of fact, and comes within the province of inductive reasoning. *Psychology* is the latest designation in use, and perhaps the most convenient one, for that science which bears the same relation to *mind*, that Anatomy and Physiology do to our *corporeal nature*. Certainly there are facts of consciousness, no less than those which are evident to sense; the human mind, to a certain extent, is a subject of observation and experiment, as the supposed seat or origin of various phenomena, that admit of number, arrangement, and classification. These phenomena, again, are not produced fortuitously, or at random, but are subject to fixed laws, more or less obvious, that may be definitely expressed. I need only refer to the great laws of association, or suggestion, which every one has occasion to observe who seeks to call up subjects that are related to each other, or to discipline his memory. The phenomena of mind, also, are often complex, and need to be analyzed and reduced to their simplest elements. Imagination, for instance, is a compound faculty, embracing simple *suggestion*, *conception*, or the picturing forth of an object, *abstraction*, and the power of forming novel combinations from the elements thus obtained.

I speak of this science as confined entirely to *mind*, without forgetting that one important point in it is the question, whether there be any such separate existence as mind distinct from matter. If this question be determined in the negative, it would appear, at first sight, that no division can be made, — that there is no room for any science separate from that which treats of the laws and properties of bodies. Yet the subject is not really affected by the determination of this doubt. Every one is conscious of *thinking*, *reasoning*, *willing*, — of *pleasure*, *love*, and *hatred;* and these qualities or phenomena are wholly unlike *bulk*, *figure*, *extension*, and other qualities usually attributed to matter. Now we do not need to assume, in the outset, that there is a separate existence, or entity, in which the first class of these attributes inhere. There is no doubt that the two sets of *phenomena* are perfectly distinct from each other; there is no danger of confounding *them*. Avoiding all hypotheses and mooted questions, therefore, it may be said that *psychology*, treating of those facts which we learn from consciousness, *is a branch of physical science*, the other subdivisions of which relate to those facts which come to our knowledge through the senses.

Metaphysics treats exclusively of the relations of ideas. — But it is certainly no part of psychological inquiry to seek after the origin of our notion of *cause*, or to analyze our idea of *infinity*. Observation cannot aid us here. In the external world, and in the succession of our thoughts, we witness only events or changes; we observe only sequences of phenomena; and to bind together the two terms of a sequence in the relation of cause and effect is the work of pure reason, unaided by the perceptive faculty. So, also, whatever we observe, whether in external nature or in the world within us, is finite, limited, and contingent; the idea of *infinity* is superadded by reason, transcending the sphere of sense and reflection, and baffling even the power of the imagination to seize or comprehend it. Our ideas, moreover, of *space* and *time* are abstract conceptions, which rise, indeed, on occasion of experience, but cannot be deduced from experience, nor explained by its teachings. To speculate on these things is the work of *metaphysical philosophy properly so called*, — of that science which goes beyond facts to principles, which begins from intuitions and ends in demonstrative certainty.

The scope and purpose of Ontology explained. — It may be said, however, that metaphysical inquiries are not concerned exclusively with relations of ideas, since Ontology, which is an important and the most abstruse branch of this science, relates avowedly, and as its name imports, to *real entities*, which are conceived to exist *out of the mind*, or independently of thought. I answer, that the realities which are the objects of ontological inquiry are few in number, and, though *supposed* to exist out of the mind, they are *known* to us only as abstract conceptions; and the sole purpose of Ontology, the only problem which it attempts to resolve, is the question *whether they are realities or not.* This point cannot be ascertained by observation and experiment, which are the great instruments of physical inquiry; it can be determined only by studying the relations of our ideas.

Take, for instance, the idea of *material substance*, which we conceive of only as *the unknown something that supports and manifests certain qualities*, even these qualities being known to us only as *the hidden causes of certain sensations*, or states of mind; and this idea, these states of mind, are the only *media* the study of which can furnish an answer to the question as to the reality of this substance. Aristotle calls this substance "the primary matter," to distinguish it from the secondary forms of matter, that are the only objects of which we take cognizance through the senses. "The primary matter," he says, "is that without which nothing could *formally* exist. It is neither earth, nor air, nor fire, nor water. It is neither hot, nor cold, nor dry, nor moist, nor solid, nor extended. It is the universal element, but can never become objective to sense." How, then, can we obtain a view of this elementary being? "We gain a glimpse of it," says the learned author of Philosophical Arrangements, "*by abstraction*, when we say that the first matter is not the lineaments and complexion, which make the beautiful face; nor yet the flesh and blood, which make those lineaments and that complexion; nor yet the liquid and solid aliments, which make that flesh and blood; nor yet the simple bodies of earth and water, which make those various aliments; but something which, being below all these, and supporting them all, is yet different from them all, and essential to their existence." Certainly, this idea is a *pure abstraction*, quite as much so as the infinitesimal quantities of the algebraist; and though reality may be predicated of it, if we believe in its existence, it is only in the same sense in which quantities infinitely small may be said actually to exist anywhere in measurable extension.

Instances of the corruption of physical science by metaphysical ideas. — And here, it may be observed in passing, we have an illustration of the radically vicious method in which the ancients undertook the study of nature; omitting altogether the observation of particular facts, and seeking to deduce from grand but vague abstractions, like this of "the primary matter," the individual truths which they disdained to collect from patient induction. It was as if a botanist should attempt to evolve by meditation the grand archetypal idea of a plant, from which to deduce, by logical analysis and strict demonstrative reasoning, the several forms which all existing plants *must* assume. We ought not rashly to infer that there is no longer any danger of committing flagrant mistakes like this in the pursuit of knowledge. Error tends to come round in cycles; and the reaction against the Baconian method, to which I alluded in the last chapter, has given some currency to speculations in natural science which seem the legitimate descendants of the reveries of the schoolmen. Take, for instance, the infant science of Morphology, applied to animals by Geoffroy St. Hilaire, and to plants by Goethe, and which has recently been made popular, at least in some of its applications, by the author of the "Vestiges of Creation." According to this speculation, "plants and animals, in the process of growing up from their germs, have a tendency to develop themselves in a much more uniform manner than they in fact do; and the differences — for example, of leaf, flower, and fruit — are mere modifications of one general phenomenon." The theory assumes, that the type, or grand purpose of nature, though constantly struggling to manifest itself, is realized only in a few cases, which are *admitted monstrosities*, the system resting on these, and *the induction from a few anomalous instances thus overriding the conclusion derived from the great majority of cases.* The doctrine naturally succeeds, that all the races of animals tend, as it were, to pass into each other, in their progress to or from the typical creature, which forms either the commencement or the end of the scale. The distinctions of species thus disappear, races cease to be permanent, and man acknowledges fraternity, or a common pedigree, with the reptile and the brute. A purely speculative notion is here superinduced upon the inductions of experience, though a lingering respect is still manifested for the Baconian method, the theory being defended by a spurious induction from a few monstrosities. And this view we are invited to entertain as a substitute for the doctrine of final causes! *

The question, whether the external world exists, is virtually metaphysical. — But this is a digression; I return to the only other question in metaphysical science which it is necessary to consider here, as a seeming exception to the doctrine that this science is concerned exclusively with the relations of abstract ideas. I refer now to the discussion respecting *the real existence of the external world*, a question distinct in some respects from the one already noticed respecting *the abstract conception of material substance.* And here a distinction is to be made between the popular belief and the philosophical doctrine, or

* Schiller made the best criticism upon this theory, when it was first explained to him by Goethe, who was one of its earliest advocates, if not its inventor. "This," said Schiller, "is not an *observation*, but an *idea*."

rather between *the causes that actually create our assent* to the proposition, and *the reasons by which*, when subsequently called upon, *we undertake to justify that assent.* Certainly, to all minds not yet accustomed to philosophical inquiries, the existence of an external world is *a fact*, and, as such, is learned by induction. There can be no reasonable doubt, I think, that the sensations of an infant are not accompanied by what we call *perception;* that they are not referred by it to an external cause; that they give it no information at first respecting outward realities, but are to it merely so many sources of pleasure or pain. By a gradual process, that is, by induction, finding that the sensations recur in a fixed order under given circumstances, that they are wholly independent of the will, that muscular exertion can sometimes be made without restraint, and at others, is checked or resisted by a foreign obstacle, the infant mind comes at last to a conception of outward things, or of existences foreign to itself.

Whether this induction is so complete, that we can consider the independent existence of brute matter as *proved* by it, is another question. It *does prove*, that there must be *some* cause of these sensations, which cause is foreign to our own minds; and this is enough to disprove the monstrous idealism of Fichte, that we create every thing from ourselves, though the doctrine of Berkeley remains quite as plausible as the vulgar belief, and rests, perhaps, on a more philosophical basis. Those who ridicule it, it is safe to say, do so from ignorance of its true character; and this remark will apply even to the great English moralist, who, when teased by his biographer about this doctrine, undertook to decide the case in his own peculiar manner. "I never shall forget," says Boswell, "the alacrity with which Dr. Johnson answered, striking his foot with mighty force against a large stone, till he rebounded from it, — 'I refute it *thus.*'" The argument implied in this act proves nothing but the essential shallowness of Johnsonian dogmatism; for it is *an appeal to facts*, to sensible evidence, *to settle an abstract philosophical question.* As mooted by philosophers, this question refers to the objective validity of our abstract idea of outward things, and as such it must be settled, if at all, by metaphysical reasons; and he who brings into this discussion the testimony of the senses, acts quite as absurdly as a metaphysician would do, who, by his abstract speculations, should undertake to confound a common man's belief in the reality of things about him.* Here, as everywhere else, the physical fact rests upon its appropriate inductive evidence; while the philosophical question must be treated philosophically, or by metaphysical considerations. The speculative attempts, extended, modified, and perpetually recurring through the whole history of philosophy, to *demonstrate* the independent existence of matter, have left the question precisely where it was, — have created nothing but an interminable logomachy, or war of words, between the realists and the idealists. The result of this warfare was pithily summed up by Dr. Brown, when speaking of the two great champions in Scotland of the opposite doctrines on this subject: "Reid bawled out, 'We must believe in an external world,' but added in a whisper, 'I own we can give no reason for this belief;' Hume cried out, 'We cannot *prove* the existence of matter,' but he whispered, 'I confess we cannot help believing it.'" †

---

* The idealist doubts not the reality of ideas and sensations, *as such*. Nature exists for him also, but only in his own mind. He fully believes the uniformity of her laws, — that like causes will produce like effects. He is confident, for instance, that the *idea* of falling from a precipice will be followed by the *idea* of exquisite pain; and if he has common sense, he will avoid those volitions which, as constant experience has taught him, will lead to its occurrence. He does not, it is true, fear the fracture of a bone; for he thinks there are no bones to break. But he dreads *the conception* of such an injury, and the pain which must attend such a conception. Since we are no further interested in our bodily frame than as it is a source of pleasure or pain, and as these feelings belong, not to matter, but to mind, the idealist is no more chargeable with inconsistency than one who attempts to prevent the recurrence of a painful dream.

† The question about the reality of the external world is very fairly stated by Prof. De Morgan, in the second chapter of his "Formal Logic."

"That our minds, souls, or thinking powers, (use what name we may,) exist, is the thing of all others of which we are most certain, each for himself. Next to this, nothing can be more certain to us, each for himself, than that other things also exist; — other minds, ur own bodies, the

Nature and logic of religious belief. — Enough has been said to show the true purpose of metaphysical philosophy, the nature of the subjects with which it is conversant, the kind of reasoning employed, and the proper limits of the discussion. Let us pass on, then, to a precisely similar inquiry respecting religion. What is the nature of religious belief, properly so called? and

---

whole world of matter. But between the character of these two certainties, there is a vast difference. Any one who should deny his own existence, would, if serious, be held beneath argument; he does not know the meaning of his words, or he is false or mad. But if the same man should deny that any thing exists except himself, that is, if he should affirm the whole creation to be a dream of his own mind, he would be absolutely unanswerable. If I, (who *know* he is wrong, for *I* am certain of *my own* existence,) argue with him, and reduce him to silence, it is no more than might happen in his dream. (It is not impossible that, in a real dream of sleep, some one may have created an antagonist who beat him in an argument to prove that he was awake.) A celebrated metaphysician, Berkeley, maintained that, with regard to matter, the above is the state of the case; that our impressions of matter are only impressions, communicated by the Creator without any intervening cause of communication.

"Our most convincing communicable proof of the existence of other things, is, not the appearance of objects, but the necessity of admitting that there are *other minds* besides our own. The external inanimate objects might be creations of our own thoughts, or thinking and perceptive function; they are so sometimes, as in the case of insanity, in which the mind has frequently the appearance of making the whole or part of its own external world. But when we see other beings, performing similar functions to those which we ourselves perform, we come so irresistibly to the conclusion that there must be other sentients like ourselves, that we should rather compare a person who doubted it to one who denied his own existence, than to one who simply denied the real external existence of the *material* world.

"When once we have admitted different and independent minds, the reality of external objects (external to all those minds) follows as of course. For different minds receive impressions at the same time, which their power of communication enables them to know are similar, so far as any impressions, one in each of two different minds, can be known to be similar. There must be a *somewhat* independent of those minds, which thus acts upon them all at once, and without any choice of their own. This *somewhat* is what we call an external object; and whether it arise in Berkeley's mode, or in any other, matters nothing to us here."

by what kind of testimony is it supported? Are we here concerned with realities, or with abstract speculations? and do we look to demonstration, or to moral certainty, as the result of the inquiry? The question is not yet, be it observed, whether the belief is legitimate, or the testimony sufficient; of that, hereafter. I do not now ask whether religion be true, but how we are to prove or to disprove it; what arguments are to be admitted into the discussion, and what considerations shut out as irrelevant. I use the word *religion* here in its most comprehensive sense, including both theology, as a system of doctrines and principles, and practical piety.

The being of a God is a fact. — The central truth of religion, on which all its other doctrines and its practice depend, is the being of a God. Is there, in very truth, a creating and sustaining Deity, or is this universe an orphan, and we, most miserable, but accidental formations from the clod, living only to consume life, relying on no support but our own strength, and looking forward to painless extinction as the happiest possible termination of our short and troubled career? Surely, we are able to say, that the Divine existence, if proved, is a fact, and the most momentous of all facts; it is at once the most consoling and the most awful of all realities. I do not forget that the name of the Supreme Being is often vaguely used; because it is said that his existence is a mystery, and his essence is unknown, for the finite creature cannot comprehend the Infinite. *So neither can we comprehend ourselves;* our own existence is a mystery, and we are surrounded with problems that we cannot solve. The lowest and the highest manifestation of *life* is alike a secret that baffles the most cunning researches of science; we can describe, meagrely and imperfectly, it is true, but we cannot explain it. If no knowledge is admissible, or deserves its name, except it be *perfect*, then indeed we are doomed to hopeless and perpetual ignorance. In this respect, the grand dogma of the being of a God is on a par with the simplest fact of physiology, or with a belief in the actual existence of any fellow-mortal whom we have never seen.

Different conceptions of a Deity. — But I go much further;

considered as a truth of religion, the being of a God is a sufficiently definite and intelligible fact, to enable us to pronounce at once on the general character of the evidence by which, if at all, it must be proved. If we discard all notion of an overruling Providence, and adopt only the Epicurean idea of the Supreme Being, as one sitting apart from his works, and allowing them to go on without interference, oversight, or regard, then indeed the question concerning the reality of such an existence is one of pure curiosity, to be ranked with other problems in science, as a matter of no immediate interest except to the student. We may sublimate that existence into an *abstract conception*, or identify it with *material nature;* and as either alternative is adopted, we may attempt to support it by physical or metaphysical reasoning. But the religious aspect of the subject compels us to bring down the question to the actual existence of a Moral Governor of the world. We care not whether the dogma, considered simply as a fact or a proposition in science, be established or refuted. Our only interest in the matter, looking at it not as philosophers, nor as students of science, *but as men*, arises from the influence which the fact, if proved, will have upon our conduct and the regulation of our hearts and lives. The question does not affect us, unless it be understood to relate to *the being of a personal God, the Creator of heaven and earth, really distinct from nature, though pervading it with his presence, all-wise and all-powerful, the conscious Cause and present Ruler of all things.* I am not taking these attributes for granted, but simply stating the question, — the only question which, as *moral* beings, we are concerned to answer. Whatever might be made of the *philosophical conception* of a Deity, or however curious and interesting to the merely rational mind might be the solution of the problem respecting the *mode* of his existence, or the reconcilement of his attributes with each other, it does not affect us, considered simply as seekers after religious truth, or as endeavoring to satisfy the longings of that *religious sentiment* which, like the desire for society, or the domestic affections, or the inherent love of right, I firmly believe to be a constituent and ineradicable principle of human nature. The proper object of that sentiment is a *person*, a moral being; its natural and even irresistible expression is in worship and prayer. We must seek to gratify it, then, just as we might attempt, if suffering under a sense of loneliness, to appease our social cravings; — first, to ascertain the fact that a companion can be found, and then to draw near to him in that spirit of loving trust, and, if necessary, of self-sacrifice, which will be sure to make him, when found, our friend.

Demonstrative evidence not applicable in this inquiry. — We cannot, then, *demonstrate* the existence of a God. If there is any force in the considerations which I have tried to lay before you, this admission is not an alarming one. We do not here attempt to weigh the abstract argument for this end, and pronounce it to be weak or insufficient; opinions might differ on this point; we put it aside altogether, as *illogical and irrelevant.* It has nothing to do with the matter in hand. We reject it for the same reason that an historian would reject, as an idle exercise of ingenuity, an attempt, made without any reference to the testimony of persons, books, or monuments, to prove, from abstract conceptions and the laws of the human mind, that a great battle *must* have been fought nearly twenty-five hundred years ago on the plains of Marathon, and that the Grecian forces in this battle *must* have been commanded by a general called Miltiades. We say that metaphysical reasoning is inapplicable here, on the same principle on which the chemist, when about to investigate the affinities of a newly discovered substance, would refuse to substitute pure mathematical analysis for the logic of the crucible, the scales, and the blowpipe. He would say, that the former mode of investigation was precluded by the nature of the case; and as the selection of the proper means of research is a question of pure logic, which is itself one of the metaphysical sciences, it would not be going too far for him to assert, that he could *demonstrate the inapplicability of demonstration.*

Why we seek to exclude metaphysical reasoning. — It may be asked, why I have taken so much pains with this preliminary matter, which is merely the logic of natural theology. Why seek to strike out abstract reasoning, and to bring the question down to the limits and principles of the inductive method, so that our researches may be governed by the rules of physical inquiry? Unquestionably, every sincere believer would be glad to accept a demonstration of the truths of religion, if it could be had; why endeavor to cut him off even from the hope of a possible future enlargement, in this way, of the grounds of his faith?

I answer, *first*, that it is of great importance so to arrange the system of our belief, that proofs of the same general character may be classed together, and the relative strength of different arguments may be clearly ascertained. They lose their proper weight in our estimation, if brought to a false standard, or tried by an insufficient test. *A pretended demonstration* of a matter of fact, if compared with the reasoning of Euclid or Laplace, *must appear*, I do not say *feeble*, but *illogical and false;* and the failure of a favorite argument is very likely to draw down with it, in the mind of the inquirer, all faith in the doctrine itself, its other supports being then disregarded or held in light esteem. I would save the earnest seeker after truth from the anguish of disappointment, in looking after what cannot be found, and thereby enable him duly to appreciate the strength of the proofs within his reach. There can be no fears for the strength of our religious faith, if it stands upon the same platform with the whole round of the physical sciences, so that no assault can reach even its outworks until the entire fabric of these sciences shall be demolished, and it be made to appear that all the boasted attainments of the last three centuries in the study of nature have been unprofitable and vain.

Kind and degree of the theological proof. — The theological argument is of the same *kind* with that which supports the conclusions of the physical inquirer; but it is superior, immeasurably superior, in *degree*. The proofs of design, for instance, which form the basis of one portion of this argument, are numerous beyond calculation. They are diffused everywhere, — above, around, and within us. They are not drawn only from a few scratches on mountains of rock, or from fossil remains here and there dug up from the earth, put together with slow toil, and their history with difficulty spelt out. They do not rest on a few experiments carefully devised and with great labor repeated. The study of years is not required before their import can be made known even to a few, while the bulk of mankind must ever remain ignorant of the doctrine, or receive it on trust. These are difficulties with which the geologist, the chemist, the astronomer, must contend. But the marks of contrivance that form the language in which the sublime dogma of God's existence is written out fill the earth and skies, and are open alike to the most elevated and the meanest capacity. They are equally obvious in the structure of every blade of grass, and in the mechanism of the heavens. They exist alike in the object perceived, and in the percipient mind ; in the hand that fashions, the ear that hears, and the lungs that breathe. They are found in the bones of extinct races, and in the habits of all living things; in the skeleton of the mammoth, and in the instinct which teaches the bee to frame its wonderful cell, and guides the waterfowl to its nest. The atmosphere, that wraps the earth in a garment, testifies His presence; and the sun bears witness to Him who lighted up its fires. "There is no speech nor language where their voice is not heard. Their line is gone out through all the earth, and their words to the end of the world."

Irrelevancy of metaphysical objections. — *Secondly*, we seek to confine this inquiry within its legitimate boundaries, because the grounds which justify the exclusion of metaphysical *proofs* show also the irrelevancy of metaphysical *objections*. It needs but little study of the evidences of natural religion to convince one, that the arguments which have been brought *against* the doctrine of the being of a God, *are, almost without exception, abstract or metaphysical* in character. They are founded on alleged imperfections in our knowledge of cause and effect; on a supposed inconsistency of the attribute of infinity with the moral qualities of God; on the assumed inviolability of abstract but personified laws; on the difficulty of conceiving of eternal duration, or of any person who is increate; on the fallacy of reasoning from what is finite to what is infinite; and last and chiefly, on the absence of demonstration itself, which, it is taken for granted, is quite as essential in this case as for establishing a proposition in geometry. To take away the whole basis of these objections, by showing that they are no more pertinent to the subject in hand than to the doctrines of physical science, is to contribute most effectually to the argument of the theist.* If it be proved, that reasoning from such premises is nugatory and inapplicable, the very groundwork of the systems of Spinoza, Hume, Kant, Fichte, and other modern infidels, is removed, and the superstructure falls. The philosophy which attempts to define and demonstrate all things, necessarily leads to fatalism. In the posthumous work of Spinoza, may be found the perfect type of these demonstration-seeking systems,—systems which can never really transcend the sphere of the abstractions on which they are founded, and therefore never can consistently admit a Deity, except in that pantheistic sense which regards God as a pure idea, that is necessarily involved in all existence, and ends in an avowed identification of the Divinity with the material universe. The title of his book, "Ethics reduced to a Geometrical System, and proved by the Geometrical Method," answers to its contents; as he begins with a list of axioms and definitions, and proceeds, by a series of theorems and proofs, to that doctrine of atheistic fatalism which has been the seminal principle of the infidel philosophy of Germany down to the present day.

Infidel systems compared with ancient mythology.—I have no fears for the security of the theist's faith, when it rests on the same basis with all the doctrines of natural science, and with all

* "If Christianity be a system of metaphysical deductions, it must of course maintain itself among other principles of the same class; and must bring all its positions into accordance with them; or must vanquish them with the weapons of scholastic warfare, and must appeal to abstract truths on every occasion of controversy. But if it be simply and solely a matter of history (as to its truth), and of verbal affirmation (as to its doctrines), then nothing can be more enormous than the attempt to bring the general fact, or the particular affirmations, into collision with the principles of metaphysical science."—Taylor's *Introduction to Edwards on the Will*, p. 140.

the conclusions which govern the daily conduct of men. To distrust such evidence, or to be incapable of acting upon it, is the common test of the folly that borders upon idiocy; and to such an unbeliever, therefore, may be literally applied the words of Scripture, "The fool hath said in his heart, There is no God." The infidel systems of modern philosophy agree very nearly with the mythology of the ancients, which admitted "Fate, Chance, Nature, Time, Space, to be real beings, — nay, even gods." "Mankind in all ages," says Mr. J. S. Mill, "have had a strong propensity to conclude, that, wherever there is a name, there must be a distinguishable separate entity corresponding, and every complex idea, which the mind has formed for itself by operating upon its conceptions of individual things, was considered to have an outward objective reality answering to it." "This misapprehension," he goes on to say, "of the import of general language, constitutes *Mysticism*, a word so much oftener written and spoken than understood. Whether in the Vedas, the Platonists, or the Hegelians, mysticism is neither more nor less than *ascribing objective existence to the subjective creations of the mind's own faculties, to mere ideas of the intellect;* and believing, that, by watching and contemplating these ideas of its own making, it can read in them what takes place in the world without." In religion, it may be added, this Mysticism leads to the most subtile of all forms of idolatry, — the only one, indeed, that is now practicable among a civilized people, — the deification of an idea, the apotheosis of an abstraction.*

The immortality of the soul is a fact. — The proposition, that *all* the fundamental truths of religion relate to *matters of fact*, and must be established, if at all, by moral reasoning, leads us to look beyond the belief in the being of a God, and to inquire

* Thus M. Cousin talks with perfect consistency about *demonstrating* the existence of a God, for he not only reasons from pure abstractions, but avowedly identifies the object of his inquiry with an abstract idea. According to his theory, the three elements of pure Reason — the idea of the Finite, the Infinite, and the relation between them — do not afford a passage to the Divine existence, "*for these ideas are God himself.*" These three elements, "a triplicity which resolves itself into unity, and a unity which

if it holds true, also, of the doctrine of the immortality of the soul. I pass over the evidences of *the moral government of the Deity,* as unnecessary to be considered here; since it is obvious that they must consist in a copious induction of examples, to prove that the reward of virtue and the punishment of vice are the great objects of all the general laws by which the world is governed. The only argument brought against this doctrine, being an enumeration of cases of a seemingly promiscuous distribution of happiness and misery in this life, is an application of the rules of physical inquiry, so that abstract reasoning is admitted to be out of place on either side. These apparent exceptions, this allotment of good and evil in a measure which often does not correspond with our sense of merit and demerit, create a presumption, it is said, that the scheme of moral government, which has only its beginning here, will be completed in a future state.

If the immortality of the soul did not open so attractive a field for general disquisition, it would be difficult to conceive of it as supported by abstract arguments, or as clouded by metaphysical doubts and difficulties. "If a man dies, shall he live again?" The question here relates to *a fact of the second order,* to *an event* which is to take place, a future occurrence; if the present, or *actual, existence* of the mind or person is a fact, so also is its *future* existence. Our means of answering the question, too, are more limited and imperfect in this case, than would suffice for the establishment of any fact in physical science. As it relates to the *future,* we can have no sensible evidence of it; and as the grave confessedly does not give up its dead to our bodily apprehension, the testimony of others, except so far as they speak of a revelation, is also set aside. The axiom re-

---

develops itself into triplicity," constitute the Divine Intelligence itself, — the *tria juncta in uno,* the mystery of the Godhead. Those who are satisfied with this conception of the Deity, can accept also Cousin's demonstrative proof of His existence. But for our own part, we want words to express our indignation at this impious harlequinade of words, — this mode of binding together three dry sticks of abstract ideas, and then baptizing the miserable fagot as God.

specting the uniformity of nature, which is the usual foundation of our reasonings from the past to the future, cannot aid us here; because we are not asking now, whether it is probable that an observed law of nature will continue in force; the question is, whether there has ever been such a law, whether a messenger has ever come back to us from that invisible bourne. Accordingly, it is distinctly admitted by the most judicious writers on *natural* theology, that the argument, after all, is but *a series of presumptions*, which we indulge the more readily, because the conclusion to which they point is one in which all persons willingly acquiesce; it agrees with the involuntary shrinking of the rational mind from the idea of utter extinction. Most of these presumptions were as well stated by the ancient philosophers, — by Socrates, and Plato, and Cicero, — as by the moderns. The *use* of such speculations is not to establish the *truth* of the point in question, but *to refute the objections* which have been urged against the possibility of the event. It *can* be shown, that the dissolution of the body does not necessarily lead us to infer the extinction of the soul, but that the presumption lies the other way. It is in this moderate form that the argument from the light of nature is stated by Butler, and it would have been well if Clarke had imitated his reserve. Immortality is no part of the positive teachings of nature; to *Revelation* alone, can we look for light and life beyond the grave.

Some unsatisfactory conceptions of immortality. — I take no account of those extraordinary speculations, which suppose the soul of man to be a ray or emanation from the Deity, which, at the dissolution of the body, will again be absorbed into its source. "This seems," says Mr. Stewart, "to have been the opinion of many of the ancient Stoics; and a similar idea has been adopted by some philosophers in modern times, who have compared the soul, when joined to the body, to a small portion of the sea inclosed in a vial; and, when separated from it, to the same water, confounded and intermixed, by the breaking of the vial which contained it, with the ocean from which it was first taken." This is but one of the applications of the doctrine of *pantheism;* and those who can give up the belief in *a personal God*, may be satisfied with this conception of the soul's futurity. But to others, the loss of distinct consciousness and personal identity or individuality, which is implied in this theory, will cause the doctrine to appear little more consoling than a belief in the termination of all things at the grave. The admitted physical fact, that of all the material particles which constitute the body at the instant of death, not one is lost, but all enter into new combinations, and pass through a ceaseless round of growth and decay, gives us an idea of the perpetuity of our corporeal frames, which answers exactly to this pantheistic notion of the immortality of the soul. To speak of *different minds being blended together and lost in one general mass of being*, is to employ a form of words which is only not injurious to sound doctrine, because it is unintelligible and absurd. *Existence is an abstract idea;* there is no such thing as existence in general, apart from individual beings, any more than there is such a thing as an audience existing separately from the men and women who compose it. To speak of the annihilation of these persons in their individual capacity, leaving their presence as a general assembly, is nonsense. To such an absurdity are we reduced by confounding *abstractions with realities*, or employing terms without attaching definite and distinct meaning to them.

The light of nature does not prove immortality properly so called. — Yet we have been told, that it is "written legibly in Nature that man is an undying being," and every thing justifies us in saying, that, "if man were made to live for ever, the impress of that intention must be distinctly visible in his very structure." Science, it is accordingly said, must decipher the marks which indicate this intention, and spell out the natural language in which every rational creature is labelled with the promise of immortality, just as it infers, from a mere fragment of a fossil bone, "the whole fashion of the animal to which it belonged, its food, its mode and sphere of existence." But the history which is deciphered by the geologist and the comparative anatomist is that of the *past;* and not even in their boldest speculations, do they attempt to pry into the secrets of the *future*, — far less, to speak confidently of an *endless* duration to come. Science can read the annals of *former* ages; but it cannot "look into the seeds of time, and see what grain will grow, and what will not." The astronomer hesitates about pronouncing upon the future stability of the system of which our earth is but a part, even on the supposition, that the laws which now seem to control its action shall continue forever in force, without restraint, limit, or interference from the Omnipotent hand which first established them. But who shall say *when* His purpose shall be accomplished? or who shall scan the designs of the Almighty? The naturalist may declare, if he can, that the flower shall droop and die at the end of a single season; but he finds no evidence that the secret principle which now vivifies it, after it has ceased to hold these material particles together, shall yet continue to be, either animating other forms, or existing apart till time shall be no more. And mental science is equally barren of any distinct promise of the future; the sharpest scrutiny of the phenomena of mind, unguided by special revelation, leaves this doctrine of immortality precisely where it was in the speculations of antiquity, — a dim though glorious foreboding, a splendid doubt.

We are not surprised, then, to find the author of the assertion just quoted rebuking those who conceive "of the eternal world as situated on the other side of the tomb," and telling them that eternity "is here and now, — that they are in it, and that it is in them." It is all a juggle of words, then, which substitutes a flight of rhetoric for the severe expression of a scientific or a religious truth, and reduces the immortality of the soul to a figure of speech. Unquestionably, it is a tolerable metaphor to say, that in good deeds there is length of years; but it is paltering with words, to hold up this trope as an enunciation or a proof of the doctrine that the soul shall never die.

It is a fact that religion enjoins certain duties. — I need not give but one other illustration of the truth, that religion is founded entirely upon matters of fact, and must be supported, therefore, by moral evidence. Religion inculcates certain duties; it enjoins some motives and modes of conduct, and forbids others, — and this, too, by the highest of all sanctions, *the com-*

mand of God. These injunctions are, in great part, coincident with the moral precepts of our own hearts; the Divine law and the law of conscience, whenever they meet, harmonize with each other, and, so far as they regard only the outward act, are reduced to one. Still, to the religious man, there is *an additional sanction, a new source of obligation;* the act, once deemed obligatory only from an instinctive perception of its rightfulness, now becomes a manifestation of obedience, a religious duty, an act of worship. Virtuous actions as such, or in themselves considered, are not religious deeds; mere virtue must be consecrated by reference to the Divine will, before it can assume even a resemblance to holiness. I do not say, that the moral sense is of imperfect obligation, so that it must be buoyed up and enforced by the will of God, before its dictates are binding upon man. *Right* is of *necessary and inherent obligation, anterior to all command.* But the precept added gives another aspect to the duty, and creates a new joy in the fulfilment of it. A life which is irreproachable before the world, which is warmed by all the kindly affections and elevated by a steadfast adherence to noble principles, is still an irreligious and godless one, if its acts are not sanctified by this reference to the Supreme Will. This is but a definition of religion, the meaning of which, as shown by its etymology and its universal acceptance, is to *religate*, or to *bind anew*, to the performance of duty, by offering an additional motive and guide; and this meaning constitutes the only possible distinction between *religion* and *mere morality.* In the family, a rule obligatory in itself acquires a new claim to observance from the command or wish of a parent, the motives of obedience and love being thus added to our almost involuntary homage to conscience. So, in the great human family, the primal duties of life, — truthfulness, temperance, justice, and charity, — become alike *more awful and engaging,* — I do not say *more binding,* — because the performance of them is the declared will of our Heavenly Father.

Observe, then, that the whole *practice* of religion depends upon our knowledge of this *fact,* that God has commanded us to do, or to abstain from doing, certain acts. It matters not how this knowledge is obtained, whether by direct revelation, or by inferring the will of the Creator from the character and tendency of his works. In either case, the light of nature, or a Divinely appointed messenger, or a miracle, announces to us a solemn, an awful *reality*, — that the moral law is His law, and transgression of it is violation of His command. I may even infer the fact only from my instinctive perception of the duty; still, the inference is one that leads to a fact, and not to an abstract principle. I argue, not from one general law to another, but from a given effect to a particular cause; not from one rule enforced by conscience to another rule enjoined by the Almighty, but from the fact that conscience speaks at all, to another fact that God also speaks, and that the voice of conscience is also the voice of God.

The practice of morality distinguished from a belief in religion. — These views, I am well aware, are directly opposed to a theory now very popular with a certain class of minds, which tends, first, to identify revealed with natural religion, and next, to merge both in the practice of a sublime but rather indefinite morality. A pure life is held up as the only true criterion of a religious character, and then as the only desirable object of attainment. Especially has this disposition been manifested when treating of the nature and functions of conscience; so that many earnest but injudicious persons have now become quite as fanatical, quite as bigoted, irrational, and intolerant, in regard to moral principle, as were formerly the wildest sect of the Puritans in respect to their religious faith. Reverence of their own nature seems to them quite as just and proper as reverence of the Deity, and a glowing though vague conception of virtue takes the place of religion as a guide of life. Nay, a sort of ecstatic contemplation of the *mere ideas* of duty and right has, with some, usurped the place of a practical manifestation of these ideas in outward conduct; and thus a species of Antinomianism has been established on ethical grounds, quite as absurd and dangerous as the same theory is, when nominally resting on Scripture. If these vagaries must exist, let them, at any rate, appear in their true character, and not borrow the name and garb of the faith which they dishonor. *Religion* is indeed an affair of the heart and the life; but a *belief in religion* is an affair of the intellect. Impulses cannot take the place of convictions, nor can morality itself find anywhere a sure and permanent support except in a recognition of its dictates as the commands of God.

CHAPTER III.

THE IDEA OF SELF, OR PERSONAL EXISTENCE.

Summary of the last Chapter. — The object of the last chapter was to draw a dividing line between the provinces of Philosophy and Religion; to show that the one was occupied with *abstractions*, and the other with *realities;* and, accordingly, that they rested upon different species of evidence, and any confusion of the two was likely to be injurious to both. During the reign of Scholasticism, says Dr. Whewell, "it was held, without any regulating principle, that the Philosophy which had been bequeathed to the world by the great geniuses of heathen antiquity, and the Philosophy which was deduced from and implied by the revelations made by God to man, must be identical; and, therefore, that Theology is the only true Philosophy." We do but invert this error in our own day, when the opinion of many seems to tend towards the conclusion, if indeed it be not openly avowed, that Philosophy is the only true Theology. Against this conclusion, I endeavored to show, by a very brief review of the questions that are chiefly considered by metaphysicians and by religious inquirers, that they differed as widely from each other as logic from history, so that reasoning from one to the other was not merely feeble and unsatisfactory, but irrational and absurd. The great truths of Religion are *the being of a*

God, the moral government of the world, the immortality of the soul, and *the promulgation of certain duties as directly enjoined by the authority of God.* These truths, I reminded you, — for no proof of a self-evident proposition is needed or possible, — are *matters of fact,* quite as much so as the existence, at some antecedent time, of a certain political community upon this earth, the authority of its first magistrate, and the enactment of laws by its legislature; that is, we rely upon sensible evidence, the testimony of others, and upon reasoning from effects to causes, — the usual media of physical and historical inquiry, — for establishing our belief in their reality.

Statement of the question respecting our personal existence. — Considering these preliminaries as established, we approach now the body of the subject, and attempt to prove the particular facts in the case, and to free them from the metaphysical speculations and difficulties by which they have been encumbered. In seeking to know the relation of God to man, we must begin by an investigation, to some extent, of *human nature itself,* as our conclusions upon this point cannot fail to affect every part of the inquiry. *What are we, considered as subjects of the Divine law, and what light is thrown by our physical constitution upon the purpose or end for which we began to exist?* or is it likely that there was no purpose in the case, but that our creation was as objectless as the gambols of an infant, — a mere freak in the disposition of matter? The common belief, that man is a complex being, made up of body and soul, has been disturbed by strange doubts respecting the possibility of any immaterial existence, and by arguments which go to destroy our confidence even in our personal identity, and consequently in our continuous responsibility to any authority. I do not say, that a solution of all these doubts is absolutely necessary before the great truths of religion can be established. Dr. Priestley was a materialist, yet he believed in the immortality of man; he was a necessarian, but he held to human accountability; and few who are familiar with his theological writings will deny, that he was even a profoundly religious person, whatever may have been his errors in scientific, political, or theological speculation. Still, it was for him to vindicate his own consistency; in ordinary minds, if such opinions are not immediately destructive of all religious belief, they certainly tend to darken and perplex it, so that a consideration of them cannot properly be omitted here. The principles already laid down do not permit us to waive the discussion as metaphysical, and therefore out of place; for the point of inquiry is a *fact*, — the continued, identical, conscious existence of a human being, — his personality, — the reality of a man to himself. Metaphysical skepticism has gone so far, that, before undertaking to establish the existence of a God, we are called upon to prove our own existence. In considering the argument upon this head, lest I should be accused of breaking my own rules, let me remind you that the testimony of consciousness has been admitted to be as legitimate a source of knowledge in physical inquiry, as the evidence of the senses themselves.

Common mode of distinguishing mind from matter. — In the attempt to disprove the doctrine of materialism, it has been usual to adopt the argument to which I briefly alluded in a former chapter; — to say, that *mind* is the seat or subject of certain phenomena, which are entirely distinct from another class of attributes or qualities which inhere in *matter*. What the substance is, in either case, we cannot determine, for our knowledge both of mind and matter is merely relative. As "we know the one," argues Mr. Stewart, "only by such sensible qualities as *extension*, *figure*, and *solidity;* and the other by such operations as *sensation*, *thought*, and *volition;* we are certainly entitled to say, that matter and mind, considered as objects of human study, are essentially different; the science of the former resting ultimately on *the phenomena exhibited to our senses;* that of the latter, on *the phenomena of which we are conscious.* Instead, therefore, of objecting to the scheme of materialism, that its conclusions are false, it would be more accurate to say, that its aim is unphilosophical." Accordingly, it is maintained to be "no more proper to say of mind that it is material, than to say of body that it is spiritual."

Insufficiency of this distinction. — This argument may be

very well as far as it goes ; but it seems to me to be insufficient, and to be very like an attempt to console us for our imperfect knowledge of one thing, by reminding us of our total ignorance of another. Besides, as mind and matter are confessedly the only constituents or parts that make up the human being, it is rather humiliating to be told, that we have only a *relative* knowledge of ourselves. When informed that matter is only the unknown substratum of certain qualities, we may acquiesce, for it has been shown that this idea of matter in general is a mere abstraction, and if it were lost altogether, it would be no serious privation, our knowledge of particular substances remaining precisely what it was before. But when a person is told that *he* is only an *unknown something* which feels, thinks, and wills, he is very likely to reluct at the conclusion, inasmuch as he considers his own existence, not as an abstraction, but a reality. The argument puts our knowledge of the material and the intellectual world exactly on a par, so that the idea of personality is left unprovided for, or it is doubtful whether the body or the mind is the person.

Second argument against materialism. — Let us look further, then, for an argument against materialism, founded on *the absolute incongruity of mental phenomena with material organization or change.* He who denies the existence of spirit must maintain that ideas and emotions are evolved, in some unintelligible manner, by the action of some part of the body, — probably of the nerves or the brain. Now we cannot conceive of any changes in these organs corresponding to the infinite variety of mental phenomena, except by the motions of their parts. But *motion* is not *thought;* the vibrations of the nerves, the agitation of the brain, the reciprocal action of infinitesimal particles on each other, is still *bodily* action, and not *mental* action. Granting, for a moment, for the sake of argument, that they *produce,* or *evolve,* thought, they *are* not thought, any more than the striking of a hammer on a bell *is* sound, or than the opening of the eyes *is* vision. A cause can never be confounded with its effect, even though it be the real or efficient cause, and not a mere invariable antecedent or concomitant event.

Let me illustrate this point a little further. Chemists and mathematicians have long been occupied with researches and speculations concerning the nature of *heat*, or caloric; at present, they can only say of it, that it is an invisible and imponderable agent or principle, which produces certain effects, — the words "agent" and "principle," be it observed, being used only for convenience of speech, and really betraying the ignorance of the speaker, who does not know whether heat is some subtile fluid, existing by itself, and tending constantly to an equilibrium by emission in straight lines; or whether it proceeds from undulations, or certain changes resembling undulations, in a fluid which exists also for other purposes; the heat in this case not being material, and never existing by itself, so that we should speak of a hot body or a cold one, just as we speak of a *smooth* surface or a *rough* surface, never supposing that smoothness is a substance, but an attribute. Now, suppose that some uninformed person, observing that heat was always evolved when one body was rubbed against another, or when it was burned, or when it was condensed from a gaseous to a liquid, or from a liquid to a solid state, should say that the problem was solved, and that *heat* was unquestionably nothing but *friction*, or *combustion*, or *condensation*. A chemist would certainly say, that this person did not even understand the question; for to know that friction *produced* heat, was quite a different thing from saying that friction *constituted* heat.

So the agitation of the brain may produce, or rather precede, or accompany thought; but it does not constitute thought. Nay, it is not even so probable that *the motion produces the thought*, as it is that *the thought produces the motion*. Fear blanches the cheek; but the paleness does not produce the fear, and, for a still stronger reason, does not constitute it.*

---

* "When we say, that the force which holds the planets in their orbits is resolved into *gravity*, or that the force which makes substances combine chemically is resolved into *electricity*, we assert in the one case what is, and in the other case what might, and probably will, ultimately be, a legitimate result of induction. In both these cases, *motion* is resolved into *motion*. The assertion is, that a case of motion, which was supposed to be *special*,

Hume's argument against the consciousness of personal existence. — Here, again, the argument appears to be sound as far as it goes; and it establishes a radical difference between *the phenomena* of mind and those of matter. Still, it does not supply the means of tying those phenomena, as it were, together, or of building up that idea of personality, or *self*, against which the sophistry of Hume was chiefly directed. This subtile skeptic directed his argument against our idea of individuality, or

---

and to follow a distinct law of its own, conforms to and is included in *the general law* which regulates another class of motions. But from these and similar generalizations, countenance and currency have been given to attempts to resolve, not motion into motion, but heat into motion, light into motion, sensation itself into motion (as in Hartley's doctrine of vibrations); states of consciousness into states of the nervous system, as in the ruder forms of the materialist philosophy; vital phenomena into mechanical or chemical processes, as in some schools of physiology.

"Now I am far from pretending that it may not be capable of proof, or that it would not be a very important addition to our knowledge, if proved, that certain motions in the particles of bodies are among the *conditions* of the production of heat or light; that certain assignable physical modifications of the nerves may be among the *conditions*, not only of our sensations or emotions, but even of our thoughts; that certain mechanical and chemical conditions may, in the order of nature, be sufficient to determine to action the physiological laws of life. All I insist upon, in common with every sober thinker since modern science has been definitely constituted, is, that it shall not be supposed that, by proving these things, one step would be made towards a real explanation of heat, light, or sensation; or that the generic peculiarity of those phenomena can be in the least degree evaded by any such discoveries, however well established. Let it be shown, for instance, that the most complex series of physical causes and effects succeed one another in the eye and in the brain to produce a sensation of color; rays falling upon the eye, refracted, converging, crossing one another, making an inverted image on the retina, and after this a motion, — let it be a vibration or a rush of nervous fluid, or whatever else you are pleased to suppose, along the optic nerve, — a propagation of this motion to the brain itself, and as many more different motions as you choose; still, at the end of these motions, there is something which is not a motion, there is a feeling or sensation of color. Whatever number of motions we may be able to interpolate, and whether they be real or imaginary, we shall still find, at the end of the series, a motion antecedent and a color consequent." — Mill's *Logic*, pp. 486, 487.

our consciousness of separate, personal existence. He reasons thus: —

"When I turn my reflection on *myself*, I never can perceive this *self* without some one or more perceptions; nor can I ever perceive any thing but the perceptions. It is the composition of these, therefore, which forms the self. Suppose the mind to be reduced even below the life of an oyster; suppose it to have only one perception, as of thirst or hunger. Consider it in that situation. Do you conceive any thing but merely that perception? Have you any notion of *self*, or substance? If not, the addition of other perceptions can never give you that notion. The annihilation, which some people suppose to follow upon *death*, and which entirely destroys this *self*, is *nothing but an extinction of all particular perceptions*, — love and hatred, pain and pleasure, thought and sensation. Philosophers begin to be reconciled to the principle, that we have no idea of *external substance*, distinct from the ideas of particular *qualities*. This must pave the way for a like principle with regard to the *mind*, that we have no notion of it, distinct from the particular perceptions. In short, there are two principles which I cannot render consistent, nor is it in my power to renounce either of them; namely, *that all our distinct perceptions are distinct existences*, and *that the mind never perceives any real connection among distinct existences*. Did our perceptions either inhere in something simple and individual, or did the mind perceive some real connection among them, there would be no difficulty in the case. For my part, I must plead the privilege of a skeptic, and confess that this difficulty is too hard for my understanding."

So far the Scotch skeptic. What some call the *mind*, and others the *person*, is, to him, simply *a succession of perpetually fleeting ideas or emotions, in nowise connected with each other*, acknowledging no common ownership, and admitting no reality or actual being, except as each, during the moment of its continuance, affirms its own existence. The mind is like a string of beads with the string taken away, each bead being seen or known to exist only by itself, and for its particular moment, as the *direct* knowledge of one must pass away before we can possibly gain a knowledge of another. For observe, that, on this theory, *mind* is really worse off than *matter;* our idea of each is but a congeries of certain qualities; but in the latter case, the qualities or attributes exist and are perceived *together*, or in a lump; while in the former, they exist *successively*, only one being known at any one time. In fine, I have a certain sensation or thought, of the reality of which, *for the moment*, there can be no doubt; but it is a fallacy, says Hume, to suppose that this thought, which is a distinct existence, belongs to ME, another distinct being, having a continuous existence. I am conscious of *the thought*, but not of *the person thinking*.

Memory cannot prove personality. — I am anxious not to overstate Hume's theory, nor to understate his argument, and hope that I have done justice to both. Perhaps it is wrong to call it *his* theory; Hume had no theory; his only object was to disprove the theories and doctrines of other people. He says only that no other doctrine than this can be *proved*, — that is, demonstrated; he acknowledges that the difficulty is too hard for his understanding. Now it is certainly an insufficient answer to his sophistry to maintain, as Dr. Brown and most of the other Scotch philosophers have done, that "our knowledge of mind is only *relative*," that "we know it only as susceptible of feelings that have already existed," and to throw the whole burden of solving the problem upon *memory*, by which one faculty, they say, "our mind, simple and indivisible as it truly is, is, as it were, multiplied and extended, expanding itself over that long series of sensations and emotions, in which it seems to live again, and to live with many lives." *Memory* is more easy to be discredited than any other faculty, on account of the mistakes with which it is often chargeable, — the frequent difficulty of distinguishing between recollections and imaginations. A remembered thought differs from an original one in the single respect of its being accompanied by a *belief* that it was in the mind before, and that it is now present for the second time. This *belief* cannot be substantiated, or proved; it may be, it sometimes is, unfounded, — a vivid conception having taken the place of a reality. Memory alone, then, cannot establish beyond a doubt the separate, continuous existence of *self*, — cannot fully support the idea of personality; and I have already given reasons for saying, that the vague and abstract notion of *substance*, being assumed as the *common* substratum of material and intellectual phenomena, leaves it doubtful whether the body or the mind is the person.

The fact of self-consciousness stated. — But we need not despair of the attempt to confirm our own personality against all metaphysical cavils, if we consider each particular personal existence as a fact, and then endeavor to prove it by the usual methods of physical inquiry; though the argument must depend, of course, on the facts of consciousness, and not on those furnished by the senses. Let me ask you, then, for a time, to discard the word *mind*, as the fruitful source of vague speculation and error, and to look at that of which it is a mere synonyme, — at *the man himself.** The sentient, thinking being, which I call *self*, is an absolute unit. Duality or complexity cannot be predicated of it in any intelligible sense. Personality is indivisible; "I" am *one*. Conceive of yourself, if you can, as divided into two persons, or as separated from yourself, or as multiplied in any manner whatever; the supposition is an absurdity, and the language in which it is conveyed is immediately felt to be ludicrous. You can conceive of an arm, or a leg, or any part of the *body*, being separated from you; there is no difficulty in that. But the idea of personality remains one and indivisible, sometimes to torture us with remorse for crime committed long before, sometimes to sustain and cheer the drooping spirit, when all else is lost, with the assured *hope*, that this unity of being is indestructible, and shall survive the dissolution of the body and the grave. For the idea of personal identity and oneness alone supports the consciousness of responsibility; the

* "That which is called 'I' is a living reality, and though *mind* were annihilated, it would remain a repository of given facts." Psychology, or the science of mind, ought rather to be called *the science of man himself;* for, as has been acutely observed, if my *mind* is not *myself*, then the universe resolves itself into *three* orders of existence; 1st, mind; 2d, matter; 3d, what I call *me*, to whom the changes of the other two are known.

guilty man cannot escape from *himself*, though human law be a feeble and tardy avenger of wrong.

Self has no plurality of organs or faculties. — This individual being, or *self*, is capable of acting in different ways; and for convenience of speech and classification, these modes of action have been arranged as the results of different faculties; though, in truth, it is no more proper to attribute to the person distinct powers and organs for *comparison*, *memory*, and *judgment*, than to give to the body separately *a walking faculty*, *a lifting faculty*, *a jumping faculty*, and so on. In the one case, these faculties are but *different aspects* of the *same mental power;* in the other, but different applications of the same muscular strength. To attribute to me *the organ of memory*, is no more than to say that *I am able to remember*, the person who remembers being one and the same with him who judges and feels. Yet this classification of mental phenomena seems to imply *a complexity of being*, and, for this reason alone, it has always furnished the chief support for the several theories of materialism. The groundwork of these systems entirely falls away, when we consider that this division of *organs* is only verbal, as the real division is of a plurality of *functions* exercised by the same being. Seeing differs from hearing, because two distinct organs of the body are exercised for different ends; but when the two acts become entirely mental, as in the case of memory, the distinction between them is done away; I recall the features of a landscape with which I was once familiar, by the same kind of effort which brings to mind the successive notes of a strain of music heard long ago. More facility may be gained by practice with one class of recollections than with another; this does not affect the nature of the process, but only its rapidity.

Immediate consciousness of self. — How we come to a knowledge of *self*, or to this consciousness of personality, — whether *mediately*, by an act of judgment, knowing that each sensation or thought must have a *substratum* or *substance* in which it inheres, and hence inferring what we are not directly conscious of; or whether we gain it *im*mediately, being equally, and at the same moment, conscious of the sensation and of the sentient being, — is a question that need not detain us long. A *thought* is but the phase, or aspect, for the moment, of *the thinking being;* it is but the abstract expression of the fact expressed in the words, "I think." If we speak of it as "a state of mind," the convenience of language compels us to regard it abstractly; but looking upon it as *an act*, we consider the real occurrence in its entireness. Take one of the appetites, for instance; to have "the sensation of hunger" is an abstract and general expression, applicable to any number of cases; but in any particular case, it signifies nothing unless interpreted to mean "*I* am hungry." The subject and object of thought are thus *inseparably blended together* in every act of thinking, and can no more be separated from each other in reality than two polar forces. When we reflect upon a sensation that has passed away, we may consider it by abstraction, — first, in regard to the object, and then it is called a sensation of color, hardness, or something else; or, secondly, in regard to the subject, and then I have a conception of *self* as performing some act, or experiencing some affection. This *apperception*, as Leibnitz calls it, or *direct consciousness of self*, seems to me an invariable concomitant of mental action.* The attention, indeed, may be concentrated on the *object* of thought, and then the personal consciousness is not remembered. Just so, a person may be absorbed in a reverie while loud music is sounding near him, and pay no attention to it; it is usually said, that he does not hear it; but this cannot be, as his faculty of hearing remains unimpaired, the vibrations *must* reach his ears, and, in fact, if

* Properly speaking, consciousness is an attribute, not of *mind*, but of *me*. When mind is *objectified*, or made an object of thought, it is not *mind* which is conscious of its own changes, but 'I' am conscious of those changes. "For to change and to be cognizant of change; for a thing to *be* in a particular state, and to be *aware* that it is in this state, is surely not one and the same fact, but two totally distinct and separate facts." Herein is a fundamental difference between *matter* and *me;* for *matter* is not cognizant of its own changes — is not *aware* of its state.

For the substance of this note and the preceding one, I am indebted to some excellent articles on the *Philosophy of Consciousness* in "Blackwood's Magazine" for 1838.

the music suddenly stops, he is roused from his abstraction by the absence of the accustomed sound, just as one dozing in church is waked when the preacher has ended his sermon. In truth, he hears every note, but instantly forgets it, from the lack of attention; and at the close, of course, he has forgotten the whole. Just so, a person thinking is never *conscious of a thought* without being *conscious of himself* at the same instant; his attention may be directed either to the object or the subject, according to the wish or exigency of the moment. If laboring under acute pain, the phrase which expresses the state of his mind at any instant is, "I suffer;" for the abstract sensation of pain would have no interest for him, except as *self* enters into or endures it.

What is personality. — If this be the correct view, and I can see no valid objection to it, the idea of personality is fixed on an immovable basis. *Self is an indivisible unit,* — a *monad,* in technical phrase, — *endowed with intelligence and activity; and we are directly conscious of it in itself, and in its passing into thought and act, without being compelled to infer its existence from these manifestations.* If we only inferred the substance from the attributes, we could not conceive of it unless in the exercise of those attributes, — any more than we can conceive of *matter* without its *qualities,* without extension, form, solidity, or color. But we can conceive of our *personal existence in the intervals both of thought and action.* A consciousness of existence underlies the exercise of every function of mental life. The celebrated argument of Descartes, "I think, therefore I am," has been objected to, and with reason, on the ground that the conclusion merely repeats what is, not merely implied in the premise, but formally stated in it. *Thought* is but *a mode of action,* and cannot be conceived as a reality without *the agent,* though it may be considered separately by abstraction. *

* From the writer, already cited, on the Philosophy of Consciousness, I borrow another illustration of the fact, that our knowledge of self is direct and immediate.

"The child's employment of language previous to his use of the word

Why self cannot be defined. — But it is said that we cannot describe *self*, or give any definition of personality, except by enumerating its attributes, or the acts of which it is capable. Hence it is inferred, that we know nothing more of it than of *matter*, which can be described only as the *unknown substratum* of certain qualities that are evident to sense. But *all simple*

'I,' may be accounted for upon the principle of imitation, or, at any rate, it must be considered as a mere illustration of the general law of cause and effect. But neither association, nor the principle of imitation, nor any conceivable modification of the law of cause and effect, will account for the child's use of the word 'I.' In originating and using this term, he reverses or runs counter to all these laws, and more particularly performs a process diametrically opposed to any act of imitation. Take an illustration of this. A child hears another person call a certain object 'a table;' and the power of imitation naturally leads him to call the same thing, and any similar thing, 'a table.' Suppose, next, that the child hears this person apply to himself the word 'I.' In this case, too, the power of imitation would naturally lead the child to call that man 'I.' But is this what the child does? No. As soon as he becomes conscious, he ceases, so far at least as the word 'I' is concerned, to be an imitator. He still applies the word 'table' to the objects to which other people apply that term; and in this he imitates them. But with regard to the word 'I,' he applies this expression to a thing totally different from that which he hears all other people applying it to. They apply it to themselves, but he does not apply it *to them*, but *to himself;* and in this, he is not an imitator, but the absolute originator of a new notion.

"Is it objected, that, in the use of the word 'I,' the child may still be considered as an imitative creature, inasmuch as he merely applies to himself a word which he hears other people applying to themselves, having borrowed the application of it from them? Oh! vain and short-sighted objection! As if this very fact did not necessarily imply and prove that he has, first of all, originated within himself the notion expressed by the word 'I,' (namely, the notion of his conscious self,) and thereby, and thereby only, has become capable of comprehending what *they* mean by it. In the use and understanding of this word, every man must be altogether *original*. No person can *teach* to another its true meaning and right application; for no two human beings ever use it, or ever can use it, in the same sense, or apply it to the same being. The word 'I,' in *my* mouth, as applied to *you*, would prove me to be a madman. The word 'I,' in *your* mouth, as applied to *me*, would prove you to be the same. Therefore, I cannot, by any conceivability, teach you what it means, nor can you teach me." — *Blackwood*, vol. xliii. p. 790.

ideas are incapable of definition, and the only mode of describing them is to enumerate the occasions on which they rise, or are suggested to the mind. Wherever there is complexity, the several parts can be distinguished, and a complete list of these will constitute a description of the object, which will be intelligible to one who has had no sensible evidence of its existence. But if the idea be simple, no account of it can be understood except by those who know it, or have had experience of it already. Colors are simple sensations, and the impossibility of defining or describing them is proved by the familiar fact, that no form of words can convey the slightest notion of them to a person blind from his birth. The word "green" may be explained by saying that it is the color of the foliage, or "blue" as the color of the sky; and this is enough for one who has seen the aspect of external nature; but it is no definition, and conveys no knowledge to him who has never had the faculty of vision.

The idea of *self* belongs to the same category with all our simple sensations, and with the more abstruse ideas of time, space, motion, and the like. All are *indefinable*, because *indivisible;* they cannot be described, because they have no complexity of parts. But who doubts our knowledge, or questions the reality, of *motion*, or *light*, or *time*, because they cannot be explained by any form of words, or, what is the same thing, cannot be resolved into simpler ideas? The unity of personality, then, which is the important point for present consideration, is established by the very argument which is brought to do away with the reality of the idea of person altogether.

The ancient philosophers and the schoolmen were guilty of much solemn trifling, in their vain attempts to define these simple ideas. Thus "motion" was *explained* to be "the act of a being in power so far forth as in power;" and "light" to be "the act of perspicuity so far forth as it is perspicuous." The inanity and uselessness of such definitions are now generally admitted, though Lord Monboddo attempted to defend them. It is justly observed by Locke, that "the modern philosophers, who have endeavored to throw off the jargon of the schools, and speak intelligibly, have not much better succeeded in defining simple ideas, whether by explaining their causes, or otherwise. The atomists, who define *motion* to be a passage from one place to another, what do they more than put one synonymous word for another? For is it not at least as proper and significant to say, 'passage is a *motion* from one place to another,' as to say, 'motion is a *passage?*' this is to *translate*, and not to *define*." The impossibility of defining or describing an idea, therefore, is no argument against the existence, either of the idea, or of the thing to which it corresponds, or against our having a distinct knowledge of it as a reality. Personality, or *self*, is as fully known, and as distinctly conceived, as motion or light.

No analogy between the qualities of matter and the acts of mind. — There is another reason for denying this parallel between mind and matter, in which it is assumed, that our knowledge of each is merely *relative*. Material substance, it is true, is known to me only as *something* which is extended, figured, colored, hard, etc., these qualities being all conceived to exist together, or at the same moment; and the conception of these qualities being taken away, nothing remains, — at any rate, nothing which is distinct and conceivable. Now mind or person may be described in a parallel manner, as *something* which thinks, feels, wills, judges, etc.; but these are not qualities, not attributes, but *acts;* and they are not conceived to exist together, or to be performed all at the same moment; they are done *successively*, and what is really attributed to the person at any one moment is, not the acts themselves, but the *capacity* of performing those acts. Of course, I can conceive of the person when *this capacity is latent*, or not exerted, — that is, of mind in the intervals both of thought and action. But I cannot conceive of any particular *body* except as the seat of all its attributes, and as continually manifesting these attributes. Imagine, if you can, a lump of matter, which has no extension, no figure, no solidity, no color, — none of its usual qualities. It is impossible. But you can conceive of *yourself* both as thinking, or as resting from thought; as sentient, or with all the senses closed; as exerting a volition, or as entirely passive.

Stating the same argument in other terms, I say that reasoning *from attributes or qualities to the substance* which supports them, is a proper inference, that being inferred which is not directly known or perceived; but *from actions to an agent* is no inference at all, but a mere descent from an abstraction to a reality, — the object of immediate knowledge or perception being, not the act, but the person acting. It is no *inference* from my perception of a triangle, to say that it has three angles; this is a part of the perception, a part of the meaning or definition of the word. But the existence of a luminous body somewhere, though it be not directly seen, is an inference from the light which it diffuses, and which is seen.

Self is one and indivisible. — I have dwelt at some length on this point, at the risk of seeming tedious and abstruse, because it is one of cardinal importance, and this doctrine respecting it has not been clearly set forth and defended, so far as I know, by any English writer on the philosophy of mind. It is the only view which seems to me to afford positive proof of the *immateriality* of the soul, or the person. Matter is essentially complex and divisible; the smallest particle of it has still an upper and an under-side, and we can conceive of these two being separated from each other. Mind, or person, as already remarked, is essentially indivisible. The being which I call *self*, or, to use the modern jargon, the *me*, is an absolute unit. For a person to speak of himself in the plural number, except as a figure of speech, is instantly perceived to be an absurdity, — as much so, as to speak of a *round square*. The doctrine of *atoms*, or ultimate particles in matter, however convenient it may be as an hypothesis, for representing the supposed groundwork of certain facts in chemistry, must always remain a hypothesis, alike incapable of proof, and even of distinct conception. "If the atomic theory be put forward," says Dr. Whewell, "as asserting that chemical elements are really composed of atoms, that is, of such particles not further divisible, we cannot avoid remarking, that, for such a conclusion chemical research has not afforded, *nor can afford*, any satisfactory evidence whatever." As a matter of fact, no one will assert that we can arrive at ultimate particles in matter, or have sensible evidence that they exist.

The body is extraneous to the man himself. — Matter, then, is necessarily divisible, or complex, in all cases; mind, or person, is necessarily indivisible; for a denial of the proposition "*I am one*," is not merely false, but absurd, this being a truth of intuition. An inevitable corollary from this doctrine is, that the complex material frame, with its numberless adaptations and arrangements, in which this being is lodged, is truly foreign from the man himself, having a kind of connection with him, in reality, but one degree more intimate than that of his clothes. The body is the curiously contrived machine through which the man communicates with the material world. It needs but little reflection to convince one, that his corporeal limbs and organs are but mechanical means and tools constantly within his reach, controlled by his single intelligence, and executing the behests of his undivided will, which is sovereign in its own domain. The eye is but his instrument to see with, the ear is his trumpet for communicating sound to him, the leg is his steed, and the arm his soldier. These outward organs and implements may tire in their uses, like willing servants that are yet overtasked; they may be worn out, become palsied, and decay; many of them may even be severed from the conscious agent whose property they are, yet the loss does not impair the sovereignty of his reason or the unity of his intelligence. The windows through which we look out upon the material world may be darkened, but the memory and the imagination are busy within, and the scenes which delighted our youth still pass before us in rapid and perpetual succession. Sleep relaxes the strained muscles, gives repose to the tired limbs, and shuts the wearied sense, the actual and material world to our apprehension ceasing to exist; but the mind, *the man*, claims no rest from his appropriate toil, but pursues his task in the world of dreams. All the proper and exclusive functions of the soul are then discharged as readily and continuously as in our waking hours Reason and recollection, judgment, fancy, the desires and the affections, still exercise their office; and the will, though it has lost control for a time of its actual servants through their fatigue, still governs an ideal kingdom, and spurs its fancied ministers. There is no good reason to believe, that sleep ever extends beyond the body, or suspends the exercise of a single function of purely intellectual life.

This view of the body as something extraneous to the man, as alike his covering and his instrument, the house which he lives in, and the nicely fashioned apparatus that executes his will and gratifies his passions, appears to me so natural and obvious, that it seems difficult to account for the practical materialism of common opinion on the subject. Even the respect which is paid to the remains of the dead, so far as it goes beyond the pleasing association which invests with a kind of sacredness every article or ornament once used by the loved and lost, — and in ordinary cases it goes much further, — seems alike irrational and unchristian. Many portions of the body may be removed, many of the organs become unfit for use, without impairing, in the slightest degree, the sufferer's conscious personality and intelligence. The particles of the whole are in a state of constant flux and renovation, so that man changes his body only a little less frequently than he does his coat.

Closeness of the temporary union of mind with body. — And viewed at any one moment, however close and intimate the union may appear, the body still seems to show its ministerial character, and to acknowledge in every part the sovereignty of one undivided and separate will. Sensation extends to every part of it, every fibre is instinct with life, and the dominion of the will is absolute and immediate over every muscle and joint, as if the whole fabric and its tenant were one homogeneous system. The mind tires not of its supremacy, and is not wearied with the number of volitions required to keep every joint in action, and every organ performing its proper function. It would not delegate the control of the fingers to an inferior power, nor contrive mechanical or automatic means for moving the extremities. Within its sphere, it is sole sovereign, and is not perplexed with the variety and constant succession of its duties, extending to every part of the complex structure of which it is the animating and directing spirit. Sensation is not cumbered with the multitude of impressions it receives, nor is the fineness of perception dulled by repeated exercise. The sharpness of its edge rather improves by use, and we become more heedful of its lightest intimations. This improvement, however, is wholly of the inner sense, the *man's* capacity being enlarged, while the external organ which is his instrument — the eye, for instance — is often injured and sometimes destroyed by excessive or unguarded use. "It does not appear," says Bishop Butler, "that the relation of this gross body to the reflecting being is in any degree necessary to thinking; to our intellectual enjoyments or sufferings; nor, consequently, that the dissolution or alienation of the former by death will be the destruction of those present powers which render us capable of this state of reflection." This consideration, indeed, affords no *proof*, properly so called, that the mind is immortal; but it rebuts the presumption, otherwise inevitable, that the death of the body is also the death of the soul. These rags of mortality, in which we are clothed, may fall off from us, and be mingled with their kindred dust; but this proves only that we have no further use for them, and and it leaves unimpaired the probability, that death, like sleep, may be only the portal to a spirit land.

I have heard of a recent case, in a town not far off, in which a young man, when just entering upon active life and the full duties of manhood, was attacked by the terrible disease which physicians call *anchylosis*, or stiffening of the joints. First one knee refused its office; and as this was accompanied with great pain, and perhaps the nature of the complaint was mistaken, the leg was amputated, in the hope that the evil would stop there. But the disease soon passed into the other limb, stiffened the remaining knee, and then crept on slowly from joint to joint, making each inflexible as it passed, till the whole lower portion of the body was nearly as rigid as iron, and the muscles had no longer any office to perform. Gradually, then, it moved upward, leaving the vertebral column inflexible; the arms and hands, which, in anticipation of its approach, had been bent into a posi ion most convenient for the sufferer, stiffened there; the neck :efused to turn or bend, and the body became almost as immovable as if it had been carved out of the rock. Years passed between the first appearance of the disease and this awful completion of its work; years elapsed *after* the hapless patient was thus hardened into stone, and still he lived. Nor was this all; his eyes were attacked; the sight of one was wholly lost, and the other became so exquisitely sensitive, that it could seldom be exposed to the light, and never but for a few moments at a time. And thus he remained for years, blind, immovable, prisoned in this house of stone, and echoing, we might suppose, the affecting exclamation of the Apostle, "Who shall deliver me from the body of this death?" But no word of impatience escaped him; the mind was clear and vigorous, the temper was not soured, the affections were as strong and clinging as ever. His good sense, his wit, his knowledge of books, his interest in the passing topics of the day, made his chamber a favorite resort even of those who might not have been drawn thither merely by sympathy for his sufferings; for not infrequently, he was still exposed to agonizing pain. But in the intervals of this distress, his active mind sought and found employment, and numerous contributions, which *this living statue* dictated for a periodical work, are now in print. The secret of his wonderful composure and gentleness may be told in two words, — religious resignation.*

---

* It cannot be indelicate now to state, that the individual here referred to was the late James Kennard, Jr., of Portsmouth, New Hampshire. A volume of selections from his writings, with a sketch of his life and character, prepared by his friend the Rev. Andrew P. Peabody, has been "printed for private circulation." Mr. Kennard died July 28, 1847, when he had nearly completed his thirty-second year. For nine years before his death he was unable to walk; but "he was occasionally brought down stairs till the summer of 1841, when he found that he could no longer bear removal, except that, with the most careful preparation, and with the utmost delicacy of touch, he was taken daily from his bed, and placed for an hour or two in his easy chair." In November, 1844, his eyes were attacked, and "the residue of his life was spent with a deep shade over his face, and in a darkened room." During the paroxysms of pain which ac-

What says the materialist to a case like this? Was that powerless *body*, maimed, stiffened, blind, hardly animate,—was *that* the person, *the man*, still active, inquisitive, industrious, generous, and affectionate? or was it only a prison-house, in which the fettered soul was compelled to await its time of release? I envy not the feelings or the intellect of him who could stand by the bedside of that patient sufferer, and still *dis*-believe that "there is a spirit in man, and the inspiration of the Almighty giveth them understanding."

Philosophy of the ancients on this subject.—We may gather instruction on this point even from the wise men of ancient times, upon whose eyes the light of direct revelation never dawned. The philosophical Athenian, in describing the death-bed of the elder Cyrus, makes the dying monarch thus address the children who were gathered round him:—"For I was never able, my children, to persuade myself that the soul, as long as it was in a mortal body, lived, but when it was removed from this, that it died; neither could I believe that the soul ceased to think when separated from the unthinking and senseless body; but it seemed to me most probable, that when pure and free from any union with the body, then it became most wise." Or take the equivalent remark,—equivalent in respect to the essential difference between mind and matter,—in which Plato anticipates the common argument for the immateriality of the thinking principle, which is founded on the constant flux and change of the material particles that make up our bodily organs:—"One would rather say, that each soul wears out many bodies, especially if it should live for many years; for

---

companied this inflammation of the eyes, and which were generally about a week in duration, "he was able to speak only in the faintest whisper, and could hardly bear the sound of another voice." But his sisters and numerous friends were eager to serve as his readers and amanuenses, and his literary pursuits were soon resumed with as much mental activity and cheerfulness as ever. His contributions, both in verse and prose, to the Knickerbocker, a magazine published at New York, may be traced by his signature of "J. K. Jr."; they were frequent, up to the very month in which he died.

if the body wastes away and is destroyed, the man yet living, while the soul always weaves anew that which is worn out, then it certainly follows, that the soul must have its last covering when it perishes, and that it dies only just before that final vesture."

I do not accumulate these arguments and illustrations to establish the doctrine of the immortality of the soul, the proof of which, from the light of nature, has been already admitted to be insufficient. The essential *unity of the person* is contrasted with the essential *complexity of matter* only to show, that the body is but the house we live in, or the garment which covers us for a season. But an indivisible atom is not necessarily indestructible, any more than it is ingenerable. If it cannot cease to exist, it must be that it exists necessarily, and, therefore, it never began to exist. Hence, the argument proves the *preëxistence*, quite as strongly as it does the *immortality*, of the soul; and it was so understood by Plato and his followers, who argue from the antecedent life of man to the subsequent, or that which follows the night of the grave.

The affections recognize the unity and continuity of self. — The continuity and identity of our personal existence amidst the ceaseless changes and renovations, the growth, progress, and decay, of the material structure which we inhabit, form the basis of the relations in which we stand to all other beings. The affections and the duties of life are equally founded upon this unity of personality; this alone makes us responsible both to human and Divine law. "*Person,*" says Locke, "is a forensic term, appropriating actions and their merit, and so belongs only to intelligent agents, capable of a law, and of happiness and misery. This personality extends itself beyond present existence to what is past by consciousness, whereby it becomes concerned and accountable, and owns and imputes to itself past actions upon the same ground, and for the same reason, that it does the present. And, therefore, whatever past actions it cannot reconcile or appropriate to itself, it can no more be concerned in than if they had never been done."

Our social feelings, also, regard this sameness of person, or self, behind the numerous and important changes which our outward frames exhibit. The body wastes, the skin shrivels, the joints and muscles languidly perform their office, and the hair becomes thin and gray. Not a line is preserved, in that bent and decrepit form, of the fresh and elastic vigor of youth, of the quick eye, ready hand, and ruddy lineaments of childhood and maturer years. The features and general aspect of the subject have wholly changed, and the artist must begin the portrait anew. Time has left no indistinct traces of his work, also, on the character and intellect. Enthusiasm is checked, impulse has given way to reflection, appetite is cooled, and the enjoyments of boisterous youth and strenuous manhood pall upon the dulled and satiated sense. But the eye of affection still discerns the *same person* beneath the altered aspect, and the father, brother, son, or friend is loved and cherished still. Instinctively, in the growth of that affection, has the real being, *the man*, been separated from his *accidents*, from his whole environment of outward circumstances, including those of form and feature, no less than of social position and the world's contumely or respect. If the feeling be true, the object of it is one and indivisible, and knows no change. Thus, in our friends as well as in ourselves, in our observation and judgment of others, as much as in the depths of our own consciousness, do we involuntarily separate the transient from the permanent, acknowledge inherent and essential oneness in the midst of complexity and transmutation, and under the fading vesture of time, a garment laid in shifting colors, discern the inflexible features of eternity.

CHAPTER IV.

THE IDEA OF CAUSE, AND THE NATURE OF CAUSATION.

Summary of the last chapter. — I have spoken of the origin and nature of our idea of personality, or rather of our knowledge of *self*, and vindicated that knowledge from the metaphysical objections and cavils that have been brought against it by abstract reasoning. The object was, to establish a distinction, not merely between material and intellectual *phenomena*, which no one can affect to question, but between the *substance* of mind or person and material substance, and thus to show that the difference between them is *essential*, instead of *phenomenal*; — or, in other words, that this difference does not depend merely on the dissimilarity of their outward manifestations. I wished to prove, that we have no idea whatever of *material* substance, except by abstraction, and no proof of its existence, except by inference from its qualities or attributes, of which alone we have any immediate knowledge. But *personality* manifests itself externally, *not by qualities, but by actions;* and these occur, *not simultaneously, but in succession;* while *self*, and the perception of self, or consciousness, *being continuous*, we know it in the intervals of thought or action, and consequently our knowledge of it is *direct*, and not merely an inference. We know, also, that *person* is absolutely simple and indivisible, and is thus distinguishable from its present house of flesh, or bodily covering, which, like all other matter, is essentially complex and infinitely divisible, and which, in fact, is going through a constant process of waste and restoration, the *man* alone remaining unchanged. This conclusion, far from being metaphysical in character, is *a fact* of universal and continuous observation, and as such is inwoven with our principles of conduct; it supports the idea of responsibility, and forms the basis of the social affections.

The idea and the law of causation. — The fact which we have thus attempted to establish is one of the first class, as it relates to *things which exist;* a consideration of the second class, or of *events which take place*, brings us to the idea of *cause*, or the beginning of existence. The inquiry into the origin and nature of this idea is a fundamental one, as in the former case; for on its issue depends every reasonable anticipation of future events, and all real knowledge of those which have passed. The exact sciences relate exclusively to *present* existences; the mathematician studies the laws of number and of space, both of which are applicable to simultaneous phenomena. Events are *successive* phenomena; and the study of them carries us both into the past and the future, and depends in almost every case upon our notion of *cause*.

The law of causation may be stated thus:—*Every event which takes place has a cause.* This law is not applicable to *things which exist*, and much confusion and unsound reasoning have arisen from the attempt to extend it to them. I cannot infer merely from the present existence of a stone, a plant, or an animal, that it must have had a cause; for all I know, it may have existed for ever. But if already aware of the fact, that at some definite epoch it *began* to exist, that time was when it was not, then I say, with absolute certainty, that that beginning of its existence must have been caused by something foreign to itself; or, more loosely speaking, that the thing itself must have had a cause. If all things in the universe were motionless and unchangeable, if no *event* whatever broke the dread uniformity and monotony of time, though all objects should remain precisely as they are at this moment, there would be no foundation for reasoning from effect to cause. The presence of a world would not enable us to prove the existence of its Creator. But the instant a *change* occurs, as soon as a sound is heard, or a leaf falls, or only quivers on its bough, we declare without hesitation, that some power or agency is at work; that the event must have had a cause. It may be a recondite one; the ingenuity of man may have been engaged ever since the foundation of the world in a vain attempt to discover it; still we say with perfect confidence, that it must have existed; there *must* have been a cause somewhere.

Efficient causation distinguished from mere succession. — I speak now of *causation* in its absolute and literal sense, — not merely of an antecedent event, but of an *efficient* antecedent, — of a cause in respect to which, if it were completely known, we could tell beforehand, or prior to all experience, what would be its effect. Those who are familiar with the speculations of philosophers upon this subject will tell me, that I am here adopting the *metaphysical* notion of cause; I admit it, but I say that it is also the *popular* notion, *the ordinary significance of a very common word,* — that people generally never think of attaching any other idea to it, and never find any difficulty in distinguishing the succession of cause and effect, properly so called, from an ordinary sequence, or from the accidental simultaneousness of two otherwise unconnected events. The falling of the spark, they say, is the *cause* of the explosion, meaning thereby the *efficient cause;* and they distinguish this case very clearly from that of two clocks striking the hour in immediate succession, never supposing, in this latter instance, that the one operates on the other, and obliges it to strike, though they may have kept exact time with each other for many years. "*Causa autem ea est, quæ id efficit, cujus est causa. Non sic causa intelligi debet, ut, quod cuique antecedat, id ei causa sit, sed quod cuique efficienter antecedat.*" This fact, that the popular acceptation of the word *cause* is also its strict and scientific meaning, it is important to remember, as will be seen hereafter.

True causes cannot be discovered in the world of matter. — Now, in ordinary physical inquiry, in the world of matter, are we able to perceive and recognize such causes? Admitting, as every rational being must do, that every event, change, or beginning of existence must have an efficient cause, can we discover this cause, and show beforehand that it must produce this particular event, and no other, and *why* it produces it? The answer may appear startling to some, but there is no doubt of its correctness. If there is any one conclusion at which both physical and metaphysical inquirers, after a long dispute, have at last arrived with almost complete accord, it is this: — that we are not able to discern the real cause of any event or change in the outward universe, and that the search after such causes is hopeless; — in the *outward* universe, or world of matter, I say, because the case of *mind* must be considered afterwards. We do not know, that the falling of the spark was the cause of the explosion of the powder; most probably, it was not. We do not know, that the man's taking poison was the cause of his death; most likely, it was not. This statement is not meant to be paradoxical, but simply explicit and clear; I hope to prove satisfactorily that it is well founded.

Observe, then, that all which we discern, in any case, is *the events themselves*, and not *the connection* between those events. I see the falling of the spark; I see and hear the explosion which immediately follows. I have sensible evidence only of this, — that two events happened simultaneously and in rapid succession. Recollecting other instances, or learning them from the testimony of others, I may have reason to believe, that these two events have always taken place together, or that the one has never occurred without being immediately followed by the other. Believing, also, that the course of nature is uniform, it seems very probable, that this succession will always take place in future. I perceive nothing but the events; I know that they are simultaneous, or nearly so; and this is all that I know. I do *not* see any necessary connection between them; and if I hastily infer, that there must be such a connection, because the two always happen in close succession, the case of the two clocks reminds me that invariable antecedence and consequence do not prove any connection whatever. *Cause* implies *power* or *force*, which is never directly perceived; but we *infer* that it exists, because the event happens, or the effect is produced.

It is often loosely said, that one event is the cause of another, when the two are, in fact, separated by quite a long succession of intermediate causes. Thus, it is said, that the stroke of the hammer on the bell is the cause of the sound which we hear; strictly speaking, however, this stroke only precedes an agitation of the particles of which the bell is composed; this agitation is said to cause a vibration in the elastic medium, the air, which extends to our ears; this vibration seems to produce a change, in the auditory nerve; which is followed, probably, by some affection of a part, or of the whole mass, of the brain; and then comes, at last, our sensation of sound. In this final sequence, which involves the connection between mind and matter, we are ready to admit, that we know only the fact, that the affection of the brain is followed by a sensation, and do not know the cause of this fact, or the reason *why* it is thus followed. We are led to make this admission, because our power of detecting intermediate sequences stops here; we cannot point out any links of connection between the effect on the brain and the sensation, as we did between the stroke of the hammer and the agitation of the nerve. The former sequence, then, is admitted to be an ultimate fact, or, what is the same thing, we say that the cause of it is inexplicable. Yet it is certain that we ought to make the same admission as to all the other sequences, each one of which, taken by itself, is an ultimate fact, and equally inexplicable. Why should a blow from a hammer be diffused over a considerable surface, so as to throw all the particles of a large bell, made of solid metal, into agitation? We do not know. But this is one instance out of a large class of similar ones; we are *accustomed* to perceive concussion followed by agitation of the parts of the two bodies which strike together, and this familiarity of the fact makes it seem less inexplicable; it is not wonderful or strange, because we know a vast number of similar cases, and, therefore, we suppose it is not difficult to be understood. In truth, we know nothing about it, except that one event is invariably followed by the other; and this knowledge of constant succession, as we have seen, is very different indeed from a perception of the efficient cause.

How the physical inquirer is said to discover causes. — What is meant, then, when we speak of the success of the physical inquirer, — the chemist, the meteorologist, or the mechanist, for instance, — in pointing out *the causes* of material phenomena? We mean, that he has succeeded in detecting some of these *intermediate sequences*, and in showing, that they are of the same character with a class of other well-known facts, all of which are *supposed to have a common cause,* though we have never thought of asking what that cause is. A phenomenon, which formerly appeared to be anomalous, or the only specimen of its class, is in this manner reduced to the same rank or class with a great number of familiar events. The discovery, then, consists in finding out *the proper classification of the fact, not in ascertaining its cause.* And, further, when we have a great number of phenomena, so similar in character that it is reasonable to believe they are all produced by one cause, though we know not what that cause is, yet we give a name to it. And afterwards, should any fact, apparently anomalous, or of a different order, be reduced to this class, then the name becomes applicable to this fact also, and we say, in ordinary parlance, that the cause of it is discovered. Let me illustrate this a little further.

Gravity is a law, but not an efficient cause. — When Newton discovered that the planets circle round the sun in the same manner in which a stone thrown by the hand describes a curve before reaching the earth, he may be said to have *explained* the former phenomenon, by bringing it into the same class with certain results which have long been familiar to us. But the explanation was only relative, not absolute. The latter phenomenon is, in reality, no more explicable than the former; he did not pretend to know the *cause* of the stone's falling to the ground, any more than of the revolution of the planets. It was something to be able to arrange these apparently heterogeneous results in the same class, and *gravity* was a convenient name to apply to the whole. But the supposition that gravity was an occult cause, inherent in matter, Newton earnestly repelled, declaring that it was inconceivable, and that the motions "must be caused *by an agent,* acting constantly according to certain laws." — So Franklin showed, that a thundercloud and the charged conductor of an electrical machine manifested the same phenomena, and might, therefore, be classed together; sparks were obtained from both; Leyden jars were charged from them; light bodies were attracted and repelled, in the same way, by both; — so that it was reasonable to believe, that the same agency *whatever it might be*, was acting in both cases. What this agency was, he did not even guess. The *cause* of electric action, whether in the excited cloud or in the excited tube, was just as obscure as ever. — Once more; chemists observed, that different substances, when brought into close contact, sometimes remained distinct, and sometimes united with each other, in various, but regular, proportions; and these capacities, of coalescing with one class of bodies, and of remaining unaffected by another, are called chemical "affinities." This is a convenient generalization, and has properly received a specific name; though the common appellation throws no light on the *cause* of the phenomenon, which remains an impenetrable secret. To say, that a certain action is *caused* by the operation of chemical affinities, is only to arrange it with a large class of other observed appearances, equally obscure as to their origin and essential character, but agreeing so far as to render it probable that one cause, *could it ever be discovered*, would be found common to them all.

Further discoveries would not reveal true causes. — Now let us go a step further, and suppose, that the progress of discovery has made known certain facts lying behind the phenomena in question, to which they may all be referred. Let us suppose, that all bodies which gravitate towards each other, are found to be embosomed in a subtile, ambient fluid, which connects them, as it were, into one system; that the positive and negative states of electricity are resolvable into the presence of two fluids, standing in certain relations to each other; and that substances show chemical affinity for each other only when they are in opposite electrical conditions. Still, we have only advanced a step in the generalization, and the real, efficient *cause* of the appearances is still hidden from us by an impenetrable veil. Gravitation is now referred to the communication of motion by impulse; electricity, to the combination and separation of different fluids; affinity, to the attraction or repulsion of these fluids. The latter classes of phenomena are more general, but not a whit more explicable, than the former. We have now fewer causes to seek for, but not one of these few has been

7 *

discovered. When we have resolved electricity, or gravitation, into the presence of an elastic medium, it is a mere figure of speech, to say that we have discovered the *cause* of the electric phenomena, or of gravity. That is just as far off as ever.

Relative distinguished from absolute knowledge. — One is often amused with the tendency of the special students of a particular science, to exaggerate the importance and precision of the lessons which it teaches, or of improvements which have recently been made in its theory. The geologist, for instance, informs us that the date of certain great changes which have taken place in the earth's crust, is fully and clearly ascertained; though he knows only, that the acts of disruption and upheaving were subsequent to the deposition of the rocks in strata, or that the Silurian formation is older than the chalk. But if asked how old the chalk is, he can only say, that it is younger than the Silurian; and to the question, when the rocks were deposited, his answer is, Before they were upheaved. We know not the dates of either of these events, or how long the intervals were that separated them, even by approximation, or within millions of years. Obviously, then, our knowledge of them is not absolute, but relative.

The case is precisely similar with the discoveries of science respecting the causes of material phenomena. The astronomer tells us, that the cause of the planets revolving in elliptical orbits is *probably* the same as that which brings a stone to the ground: but if asked why the stone falls, his answer must be, Probably from the same force which carries our earth round the sun. Observe, now, the errors that arise from the use of language, and the facility with which *words* are often imposed upon us in the place of *knowledge.* To this unknown cause, which is only conjectured to be the same in the two cases, the name of *gravity* is applied; and then, to either of the questions that I have propounded, the man of science wisely answers, that *gravity* is the cause of the phenomenon; and by most persons this answer is held to be sufficient, as it seems to offer a known and adequate cause. But it is not so; *gravity is only the mode in which the machine works,* — *not the cause* of that motion. If asked by a child, why the hands of a clock move so steadily and uniformly round its face, it would not be very satisfactory to reply, that *regularity* is the cause of the motion; to give the little inquirer any real light upon the subject, we must open the case, show the internal machinery, and trace back the complicated action to the descent of a weight. Just so we can observe the regularity with which the hands move over the great dial-plate of nature, which marks out time for us in the heavens; and we may call that regularity *gravitation*, if we please; but human beings are like children, who are not permitted to open the clock-case.*

* What are *general laws*, or *laws of nature*, as they are generally termed? Few phrases are more frequently and glibly used than these, yet in the minds of most persons, they have but a vague and uncertain signification. It is worth while, then, to attempt to gain some clear and precise notions respecting them.

A *law of nature* is nothing more than a *general fact*, or rather *a general statement, comprehending under it many similar individual facts*. A *law* is the result of a *classification*, and individual things are classed together on account of some similarity or uniformity that has been discovered between them.

1. *Objects that exist* are classed together on account of their resemblance to each other. Such classification may consist of several successive steps, and is the proper work of Natural History. Thus, all objects whatsoever are divided into three great kingdoms, the Animal, the Vegetable, and the Mineral. The Animal kingdom is subdivided into four classes, Vertebrates, Molluscs, Articulates, and Radiates or Zoöphites. The *General Fact*, that all the animals so classed possess the organ or property, which is the characteristic of the class, is called a *Law of Nature*. It is a Law of Nature, for instance, that all Vertebrates have a spinal cord and a skull inclosing the brain. Another Law of Nature is, that every animal is produced from an egg.

2. *Events that take place*, also, are classed together on account of their uniformity. Thus, it is a General Fact, or Law of Nature, that pressure on a fluid is propagated equally in all directions, and that a heavy body, if unsupported, falls to the earth. Many of these General Facts are so familiar, that we never think of formally enunciating them; "no science," says J. S. Mill, "was needed to teach men that food nourishes, that water drowns, or quenches thirst, that the sun gives light and heat, that bodies fall to the ground." These laws, also, are not necessary truths, but are founded on mere induction, — often on a not very extensive one. A newly discovered metal, being found, by a single experiment, to be fusible

Uniformity of the effects does not always indicate a common cause. — I have said, that the unknown cause is only *conjectured* to be the same in the two cases; this is an important further limitation of our knowledge of the subject, and naturally leads us to ask, how trustworthy are the grounds of this conjecture. If an observer from another planet, utterly ignorant of the actions, and the reasons of action, of men like ourselves, were to survey, from a distance, the evolutions of large bodies of troops on a parade-ground or a battle-field, he could not fail to be struck by the precision and uniformity of their movements, the preservation of the ranks and files in right lines, and the simultaneous changes in the position and direction of their arms. If he were to inquire, upon the principles of human science, into the cause of these regular and parallel motions, he would prob-

---

at a certain temperature, it is at once declared to be a Law of Nature, that it does melt, always has melted, and always will melt, at the ascertained degree of heat. It is certainly possible, though not probable, that another piece of the metal may be discovered which will not melt at this temperature. A particular event, comprehended under the statement of a Law, is not properly said to be *be caused by the Law,* but only to be *a case,* or instance, *happening under the Law.* A cow does not suckle its calf *because* it is called a Mammifer, but it is called a Mammifer because it suckles its calf. So, it is not a law of Hydrostatics, which causes water to remain at the same level in the two arms of a bent tube; but the fact, that the water stands at this level, is ranked among many other facts, which are comprehended under the general statement, *called a Law,* of Hydrostatics. Gravitation does not make the stone fall, but the particular fact, that this stone fell, is comprehended under the General Fact, *or Law,* of Gravitation. In like manner, Gravitation does not make the earth revolve in an elliptical orbit round the sun; but the fact that the earth revolves in this manner, is ranked with the falling of a stone, and with many other facts *of a similar character,* under the general statement, or Law, of Gravitation.

Hence it is abundantly evident, to adopt Mr. Mill's language, that "the expression, Laws of Nature, *means* nothing but the uniformities which exist among natural phenomena, when reduced to their simplest expression." The Laws of Nature *do not account for,* or *explain,* the phenomena of nature; they only *describe* them. Description and classification are the sole employments of Physical science.

To account for, or explain, the operations of nature, we must have recourse to *Metaphysics* — to something *after,* or *above,* nature. We must ascend to the notion of *Cause.*

ably attribute it to the action of some *one* force, inexplicable to him, situated at the centre of the field, and operating uniformly on every rank, and on every individual in the ranks; and he would proceed to lay down the laws of its operation, — that is, to note the order of the marches and countermarches, and to make out the whole theory of these complicated evolutions. So long as discipline continued, his theory, doubtless, would be a very satisfactory one. But if he waited till the order of review or battle was broken up for the night, he would see, to his astonishment, the soldiers scattering in all directions, and a universal hubbub following that scene of order and method. He would perceive that there was nothing *mechanical* in the whole matter, but that each soldier had a distinct principle of action, a separate will and a separate power of motion; and although, for some unknown reason, all had determined to act in concert for a time, preserving their ranks and mechanically imitating each other, still, for each movement of each individual, there was an independent volition and a distinct personal cause. It is not necessary for me to apply the illustration; substitute weighty bodies, or masses of matter, for soldiers and companies of soldiers, and you have in this theory the exact counterpart of the scientific man's theory of the universe, *as it is commonly understood.* I do not yet say that the theory is false, especially if it be rightly interpreted; I am only showing what is the nature of the evidence which entitles us to attribute all similar phenomena to the operation of a single cause, when we know not, and never can know, the nature of that cause.

But I have gone far enough, perhaps, to vindicate the assertion with which I began, — that we are not able to discern the real or efficient cause of any event or change in the outward universe. This inability is now admitted, so far as I know, by every scientific writer of any reputation, either in physics or metaphysics, excepting Dr. Whewell, whose anticipations of the triumphs of science are rather more glowing than profound. I borrow a clear statement of the truth on this subject from Mr. Mill, as a single authority will be enough.

"What is called *explaining* one law of nature by another," he observes, "is but *substituting one mystery for another*, and does nothing to render the *general* course of nature other than mysterious; we can no more assign a *why* for the more extensive laws than for the partial ones. The explanation may substitute a mystery which has become familiar, and has grown to *seem* not mysterious, for one which is still strange. And this is the meaning of *explanation* in common parlance. But the process with which we are here concerned often does the very contrary; it resolves a phenomenon with which we *are* familiar, into one of which we previously knew little or nothing; as when the common fact of the fall of heavy bodies is resolved into a tendency of all particles of matter towards one another. It must be kept constantly in view, therefore, that when philosophers speak of explaining any of the phenomena of nature, they always mean, pointing out some, not more familiar, but merely some more general, phenomenon, of which it is a partial exemplification, or some laws of causation which produce it by their joint or successive action, and from which, therefore, its conditions may be determined deductively."

How physical science is useful. — Lest some should think that this doctrine tends to discredit physical science, by pointing out the narrowness of its scope, and the hopelessness of all attempts to go beyond it, let me observe, that the field of research is not at all diminished, but the objects in it are called by their right names, and made to appear in their true character. These sequences of phenomena, or *invariable conjunctions of events*, which were improperly supposed to be related to each other as cause and effect, are still, when stripped of this supposititious relation, *important objects of study, and the discovery of new ones will affect the calculations and conduct of men just as much as ever.* To return to the examples first given, we do not know that the spark was the *cause* of the explosion, or that taking poison produced death; but we do know, that the two events *are always united*, that one is the invariable consequent of the other, and *this is enough to direct us in action.* Experience loses none of its value as a trustworthy *guide of life*, though it is deprived of some of its factitious importance as a *source of knowledge.* The discovery of invariable sequences, of regularity in the succession of events, is the true aim of physical science. To distinguish accidental, and therefore infrequent, conjunctions from such as are constant, to separate the casual proximity in time of two events, from their permanent relation to each other as antecedent and consequent, is the only object of the inquirer. An eclipse of the sun *may* be followed by a pestilence; a troubled dream *may* very soon be succeeded by some great domestic misfortune. But a brief experience of eclipses and of dreams will satisfy us, that there is no *permanent* relation between these two events, nothing but a *fortuitous* conjunction of them. On the other hand, the application of heat is *always* followed by the boiling of the water, and the sensation of coldness never fails to result, if the warm hand be placed upon ice. *Permanent sequences are thus distinguished from casual ones;* but of the true relations of the two events to each other, of the reason or cause of their proximity, we are just as ignorant in the latter case as in the former. Previously to all experience, we have no more reason for supposing that powdered sugar will dissolve in water, and powdered marble will not, than for believing that an eclipse of the sun will be followed by an earthquake. "*Causis autem efficientibus quamque rem cognitis, posse denique sciri, quid futurum esset.*"

To distinguish invariable sequences from necessary connections, Dugald Stewart and others have proposed to call the former '*physical* causes,' and the latter '*efficient* causes.' This nomenclature is good enough in one respect, as the former are the only objects of physical inquiry; but it is faulty, in so far as it connects the idea of *cause* in any manner whatever with such relations. 'Physical causes,' as they are termed, are only the constant forerunners and signs of certain natural events; the word *cause* is almost universally understood to mean nothing but *efficient* cause.

How invariable sequences are distinguished from accidental ones. — To show both the importance and the difficulty of distinguishing invariable sequences from accidental and unessential conjunctions, I borrow an illustration from Mr. Stewart. "Let us suppose that a savage, who, in a particular instance, had found himself relieved of some bodily indisposition by a draught of cold water, is a second time afflicted with a similar disorder, and is desirous to repeat the same remedy. With the limited degree of experience which we have supposed him to possess, it would be impossible for the acutest philosopher in his situation to determine, whether the cure was owing to the water which was drunk, to the cup in which it was contained, to the fountain from which it was taken, to the particular day of the month, or to the particular age of the moon. In order, therefore, to insure the success of the remedy, he will very naturally, and very wisely, copy, as far as he can recollect, *every* circumstance which accompanied the first application of it. He will make use of the same cup, draw the water from the same fountain, hold his body in the same posture, and turn his face in the same direction; and thus all the accidental circumstances in which the first experiment was made, will come to be associated equally in his mind with the effect produced."

The man of science, Mr. Stewart might have added, will repeat the experiment a number of times, leaving out at each trial one of the attendant circumstances, till he falls upon one, after the omission of which the desired result no longer follows. He is then popularly said to have found out the *cause* of the cure; but his reason for believing in the efficacy of this *one* antecedent, in its necessary connection with the result, *is precisely the same that the savage had* for believing in the necessity of *all* the attendant circumstances; — namely, that *the application was made, and the cure followed.* And were he to repeat the experiment a thousand times, *he could learn no more* than this, — the invariable attendance of one event upon the other. *Why* the cure takes place, he knows not. Lest I should be accused of taking an extreme case from so imperfect a science as medicine, let me say, that the power of water to slake one's thirst is ascertained in precisely the same manner. After the draught, we feel no longer thirsty; and this succession of the one event to the other is all that we know about it.

The theory which denies that we have any idea of an efficient cause. — I pass now to a consideration of an error in the theory of causation of precisely the opposite character to that which has thus far occupied our attention. So evident does it appear to some philosophers, that we never discern any efficient causes in nature, that they deny our having any knowledge of them, or *any conception of their existence.* The word *cause,* they say, whether it be called *efficient* or not, *means nothing* but invariable antecedence. The idea of efficiency, of power, of energy, is a mere figment of the brain; it denotes nothing but constancy of succession. Dr. Brown's words are, — "We give the name [*cause*] to that which *has* always been followed by a certain event, *is* followed by a certain event, and, according to our belief, *will continue to be* followed by that event, as its immediate consequent; and causation, power, or any other synonymous words which we may use, *express nothing more* than this permanent relation of that which has preceded to that which has followed." So well satisfied was he of the truth of this doctrine, that he said his elaborate argument in favor of it appeared to him very much like an attempt to prove the correctness of the multiplication-table. Hume and Brown are followed in this respect by Mr. Mill, who denies that we have any notion whatever of *power,* or *force,* apart from the substances or events in which they are supposed to inhere; he says, "there is nothing in causation but invariable, certain, and unconditional sequence;" and that "reason repudiates," though the imagination may retain, the idea "of some more intimate connection, of some peculiar tie, or mysterious constraint exercised by the antecedent over the consequent." He even denies the universality and necessity of the law of causation, — or, as he understands it, the law of invariable antecedence, — saying, that although, in this world of ours, every event is preceded by some other event, the two forming a constant sequence, yet, for aught we know, "in some one, for instance, of the many firmaments into which sidereal astronomy now divides the universe, events may succeed one another at random, without any fixed law."

Confutation of this theory. — Against skepticism so extravagant as this, it is only necessary to adduce the fact of which I reminded you at the beginning of this chapter, — that the popular significance of the word *cause* is the scientific and metaphysical meaning of it, the idea being that of *efficient* cause, and not merely of a constant forerunner or sign of any event. I appeal to the consciousness of every one who hears me, if, by the relation of cause and effect, he does not understand a fixed and essential relation, — one perfectly distinct from that of mere succession, — the former event being necessarily followed by the latter, and the existence of the latter being inconceivable except as both preceded and produced by its antecedent. When you say, that the falling of a spark *caused* the explosion, you mean something very different from the mere proximity of two successive strokes upon a bell. The idea of *power*, or *force*, is perfectly clear and distinct in your mind; I ask not now how it came there, — whether it be legitimately acquired, or a mere figment of the imagination; but IT IS THERE, — as distinguishable from all your other notions as the idea of *unity*, or of *self*. "What convinces me," says Dr. Reid, "that I have an idea of *power* is, that I am conscious that I know what I mean by that word, and, while I have this consciousness, I disdain equally to hear arguments for or against my having such an idea." As the idea is not complex, it cannot be analyzed, and is therefore indefinable; but in this respect, it is only on the same footing with all other simple conceptions.

Paradoxical result of the inquiry. — Observe, now, to what point the discussion has brought us; — to the acknowledgment that the idea of power, or efficient cause, is one of the *simplest and most familiar* conceptions of the human mind; yet that we can find *no reality corresponding to it* in the outward universe. Every change, every phenomenon, which begins to exist, *must* have an efficient cause; we can no more question this proposition than we can deny the axioms of the geometer. But the closest observation, the most refined analysis, nowhere discovers such a cause in the external world; it detects nothing, it never can detect any thing, but invariable antecedence, — a relation which differs from that of cause as widely as the idea of person, or self, differs from that of material substance. Whence came the idea, then? Why do we suppose the existence of such a cause, or attribute to it every outward phenomenon, when it is nowhere discoverable? This is the problem which we must now undertake to solve.

Origin of the idea of cause. — Two answers are possible to this inquiry. One is, that the idea of cause is *a conception of pure reason;* an original and spontaneous intuition of the soul; not furnished by experience, though first developed on occasion of its exercise; a part of the primitive constitution of the human mind; in short, an innate idea. Those to whom this answer is satisfactory, of course, need go no further. The existence of such primitive ideas is a mere dogmatic assertion, admitted to be incapable of proof, and affirmed to be in no need of it, but to occupy a position above all argument. No inquiry into their origin, or genesis, is possible, for they had no origin, except with the birth of the mind itself; no process of legitimating them, or establishing their objective validity, is required, as they constitute the grounds of reasoning about other things, and so cannot themselves be reasoned about. If you deny the existence of them, you are a skeptic, or a materialist, and there is an end of the matter. Now, for the purposes of this inquiry, I do not feel concerned either to affirm or deny them. Those who believe in them, as I have said, need go no further; the conclusion to which they have come is perfectly satisfactory, though they have jumped to it; and I freely concede this point, that the idea of cause has a better claim to be considered original and spontaneous than any other. If there are any innate ideas, this surely is one. Those who are not satisfied with this compendious and dogmatic method of solving the problem, may accompany me in a consideration of the second possible answer to the question proposed; — namely, that *the idea of cause has its origin in internal experience, in the consciousness of volition and action.*

The human will is an efficient cause. — Our theorem is, that we have the direct evidence of consciousness, arising from every volition or voluntary act, that the human will is a cause, — an efficient cause, not a mere antecedent, — a *limited* cause, indeed, but supreme within its proper domain, — not always *suf*-ficient for the end proposed, but always *ef*-ficient, or expending force or power, which is real, though often inadequate. Thus, if I will to move a limb which has been paralyzed, though the limb does not move, I am conscious of *making an effort* to move it, and this *consciousness of effort* is a consciousness of force exerted, of *power in action, which is necessarily causal* or *causative*, though in this instance too weak, or too little, for the end proposed. By this "effort," I do not mean the mere straining of the muscles, or muscular effort. I mean the strong purpose, the vigorous exertion of will, a purely mental effort, — which will be best illustrated, perhaps, by an action confined entirely to mind.

Consider, then, the strong effort of the will to fix the attention upon a particular subject of thought, when a variety of distracting circumstances calls off the mind to other topics, — when grief, terror, anxiety, or anger darkens and disturbs the soul. The success of the attempt in such a case, the issue of the struggle, may be doubtful; but we are conscious that it *is* a struggle, that power is put forth towards the end in view, and this power is a true cause. A man of great energy, of indomitable resolution, is said truly to possess great *force* of character, however puny may be his bodily constitution, however meagre and insufficient may be the outward means at his disposal for the accomplishment of his object. In a successful contest with the passions, in resistance to temptation, there is a consciousness of power exerted, which no mere material exertion, no stiffening of the sinews and summoning up the blood, can ever equal. *Our real activity resides solely in the will.* An effort to lift the arm is, so to speak, an *outward* effort, like the attempt to rend an oak; it may or may not succeed; that depends on the material constitution of the nerves and muscles. But *the act was really completed in the volition*, or in putting forth *conscious energy* towards the end proposed; and *this always succeeds.* The limbs may be palsied, the muscles may refuse to bend, and this tenement of clay in which we live may no longer obey our wishes, or minister to our necessities. But the kingly *will* still governs and acts within, and is still responsible for its acts at that dread tribunal where not the outward movements, but the purposes of the heart, come into judgment.

Power may be exerted, though no outward effect follows. — I contend that, in the action of will, we have all the marks or tests, by which efficient causation is distinguished from mere antecedence. In the case of material phenomena, as we have seen, the result can be ascertained only by experience; we learn only by trial that one substance is soluble, and another not, — that iron expands, and clay contracts, in the fire. But in the case of mental exertion, the result to be accomplished is *pre-considered*, or meditated, and is therefore known *à priori*, or before experience; * the volition succeeds, which is a true effort,

* To this statement, Mr. J. S. Mill objects, "This is merely saying, that when we will a thing, we have an idea of it. But to have an idea of what we wish to happen, does not imply a prophetic knowledge that it will happen."

Certainly it does not; but a *mental* sequence between a volition and a bodily motion, is hereby distinguished from a sequence between *two external* events, because, in the latter case, the antecedent gives us no idea at all *what* the consequent will be, and no assurance that there will be *any* consequent; while, in the former case, the antecedent does inform us, through consciousness, and prior to experience, *what* the consequent will be, if any, and also that the volition will *tend* to produce this particular consequent, even if the effort, or the force of the volition, should not suffice to produce *the whole* of the intended result; — just as I may be conscious that I push against a pane of glass, though I do not push hard enough to break it. It is something to establish this distinction, as we thereby negative Mr. Mill's previous assertion, that "our will causes our bodily actions *in the same sense, and in no other*, in which cold causes ice."

Again, — though "the idea of what we *wish* to happen" does not imply a prophetic knowledge of what will happen, yet the idea of what we *will* (that is, the consciousness of a volition,) does imply, if not a *prophetic* knowledge of what *will* happen, yet an *immediate* knowledge of something that *does* happen. It is a consciousness of an action — of something *done* — of power exerted, whether the future result of that action be precisely what we intended or not. An act of the will is at the same moment a volition and an action; it is but one state of mind considered under two different relations. It is a volition, in so far as it is directed to one purpose or a power in action; and this, if the power be sufficient, is *necessarily* followed by the effect. It was from overlooking this distinction, that Hume, Kant, and Brown, and such metaphysicians of the present day as Bailey and Mill, have been led to deny all knowledge of causation even in the action of mind. They confounded *sufficiency* with *efficiency*, and supposed, because the power or volition did not *always* accomplish the object, that it did not *tend towards* it, or exert any effect upon it. But I quote Mr. Mill's language against himself; for when he is looking only to physical causes and material results, he lays down this distinction with admirable clearness.

Alluding to the direction and velocity with which a body moves when acted upon by a certain force, he says, "The body does not only move in that manner, unless counteracted; it *tends* to move in that manner, even when counteracted; it still exerts in the original direction the same energy of movement, as if its first impulse had been undisturbed, and produces, by that energy, an exactly equivalent quantity of effect. This is true, even when the force leaves the body, as it found it, in a state of absolute rest; as when we attempt to raise a body of three tons' weight, with a force equal to one ton. For if, while we are applying this force, the wind, or water, or any other agent, supplies an additional force just exceeding two tons, the body will be raised; thus proving, that the force we applied exerted its full effect, by neutralizing an equivalent portion of the

---

or another; it is an action, in so far as it is something *done*, (and *something*, therefore, *for which our conscience holds us responsible*,) whether the ulterior purpose in view is answered or not. Mr. Mill's ingenious periphrasis for a volition — "an *idea* of what we *wish* to happen" — cannot be accepted. Merely "to have an idea" of a thing, is not *to do* that thing. I may "have an idea" of committing murder; but I do not thereby commit murder. The mind is entirely passive, when it is occupied with mere contemplation, or is merely entertaining ideas. But on the other hand, if I *will* to commit murder, and, as a necessary means to this end, *will* to pull the trigger of a pistol, then, *in foro conscientiæ*, I am guilty of that murder, *because I have done something*, though, from the rustiness of the lock, the trigger should not move, and the life of the intended victim should thereby be saved.

weight, which it was insufficient altogether to overcome. And if, while we are exerting this force of one ton upon the object in a direction contrary to that of gravity, it be put into a scale and weighed, it will be found to have lost a ton of its weight, or, in other words, to press downwards with a force only equal to the difference of the two forces.

"These facts are correctly indicated by the expression *tendency*. All laws of causation, in consequence of their liability to be counteracted, require to be stated in words affirmative of *tendencies* only, and not of actual results. In those sciences of causation which have an accurate nomenclature, there are special words, which signify a tendency to the particular effect with which the science is conversant; thus, *pressure*, in Mechanics, is synonymous with *tendency to motion*, and forces are not reasoned upon as causing actual motion, but as exerting pressure."

How language so precise as this is to be reconciled with the writer's denial of the fact, that we have even any idea of efficient cause, is a question for Mr. Mill to answer. I have no concern with it, except to remark, that the *energy*, or power exerted, which is not followed by any actual effect, but only tends to produce one, cannot with any propriety be considered as a mere *antecedent* event, *for it has no consequent.* It is no fact of observation, inasmuch as no result is perceived; and therefore it does not conflict with our doctrine, that we nowhere discern efficient causes in the material world. But *tendency cannot even be conceived of*, much less so clearly explained as it is by Mr. Mill, *except as the effect of power in action*, and therefore as implying a real cause.

However this may be, the illustration amply vindicates our knowledge of efficient causation in the phenomena of mind, against which no objection can be brought, except the alleged necessity of waiting till experience informs us whether the volition is effective or not, so that we cannot say *à priori*, as we should do of a true cause, that it will be, it must be, effective. We *can* say this beforehand of mental activity, or will; the volition is always effective, if not to the full extent of actually producing the whole result in view, at least as *tending* to produce it, so that it is an efficient cause.

How the idea of cause is expanded into the law of causation. — The difference between voluntary and involuntary states of mind, — between *attention* and *sensation*, for example, — is soon recognized. We *know* that power is exerted in the former case, that every act is preceded by a volition, and that this volition is the sole and efficient cause of the act. Nay, *within the proper domain of the will*, it is even inconceivable to us that any event or change should take place without the agency of the will; and hence, as I am inclined to believe, by a natural association of ideas, we are led to the doctrine of *universal* causation, — to the belief that no event whatever, whether in the mind or in the outer universe, can take place without an efficient cause. In most cases, we are ignorant what that cause is, for undoubtedly the majority even of our mental states is involuntary; we *must* believe and perceive, when evidence or objects are presented to us. These cases we are not completely acquainted with; strictly speaking, the efficient cause of them comes not within the range of our knowledge. But voluntary acts we do know thoroughly; the efficient cause of them — namely, our own will — does lie entirely within the sphere of our consciousness, and is known to be in immediate contact, as it were, with the effect. Hence, association leads us to believe that every other event must have a cause, and that, if we had the thorough knowledge of it which we have of a voluntary act, it would be *seen* to proceed from a cause; and this cause is naturally sought for in the immediately antecedent event. Every action of our lives, every volition, appears in this character; so that it is by no narrow and insufficient induction, but by one that is coëxtensive with our whole conscious existence, the acts which form its basis recurring at every instant, that we are led to the general law, that *no phenomenon occurs without a cause.*

The *universal* and *necessary* character of the law of causation, that "every event must have a cause," may be accounted for in another way. It may be traced to our intuitive appreciation of the fundamental and essential distinction between *matter* and mind, — to the first act of self-consciousness by which the *me* is distinguished from the *not-me*.* In that primitive cognition, we are directly conscious of the *me* as essentially active, and the *not-me* as essentially inert or passive. This is the necessary antithesis which the thinking being establishes between himself and the outward world, just as soon as he arrives at a consciousness of either. He necessarily attributes power and activity to himself, for he cannot imagine, he cannot even think, himself deprived of *power*, or, what is the same thing, of *will*; for in our analysis, the two things are identical. Imagine yourself, if you can, deprived even of the power to will; you cannot do it. Outward restraint is nothing; bars and fetters cannot bind the soul. Paralysis is nothing; we can yet *will* to move the limb, though it remains fixed. The effort may be apparently powerless as to its effect upon the limb; but it is still an effort, and can always be made. You cannot cease to be conscious of a power to will without ceasing to be conscious of yourself.

---

* I here adopt an important distinction from Mr. De Morgan, who first clearly stated it in his "Formal Logic."

"When a name is clearly understood," he observes, "the name applies to every thing, *in one way or the other*, [i. e. positively or negatively.] The word *man* has an application both to Alexander and Bucephalus; the first *was* a man, the second *was not*. In the formation of language, a great many names are, as to their original signification, of a purely negative character; thus, *parallels* are only lines which do *not* meet; *aliens* are men who are *not* Britons, (that is, in our country). If language were as copious and as perfect as we could imagine it to be, for every name which has a positive signification, we should have another which merely implies *all other things*; thus, as we have a name for *a tree*, we should have another to signify every thing that is *not a tree*. As it is, we have sometimes a name for the positive, and none for the negative, as in *tree*; sometimes for the negative, and none for the positive, as in *parallels*; sometimes for both, as in a frequent use of *person* and *thing*."

"Let us take a pair of contrary names, as *man* and *not-man*. It is plain that, between them, *they represent every thing imaginable or real, in the universe*."

Obviously, then, every judgment founded upon the antithesis between the *me* and the *not-me* must be a *universal* judgment; for these two terms, between them, comprise the universe.

Now, the outward world first manifests itself to us as an obstacle, a limitation, a resistance to be overcome. Our first knowledge of its existence is a perception of its inertness, or want of power,—its essential passivity. We cannot cease to recognize this quality in it, without losing consciousness also of that which renders it different from ourselves. Every thing which is foreign to the perceiving mind is perceived to be in antagonism with it; as the one is known only under the conditions of life and activity, the other is recognized only as dead and motionless. Because matter is perceived, through its antagonism with mind, to be essentially inert, we say that every change in its state must have a cause, or that mind, the only true *energy*, or source of power, with which we are acquainted, must be acting upon it, either from within or without. As all actual and all imaginable existence must be either identified with the *me*, that is, with *mind*, or considered as foreign to it, that is, as *matter*, it must also be conceived either as essentially active, or essentially inert. Here, then, we find a basis for the *universal* law of causation.

All the phraseology of causation is borrowed from mind.— This doctrine derives confirmation from the fact, that all the phraseology employed in speaking of the successive generalizations of the science of events is borrowed from the action of mind. The word *action* itself has no real significance, except when applied to the doings of an intelligent agent; we cannot speak of the *doings* of matter, as we could if the word *action* were applicable to it in any other than a figurative sense. Let any one conceive, if he can, of any *power*, *energy*, or *force* inherent in a lump of matter,—a stone, for instance,—except this merely negative one, that it always and necessarily remains in its present state, whether this be of rest or motion. Again, in speaking of the similarity of facts and the regularity of sequences, we refer them to a *law* of nature, just as if they were sentient beings acting under the will of a sovereign. Chemical *affinities*, also, are spoken of, as if material elements were united by family ties, and manifested choice, or affection and aversion. We attribute *force*, or *power*, to the particles of matter, and speak of their natural *agencies*. Just so, we talk of *tone* in coloring, and of a *heavy* or *light* sound; though, of course, in the proper significance of these words, *tone* belongs only to sound, and *heaviness* to gravitating bodies. These modes of speech are proper enough, if their figurative character be kept in view; but we ought always to remember, that *agency* is the employment of one intelligent being to act for another; *force* and *power* are applicable only to *will;* they are characteristic of *volition*. Of course, it is a violent trope to apply either of them to senseless matter.

The doctrine of immediate divine agency. — An obvious corollary from these remarks is, that all *causation* is an exertion of *mind*, and is applied only by metaphor to the *material* universe. It necessarily implies power, will, and action. It is a universally admitted truth, that an efficient cause is nowhere discoverable in the world without us; we know what it is only from consciousness, and all our language respecting it is borrowed from mental phenomena. This doctrine places the material universe before us in a new light. The whole framework of what are called "secondary causes" falls to pieces. The *laws of nature* are only a figure of speech; the powers and active inherent properties of material atoms are mere fictions. Mind alone is active; matter is wholly passive and inert. Mind alone *moves;* matter *is moved.* There is no such thing as what we usually call the "course of nature;" it is nothing but *the will of God producing certain effects in a constant and uniform manner;* which mode of action, however, being arbitrary, or dependent upon will, is as easy to be altered as to be preserved. All events, all changes, in the external world, from the least even unto the greatest, are attributable directly to his will and power, which, being infinite, are always and necessarily adequate to the end proposed. The laws of motion, gravitation, affinity, and the like, are only expressions of the regularity and continuity of one infinite cause. The order of nature is the effect of Divine wisdom; its stability is the result of Divine beneficence.*

* Sir William Hamilton enumerates and criticizes eight different theories that have been framed by philosophers to account for the origin of our

"judgment of causation," or irresistible belief that every event must have a cause. Four of these are based on experience, and affirm that the idea or the judgment is derived from observation; the other four regard this judgment as an *à priori* cognition, — that is, a law of thought, or a condition of experience.

1. The opinion that we are able to detect efficient causes even in the *outward world*, the true *nexus*, or bond of union between the phenomenon and its cause, being exposed to observation, though it continues to be the belief of the vulgar, is now generally abandoned by the learned. Dr. Whewell is the only writer of eminence, since the days of Hume, who has ventured to maintain this doctrine. We have already proved that no true cause has been, or ever can be, discovered in the material universe.

2. The theory maintained in this chapter, that the idea of cause has its origin in *internal* experience, in the consciousness of volition and action.

3. We obtain our knowledge of causation by a process of induction, just as we trace out other recondite laws of nature. After we have repeatedly observed a certain event to be immediately followed by another, and have never seen one without the other, we infer that there is a necessary union between them. When observation has brought to view a multitude of such instances, we generalize the fact into a law of nature. The objections to this theory are, first, that immediate succession is not causation, and secondly, we cannot affirm that *all must be*, because *some are*. This doctrine would allow us to say, that an event as yet unobserved by us *may* take place without a cause; which is contrary to the judgment of causation, that *every* event *must* have a cause.

4. The judgment is the result of custom and the association of ideas. But Hamilton answers, "the *necessity* of so thinking cannot be derived from a *custom* of so thinking. The customary never reaches, never even approaches, to the necessary. On this theory, also, when the association is recent, the causal judgment should be weak; and rise only gradually to full force, as custom becomes inveterate. But we do not find that this judgment is feebler in the young, and stronger in the old."

These are all the theories which are based on experience; we pass to an enumeration of those which give an *à priori* origin to our idea of cause, or resolve it into a law of our mental constitution.

5. The causal judgment is a primary revelation to the intellect, or an ultimate principle, the genesis of which does not admit of explanation. This opinion is adopted by Reid, Kant, Stewart, and Cousin, and is now more generally received than any other. But, *entia non sunt multiplicanda præter necessitatem;* we must not admit any phenomenon to be an ultimate fact, till all the modes of explaining it are proved to be unsound. This opinion, therefore, can only be admitted provisorily; it falls, of course, if what it would explain can be explained on less onerous conditions.

6. Dr. Brown would identify our *conviction* of the causal dependence with our *presumption* of the constancy of nature. But our belief in the

permanency of the laws of nature only *inclines us to expect* that, when *two* events *always have* happened in immediate succession, one of them *always will be* followed by the other; while the causal judgment affirms of any *one* event, though seemingly isolated, that it must have a cause. This *necessity* to suppose a cause for every phenomenon, Dr. Brown keeps cautiously out of view, thus virtually eliminating all that requires explanation in the problem.

7. The next theory is an endeavor to demonstrate the causal judgment by abstract reasoning; in other words, to prove by argument that every event must have a cause. The attempt is vain, because our knowledge of causation is not involved or implied in any higher act of judgment or self-evident proposition, from which it can be deduced by analysis. The reasoning which would trace it to any higher principle is now universally admitted to be inconsequent.

8. Sir William Hamilton's own theory resolves our positive affirmation, that every event must have a cause, into a mere negation, or a result of the incompetency of the human intellect. *E nihilo nihil fit;* as we cannot imagine something to be created out of nothing, when a new phenomenon appears, we are compelled to believe that it had previously existed under other forms. These "other forms," under which it previously existed, are *the causes* of the phenomenon. We object to this theory, that it seems to confound *being* with *doing*, or existence with causation. It does not say, that the cause *produces* the effect, but that the cause *is* the effect; it boldly identifies the two, and thus falsifies the conditions of the problem. If we believe that the phenomenon must have a cause, only in order to avoid believing that the sum of existence is increased, then the cause and the phenomenon are really the same existence, and no change, no event, has taken place. Again, the causal judgment cannot be resolved into the maxim *e nihilo nihil fit*, for the former is the more comprehensive of the two; it would be less natural to deduce the judgment from the maxim, than the maxim from the judgment. The inference, *something cannot be created out of nothing, because every thing must have a cause,* is surely more natural and more logical than to say, *every event must have a cause, because something cannot be created out of nothing.* Still further; the theory shows only the necessity of thinking that the succession of events is continuous — without break before or after — each phenomenon being only a disguised repetition of its predecessor — and no one phenomenon either really beginning to be, or really ceasing to exist. It does not prove or explain (what we are still obliged to believe,) that each event is produced or evolved by some exertion of *force* — some *power* in action. Hamilton's theory, indeed, totally overlooks this notion of *power*, or *force*, though it is a necessary element in our idea of causation. The theory explains only the succession, or continuity of events.

CHAPTER V.

FATALISM AND FREEWILL.

Summary of the last chapter. — The question respecting the origin and validity of our idea of cause, which formed the topic of the last chapter, has been greatly obscured and perplexed, because it involves several distinct inquiries, which are too frequently confounded with each other. I endeavored to separate them, and to consider each one by itself in the natural order. First, the popular acceptation of the word *cause* was observed to be also its strict and metaphysical meaning; as *efficiency* is universally attributed to causation, and a *necessary connection* is believed to exist between cause and effect. But in opposition to the common belief, it was proved that we can nowhere detect such causes in the material universe; the observation of external nature never has led, and never can lead, to the discovery of any thing beyond the invariable *succession* of events, or the fixed relation of antecedence and consequence, — a relation which differs as widely from that of cause and effect, as any two distinct conceptions, which the mind is capable of forming, do from each other. But our inability to discover such causes in the world of matter, is no proof (1.) that they are not to be found anywhere; for there is clear and indisputable evidence that they exist in the world of consciousness, — every act, every volition, of a conscious agent being a true cause. This inability does not even prove (2.) that there are no such causes operating in external nature, as the limits of our faculty of investigation and discovery are not, surely, the limits of the possibility of things; — and the general proposition, that every change or event must have a cause, is one that we can no more doubt than we can disbelieve that two and two make four. For a still stronger reason, this inability does not prove (3.) that we have no *idea* of efficient cause, and therefore no knowledge of what the word *power* means; — for the very existence of the problem, this very search after real causes, shows that we have a clear idea of some connection between two events which is fundamentally different from mere succession, or contiguity in time. The arguments and illustrations which I adduced, went to disprove these three forms of skepticism, these three unfounded conclusions, or false inferences from the admitted fact, that our feeble powers of observation and analysis cannot *discover* any efficient cause whatever in the material universe.

The doctrine of immediate Divine agency. — In arguing against these skeptical views, we were led incidentally to state and defend what I believe to be the true doctrine of causation; — namely, that one particle of matter never *acts* on another particle; for nearly all philosophers admit that we have no proof of such action, and when we come to look closely into the subject, it appears even inconceivable that inert matter should thus *act*, or have any real *power*. In truth, *action* is never even attributed to *matter*, except by a metaphor, or figure of speech, as is clearly shown by an examination of the language usually employed. *The only real action,* of which we have any knowledge or distinct conception, *is that of mind or person;* and the field of this activity is not only the mind itself, but the material structure, the congeries of bones, muscles, and nerves, which we inhabit, all the voluntary motions of which are produced and governed by the indwelling spirit, the kingly and indivisible *will.* Thus we came to the conclusion, that *spirit alone moves, while matter is moved,* and that this union, for a time, of a body with our personality, shadows forth a connection between the material universe and the Infinite One. How else, indeed, can we attach any meaning to the attributes of *Omnipresence* and *Omnipotence?* The unity of action, the regularity of antecedence and consequence in outward events, which we commonly designate by the lame metaphor of *law,* then become the fitting expression of the consistent doings of an all-wise Being, in whom there is no variableness, neither shadow of turning. Our bodies, then, are kindred to organic nature, or the external universe, in a double sense; both are fashioned

from the same materials, from particles of brute matter, and both are informed, actuated, and controlled by an indwelling person; every atom in this tenement of clay being really subject to his sovereign will, though in the one case, that *will* or *power* (for the two expressions are synonymous) is *infinite*, and in the other it is *finite*, or limited, so that the *whole* result which was contemplated does not always follow. The Creator, then, is no longer banished from his creation, nor is the latter an orphan, or a deserted child. It is not a great machine, that was wound up at the beginning, and has continued to run on ever since, without aid or direction from its artificer. As well might we conceive of the body of a man moving about, and performing all its appropriate functions, without the principle of life, or the indwelling of an immortal soul. The universe is not lifeless or soulless. It is informed by God's spirit, pervaded by his power, moved by his wisdom, directed by his beneficence, controlled by his justice. The harmony of physical and moral laws is not a mere fancy, nor a forced analogy; they are both expressions of the same will, manifestations of the same spirit. The sublime language of the poet, then becomes the simple expression of a philosophical and religious truth: —

> "I have felt
> A presence that disturbs me with the joy
> Of elevated thoughts; a sense sublime
> Of something far more deeply interfused,
> Whose dwelling is the light of setting suns,
> And the round ocean, and the living air,
> And the blue sky; . . . . .
> A motion and a spirit, that impels
> . . . . . all objects of all thought,
> And rolls through all things."

The admirer of Wordsworth will perceive that I have omitted portions of lines, which deform this sublime conception with the dark and mystical doctrine of *pantheism*, — a doctrine which no one will confound with the system here developed, who remembers that the complex structure, which is our outward integument for a season, is really foreign to the person, and distinct from the will, or power, by which it is moved and gov-

ened. *Pantheism* is to the Deity what *materialism* is to man, a mere denial of any spiritual existence, and the extinction of all idea of personality.

Objections to this theory considered.—The objection to this theory of causation, that it is *beneath the dignity* of the Almighty to put his hand to every thing, is founded on a false analogy, as is seen by the form in which Aristotle states it. "If it befit not the state and majesty of Xerxes, the great king of Persia, that he should stoop to do all the meanest offices himself, much less can this be thought suitable for God." The two cases do not correspond in the very feature essential to the argument. An earthly potentate, *unable* to execute with his own hand all the affairs of which he has control, is *obliged to delegate* the larger portion of them to his servants; selecting *the lightest* part for himself, he gratifies his pride by calling it also *the noblest;* though the distinction is factitious, there being no real difference, in point of honor or dignity, between them. But Omnipotence needs no minister, and is not exhausted or wearied by the care of a universe. Power in action is more truly sublime than power in repose; and surely it is not derogatory to Divine energy to sustain and continue that which it was certainly not beneath Divine wisdom to create and appoint. Rightly considered, to guide the falling of a leaf from a tree is an office as worthy of Omnipotence as the creation of a world. "Are not two sparrows sold for a farthing? and one of them shall not fall on the ground without your Father."

Equally lame is the oft-repeated comparison of the universe to *a machine* of man's device, which is considered the more perfect the less mending or interposition it requires. A machine is a *labor-saving* contrivance, fitted to supply the weakness and deficiencies of him who uses it. Where the want does not exist, it is absurd to suppose the creation of a remedy. Human conceptions of the Deity are for ever at fault in imputing to him the errors and deficiencies which belong to our own limited faculties and dependent condition. Hence the idea of the Epicureans, that sublime indifference and unbroken repose are the only states of being worthy of the gods. Viewed in the light of true philosophy, no less than of Christianity, how base and grovelling does this conception appear! Substitute for it the Christian idea of the unceasing watchfulness of a Parent, and the active and constant beneficence of an Almighty Father and Friend, and it sinks into its true character, as a degrading doctrine of heathen mythology.

Divine action equally incessant in the physical and moral universe.— In truth, we have only to decide whether it is more likely that the complex system of things in the midst of which we live, — the beautiful harmonies between the organic and the inorganic world, the nice arrangements and curious adaptations that obtain in each, the simplicity and uniformity of the general plan to which the vast multitude of details may be reduced, — whether this system, I say, *is* NOW *sustained,* and prevented from falling into nothingness and ruin, by one all-wise and all-powerful Being, or by particles of brute matter, acting of themselves, without any immediate direction, oversight, or control. Remember we have no proof, that such particles can exert any causal agency whatever; that science never has discovered, and never can discover, a single efficient cause, properly belonging to matter, in the whole material universe; that the only power in action with which we are acquainted, is that of mind upon matter, and upon itself, as evinced in our own consciousness, and in the voluntary movements of our bodies dependent on the will or person within; and that the almost unceasing movement and change of all the material particles around us, that are not dependent upon our own wills, is a fact to be accounted for by some efficient and adequate cause. The *moral* government of God is admitted to be direct, incessant, and continuous, by all theists who admit his moral attributes, and who thereby furnish a basis for religious faith and practice. This is evident from all the ordinances of religion; prayer being a mockery, unless we believe it is heard, and worship not really obligatory, unless it is specially enjoined. Then why is not his *physical* government, so to speak, his causation and control of movement and change in the material universe, equally immediate and unceasing?* I believe that it is, and when rightly viewed, the flut-

* In his strictures upon this doctrine and the reasonings by which it is supported, Mr. J. S. Mill objects to "the inference that, because Volition is an efficient cause, therefore it is the *only* cause, and the direct agent in producing even what is apparently produced by something else. Volitions," he says, "are not known to produce any thing directly except nervous action, for the will influences even the muscles only through the nerves. Though it were granted, then, that every phenomenon has an efficient, and not merely a phenomenal cause, and that volition, in the case of the particular phenomena which are known to be produced by it, is that efficient cause; are we therefore to say, with these writers, that since we know of no other efficient cause, and ought not to assume one without evidence, there *is* no other, and volition is the direct cause of *all* phenomena? A more outrageous stretch of inference could hardly be made." And again, "The supporters of the Volition Theory," which is the name he gives to the doctrine of the Immediate Agency of the Deity, "ask us to infer that volition causes *every thing*, for no reason except that it causes *one particular thing*; although that one phenomenon, far from being a type of all natural phenomena, is eminently peculiar; its laws bearing scarcely any resemblance to those of any other phenomenon, whether of inorganic or of organic nature." — *System of Logic*, 3d ed. vol. i. pp. 370–372.

We presume Mr. Mill will admit it to be a sound logical maxim, that *no more causes must be assigned than what are absolutely necessary to account for the phenomena.* The reasoning to which he objects may be briefly stated thus: — Volition is the *only* known *power* in the universe; changes in matter are the phenomena to be accounted for; and as many such changes (to wit, the movements of our own limbs and bodily organs,) are confessedly produced by *human* volition, the residue of them must be attributed to some other *Will*, which, by its omnipresence and omnipotence, is capable of producing them.

We contend that this reasoning is eminently logical, and in proof of this assertion, we once more cite against Mr. Mill his own *System of Logic.* The reasoning here employed is what he calls the method of "induction by simple enumeration," — a law being assumed to hold good in *all* cases, because it has been found to hold good in *many* cases, and not one instance has been found to the contrary. It is curious to find Mr. Mill, in the following passage, asserting that this process is entirely valid and legitimate in reference to the law of universal causation, the very instance to which we are here applying it.

"Induction by simple enumeration," he says, "or, in other words, generalization of an observed fact from the mere absence of any known intering of a leaf to the ground, after it has been disengaged from its parent bough, furnishes evidence of Divine agency as direct as if the grave should give up its dead.

> "Estne Dei sedes, nisi terra, et pontus, et aer,
> Et cœlum, et virtus? Superos quid quærimus ultra?
> Jupiter est quodcumque vides, quocumque moveris."

Birth is surely as wonderful — as miraculous, if that term be preferred — as *resuscitation;* and birth is constantly going on all around us. The greater frequency of the act certainly does not lessen its marvellousness, or render it easier of accomplishment; though the repetition exhausts and deadens our emotion of wonder, and we then conceal under the lame metaphor of

---

stance to the contrary, is by no means the illicit logical process in all cases which it is in most. It is delusive and insufficient exactly in proportion as the subject-matter of the observation is special and limited in extent. As the sphere widens, this unscientific method becomes less and less liable to mislead; and the most universal class of truths, *the law of causation, for instance,* and the principles of number and geometry, *are duly and satisfactorily proved by that method alone, nor are they susceptible of any other proof.*" — *Id.* Book III. ch. xxi. § 2.

The case we are now considering is one of *universal* generalization; it embraces *all* the phenomena of the material universe, *every* change in which requires a cause. Human bodies, of course, are a part of this universe, — as much so as the ground these bodies tread upon, or the air they breathe. All the voluntary movements of these bodies, which are repeated and varied till their number exceeds all calculation, are known to proceed from the *Will* as their efficient cause; and *the Will is the only known instance of efficient causation in the universe.* The law of "induction by simple enumeration," then, is strictly applicable in this case; and the conclusion to which it leads us, is, that all other physical events — from the quivering of an aspen leaf up to the flight of the planets in their courses — are also attributable to *Will,* and *that* Will must be one proportioned in power and comprehensiveness to the variety and grandeur of its effects. That this Will belongs to a Being differing from all those whose existence is made known to us by the testimony of the senses, is not a circumstance which vitiates the argument, for the reasoning is addressed only to the Theist. The muscular movements of different individuals are ascribed respectively to the volitions of those individuals. The Will has efficient causative agency *as such,* and not because it is the Will of one man or another — not because it is human or divine.

law, and the blank hypothesis of machinery, the direct and perpetually recurring action of Deity.

The argument for the Divine existence, then, is ever freshly presented to us by the continuance, no less than by the beginning, of all things. It proceeds not only from the creation of the race, but from the birth of the individual. In the seed which swelled under the last night's rain, in the shoot which appeared under this morning's sun, we find proof of ever-present and ever-acting power. To the reflecting theist,

> "The world's unwithered countenance
> Is bright as at creation's day,"

and reflects its Maker's image just as clearly.

The fatalistic doctrine of causation. — The doctrine of causation which I have thus endeavored to develop, stands in striking contrast with the only other theory of it which I find occasion here to notice, — a theory, indeed, which does not rest upon any new fundamental principle, but, beginning with the general law of causation as applied to the physical universe, carries it out in all its universality, with an affectation of great logical rigor, to its inevitable conclusion in a sweeping system of fatalism. It would be difficult to find a more impressive illustration than is afforded by this theory, of the danger of commencing with a single *abstract* proposition, asserted to be original and spontaneous, a necessary and universal law of human belief, and pushing it, in all its strictness, to its remotest consequences, unchecked by facts, and unappalled either by the irrational or the revolting character of the principles to which it leads. It furnishes the most striking example of the mischief of applying metaphysical reasoning to practical subjects.

The theory begins with the general law of causality, — that every event must have a cause, — this being understood either absolutely, or, as in its application to material phenomena, to signify only invariable antecedence and consequence. The whole doctrine depends on this word *invariable*, taken absolutely, and on the assumed universality and *necessary* character of the law itself, in virtue of its primitive and categorical nature.

Every event, of course, is surrounded by other events, and must be considered as being at the same time both antecedent and consequent,—as *necessarily* resulting from those which preceded, and *necessarily* followed by those which come after it,—and thus, as forming one link in an adamantine chain which extends from eternity to eternity. All occurrences whatever have their environment of circumstances, with which they stand in necessary and fixed relations by an absolute law; and the state of the universe at any one moment, in all its parts, from the creation of a world to the stirring of an aspen leaf, could not possibly have been different from what it is. Still further, the system is not content, after thus "binding Nature fast in fate," to "leave free the human will." Every volition, every act, of a conscious agent is preceded by certain states of mind, certain sensations, beliefs, and emotions, *all involuntary*, upon which it is necessarily consequent; and it could no more have been unlike what it is, than our earth could suddenly and causelessly cease turning upon its axis, and revolving round the sun. Nay, more;—with a Titan-like audacity of speculation, we must scale the throne of Omnipotence itself, and say—if the utterance of such a doctrine be not blasphemy—that every thought and act even of the Almighty is but the inevitable consequence of all that has gone before, the necessary cause or forerunner of all that comes after it.

Consequences of this doctrine.—I have endeavored to present this astounding theory in its simplest and most abstract form, in order to show clearly the grounds on which it rests, and the nature of the reasoning by which it is supported. It is the consistent and thorough application of a single abstract principle, assumed to be a primitive and necessary law of the human understanding, to the whole order of actual, possible, and conceivable events. Unlike the skepticism of Hume, which aims merely to shake all convictions, and to reduce all principles to uncertainty and doubt, this system appears as the dogmatism of infidelity, the demonstration of fatalism. If we are entitled to reason *à priori* about matters of fact, these are the conclusions in which we must rest. Belief in a miracle, of course, is an absurdity; a revelation from God to man is an impossible idea. All evidence, all testimony, adduced in proof of such events, must be rejected at once, and without examination; it can be nothing but moral evidence, made up of contingent truths, which, in the presence of necessary convictions, or truths known *à priori*, vanish like mist before the sun. This theory is the pivot on which the whole system of Spinoza rests and turns, and it is the avowed essence of German Transcendentalism. As such, it is taken up and expounded with singular clearness and method by Fichte, who is far the ablest reasoner in that school, not even excepting Kant. In Fichte's work on the Destination of Man, which contains a summary of his philosophical opinions, it is so fully developed, that I shall give you the application of it mostly in his own words.

Fichte's exposition of Fatalism. — "Why, then, has Nature," asks Fichte, "amidst the manifold, infinite, possible varieties of being, assumed precisely these, and no others? For this reason, — that certain others had preceded them, and these, in the same manner, will determine those which shall follow; and these again, others, to infinity. Were the smallest thing at the present moment different from what it is, then necessarily, in the following moment, would something else be different, and again in the succeeding one, and so on for ever. . . . . .

"In every moment of her duration, Nature is one connected whole; in every moment must every individual part be what it is, because all others are what they are; and a single grain of sand could not be moved from its place, without, however imperceptibly to us, changing something throughout all parts of the immeasurable whole. Every moment of duration is determined by all past moments, and will determine all future moments; and even the position of a grain of sand cannot be conceived other than it is, without supposing other changes, to an indefinite extent. Let us imagine, for instance, this grain of sand lying some few feet further inland than it actually does; then must the storm-wind that drove it in from the sea-shore have been stronger than it actually was; then must the preceding state of the atmosphere, by which this wind was occasioned, and its degree of strength determined, have been different from what it actually was, and the previous changes which gave rise to this particular weather, and so on. We must suppose a different temperature from that which really existed,— a different constitution of the bodies which influenced this temperature: the fertility or barrenness of countries, the duration of the life of man, depend, unquestionably, in a great degree on temperature. How can we know, since it is not given us to penetrate the arcana of nature, and it is therefore allowable to speak of possibilities,— how can we know, that in such a state of the weather as we have been supposing, in order to carry this grain of sand a few yards further, some ancestor of yours might not have perished from hunger, or cold, or heat, long before the birth of that son from whom you are descended, and thus you might never have been at all; and all that you have ever done, and all that you ever hope to do in this world, must have been hindered, in order that a grain of sand might lie in a different place?

"I myself, with all that I call mine, am but a link in this chain of rigid natural necessity. There was a time,—so others tell me, and although I am not immediately conscious of it, I am compelled by reason to admit it as a truth,— there was a time in which I was not, and a moment in which I began to be. I then only existed for others, not yet for myself. Since then, myself, my conscious being, has gradually developed itself, and I have discovered in myself certain faculties and capacities, wants, and natural desires. I am a definite creature, which came into existence at a certain time. I have not come into existence by my own power. It would be the highest absurdity to suppose that, before I was at all, I could bring myself into existence; I have, then, been called into being by a power out of myself. And what should this be but the universal power of Nature, of which I form a part? The time at which my existence commenced, and the attributes belonging to me, were determined by this universal power of Nature; and all the forms under which these my inborn attributes have since manifested themselves, have been determined by the selfsame power. It was impossible that, instead of me, another should have arisen; — it is impossible that, at any moment of my existence, I should be other than what I am.

"That my successive states of being have been accompanied by consciousness, that some of them, such as thoughts, resolutions, and the like, appear to be nothing but various modifications of consciousness, need not perplex my reasonings. It is the nature *of the plant* regularly to develop itself; *of the animal* to move towards the attainment of certain ends; *of the man* to think. Why should I hesitate to acknowledge the latter as an original power of Nature, as well as the first and second? *Thought* is assuredly a far higher and more subtile operation of Nature, than the formation of a plant, or the motion of an animal; I cannot explain how the power of Nature can produce thought; but can I better explain its operation in the production of a plant, in the motion of an animal? Thought exists in Nature, as well as the creative power which gives birth to the plant. The thinking being arises and develops himself by natural laws, and exists through Nature. There is, therefore, in Nature an original thinking power, as well as an original plant-creating power. . . . . .

"Figure, motion, thought, in me, are not consequent on one another, but are the simultaneous and harmonious developments of what might be called the *man-forming* power, necessarily manifesting itself in a creature of my species. I am not what I am, because I think so, or will so, — nor do I think and will, because I am, — but I am, and I think, both absolutely and necessarily. I am that which I am, because, in the connection of the great whole, only such a one, and absolutely no other, was possible; and a spirit who could look through all Nature, would, from the knowledge of a single man, be able to determine what men had been before, and what they would be at any moment. In one person, he would obtain the knowledge of all. All that I am and shall be, I am and shall be of necessity, and it is impossible that I should be otherwise. Give to Nature a single definition of a person, let it be ever so apparently trivial, — the course of a muscle, the turn of a hair, — she would be able, had she a universal consciousness, to declare what would be his whole course of thought during his whole course of being. Most certainly I cannot, by all my repentance, by all my resolutions, produce the smallest alteration in the appointed course of things. I stand under the inexorable power of rigid Necessity; should she have destined me to become a fool and a profligate, a fool and a profligate without doubt I shall become. Should she have destined me to be wise and good, wise and good I shall doubtless be. There is neither merit nor blame to be ascribed to her or to me. She stands under her own laws, — I under hers. It would therefore contribute to my tranquility to subject even my wishes to that power to which my existence is entirely subject. — O, these rebellious wishes!"

Practical results of fatalism. — There is no ambiguity in this language, no reserve in the statement of the doctrine. Fichte was a daring speculatist, and did not shrink from the enunciation of the theory of philosophical necessity in all its rigor and completeness. The practical lesson, the rule for the conduct of life, which is deducible from this theory, may be very briefly stated; it is the practical fatalism of the East: — *Make no vain efforts to alter that course of things which proceeds by its own irresistible laws; do not contend with your destiny.* Submit to be carried along, like a leaf floating on the waters, whithersoever the stream may lead. Embosomed in nature, and borne along with it, let your passive intellect reflect like a mirror whatever images may stray over its surface. Utter the word that is in you, perform the act to which you are prompted, and spend no thought about the consequences of either; these will inevitably come as they are determined, be your strivings and exclamations what they may. Strictly speaking, you do not act, but are acted upon; contemplation, and not action, is your fate.

Exposition of Spinoza's system. — I have said that Spinoza's system is but the development and completion of this theory. As nature is one connected whole, and I am but a part of it, and every individual part of it must be what it is, because all others are what they are, there is truly but one substance, and that exists by necessity. Thought and extension are its attributes, and both are infinite, like the substance in which they inhere. The essence of a thing, or its formal cause, is its internal constitution, or that which makes it what it is. In this sense, we may speak of a cause of all things, or of nature; but it is an *indwelling*, or *immanent*, cause,—and not one which is really distinct from the thing itself, and operates upon it from without. We may contemplate Nature as a cause, that is, as operating on itself, and causing all things in itself by its own inherent necessity, every event being the necessary result of all other events, and every part being determined, or made what it is, by all the other parts;—this is the first conception, and in this sense, Nature *is* a cause, but a cause only of itself; it is, in technical phrase, *natura naturans*, or Nature working out itself; and thus understood, Nature is God. But we may also contemplate nature as an effect, as something produced, *natura naturata*, nature worked out, or made what it is; yet, as before, it is so made, or worked out, only by itself, and by virtue of its own inherent and necessary laws;—in this sense, there is nothing but nature, and there is no God.

The doctrine is abstruse; but as it is only the logical development of a single principle, a train of consequences drawn from one axiom, we cannot complain that it is unintelligible. We hear so much about Spinozism at the present day, its spirit pervades so large a portion of the reputed philosophy of our times, and so many of its doctrines, or corollaries from those doctrines, are pressed home upon us, without any distinct indication of their source, that it is worth while to give some effort and attention to the attempt to understand it.

The conception of an immanent cause illustrated.—In illustration of what I have stated, then, let me ask you to contemplate a particular substance,—a piece of iron, for instance; it has certain qualities, or attributes, such as hardness, weight, malleability, etc.; and these qualities may be considered as the results, or effects, of the internal constitution of the iron, or the relation of its primary particles or atoms to each other. This internal constitution being altered or affected in any way, the qualities which result from it, or are caused by it, are altered also; it becomes more or less hard, weighty, malleable, etc.; perhaps it loses some quality entirely, as when it ceases to be malleable. This internal constitution of the body, the old philosophers called *its essence*, or that which makes it what it is; and they wasted a great deal of labor in searching after the essences of things; for, as all the qualities are derived from the essence, and depend upon it, if we knew the essence, we could tell beforehand what all its qualities must be, they being deducible from it; just as the geometric properties of a triangle are deducible from the geometric definition of a triangle. Now, as the qualities of a substance form our whole distinct conception of that substance, and as the essence produces, or causes, these qualities, it is quite intelligible, in one sense of the word *cause*, to say that the substance *causes* or determines itself; and this is what Spinoza means when he speaks of *natura naturans*, Nature causing itself, or being a cause; — in which sense, Nature is God, or, in other words, God is the indwelling, or immanent, cause of nature; — not a foreign cause, acting upon it, or creating it, from without, but its essence, or internal cause; — that is, its internal constitution, on which all its qualities depend.

Again, we may contemplate the piece of iron without reference to the internal origin, or source, of its qualities, but simply as a particular substance manifesting certain attributes. This is the idea of *natura naturata*, or nature worked out, and existing as a whole; in this sense, there is nothing but nature, and there is no God. Observe further, that these two ideas of nature differ only formally, and not objectively, from each other; they are but two aspects of, or two modes of considering, one and the same Nature. So the iron is one and the same body, whether we regard its qualities as constantly produced or manifested — that is, *caused* — by its internal constitution, or essence, or look at it merely as an aggregate of those qualities, inhering in one *substratum*. The criticism of Dr. Reid, then, is well founded, when he says, that in Spinoza's system "there neither is, nor can be, a cause at all; nothing acts, but every thing is acted upon; nothing moves, but every thing is moved; all is passion, without action, — all instrument, without an agent; and every thing that is, or was, or shall be, has that necessary existence in its season, which we commonly consider as the prerogative of the First Cause." The *cause* that is spoken of in this system is not an *efficient*, but a *formal*, cause; that is, the inherent necessity of the thing to exist, and to be what it is. The universe, or the totality of things, is presented by Spinoza as one connected whole, but under a double aspect: — first, as necessarily existing, its existence at any one moment being absolutely determined, or caused, by its existence at the preceding moment; and in this view, God is identified with nature, and we have a system of pantheism; — secondly, as the only substance or necessary being, without regard to the manner in which its successive states of being are manifested or developed; and in this view, there is nothing but nature, and the scheme is one of atheistic fatalism. The germ of this latter doctrine may be found in the ancient speculation of Democritus and Leucippus, amounting to an atheistic fatality founded on the mechanical or corpuscular philosophy. Dr. Reid justly says of it, that it is "the genuine and most tenable system of necessity;" and if it be true, all reasoning to prove the existence of a First Cause 'must be given up as fallacious."

Spinozism the logical consequence of attributing efficient causation to matter. — It would not be difficult to show, in respect even to the modified scheme of necessity that is presented by so cautious and temperate a speculatist as Mr. Mill, either that it is wholly unfounded, a baseless dream, or that it must be carried out, by the legitimate and consistent extension of the argument on which it rests, to the gigantic system, the absolute and universal Fate, of Spinoza.* No compromise is possible with this

* Having asserted that "*there is nothing in causation but invariable, certain, and unconditional sequence,*" and having thus got rid of the idea of any active *force* or *power*, Mr. Mill thinks he has thereby effectually exorcised the bugbear of Fatalism, which has so long obstructed the reception of the doctrine of Necessity. He avows that he is a Necessarian, but he stoutly denies that he is a Fatalist. Men are unwilling to admit, he says, that

doctrine; we must deny secondary causes altogether, or we must go on to Asiatic and atheistic fatalism. It is the boast of

there is any "peculiar tie" between a man's previously formed character, together with his motives, on the one hand, and his actions on the other, so that the latter are under "a mysterious constraint" from the former. No; a man's motives do not *compel* or *force* his character. There is no *compulsion* in the case; there is no such thing as *force*. If there were, Fatalism would be the only true doctrine. But a man's actions are "the invariable, certain, and unconditional" results or consequents of his motives and his character. The actions *must* have been what they are, and *must* be repeated, if the same antecedents should again occur; the man could not have willed otherwise than he did; and under the same circumstances, the same volition would inevitably be repeated. B invariably follows A, and always *must* follow it; yet, so long as A does not *compel* B to follow it, but the inevitableness of the sequence arises from some other source, — say, from the nature of things, or from a logical necessity, — then the doctrine is not one of Fatalism, but only of Necessity.

Mr. Mill finds great comfort in this distinction; but we must avow our opinion, that it is a distinction without a difference. We do not object to the Fatalist's doctrine so much on account of *what he asserts*, as on account of *what he denies*. He asserts, that the strongest motive constrains the will with a despotic power, so that the volition could not have been otherwise than what it was. This is bad enough, and even Mr. Mill does not agree with him, but affirms that the motive does *not* constrain the will, because no one thing ever constrains or causes another thing. There is no such thing as "a peculiar tie or mysterious constraint" in any case. But the Fatalist denies that *we* are the free causes of our own actions; and here, unfortunately, Mr. Mill agrees with him, and for the same reason as that alleged in the former instance, namely, that there is no such thing as efficient causation. If this be so, we are just as badly off as ever; for remorse is illusory, and repentance is vain, if the action repented of was the "invariable, certain, and unconditional" consequence of what preceded it, so that it could not have been changed by any exertion of the will alone, unaided by a change of circumstances.

Conscious, however, that man needs a little consolation under the fearful doctrine that all his volitions and actions are the inevitable consequents of circumstances over which he has no control, Mr. Mill tries to administer a drop of comfort by suggesting, that, if a person *wishes* to alter his character, (that character being *one* of the antecedents which his volitions follow,) then the *wish* itself is a new antecedent, "and by no means one of the least influential," and it necessarily tends towards its own fulfilment. In other words, if the wish exists to modify the character, the character really **is** somewhat modified by that wish. But then, this wish "is given us, not by

the followers of Spinoza, that their reasoning is mathematical and demonstrative from beginning to end; all the forms and

---

any efforts of ours, but by circumstances which we cannot help; it comes to us either from external causes, or not at all." "Most true," responds our author; yet if circumstances have not given us any desire about the matter, then we have no reason to be troubled. If we have not the wish, we cannot complain of its non-fulfilment. In this case, we are dumb cattle, driven forward by an inexorable master, Fate; but luckily we are *blind* cattle, and do not therefore lament our destiny, because we are ignorant that the path along which we are driven terminates on a precipice.

We cannot find much comfort in this suggestion. In no proper sense are we masters of our own destiny, if the mastership is given or withheld only by some circumstance over which we have no control; and it is a very imperfect mastership at best, as the existence of the wish is only *one* out of the many antecedents, independent of our own will, which determine our whole conduct. A faint wish would have little or no effect. "If what we do depends on our wishing to do it," says Dr. Walker, "and our wishing to do it depends not on ourselves, then nothing depends on ourselves, except to be the willing and active instruments of destiny." The most decided Fatalist will readily admit, that the thoughts and wishes which come into our minds without any agency on our part, and whether we will or not, are *among* the circumstances which regulate our actions and shape our destiny.

In all other respects, save the two qualifying doctrines (if they can be called such) which we have now fully considered, Mr. Mill is a consistent and rigorous Fatalist. He is too good a logician to stop short of any legitimate inferences from his doctrine, and too bold and independent a thinker to shrink from avowing these inferences, whatever they may be.

"There is no Thing produced, no event happening, in the known universe, which is not connected by a uniformity, or invariable sequence, with some one or more of the phenomena which preceded it; insomuch that it will happen again as often as those phenomena occur again, and as no other phenomenon having the character of a counteracting cause shall co-exist. These antecedent phenomena, again, were connected in a similar manner with some that preceded them; and so on, until we reach, as the ultimate step attainable by us, either the properties of some one primeval cause, or the conjunction of several.

"The state of the whole universe at any instant we believe to be the consequence of its state at the previous instant; insomuch that one who knew all the agents which exist at the present moment, their collocation in space, and their properties, — in other words, the laws of their agency, — could predict the whole subsequent history of the universe, at least unless some new volition of a power capable of controlling the universe should supervene." — Vol. I. pp. 357, 358.

requisitions of mathematical logic are complied with in the work of their master; the reasoning is perfectly abstract, the technicalities of the geometer and algebraist are preserved, and no flaw can be found in the demonstration. I fully admit the justice of this boast; if you grant Spinoza's premises, there is no stopping short of Spinoza's conclusions. Once admit that efficient causation belongs to matter, that one particle really *acts* on another particle by its inherent power or principle, and necessitates a change of its state, and it follows that the displacement of a grain of sand *must* alter the history of the universe. Each event is bound by iron necessity to all preceding and all subsequent events, the chain of Fate extending from the fall of an atom up to the throne of God. Admit further, that the volitions and acts of a conscious agent are events of the same order with occurrences in the material universe, having their antecedents and consequents, with which they equally stand in invariable relations, and man himself is like a grain of sand, controlled and blown about by the winds of destiny. Thought and extension, then, are attributes of one infinite substance, both being manifested by the same inherent necessity, both being what they are because other things are what they are.

> "All are but parts of one stupendous whole,
> Whose body Nature is, and God the soul;" —

the word *soul* being here understood in the same sense as internal constitution, or essence, — as if we should say, that it is the nature, or *soul*, of iron to be hard, weighty, and malleable. The parts of the great whole being thus bound together, each being the result of all, and all of each, it follows, — to repeat Fichte's illustration, — that, the slightest particular being given, the course of a muscle, or the turn of a hair, in a certain individual, and if Nature could answer, she would be able to foretell all his good and evil deeds, from the beginning to the end of his life. An inwrought necessity extends through the whole web of events physical and mental, reaching from infinitude to infinitude; and this necessity is God. Nothing acts; every thing is acted upon; nothing moves, every thing is moved; this necessity itself, being the inherent nature of things, and not an external force, operating from without, is said only formally *to compel*, or *to act*, — since it is passive, not efficient. Thus the system of Spinoza is but the consistent and universal application of the law of causality, (wrongly interpreted, as I believe,) but taken absolutely, to all conceivable events; it is but the extension of this principle, that every event must have a cause.

It cannot be denied, that there is a kind of awful sublimity in this appalling doctrine, in its simplicity, consistency, and universality, which renders it very impressive to the imagination, and accounts, in a great degree, for the favor with which it is received by many persons of a poetical temperament. An Oriental fable, says Mr. Stewart, "places the import of the doctrine in a more striking light than I could do by any philosophical comment. The Arabians tell us, that as Solomon (whom they supposed a magician, from his superior wisdom) was one day walking with a person in Palestine, his companion said to him, with horror, 'What hideous spectre is that which approaches us? I do not like his visage. Send me, I pray thee, to the remotest mountain of India.' Solomon complied, and the very moment he was sent off, the spectre arrived. Solomon,' said he, 'how came that fellow here? I was to have fetched him from the remotest mountain of India.' Solomon answered, 'ANGEL OF DEATH, thou wilt find him there!'"

Spinozism contrasted with the doctrine of immediate divine agency. — I have chosen to present this terrible dogma of universal fatalism, for the first time fully and scientifically developed by Spinoza, in immediate juxtaposition and contrast with that view of causation to which we were led by the principles adopted in this work; — with the doctrine, that is, which denies that there is any power or efficient agency whatever in brute matter, even by transmission, or as derived from a higher source, and which ascribes all causation to spirit, or person, — whether finite, and therefore often inadequate, and always limited in its sphere of action, — or infinite, and so necessarily adequate to all occasions, both controlling and *sustaining* the universe of things, from the fall of a leaf up to the creation of a world. The two doctrines are the opposite extremes of this question they are the antipodes of each other. But I believe they are also the only logical and consistent creeds which we can entertain upon this subject, all intermediate views being imperfect and inconsequent. Begin with any event you please in the material universe, not immediately connected with the agency, real or supposed, of man, and but two suppositions respecting its cause are possible. Take, for instance, the melting of wax in the flame; if you believe that the flame really *acts* on the wax, that there is an inherent and underived power in the former to melt, and a necessity in the very constitution of the latter to be melted, when the two are brought together, then you cannot consistently stop short of Spinozism; you must also believe that the fall of a leaf from a tree is at once a cause and a consequence directly connected with the destruction of empires, and with the movement of the planets round the sun. But if you believe that the flame has no power or causality of its own, — and all agree that none can be detected in it, — if you admit that the two events (namely, the bringing of the two substances together, and the melting of one of them) are related to each other only as antecedent and consequent in time, though invariably thus related as far as our experience extends, then all action is personal, or begins from mind, and what we call the course of nature is but the infinite activity, the constant government, of God.

Hypothetical character of Spinoza's system. — For a refutation of Spinoza's system, therefore, we have only to recapitulate the principles that have already been advanced. The *first* argument against it is, that it is, throughout, *an application of abstract, metaphysical reasoning to matters of fact.* The idea of *cause* is metaphysical, or rather hyperphysical, as it is nowhere furnished by external nature, which gives us an idea only of the sequences of events; and as Spinoza rejects the doctrine of the independent personality of the will, he could not derive it even from internal experience. To him, *cause* is a mere abstraction, denoting invariability in the *succession* of events; and to consider it, therefore, as accounting for the *origin* of these events is a mere assumption. The reasoning begins with an abstraction and an hypothesis; given the idea of cause, or abstract invariableness of succession, and supposing that all events are of the same order, that is, that the active states of mind do not differ from the passive capacities or susceptibilities of matter, and certain results follow. Logically, then, the reasoning must end where it began; that is, in an ideal or hypothetical universe, in which we may suppose that this abstraction is a reality, and this assumption a fact. In its application to real occurrences, or the actual universe, it must be fallacious. Spinoza uses demonstrative reasoning exclusively, and it has been proved that this can lead only to abstract conclusions.

Spinozism confounds mind and matter. — The *second* objection to the system is, that it requires thought and extension to be considered as attributes of one and the same substance; the phenomena of mind must be placed in the same order with material events, and thus equally subjected to the iron rule of necessity. But it has been proved that person, or self, is essentially distinct from matter, as it is *indivisible*, and has the *consciousness of activity*, or of power in action; while matter is *infinitely divisible*, and can only be *acted upon;* its inertness, or passive submission to any forces that are applied to it, having no internal force wherewith to resist them, is in truth the only reason for believing that all its changes of state are necessary. We say that the movements and changes of matter are inevitable or necessary, *because we perceive that matter has no power to act of itself*, so that it must be operated upon from without; and we derive this belief of power of some sort as essential to action from the phenomena of consciousness. If it were not from observing, that, within the proper domain of the will, no act takes place unless preceded by a volition, that is, by a consciousness of effort, we never could have arrived at a knowledge of the law of causality, namely, that every event must have somewhere an efficient cause. Now, it is the vice of Spinoza's system, that it ignores the idea of power altogether; every thing is caused, nothing causes; every thing is moved, nothing moves; power is transmitted, as it were, from one event to another, each one being compelled or necessitated by that which preceded it, and in its turn compelling its consequent, and yet this power, thus transmitted, and thus enforcing the law of necessity, has its origin nowhere. We pursue its fleeting shadow through a series of events, but can never overtake it, for the series is infinite. The powder exploded because the spark fell upon it; the spark fell, because the flint excuded it from the steel; the flint and steel were struck together by the action of a man, this action being the result of a volition, and this volition being necessarily determined by certain antecedent emotions and beliefs, these states of mind being inevitably consequent on certain sensations, and these again, on some preceding physical events; — and so we proceed, tracing the chain once more through the world of matter, then perhaps again to a conscious mind, and so on to infinitude. Nature, then, according to Spinoza's system, is not only infinite in extent, but eternal; strictly speaking, nothing ever began to be, and creation is but a dream. The power, or necessity, which now is, has existed from eternity, and has travelled down to us through an infinite series of events, never relaxing its iron grasp, never varying in intensity or diminishing in strength, — a blind and unconscious God.

Power is not transmitted, but is always primitive. — Against this terrific and incredible conception, the Ἀνάγκη of the Greek tragedians, place the theory of power, or causation, which I have endeavored here to develop. Consider *power* really as such, that is, as exerted with freedom, — not as caused, but as causing, not as merely transmitted, but originating afresh in every act. Replace mind as a distinct existence by the side of matter; restore personality, or self, as the most fundamental and the most frequently repeated of all our conceptions; and thus dethrone this blind spectre of Fate, and replace a conscious Deity on the throne of the universe. Volition is necessarily followed by the act, and thus we gain the idea of the necessary connection between cause and effect: but that this act propagates itself, or produces, by its own inherent energy, another event in the external universe, is what we have no evidence of whatever, either by sensible observation, or in the world of consciousness. Matter is essentially inert and passive, and for this reason, among others, we say that every change in its state must have a cause; or that mind, the only true energy or source of power with which we are acquainted, must be operating on it from without or within. We do not find that agency in an antecedent physical event; and it is not true that one event is, at the same time, or in two consecutive instants, both effect and cause, or produced by one phenomenon, and producing another. Power, or efficient agency, is needed at each step; and to find whence it comes, we must look to mind or person, that is, to an agency not caused or necessary, but voluntary. That favorite metaphor, of a *chain* of causes and effects, when literally construed, has no meaning; it is contradictory, for it affirms and denies the existence of active power at each link.

Motives do not constrain volitions. — That mental phenomena take place in succession, and therefore, that each volition is invariably preceded by motives, desires, and beliefs, is a circumstance that need not perplex our argument. The relation between *the motives* and *the act* is that of mere *sequence in time*, not accompanied by any consciousness of power exerted; while the relation between the volition and the act, as in the case of forced attention, is truly causative, the consciousness of effort or exertion being perfectly distinct. To say that the motive *causes* the action, is to make the will inoperative altogether, or non-existent. Whatever may be the operation of motives, they operate on the man, or on *self;* whatever may be the nature of the action, it is not the motives which act, but the man acts. We must not lose sight of the absolute indivisibility of person, and the consequent fact, that what are called the separate faculties of mind are but different and successive states, or conditions of being, of the same individual. There is no *will*, but only the *man willing*, — no *motive*, only the man contemplating various objects of desire. Now, two successive states of the same substance do not cause each other; we might as well say, that the heat of a bar of iron, when just withdrawn from the fire, causes its subsequent coldness after it is exposed to the air. One state *precedes* the other, but does not *cause*, or necessitate, the other.

Neither external nor internal causes determine the will. — If a lump of matter changes its state, if from a solid, it becomes a liquid, or assumes a new color or a new shape, we look for the cause of this change to something existing out of the substance itself, and operating upon it from without. We do so, from our intuitive perception of the fact, that it is *incapable of acting on itself,* — or, in other words, of changing itself. But if incapable of acting on itself, how can we suppose that it is *capable of acting on something else?* If it cannot change itself but through the intervention of a foreign cause, how can it change the state of another substance? We deny, then, that one physical event depends on another of a similar character; and Fichte's long chain of causes, from the displacement of a grain of sand up to the creation of a world, drops asunder at every link. In the world of consciousness, moreover, since there is often no *external* event to which a particular change or determination of the will can be attributed, the necessarian, in seeking for a cause of the phenomenon, is obliged to look to an *antecedent state of the man himself,* — that is, to a motive, a preëxistent or concomitant longing or desire. He thinks to make out his theory, then, by saying, that *the strongest motive* causes the change, or, in other words, determines the will. But as the mind or person is *absolutely single,* and only exhibits itself under different phases, or as variously employed, *the motive* means nothing but *the man himself wishing for some object;* and the determination of the will means nothing but the same person acting. The assertion, that the motive determines the will, therefore, is only an abstract statement of the fact, that the *man wishing* determines the *man acting,* or that the will determines itself, — which is precisely the theory of the advocate for human freedom. The necessarian theory is absurd, for it assigns an abstraction as the cause of a reality.

CHAPTER VI.

THE ARGUMENT FOR FREE AGENCY CONTINUED: REASONING FROM EFFECT TO CAUSE.

Summary of the last chapter. — The two theories of causation, which I have endeavored to develop, terminate respectively in the system of Spinoza, which is atheistic fatalism, and in that of freewill, which ascribes all action to mind or person, and therefore attributes all changes that take place in the universe, except those which are caused by man, to the *immediate* agency of the Deity. These two theories are the only ones with which we need concern ourselves, for they alone are logical, consistent, and complete. No compromise is possible between them. Take the doctrine of necessity in its mildest and most liberal form, as expounded by those who shrank from the awful consequences that Spinoza deduced from it, and it will not be difficult to show that it is partial and inconsequent; the premises on which it rests, as we might expect from the demonstrative character of the reasoning employed, leading either to universal conclusions, or to no conclusions at all. Spinozism in itself is utterly incredible and absurd, no sane man ever having actually believed it, or entertained it in any way, except as a mere exercise of the intellect, — the fanciful scheme of a hypothetical universe, in which abstractions are taken for realities and assumptions for facts.

I endeavored to show further, that the argument in support of this monstrous system, being a mathematical one, needs to be complete and certain in all its parts, so that if a breach be anywhere made in it, the whole fabric must fall. To prove the falsity of any one doctrine, that is really involved in it, is to disprove the whole system. Observe, then, at how many points it is refuted by the principles which we have already established by independent evidence. *First,* it begins with the assumption, that every physical event is caused, or necessitated, by the antecedent physical event; while it is now admitted on all hands, that we never have discovered, and never can discover, between two physical events any necessary union whatever. *Secondly,* the system requires us to believe, that there is no distinction between mind and matter, but that thought and extension are attributes of the same substance; while it has been proved that personality is essentially distinct from materiality, and that the acts of the will do not belong to the same class with changes in matter, so that reasoning from the latter to the former is wholly fallacious; they have not even any qualities in common. *Thirdly,* Spinoza denies that there is any such thing as active power, and teaches that every event is necessarily produced by the inherent passivity, so to speak, of all objects, there being nowhere an agent, a mover, or a primal source of power; while it has been shown, that in the phenomena of will, there is a consciousness of effort or exertion, which is a direct perception of original, and not of merely transmitted, power. *Fourthly,* a cardinal point in the system is a denial of the freedom of the will, and the consequent doing away with all sense of moral obligation, all consciousness of merit or remorse for crime; while the voice of conscience imperatively declares, what we can no more disbelieve than we can distrust the multiplication-table or the axioms of the geometer, that man is accountable for his actions, and incurs merit or blame for deeds which he was free to commit.

Argument for the freedom of the will continued. — In regard to the freedom of the will, I argued further, what all experience teaches, that, *of two successive states of the same substance, the former is not the cause of the latter, but only its antecedent.* Daylight is not the cause of darkness; a headache does not produce the freedom from pain which follows it. The consideration of *motives and the subsequent volition are two successive states of the same person;* if there were a causal or necessary union between them, the latter would *immediately* succeed the former; for when the cause is present, the effect cannot be delayed. But we often and involuntarily pause and dwell upon various motives, holding them up in various lights, and balancing them against each other, the will remaining quiescent during this process, the understanding and reason alone being active. Now, if the strongest motive is necessarily followed by the volition, why is it not *immediately* so followed, the motives being certainly before the mind? If you assert, that there is an immediate determination of the will in such a case, namely, a determination to remain quiet, or to postpone the particular action in view till the motives have been fully weighed, I deny the fact. *The will certainly may remain dormant* for a time, without a particular volition to that end. Take the case of a man absorbed in some operation of pure intellect, — considering, for instance, the various steps of a mathematical problem; there is no action of the will here, not even a volition to suspend volition. But the balancing of motives is as much an intellectual operation as mathematical research; why, then, I repeat, if motives necessarily act on the will, do they not determine it immediately? I see not how it is possible for the necessarian to answer this question in conformity with his theory.

The will is a source of power, and is not an effect. — But it is argued against the doctrine of the freedom of the will, that it requires us to believe in an uncaused event, and thus denies the universal application of the law of causality. How can a volition, it is asked, take place without a cause, if it be true that *every* change, every thing which begins to exist, must have a cause? I reply, that *the law of causation is founded on the acknowledged inertness of matter;* because matter cannot act on itself, we say that every change *in matter* must have a cause; but it does not follow that this cause is also in its turn an effect, and must have been caused by some antecedent event, and that again by another cause, and so on to infinity. This notion of a chain, or infinite series, of causes has already been refuted, because it really banishes all idea of efficient agency from the universe; we chase the phantom of a cause along the line for ever, without the possibility of overtaking it. The true maxim is, that every physical event, every *material* phenomenon, must have a cause, *because it cannot act of itself;* but *it does not fol-*

low that this cause must also have a cause, for it is itself a source of power; it is *mind*, or *person*, which, unlike matter, *can act of itself*, and therefore does not need a cause. It is an unauthorized extension of the law of causality, to say that every *action* of a conscious agent must have a cause, just as much as a material phenomenon. This would be begging the question in the present case, and it is refuted by the direct evidence of consciousness, which teaches us that the will is a true source of power in itself. We must get rid of this notion of transmitted power, or a chain of causes and effects, which is a mere fiction, founded on the interminable succession of material phenomena; this succession, as we have shown again and again, is not causation, but mere sequence in time. Each event in that succession must have a cause; but this cause is not found, and never can be found, in the antecedent physical event, but only in some power, or being, acting out of the line; and to ask for the *cause of this being*, that is, for the *cause of this power*, or *cause of a cause*, is absurd.

Reid's statement of the doctrine of causation. — Thus, the doctrine of the freedom of the will brings us back again to the grand dogma of the immediate agency of the Deity throughout creation, that is, to the omnipresence and omnipotence of God. In some recently published letters, from the private correspondence of Dr. Reid, I find a part of this theory of causation so clearly stated and illustrated, that a few passages from them may well be cited here. "In the strict and proper sense," says this philosopher, "I take an efficient cause *to be a being* who had power to produce the effect, and exerted that power *for that purpose.* Power to produce an effect supposes power not to produce it; otherwise it is not power, but necessity, which is incompatible with power taken in a strict sense. I am not able to form a conception how power, in the strict sense, can be exerted without will; nor can there be will without some degree of understanding. Therefore, *nothing can be an efficient cause*, in the proper sense, *but an intelligent being.* I believe we get the first conception of power, in the proper sense, from *the consciousness of our own exertions;* and as all our power is exerted by will, we cannot form a conception how power can be exerted without will. Matter cannot be the cause of any thing; it can only be an instrument in the hands of a real cause."

"Suppose, now, that you take the word *cause* in this strict sense; its relation to its effect is so self-evidently different from the relation of a motive to an action, that I am jealous of a mathematical demonstration of a truth so self-evident. Nothing is more difficult than to demonstrate what is self-evident. A cause is a being which has a *real* existence; a *motive* has no real existence, and therefore can have no active power. *It is a thing conceived, and not a thing that exists;* and therefore can neither be active, nor even passive. To say that a motive really *acts,* is as absurd as to say, that a motive drinks my health, or that a motive gives me a box on the ear."

"We are early conscious of some power in ourselves to produce some events; and our nature leads us to think that every event is produced by a power similar to that which we find in ourselves, — that is, by will and exertion; when a weight falls and hurts a child, he is angry with it, — he attributes power and will to every thing that seems to act. Language is formed upon these early sentiments, and attributes action and power to things that are afterwards discovered to have neither will nor power. By this means, the notion of action and causation is gradually changed; what was essential to it at first [namely, will,] is left out, while the name remains; and the term *cause* is applied to things which we believe to be inanimate and passive."

How it came to be believed that matter is a cause. — Again, — "It is a curious problem in human nature, how, in the progress of life, we come by the lax notion of power, agency, cause, and effect, and to ascribe them to things that have no will nor intelligence. I am apt to think, with the Abbé Raynal, 'that savages,' (I add children, as in the same predicament,) '*wherever they see motion that they cannot account for*, there they suppose a soul.' Hence, they ascribe active power and causation to sun, mocn, and stars, rivers, fountains, sea, air, and earth; these are conceived to be causes in the strict sense. In this period of society, language is formed, and its fundamental rules and forms established. Active verbs are applied only to things that are believed to have power and activity in the proper sense. Every part of nature which moves, *without our seeing any external cause* of its motion, is conceived to be a cause in the strict sense, and therefore is called so. At length, the more acute and speculative few discover, that some of those things which the vulgar believe to be animated like themselves are inanimate, and have neither will nor understanding;" but they must still "speak the common language, and suit it to their new notions as well as they can; just as philosophers say with the vulgar, that the sun rises and sets, and the moon changes."

Metaphysical reasoning not needed to prove the being of a God. — With these quotations from Dr. Reid, I conclude the more abstract portion of the discussion in which we are engaged. To some it may appear, that we have been wandering a long time in a mere wilderness of logic and metaphysics, "whence issuing, we again behold the stars." I certainly do not believe that it is necessary to pass through all the abstruse reasoning, which has thus far occupied our attention, before we can obtain any firm and well-grounded faith in the great doctrines of religion. It would be an impeachment of the goodness of the Deity to suppose, that he has given to his creatures only such intimations or proofs of his own existence and his will as the most cultivated and ingenious minds can follow slowly and with great effort. On the contrary, the conclusions in this great argument are so obvious and direct, lying but a step from the premises, which are numberless, and so nearly akin to the mental processes which we are compelled to use for the daily purposes of life, that the child or the savage cannot avoid resting in them with sufficient confidence. It is no doubtful inference, no long and tedious process of reasoning, which connects all events in the history of the universe with the being and attributes of a God. The conclusion is so obvious, the connection so close and striking, that it is difficult to believe that any mind not wilfully obtuse, or not perverted by logical subtilities and metaphysical abstractions, ever failed to receive it with perfect trust at the first view.

How far metaphysical reasoning is useful.—But the importance of these preliminary considerations appears from the fact, that they afford a complete answer to the objections urged by skeptics so formidable as Spinoza, Hume, Kant, and the later school of German infidels. Those who are not conversant with the objections may safely pass over the answers to them; but to many others, they may be of use from their tendency to do away with an impression,—now, it is to be feared, quite too common,—that the common proofs of the being of a God, however satisfactory to the vulgar, will not bear the test of a sound philosophy or of strict logical analysis. They tend, at any rate, to clear the ground, to establish certain *data*, or sound premises for the argument, and to furnish logical rules for the conduct of the inquiry. Let us hold fast, then, to the ground which we have acquired, and having established certain principles, let us use them without doubt or hesitation for the remainder of the discussion. Let no one imagine, for instance, that reasoning from the effect to the cause, as we shall have occasion to do, is illogical, because Hume and others have demonstrated that physical causes, so-called, are mere antecedents, and that no power, or efficient energy, can be detected in them. All this is admitted; but the only consequence of it is, not to banish the notion of cause altogether, but to substitute for *material* causes and transmitted power the idea of direct *personal* agency, accompanied by intelligence and will. Neither let the grim dogma of necessity, or absolute fate, any longer shadow the faith of the believer with the fear, lest the commands of the Almighty should be nugatory from his own moral inability to comply with them. The doctrine of freewill rests upon foundations which are not to be shaken by the utmost force of philosophical skepticism.

Above all, let us know what we are to expect as the result of the inquiry, and what weight is to be given to the disparaging remark, that truths supported only by moral evidence are at best but contingent, and that demonstration of a fact is impossible. The evidence which supports the fundamental truths of religion is precisely the same with that which directs all our conduct in life, and, in ordinary cases, no one thinks of complaining that it is insufficient. To say that it is moral, instead of being demonstrative, is only to admit that the truths themselves are practical, and not speculative. I repeat it then, there can be no fears for the strength of our religious faith, if it stands upon the same platform with the whole round of the physical sciences, so that no assault can reach even its outworks, till the entire fabric of these sciences shall be demolished, and it be made to appear that all the boasted attainments of the last three centuries in the study of nature have been unprofitable and vain.

Analysis of the common argument à posteriori. — The common argument *à posteriori* for the being of a God is divided into *two* branches, according as we seek to establish the reality of *some* cause, no matter what, simply from the presence of an effect, or as we endeavor to determine *the nature of that cause* from the peculiarities of the effect; the one is reasoning from efficient, the other from final, causation. The one proceeds simply from nature up to nature's God, as from a fact otherwise inexplicable to that which is at once the origin and the explanation of that fact; the other infers, from the peculiar character of the works of creation, that *a purpose or design* is accomplished in them, and consequently assumes that this design must have been previously entertained by *an intelligent being*, having power adequate to the work. Thus, the geologist infers, from the dislocated and upheaved position of certain strata of rock, that there must have been *some* cause of the disturbance and elevation; this is his first conclusion, and it is quite distinct from his subsequent inquiry, as to *the time, nature*, and *extent* of the convulsion which produced the phenomena that he now seeks to explain. This later inquiry must proceed from careful observation of the particular facts in the case, of the minor circumstances which go to prove that the grand change was produced by one cause rather than another. It is the former and more comprehensive conclusion, the validity of which we are now to examine.

Criticism of Dr. Clarke's argument. — The argument is

stated in its simplest, but not, as it seems to me, in its most logical or conclusive form, by Dr. Clarke. He reasons thus: "Something must have existed from all eternity, — otherwise, the things that now are must have been *produced* out of nothing, absolutely and without cause, which is a plain contradiction in terms. For to say a thing is *produced*, and yet that there is no *cause* at all of that production, is to say that something is *effected by nothing*, — that is, it is *not effected at all*." I pause here to remark, that Dr. Clarke, in his anxiety to make his reasoning exclusively metaphysical, and consequently to avoid all reference to matters-of-fact, makes two unfounded assumptions: — first, that we have a metaphysical knowledge of "the things that now are," — a loose and indeterminate expression, which means, if it means any thing, the universe of animate and inanimate being, though the existence of this universe is certainly made known to us only by physical evidence, — that is, by experience, whether by observation through the senses, or by consciousness; — and secondly, his assertion, that "otherwise the things that now are must have been *produced* out of nothing," must be understood to mean, that the things which now are must have *begun to be* without an antecedent cause; inasmuch as to say that they were *produced*, is begging the question as to their *producer*. The reasoning is worth nothing, unless it is supported by the general law of causality, — the law, that is, that every thing which begins to be must have a cause; — and this law, for reasons already alleged, must be considered as the dictate of experience. Of course, Clarke's argument is of a metaphysical or *à priori* character only in name; it is just as much founded on physical testimony as the argument from design. It proceeds from the existence of realities, made known to us by the senses and by consciousness, to the *cause* of these realities, the ground of the inference being a general maxim, the truth of which is collected from experience.*

---

* Dr. Clarke has proposed another argument, which is more metaphysical, and therefore less conclusive, than the one considered above. This second form of proof, briefly stated, is as follows.

"Space and time are alike infinite and necessary, for we cannot even

Still, the argument thus far, whatever may be its technical designation, is a valid one, and is in truth unanswerable. From the universe of things that are, we infer, either that these things have existed for ever, or that they began to be; and if the latter, then there must have been a cause of their beginning of existence; and this cause must either have existed from eternity, or else it also had a cause, — and so on. Hence we are reduced to the alternative of admitting the existence, either of one eternal being, or of an infinite series of dependent beings, each one having been produced by its predecessor. So far, the argument is sound; but Clarke proceeds to urge several metaphysical reasons, which seem to me quite unsatisfactory from the very

---

conceive of their limitation or their non-existence. They are not in them selves *substances,* but attributes, and as such, *necessarily presuppose a sub stance,* without which they could not exist; and this *substance* is, consequently, infinite and self-existent."

But the word *substance,* as here used, is entirely indefinite; the idea of it includes neither personality nor intelligence. The argument, at the utmost, proves only that *something* exists, to which these attributes belong; and this *something,* Clarke immediately assumes to be *a particular Being.* The sophism consists in this illogical transition from the general to the particular, from the abstract to the concrete; and a more palpable one can hardly be imagined.

Besides, the proposition that space and time are attributes, if not wholly unintelligible, must be understood in the same sense as the proposition, that human beings *exist in* space and time. *Finite* space and time are qualities of *man,* in the same way that eternity and immensity are attributes of the Supreme Being. Now, human beings are not necessary or self-existent. And if finite space and time do not necessitate a finite substance, so neither do the ideas of immensity and eternity compel us to believe in an infinite substance.

The whole argument rests on an abuse of language. Time and space are not attributes, but *conditions of being.* We cannot conceive of any thing except as existent under these conditions; but we may conceive that the conditions are fulfilled, while the reality is wanting. Atmospheric air, for instance, is a condition of man's bodily existence; he cannot live without it. But air may be, as at the North Pole, where man is not. In Clarke's argument, the prerequisite is made to change places with the reality, or the thing conditioned. He infers the presence of the thing, from the fulfilment of the conditions, which is precisely inverting the two terms of the only legitimate inference.

fact that they are metaphysical, for rejecting the hypothesis of an infinite series of created beings, and hence for resting in the conclusion that there is but one eternal being, who is God. The truth is, Clarke quite confounds *two* perfectly distinct meanings of the term *necessity;* and on this fallacy, this confusion of terms, the whole of his subsequent reasoning depends. In a syllogism, the conclusion necessarily follows from the premises; and this we call a *logical* necessity. For an instance of the other kind, take the necessary and unlimited existence of space. *Space is indestructible;* we can conceive of the annihilation of matter, but not of the space which matter now occupies. Imagine, if you can, the destruction of the room or space which this building now occupies. You can conceive easily enough of the annihilation of all objects within it — that this space should be made empty or void; but you cannot conceive of the space itself as annihilated, or as no longer affording room for other objects. Now *this necessary existence of space* we may call, for want of a better term, *a physical necessity.* Clarke quite confounds these two significations of the word; having shown by argument which he holds to be demonstrative, that God *must* exist, that is, that there is *a logical necessity* for our believing in his existence, he goes on to reason as if he had established *a physical necessity* of the being of a God; that is, he thought to prove that we can no more conceive of his non-existence, than we can of the non-existence of space or time. If this were so, *atheism were impossible,* and then it would be difficult to tell why any argument was needed, or why Clarke thought it necessary to write his book, if there was nobody to be convinced by it. As to the possibility of atheism, if a man can be so far blinded by metaphysical subtilties as to doubt his own existence, I do not see why he cannot go on to deny the being of a God.

The universe must have had a cause. — But it was not my object to show that the reasoning of Clarke is fallacious, but only to select that portion of it which is open to no cavil or objection, and from this, if possible, to proceed to a satisfactory conclusion. Let us go back, then, to the proposition, sufficiently established by him, that *we must believe either in one eternal being, or in an infinite series of created beings.* Are there sufficient reasons for rejecting the latter branch of this alternative? *Metaphysical* reasons for rejecting it I cannot find; I frankly admit, that the bare conception of such an infinite series is no more impossible in this argument than it is, for instance, in mathematics, where the mere tyro will present to you the law and the sum of such a series without difficulty or hesitation. The presence of it is no more perplexing to him in the calculation, than is that of the expression for the root of a number which is not a perfect square or other power. But in mathematics, as in natural theology, the infinite series is possible as an abstraction, *but not as a reality.* There are physical considerations, so to speak, which are conclusive against the hypothesis that this vast machine of the universe, even on the supposition that it is continually propagating and renewing itself by the laws now in force considered as real causes, had no beginning, but has existed from all eternity in an infinite series of changes, decay, and restoration. I speak now of *the universe, not as a mere aggregation of brute matter*, which it is not, *but as a vast and complex organism,* all the parts of which are in constant and harmonious activity, and tenanted by various orders of life, each of which is continued in one direct line, and, so far as human observation has extended, under a permanent type. It would not be difficult, I believe, to establish this proposition in reference to the whole system of worlds, the solar and starry kingdoms, of which our earth is but so small a part. But we know so little of these, beyond the general facts that they exist, and move, or are moved, in accordance with the law of gravitation, that an argument either for or against their eternal existence in their present form, and under their present laws, would have too much the aspect of an appeal to human ignorance. We could only say, either on the affirmative or the negative side, that it might be so for aught that we knew to the contrary; — a conclusion unsatisfactory in itself, likely to be overthrown by the progress of discovery, and almost sure to be disproved by that knowledge which we may conceive a superior spirit to possess, both of their external and internal economy.

For a similar, but still stronger reason, I put aside here the question as to the eternal existence of *inorganic matter*, which is, at best, but *the brute material* out of which worlds are fashioned. Whether this exists at all, according to the ordinary conception of it, is doubtful; and it is certain that we have no knowledge of it, that we cannot perceive it, that we cannot distinguish between the qualities properly belonging to it in itself, and those imposed upon it either by our own faculties of observation, or by an external power.

Physical proof that the world did begin to be.—I confine the inquiry, then, to the past duration of the only world with which we have any immediate concern, to the antecedent history of this earth, to the assumed continuance, through the endless ages that are past, of the various lines and races of animate and organic being, upheld only by the inherent energy of the laws, so called, which support or direct their present existence. Have we proof or disproof of infinite series here? I contend that we have testimony, clear, unquestioned, scientific, admitted by all physical inquirers who have any acquaintance with the subject, even by those most prejudiced against the conclusions which I wish to establish, that *organization and life on this earth*, through all their myriad forms, throughout the vegetable and animal—aye, even the mineral—kingdoms, *did begin to be*, and that within definite periods of time. We even pronounce with certainty on their relative ages, and map out chronologically the history of the world, from chaos down to the time when man, the last comer, was introduced upon a scene which was, by comparison with those which had preceded it, one of perfect symmetry and order. Geology declares without hesitation, and with as much distinctness as Holy Writ, that *time was when the earth was without form and void*, and before the dry land appeared. Thence it traces down the annals of things:—first, the successive induction of those circumstances which rendered even the lowest forms of life possible; then the creation of those low forms; their subsequent utter extinction, so that they have no representatives among us at the present day; the filling of their place by higher orders of being; and so on, through successive transformations of life, down to the appearance of man.

I am not dwelling now on any of the more obscure and disputed doctrines of geological science. I am not resting this great argument on any of the theories, often contradictory, or very questionable, respecting the particular circumstances under which certain strata of rocks were raised from the bottom of an ocean, or certain mountains upheaved from the plain. All that is needed for the purposes of the present discussion may be found in those first principles and elementary facts of geology, which are now universally admitted, and which, indeed, cannot be denied without impeaching the trustworthy character of the evidence on which all physical science depends. Your own eyes have probably seen the fossil forms of those extinct races which once peopled the earth that is now our home. You have heard or read the history of these lost tribes, and various speculations about the catastrophes or gradual changes which swept them away, and the new forms of life which succeeded them. You have seen the marks of igneous formation or alluvial deposit in the very stones on which you daily tread, and have had your thoughts thus carried back by necessary inference to periods when the first continents were raised from the bosom of the deep, when mountains of ice floated over what are now fertile tracts peopled by myriad forms of terrestrial life, or when the incandescent surface of the earth still glowed with the heat which even now rages but a few miles below its outer rind. Then occurs to us, with a more impressive significance, the awful question which the Hebrew poet seemed to hear, as coming out of the whirlwind: — "*Where wast thou,* when I laid the foundations of the earth? Declare, if thou hast understanding."

I say, then, that *the past continuance, through an infinite series of years, of that order of things which we now behold,* under laws similar to those which now direct or express that order, *is disproved by an amount of physical testimony that is absolutely conclusive.* Ignorance may deny this proposition, but the instructed skeptic must admit it. Remember that the point we are now seeking to establish is *a fact,* and that I am arguing it by *an appeal to facts.* You can judge whether the conviction produced by the mass of evidence, to which I have merely alluded, would be, to any appreciable extent, either confirmed or shaken by *a metaphysical discussion* of the abstract possibility of an infinite series of dependent beings.

Application of the argument from effect to cause. — We have, then, the starting point for the application of the argument from the effect to the cause. *Certain things began to be.* At a certain period, which is not even a very remote one, when considered in that gigantic chronology which geological science obliges us to contemplate, all the present races of living things, all organized forms that we now behold, were not. There was no firm-set earth on which they could tread, there were no articles for their aliment and sustenance, there was no atmosphere which they could breathe. They have subsequently come into existence. *Whence came they?* I choose to put the question in this, its simplest, form, in order not to perplex you with any further discussion, here unnecessary, of the law of causality. It is not enough to say, that you cannot believe, — you cannot even imagine, that this earth, once without one germ of organic life in its vast bosom, suddenly became tenanted with countless forms of living beings, without some foreign and adequate cause. Give the largest significance you may to what are called the laws of nature; confound, if you will, physical with efficient causes; say that the birth of an individual in the race is but the mechanical effect of the powers inherent in the organism of the parent; — still the beginning of that race, the beginning of all races, goes utterly beyond the laws of nature, and obliges you to look up to nature's God.

The laws of nature do not account for the introduction of a new species. — The skeptic's first principle is, that *we must not admit any laws of nature, or modes of action, but those which we now actually perceive going on around us;* we must not *invent* causes to account for certain phenomena, until we are fully satisfied that the known and familiar agencies of nature are insufficient to that end. I take him at his word. *The physical laws which are now exposed to the observation of mankind will not* *explain the introduction of a new species, a new race,* among those formerly in being, and certainly not the beginning of life itself in a world till then inanimate. If you say that the lower forms of life may be spontaneously generated from the dust,* or that higher types of being may be evolved from those next below them in the scale, without the exertion of any new power you assert what the most careful observation, the minute and long continued researches of science, have failed to verify. *Permanence of type* is one of the most firmly established of those very laws of nature to which you ascribe inherent power, and which you claim to be immutable. It is the grossest incon-

---

* All the races of animated beings, which are entirely within the range of our powers of observation, — which have such a size and locality that we can study and accurately determine their organization and habits, — are unquestionably produced from parents of their own kind. Only the minute microscopic animals are now supposed to be generated spontaneously; and this alleged fact rests not on direct proof, but only on our inability in certain cases to trace the process of their production in the ordinary way. As many of these animals, in their perfect state, are not more than the twelve thousandth part of an inch in diameter, it is not much to be wondered at, that we should not be able in all cases to discover their ova, or to follow these ova through all their stages of development into the complete being. It is further remarkable, that these animalcules, when once produced, whether by spontaneous or natural generation, are all found to be provided with the organs or requisite means for continuing their species, and, in fact, for multiplying their number from themselves with astonishing rapidity. As they certainly have children, it seems reasonable to suppose, according to the analogy of all the higher animated tribes, that they also had parents. The ancients supposed, that the worms and insects which appear in decaying organic matter were generated there by the decomposition of the substance, without the previous agency of individuals of the same stock. Every schoolboy is acquainted with Virgil's mode of obtaining a new swarm of bees from the decaying carcass of a heifer Subsequent researches, made with more care, and perhaps with better instruments of observation, have entirely disproved the hypothesis, and show that the maggots were produced in every case from eggs deposited by flies or other insects, and were afterwards themselves developed into the state of perfect insects. Then it seems reasonable to believe, that the improved observations of future times will clear up the only remaining difficulty and shew how the infusory animalcules also are generated from beings of their own kind.

sistency on your part to attempt to set aside, in this single case, those very principles, on the assumed unchangeableness, the inherent power, and infinite duration of which, your whole theory depends. In that *ordinary course of nature*, to which you would fain reduce all phenomena, so that all may seem to be mere *continuance*, and nowhere may appear a *beginning* of existence, so as to avoid any necessity for the interposition of any new cause or foreign power, — in this ordinary course of nature, I say, quadrupeds are not born from birds, nor birds from reptiles, nor reptiles from fishes, nor fishes from invertebrate animals; *

* The point chiefly relied upon to show the credibility of this doctrine here alluded to is the fact, that the higher animals, in their embryotic existence, pass through a series of changes resembling the permanent forms of the lower tribes. The first form of man himself resembles that which is permanent in the animalcule; and thence he comes to resemble successively a fish, a reptile, a bird, and the lower mammifers, before he attains his specific maturity. It is held, then, that a premature birth from an animal of a higher kind might have instituted a new race of a lower type; and that a birth unusually delayed, permitting an embryo to be still further advanced in the line of organization, might have created a new species of a higher order than the parent. Here, every thing depends on the *absolute identity* of the germs of all animals, in the lower stages of their growth. General resemblances and analogies are of no weight whatever; the essential internal organization of the ova of different species must be the same; otherwise, however ripened into a mature being, whether the birth be advanced or postponed, the individual must still belong to its parents' species, of which it possesses the distinctive peculiarity. Now, this point of *the identity of germs is a mere assumption;* not only is it destitute of proof, — the whole evidence is against it. There is a degree of outward resemblance, but there is no sameness. When we trace the origin of life back to the remotest point to which our powers of observation extend, when we come to microscopic vesicles that can be discerned only by the highest magnifiers, general similarity of outward shape is all that can be predicated of them. The specific differences lie below this general resemblance of outward form; we cannot discern them, but we *know* that they must exist, and that they are *essential* differences; for each one of these vesicles is invariably developed, if at all, into an individual of the species to which its parent belongs. The germinal vesicles of a tree and a quadruped are somewhat alike, outwardly; so, to the hen's eyes, there is no difference between her own eggs and the duck's eggs which the farmer's wife has put into her nest. But when she has hatched her brood, part of them are

but *each of these races continues itself by producing young after its own kind.* It is not pretended that there is *any known instance* of the transmutation of species, or of the evolution, in the ordinary way, of any being specifically different from its parents. The same animal, indeed, may pass through different grades of development; but these changes affect only the individual, not the race. The progeny of this animal must begin at the same point where its parent did, and run precisely the same cycle. The tadpole becomes a frog, but the young of that frog are tadpoles; the worm becomes a winged insect, but the eggs of that insect are hatched into nothing but worms. These changes in the life of the individual, like the successive periods of the embryotic state, of infancy, and of manhood in the human being, are perfectly consistent with persistence of type in the race, and do not indicate even the possibility that a new species may be developed out of an old one. On the contrary, the germ must be considered as *potentially* equivalent to the whole future being, for it is invariably developed into that being. If there be any one fact unquestionably established by observation, it is, that *each species invariably produces its like.* "All the phenomena," says Müller, one of the first physiologists of the day, "all the phenomena at present observed in the animal kingdom seem to prove, that the species were originally created distinct, and independent of each other. There is no remote possibility of one species being produced from another."

Result of this branch of the argument. — Here, then, we rest the first and lowest branch of the argument *a posteriori*, considering it as an established fact in physical science, that *organization and life on this earth did begin to be, within a definite period of time,* and that *none of the physical causes now in opera-*

---

found to be webfooted, and these, to her great astonishment and distress, immediately take to the water. Those who uphold this theory commit the same blunder as the poor hen. This want of consciousness that they have got to the end of their tether, this inability to believe that any difference can exist where they are not able to see it, though it is invariably indicated by future consequent differences of the most striking nature, is perfectly characteristic of the rash theorist in science.

tion is adequate to account for that beginning. We are led, then, irresistibly up to the agency of a First Cause, a power not inherent in nature, but in one sense external to it and acting upon it, and which, for the reason already stated, must have existed from everlasting.

I have called this the *lowest* branch of the argument, because, though the conclusion seems to me to be legitimate, and even unavoidable, it does not fully answer our desires, nor satisfy the aspirations of the religious sentiment in man. To prove the being of a Creator only from an act of creation assumed to have been completed long ago, if a useful, is still a frigid, result of the inquiry. It seems too much like establishing some remote fact in history, which ceased long since to have any immediate interest, as its direct consequences are no longer traceable. We seek to bring the argument and the doctrine home by proofs of the repeated, if not the continuous, agency of Omnipotence, so that what is almost the abstract conception of a First Cause may be changed into a well-grounded faith in the existence of an infinite and ever-watchful Father.

The work of creation frequently renewed and extended. — One step, and an important one, towards this conclusion, we are able immediately to take. The work of creation was not a single act, begun and ended by a solitary exertion of power; it was often renewed, and it extended over a lapse of ages which the imagination vainly strives to comprehend. Science has discovered an ineffaceable and undoubted record of a multitude of cases, in which preceding laws of nature, that had been unbroken for ages, were interrupted by special exertions of a foreign power. Mighty revolutions have often swept the face of this planet, hurrying nearly all former orders of life into ruin; and each time, the desert was peopled anew with animated tribes wholly unlike their predecessors. Geology is but the history, chronicled in stone, of many miracles performed before man was, and extending far back into a past eternity. *There is not an animal or a plant on this earth, which, as a race, is not older than man.* Science does not contradict, it rather confirms, that voice of revelation or tradition which assigns about six thousand years as the period of man's residence upon the earth. One of the latest events in the geological history of the world, we are told, was a great submersion of the land, by which "terrestrial animal life was extensively, if not universally, destroyed;" so that the creation of the species now in being — at least, all the higher species — was "a comparatively recent event, and one posterior generally speaking, to all the great natural transactions chronicled by geology." From this "recent event," back certainly as far as the time when those races began to be, the remains of which are now found entombed in the lowest Silurian rocks, the period of creation extends, — a drama of many acts and countless shifting scenes, each one of which leads us up to a knowledge of its Infinite Author.

In truth, the assumed invariableness of the laws of nature, considering these only as the necessary manifestations of powers inherent in the substances themselves, is a doctrine which loses all meaning, as well as probability, when we look to the annals of the universe for guidance, and not merely to the story of one life, or even of one order of being. The history of God's providence is not the story of a day, nor can it be interpreted by the experience of an hour. We must decipher even the record, inscribed on the rocks, of *the mutations which this solid globe has undergone, in the vast series of ages that elapsed before it was peopled with beings like ourselves.* If we would climb to the heights of this great argument, our view must be expanded in feeble imitation of His vision with whom a thousand years are but as one day. Perhaps it will be found, that these supposed breaks in the continuity of the inferior laws of nature are but the intercalations of a higher law, working for a nobler end; that *what appear as special exertions of Divine agency, are but the ordinary mode in which infinite wisdom works and governs;* that the physical is subordinate throughout to the moral universe; and that what man calls interruptions of the usual course of nature, are precisely what he might most reasonably and naturally expect from omnipotence and infinite benevolence combined.

Parallel between human and Divine action. — The action of

a human being, though generally inconstant and wavering, from his unsettled will, so that the future cannot be predicted from the past, is also often directed through long periods by a fixed purpose, and rendered uniform through the facility acquired by habit; so that, if it were watched by a being of a different race, ignorant of the human constitution, and very limited in his period of observation, it would appear mechanical, and, like the regular working of a machine, to be attributable only to an impulse given to it at the commencement, and not afterwards renewed. If, however, the observation were continued for a longer time, or if a record could be found of the man's whole history, the changes of action induced by altered circumstances, or a fluctuating purpose, would be manifest. Geology is such a record of the history of the universe, showing those breaks in the succession of events, which prove the frequent interposition of directing will and sustaining power; each of them being an insoluble problem, unless we admit that such a will exists. If it be objected to the probability of such interruptions, that it is inconsistent with the attribute of Divine wisdom to suppose that the Deity ever changes his plan, or alters his purpose, I answer, *first*, he who declares that infinite wisdom necessarily dictates invariability of action, also assumes that he possesses infinite wisdom himself; and *secondly*, a *change in the mode of action does not necessarily imply a change of purpose.* The emergency may have been foreseen, the extraordinary action by which it was to be met may have been predetermined, from the foundation of the world. At any rate, this consideration is one with which, for our present object, the proof only of the being of a God, we have nothing to do. The facts are unquestionable; that such interruptions have taken place, whether they argue a change of the Divine purpose or not, cannot be denied. Huge strata of earthbound rock, the solid framework of the globe itself, in characters which the school-boy now may read, testify to the unceasing guardianship, the frequent intervention to repair, renew, and improve, of Him who created the heavens and the earth, and laid the corner-stone thereof. The world was never an orphan, never left to the dominion of cl ance, or — what is little better — to the blind and unbroken operation of what are called natural laws. A Father's care watched over it, a Father's hand peopled it again and again with tribes of living things, — not by inflexible ordinances, nor by vicarious government through secondary means, — but even as an earthly parent careth for his children.

The argument applied to the beginning of man's existence. — But we may go much further, and find sufficient proof of far more frequent intervention of Divine power in the affairs of the universe than that which is confirmed by geological evidence. Admitting, for a moment, the general principle, which I regard as wholly indefensible and unphilosophical, that in the *material* universe, the argument from the effect to the cause finds place only at the beginning of a succession of beings, and not at any one link in that succession, in the world of *mind* we have irrefragable evidence, at every step, which leads us up from the created directly to the Creator. This evidence appears in *the essential unity of personality*, in that recognition of the indivisible *self* in consciousness, on which so much stress has already been laid. Each person can say of himself, "*I* have a separate and indivisible existence." We may borrow again the language of Fichte, as it is the unwilling concession of an opponent: "I have not come into existence by my own power. It would be the highest absurdity to suppose, that before I was at all, I could bring myself into existence: I have, then, been called into being by a power out of myself."

Starting from this admission, we say that the theory which Fichte adopts, and which we are here taking for granted in respect to the world of matter, — *which refers the beginning of an individual's existence to the first creation of the race to which he belongs*, which considers intelligent life as continuous through a succession of beings, one springing out of another, and then giving birth to a third, by virtue of principles infused or machinery contrived in the race, when the original progenitor of it was formed, — this theory, we say, *will not hold in the present case.* It may account for the origin of the material framework, the habitation of clay, in which I live; but it will not account for the origin of *me*. It is contradicted by the great fact of my existence as an indivisible unit. Complexity of parts, according to the materialist's hypothesis, is essential to the propagation of existence. The seed exists in the fruit; the germ exists in the seed. It is afterwards taken from the fruit and the seed, and begins to exist as a distinct plant. But this is the commencement of its *separate*, not of its *total* being. It existed before; it was in the parent plant, as a part of it; and its birth was not a creation, but a division of existence. The beginning of any material life, a tree, a flower, an animal, is not the creation of any thing new, says the materialist, but the development of a germ which existed ages before, — which has lived ever since the world was. But *the beginning of intellectual life, the essential unity of which is attested by consciousness, cannot be explained by mere separation.* It cannot give birth to another by division of itself. In fine, the materialist affirms, that birth is but a separation, and growth but an accretion and assimilation, of parts that previously existed, though in an inorganic state; for it is a necessary part of this hypothesis, that the number of primary particles in the universe is neither more nor less than it was at the creation. Meeting him on his own ground, we reply, that his own personal existence is certain proof, that at least one unit has been added to the mass of being since the formation of the universe. Of course, we have every reason from analogy to believe, that *the beginning of life in all cases*, even animal and vegetable, *is the addition of a unit to the sum of being, and therefore a direct act of creation*, as much so as the building of a world or a system. But only in intellectual life have we positive evidence of this fact from consciousness.

CHAPTER VII.

ALL EVENTS IN THE MATERIAL UNIVERSE A PROOF OF THE PRESENCE AND THE AGENCY OF GOD.

Summary of the last chapter.—After completing, in the last chapter, a very brief exposition of the freedom of the will, the subject of the common argument *a posteriori* to prove the being of a God was taken up with a view, not so much to restate it or to enter into its details, as to determine its logical character, and to consider its claims as a just and philosophical specimen of reasoning. Having shown, on a former occasion, that the doctrines of *theology* related to matters of fact, I endeavored to prove that the evidence in their favor was such as might be expected in *physical science*,—that it was to be gathered from observation and experience. The other sciences are to be laid under contribution for this end; *geology*, in particular, considered as a record of the antecedent history of this earth, might be expected to furnish proofs of the agency of that Being by whom this earth, with all that it inhabit, was created and sustained.

Taking the first, and certainly the more abstract, branch of the argument,—that which infers the reality of a cause simply from the presence of the effect, without regard to the peculiarities of that effect,—I attempted to show, even from the most recently and best established facts in geology and zoölogy, that events had taken place, or things had begun to exist, which the ordinary *laws of nature*, as they are called, cannot account for, and which, consequently, must be referred to the agency of the great First Cause. If you reject this inference, you must deny, either that organization and life on this earth did begin to be, that is, you must reject many of the best accredited conclusions of modern science, on which, indeed, some entire sciences exclusively depend; or you must assert, that *an event can take place without a cause*, and thus contradict what is either an intuitive axiom, or a principle founded on the largest induction of which the human mind is capable. The metaphysical reasoning of Clarke on this subject was shown to be unsatisfactory, chiefly on the ground that it is metaphysical; and therefore the conclusion, which is a *fact*, cannot be inferred from the premises, so far as these are mere *abstractions*, without really begging the question. It was further proved, that creation was not a solitary act, begun and completed long ago, but rather that it consisted of numberless acts, extending over vast periods of time; and thus that it afforded not merely increased proofs of the Divine existence, but satisfactory evidence, also, of the renewed and repeated, if not the continuous, exertion of Divine power. This last conclusion was strengthened and brought still nearer home through the testimony of consciousness, that person, or self, is indivisible, and therefore immaterial; and thus, that the creation of every human soul cannot be accounted for, except as the direct act of Omnipotence.

All events in the material universe evince the being of a God.—It is but a short step, then, to take in the extension of this argument, to say, that *all events whatever in the material universe*, except those which are caused directly by human will and power, *are in truth the doings of the Infinite One.* Hitherto, this doctrine of immediate Divine agency has been considered only in its place with other theories of *causation*, as the most plausible, if not the only possible, explanation of the phenomena of nature. We are now to consider whether the evidence on which it rests is not so strong, that it may well be classed with other proofs of the being of a God, and in one respect, indeed, be viewed as more satisfactory than any other, as it is the only one from which we infer directly his *present* existence. The argument, both from creation and design, proves immediately that he *was;* here we find direct evidence that he *is.* The phenomena of nature, so far as they show action or change, from the breaking of a bubble on the stream, up to the swift flight of the celestial orbs in their appointed paths, do not merely prove, but directly manifest, his existence and his glory

Let me not be understood as depreciating the value of the other proofs, in order to rest the whole weight of the argument here. I mention the distinction only to characterize more definitely the nature of this mode of reasoning, and not to lessen the cogency of the other forms of proof.

How we recognize God in nature. — We recognize the presence of God in nature in precisely the same manner in which we come to know that any intelligent, though finite, being exists besides ourselves. The outward form surely is nothing; a statue or an automaton may be moulded into a perfect external likeness of a man. But the actions of the living man show that he is animated by a spirit kindred to our own, by something distinct from the mere framework of bones and muscles which he inhabits, and which we distinguish as clearly from the person within as we do our own bodies from ourselves. *I* am conscious of power dependent on my will, and I perceive the effects produced on matter by the exertion of that will; I perceive, also, perfectly similar effects, which I can attribute only to my brother man, and I infer, therefore, that *he* exists, and that his will is equally active in producing those effects. I do not imagine that his limbs *move themselves*, but that *he* moves them; I do not think that his eye turns towards me of its own accord with a glance of affection, or that his hand comes to meet mine in a friendly grasp from an energy that is inherent in that hand alone. In like manner, then, I say, if *His* sun rolls over my head and warms me, if His wind cools and refreshes me, if His voice speaks to me, whether in the thunder at midnight, or in the whispers of the forest, or but in the rustling of a leaf, if His seasons still come round to me in their grateful vicissitude, and wherever I look in outward nature, I behold constant action, change, and joy, I do not suppose that brute and senseless matter causes all this by its inherent power whether original or derived, but that the spirit, the Person within, controls, vivifies, and produces all.

"These, as they change, Almighty Father, these
Are but the varied God. The rolling year
Is full of thee. . . . . .

But wandering oft, with brute, unconscious gaze,
Man marks not thee, marks not the mighty hand
That, ever busy, wheels the silent spheres."

Do not say, that this is mere poetical enthusiasm, or devotion, but not truth; it is the highest form of poetry, precisely because it is the *literal* truth. It is a conclusion founded on the most accurate researches of science, no less than on the instinctive promptings of our human nature, and on the aspirations of the religious sentiment within us; it is alike the doctrine of the intelligent mind and the dictate of the upright heart. We know not of any direct agency, we find no proof of any active power, but that which is the attribute of personality, which is directed by will, and witnessed by consciousness. External nature, when questioned as to the reality of power originating in itself, or inherited in its own right, hears not and answers not; no efficient cause, that is, no cause at all, in the proper signification of the word, has ever been discovered in it. Whence come, then, its countless changes, its incessant activity and life? It is no answer to this question to say, that events constantly succeed each other in regular sequence, or even to give a name to that order, and call it *law*, or *physical* cause. You cannot believe, you cannot even imagine, that any one of these events takes place without a *real* cause, an efficient energy, without which it were not. If matter be considered entirely apart from mind, it is dead, formless, and motionless; no winds agitate the surface of a chaotic ocean, no tides heave its waters, no waves break upon its silent shores. No eye can penetrate

"The secrets of the hoary deep, a dark
Illimitable ocean, without bound,
Without dimension, where length, breadth, and height,
And time and place, are lost; where eldest Night
And Chaos, ancestors of Nature, hold
Eternal empire. . . . . . In this wild abyss,
The womb of Nature, and perhaps her grave,
Is neither sea, nor shore, nor air, nor fire,
But all these in their pregnant causes mixed
Confus'dly."

Milton's conception of inorganic matter left to itself, without an indwelling soul, is not merely more poetical, but more philosophical and just, than the scientific romance, now generally repudiated by all rational inquirers, which represents it as necessarily imbued with the seminal principles of organization and life, and waking up by its own force from eternal quietude to eternal motion.

But I need not here renew the argument, already considered at sufficient length for our purposes, in favor of attributing all the active phenomena of nature directly to the omnipresence and omnipotence of God. A few considerations, which tend rather to illustrate than to prove the doctrine, and to account for the general reception of the popular fallacy which ascribes efficient causation to matter, will close the review of this branch of the subject.

This reasoning applied to the phenomena of gravitation. — Of all the classes into which the motions and changes of material objects are divided, with reference to their general similarity, and hence to a supposed unity of cause, the most comprehensive and important are those of *gravitation* and of *life*, — the latter term being understood, as in the vegetable kingdom, to signify merely *the law of formation and growth*, without supposing that any inherent principle exists in the plant distinct from its organic arrangement. As to the former class, the fact that *all particles of matter constantly tend towards each other* is the great conservative or sustaining principle of the material universe. Though often suspended or overbalanced by a stronger agency, as in all cases of life, the instances of it falling under our immediate observation are still so numerous, that we suppose there is no mystery in it. A weight that is no longer supported falls to the ground; and this phenomenon, from the frequency of its occurrence, excites no wonder. If it ever occurs to us to ask after its cause, we are contented with the answer, that it is probably *the same cause which makes other weights fall* under similar circumstances, though this certainly is no answer at all to the main question. That this gravity, or tendency to fall, is no *primary quality* of the substance itself, necessarily entering into our conception of it, as its *extension* does, is evident enough from the fact, that before any observation or experience of motion from gravitation, we should no more expect the body to fall downwards than upwards, like a balloon, or sidewise, like a bird. The vicinity of the body to the earth is now known not to be the characteristic feature of the phenomenon, as gravity is found to be the law of the material universe.

Consider, then, one of the great orbs which hang suspended in void space, isolated by millions of miles in every direction from other objects, and in reference to the motion of which, therefore, the words *upwards* and *downwards* hardly seem to have any meaning. Why should this body *fall* towards another orb which is more than ninety millions of miles off, in preference to moving in any other direction? You will doubtless say, that it is the attraction of the sun, which draws it. But examine carefully, I pray you, whether this answer be in truth the assignment of a cause, or merely another expression, an expression in different words, of the fact that the body does tend to move towards the sun, which is the phenomenon itself that we seek to account for. No axiom seems more self-evident than the old adage, that *nothing can act but where it is;* or if you hesitate to accept this maxim in all its generality, you will surely admit that *brute matter* — a collection of extended, impenetrable, and insensate particles — cannot act where it is not. It is a sufficiently violent hypothesis, to imagine that it can really *act* at all, or have any real force even within its own limits. But that it can exert any influence beyond these limits, is demonstrably absurd; for *action is a state of being*, and that a body should act where it is not, is therefore equivalent to saying that it is possible for *the same thing to be and not to be* at the same moment, which is a contradiction. How, then, can the sun *act* upon a body which is eighteen hundred millions of miles off, which is the distance of Uranus, to say nothing of the newly discovered planet, which is nearly twice as far, this immense intervening space being entirely void? I say, then, the supposition, that the sun, or any other material substance, really acts on another body, at a distance from it, is not merely extravagant, it is inconceivable; and as the point of greater or less distance is really of no importance, except to aid us in conceiving the question distinctly, the falling of a stone to the ground, either by its own inherent power, or by that of the earth, is equally inconceivable.

But along with gravity, another property is attributed to brute matter; namely, that when once set in motion, it tends to move onwards in a straight line, with a uniform velocity, for ever. The hypothesis here is of the same character, and quite as extravagant, as in the former case; but no matter; let us, for the present, take it for granted. The planets, and all the other heavenly bodies, do *not* move in straight lines, but in curves; and the mathematician will therefore tell you, that *at every instant* they are deflected, or turned aside from their proper course, by some agency foreign to themselves, which operates on them uniformly, with a constant force, tending towards a fixed point, thus keeping them within their appointed bounds. What is this agency? Or rather, *whose* is it, but His "who spake the word, and they were made? who commanded, and they were created? who hath made them fast for ever and for ever, and hath given them a law which shall not be broken?"

The purpose of the astronomer's calculations. — This view does not conflict with a just conception of the manner in which mathematical reasoning is applied to matters of fact, but tends rather to elucidate and confirm it. The real object of the astronomer's calculations is to express the *law*, that is, the *uniformity*, of the motions of the heavenly bodies, with little regard to any theory as to the origin or cause of those motions. *The motion alone is mensurable*, depending on the relations of space and time; and therefore it alone is calculable; *the cause of it cannot be measured*, for it cannot even be perceived. The mathematician, indeed, for the sake of clearness, begins with certain arbitrary hypotheses as to the origin and nature of the phenomena; but his calculations do not rest upon the truth in fact of those hypotheses, but only on the phenomena themselves, which he supposes to result from them. These hypotheses are not the actual structure, the foundations and walls, of his building, but the temporary scaffolding by the aid of which he erects those walls. They form the theory which enables him to *express in mathematical language* the facts or actual phenomena, — to recur to the preceding metaphor, the separate stones of which the walls are composed; and there may be several theories, directly conflicting with each other, which will answer this purpose equally well.

Thus, nearly all the phenomena of *light* are equally explicable on the theory either of *emission* or of *undulation;* from whichever of these two hypotheses the mathematician starts, the results of his calculations agree equally well with the observed phenomena; and yet, be it observed, the two hypotheses differ fundamentally, radically, from each other; they are contradictory. But as they are used only for a temporary purpose, just like the abstractions and postulates which constitute the first principles of pure mathematical science itself, the correctness of the result in nowise depends on their reality, their truth or falsity. They are mere scaffolding. Hence it was, that, until some crucial experiments were recently devised, which really determined that the undulatory theory was more satisfactory, or came *nearer* to the truth, than that of emissions, it was actually proposed as one reason for preferring this hypothesis to its rival, that it was more convenient for calculation; — it was a handier tool to work with.

What are forces in physical science. — We now see the reason why there is so much talk about various *forces* in physical science, especially in mechanics, when the mathematician seeks to express the facts in his own language. An objector to my argument might ask, How is it that you say there is no real power or force discoverable in the material universe as such, when a Laplace or a Bowditch, who deals with the most rigorous and accurate of all sciences, is constantly speaking of a great number of forces, and clearly distinguishes them from each other, and measures with the nicety of a hair's breadth their respective results? I answer, what the physical inquirer calls *force*, is merely a mathematical expression for the law, or order, with which certain observed results of a *supposed* force succeed each other. The calculation actually represents those phenomena, their time, character, and sequence, — and nothing else; as is seen at the close of the process, when the calculated results are tested by comparison with the last-observed phenomena. The calculator, in the midst of the process, often supposes several forces, recognized by him at the time to be fictitious or imaginary, for the mere purpose of facilitating his labor.* A body moving along the diagonal of a parallelogram

---

* Newton's theory is not an empirical law, but a hypothetical one. He does not say, that an attractive force between the particles of matter actually exists, but only that all bodies move or rest *as if* such a force existed. In respect to the solar system, it would be an equally correct statement of his doctrine to say, that the motions of the planets relative to the sun and each other, and of all satellites relative to their primaries, are such *as if* these bodies were bound to each other by elastic material ties, the strength of which varies directly as the masses of the bodies which they connect, and inversely as the squares of their own length. Newton no more believed in the actual existence of an attractive force, than in the actual existence of such elastic bands.

I have already shown, that mathematical science can offer no proof whatever of a physical fact; it can *prove* nothing but abstract propositions. When applied in the Mixed Sciences, it simply enables us to make a more strict and exact comparison, than would otherwise be possible, of the results of theory with the facts of nature. The only test of any hypothesis respecting the relations of certain phenomena to each other, is observation and experiment; and a competent knowledge of mathematics will enable us to apply this test with the utmost precision. With it, we can calculate, to a hair's breadth, the necessary results according to theory; and then, with the immense improvements of modern times in the instruments of observation, we can determine with equal accuracy the character and limits of the phenomenon. The astronomer, in his observatory, can determine the time at which the occultation *did* take place, within the tenth part of a second; and the mathematician, in the room below, can fix the time when, according to theory, it *ought* to take place, within the hundredth part of a second. The nice coincidence thus made out affects us with wonder, and seems to common minds a mathematical, and therefore incontrovertible, proof of the truth of the theory. But the coincidence itself can be made out, in a rough way, with the naked eye as the only means of observation, and by a train of reasoning from the theory so consequent

is really propelled by a single force, as when moving over any other straight line; but it is often convenient to *suppose* it impelled at the same instant by two forces, corresponding in direction and intensity to two adjacent sides of the figure.

The Ptolemaic system of astronomy. — My next illustration, being taken from astronomy, comes more nearly home to our leading subject. It is hardly possible to conceive of two theories of the motions of the heavenly bodies, which should differ from each other more widely than do those of Hipparchus and Copernicus. The complex and intricate system of the former has become, though unjustly, the derision of modern science; Milton ridiculed it long ago, in the counsel which he makes Raphael give to Adam, not to seek too eagerly to pry into those secrets of the heavens which "the great Architect did wisely to conceal:" —

"He his fabric of the heavens
Hath left to their disputes, perhaps to move
His laughter at their quaint opinions wide
Hereafter, when they come to model heaven,
And calculate the stars; how they will wield
The mighty frame, how build, unbuild, contrive,
To save appearances; how gird the sphere
With centric and eccentric scribbled o'er,
Cycle and epicycle, orb in orb."

The same complex system, when explained to Alphonso, king of Castile, gave rise to his noted remark, "that if God had consulted him at the creation, the universe should have been on a better and simpler plan." Now the truth is, that this complicated and fantastic theory of the heavens, with its operose contrivances of eccentric wheels, and circles riding upon circles, and which, in point of fact, is false from beginning to end, is

---

and direct, that a mind of great analytical power could follow it without the use of one mathematical symbol. And the coincidence itself, whether roughly or nicely determined, affords just as much proof of the theory, as would be gained in favor of any hypothesis as to the manner in which my neighbor's house caught fire, by showing, experimentally, that my own house might be so fired under precisely similar circumstances.

just as correct a basis for astronomical calculations as the simpler, more beautiful, and more truthful system of Copernicus. The language of Mr. Whewell, whose authority on a point like this no one will dispute, is, "As a system of calculation, [it] is not only good, but in many cases no better has yet been discovered." The Hipparchian or Ptolemaic theory represents the *apparent* motions of the heavenly bodies as *actual* motions; the Copernican deduces these *apparent* motions from a totally different system of revolutions, which it considers as the real one. Both systems are true or correct in this, — that *they represent those apparent motions rightly;* and this is all that is needed for the mathematician's purposes, all that the calculator wants in order to predict what will be the aspect of the heavens, or the exact position of a particular body, at some future time.

Astronomical theories are mere geometrical conceptions. — The office of theory, then, in physical science, is not to explain the cause or the origin of phenomena, but simply to represent with precision the phenomena themselves, and the order in which they succeed each other. In order to do this with clearness and simplicity, the theorist feigns certain causes, operating in an imaginary way, and thus gives unity to the phenomena by "making believe" that they all proceed from one source, the internal constitution of which is such that it can produce just these phenomena as they have been observed, and no other. Ptolemy had a correct notion of the Hipparchian theory in this respect; for although his predecessors and many of his disciples taught that the celestial spheres were real solid bodies, "they are spoken of by him as imaginary; and it is clear," says Mr. Whewell, "from his proof of the identity of the results of the hypothesis of an eccentric and an epicycle, that they are intended to pass for no more than geometrical conceptions, in which view they are true representations of the apparent motions." Now the several *forces*, by which, in the language of modern mathematicians, the heavenly bodies are represented as moved and directed, are just such "geometrical conceptions" as those of an eccentric and epicycle; rightly speaking, they are *not even conceived to be realities, but only convenient fictions,* just like the great circles, — the equator, the ecliptic, the meridians, etc., — which not even the school-boy supposes to be real and material arches over and around our universe. Newton found that the elliptical motions of the planets could not be mathematically represented by the hypothesis of *one* mechanical force, operating on them constantly and uniformly; and so he *imagined* two forces, one being that of gravitation, which tends constantly towards the sun, and another by which they tend to fly off at a tangent from their orbits; or the latter may be considered rather as the result of the primitive projectile force, with which the planets were originally launched in space. From these convenient fictions, he found he could deduce mathematically their true motions. It is possible, though certainly not probable, that some mathematical theory will hereafter be invented, which will account for the motions of the system on the hypothesis of a single force; if so, it will immediately take the place of the present theory, on account, not of its superior truth, but of its greater simplicity.*

Gravity is only a hypothetical force. — What shall we say, then, of a hypothetical history of the universe, which pretends to explain both the genesis and the progress of all material worlds by the aid only of this imaginary force, this mathematical fiction? What but this, — that it affords a striking proof of the manner in which language reacts on the ideas or opinions that it is intended to express, and thus leads men to talk non-

* I am able to quote the admission of M. Comte himself, a mathematician who will not be accused of any religious tendencies, that this remark is well founded. "In my dread of our resting in notions of any thing absolute, I would venture to say, that I can conceive of such a thing as even our theory of gravitation being hereafter superseded. I do not think it probable; and the fact will ever remain, that it answers completely to our present needs. It sustains us, up to the last point of precision that we can attain. If a future generation should reach a greater, and feel, in consequence, a need to construct a new law of gravitation, it will be as true as it now is, that the Newtonian theory is, in the midst of inevitable variations, stable enough to give steadiness and confidence to our understandings." — Martineau's *trans. of Comte's Phil.* Vol. I. p. 184.

sense without knowing it? To say that *gravitation* not only accounts for the present motions of the heavenly bodies, but that, on an easily conceivable theory, it may be made to explain *the origin of these motions*, and their several stages of progress, so to speak, to their present state or law, is the same thing as to say, that I can frame a hypothetical history of an imaginary universe, all the phenomena of which, and all the supposed changes in the *law*, or mode of succession, of those phenomena, can be calculated on the same mathematical principles; that is, by the aid of the same postulates, abstractions, and fictions, through which the mathematician deduces by exact computation the future positions of the real heavenly bodies from their past states and revolutions; or in other words, that mathematical science is a very general organon of calculation, which enables us to compute, not only the actual motions and changes of the actual universe, but the imaginary states and changes of a great number of fictitious, but easily conceivable worlds. This I conceive to be the exact meaning of Herschel's nebular hypothesis, and Laplace's theory of the genesis of our system by planets peeled off from the sun. Very different, and far more philosophical, was the view of gravitation which was taken by that great mind which first conceived the theory, and verified it by application. "That gravity," says Sir Isaac Newton, "should be innate, inherent, and essential to matter, so that one body may act upon another at a distance through a *vacuum*, without the mediation of any thing else, by and through which their action and force may be conveyed from one to another, is to me so great an absurdity, that I believe no man, who has in philosophical matters a competent faculty of thinking, can ever fall into it. *Gravity must be caused by an agent acting constantly according to certain laws.*"

Gravity is the basis of mechanical theories of the universe. — I have detained you too long, perhaps, with speculations respecting the true nature of the chief element in mechanical and astronomical calculations. But the popular conception of gravity seems to me so wholly unlike the just and philosophical view of it, and the part assigned to it in atheistic schemes of cosmogony is so prominent, and at the same time, when rightly considered, so unintelligible, that it was worth while making some attempt to rise to a clear comprehension of the subject. If I have at all succeeded in this explanation, it is evident that, in regard to efficient causation, or the great motive *power* of the universe, *the theory of gravitation, with all the calculations and hypotheses that are founded on it, leaves us precisely where it found us;* it accounts for nothing, it explains the origin of nothing; it is a simple statement, in a form convenient for scientific purposes, of the order and manner in which certain phenomena recur, leaving us to find a *cause* for those phenomena where we may. The conclusion remains as before, that this cause can be nothing but personal agency, which is to us the only known source of power, the only Œdipus that can explain the riddle of that great Sphinx, the universe. Yet the phenomena ranged under this class are so clearly distinguishable from all others, they are so simple and so frequent in their recurrence, that they suggest very forcibly *the action of a machine* of man's device; and for this reason, they have always been the chief support of all mechanical theories of causation. Yet a moment's reflection might satisfy us, that as in a machine, though human ingenuity devised it, it is not human power which keeps it in action, but rather (to use the common metaphor) the powers of nature, such as the weight of falling water, the elasticity of steel, or the expansive action of steam, — powers which we economize, direct, and apply to use, but do not create, — so these powers of nature themselves are not the source of the energy or true cause, but only the mode in which it is applied.

Tendency of mechanical calculations. — But as these phenomena suggest so strongly the action of a machine, they have been the chief support of the doctrine, that active power is in some way inherent in matter; the theory of gravitation has been the starting-point and the strong-hold for all mechanical theories of the universe. If the often quoted remark, that "the undevout astronomer is mad," be understood to mean only that astronomy is better calculated than any other branch of physical science to lead to correct views of the providence of God, I may be permitted to doubt its correctness. The vastness of the objects contemplated, and the sublimity of the phenomena, tend forcibly, it is true, to lead the partially instructed mind from the finite up to the infinite; but one who is conversant with the details of the science is apt to be blinded by their simplicity and uniformity, to be elated by his seemingly entire knowledge of them, and his power of predicting their recurrence, till he comes to imagine, that vast and magnificent as creation is, it is but a simple affair after all, — that the theory of gravitation unlocks the whole mystery of it, and places the secret, not only of the continuance of the system, but of its origin and growth, completely within the grasp of the human intellect. Newton was a believer, as minds of the highest order always will be; but Laplace, a man of great talent rather than original genius, immersed all his life in mathematical calculations, and inordinately vain of his success with them, doubted or denied; and the very title of his great work, the *Mécanique Céleste*, suggests the cause of his doubts. He thought he had reduced nature to *a vast piece of mechanism*, and that he could calculate to a fraction the strength of all its parts, and the intensity and mode of action of all its motive forces.* His accurate knowledge of the details of

* Since the passage in the text was written, Sir William Hamilton has made a similar observation. In the last edition of his "*Discussions*," (page 310,) he says, "It has been poetically said, 'an undevout astronomer is mad.' This, however, if poetical, is not true. For if, as has been quaintly but significantly expressed, '*Nature* is a Hebrew word written with mere consonants, to which *philosophy* must place the points,' certainly the '*mechanism* of the heavens' itself is not the grammar from which we can ever learn 'to syllable the stars.' Historically, a larger proportion of astronomers have been religious skeptics, in the last and worst degree, than any other class even of mere physical observers."

He afterwards quotes, (page 312,) as an illustration, the following shallow and impious remark from M. Comte, the most eminent infidel philosopher among the mathematicians of the present day. "To those unfamiliar with a study of the celestial bodies, Astronomy has still the character of being a science preëminently religious; as if the famous text, '*The Heavens declare the glory of God*,' retained its old significance. But to minds familiar with true philosophical astronomy, the heavens declare no astronomical science, in which the universe is considered only as a great system of revolving orbs acting on each other, prevented him from taking comprehensive and philosophical views of it as a whole.

Limited aims of astronomical science. — One reflection alone might have convinced him of the hollowness and vanity of his pretensions. Astronomy is a very finished science only because it is very limited in its objects. It contemplates nothing but motions and positions. Of the physical constitution even of the other bodies in our own solar system we are profoundly ignorant; we form a few faint guesses about the irregularities on the surface of the moon, which is the nearest of them, and here we stop. The stellar universe is to us only a grouping of points of light, seen from an immeasurable distance, in which a few slight changes of relative position have but recently been discovered. Of the external and internal economy of these orbs, of the forms which organized matter there assumes, the modes in which active energy develops itself, and the living races, if any, which tenant them, we are so far from knowing any thing, that we do not pretend even to study them. To explain the action of the planets and stars themselves, merely as it is investigated by the astronomer and the mathematician, — that is, to

---

other glory than that of Hipparchus, of Kepler, of Newton, — in a word, of all those who have aided in establishing their laws."

To this poor sophistry, it is certainly competent for us to reply, as we have done in another place, that the grandeur of astronomical science, after all, depends far more on the sublimity and perfectness of the objects of study, than on the ability and success with which they have been studied. The wonder is, not so much that man should be able to foresee the return of an eclipse, even to a second of time, as that the arrangement of the vast system of worlds should be so perfect, and their mutual action and dependence so accurately balanced, that the two bodies should return from their vast journey at the precise moment, and to the previously defined point in the heavens. M. Comte would have us believe, that the ingenuity of a person who should ascertain, after long study, that the movement of the hands on the face of a clock correctly indicated the hour of the day, was greater than that of the artisan who invented and constructed the instrument.

expound a theory of their relative motions and positions, — is to lay open but an infinitesimal part of the secrets of the celestial universe, and this the simplest and most conceivable part. Our idea of the mechanism of the heavens comes almost immeasurably short of the truth of things; and hence our notion of efficient cause, or active power, so far as it is derived only from this mechanism, or applied only to an explanation of it, is imperfect and vain. Notwithstanding the boasted triumphs of science in this department, the philosophical observer, seeing how vastly the subject still transcends the human intellect, instead of indulging the vanity of Laplace, will say rather, with the Psalmist of old: — "When I consider the heavens, the work of Thy fingers, and the moon and stars which Thou hast ordained, what is man that Thou art mindful of him, and the son of man that Thou visitest him?"

The same reasoning applied to the phenomena of life. — We gain a clearer idea of the limitation of our knowledge in this respect, when we consider the second class of phenomena to which I proposed to direct your attention, — those, namely, which are ascribed to *life*. Here, our observation is at once restricted to this earth; and the lessons which it teaches us, if deeply pondered, seem even more profound and impressive than those offered by the vast scale on which material attraction acts. *Gravitation is the simplest and most regular* of all the modes in which active power develops itself, while *life is the most complex and varied.* The two classes of phenomena ranged under these heads are thus taken from opposite ends of the scale; which is the reason why I have chosen them to illustrate the true doctrine of causation, instead of the intermediate classes, such as *chemical affinity*, and the imponderable agents, *electricity*, *heat*, and *magnetism*. Whatever is established as to the nature of the power exerted in these two classes, will very readily be admitted of all the ranks and divisions which lie between them. My present point is this, — that if the simple, regular, and frequently recurrent phenomena of gravitation cannot be explained on the hypothesis, that the universe is a machine, a clock that was wound up at creation, and which never runs down, then, for a still stronger reason, the myriad forms of life, the infinitely diversified modes in which creative and sustaining energy here shows itself, are not mechanical, but personal and Divine. If the hypothesis, that brute matter is necessarily endowed with a native and inherent activity, is utterly insufficient to explain even the simple fact, that all particles of that matter tend to move towards each other, and that aggregations of those particles into vast orbs uniformly circle round each other at immense distances with ceaseless motion, then, surely, the same hypothesis will not account for the mystery of life, as shown by the infinitely diversified motions of the motes which people a sunbeam, or of the animalcules which find an ocean in a drop of water, or of the vegetative forms, which cover the earth's surface with beauty, and minister to the wants of man, from the tiniest flower up to the grandeur and endurance of the firm-set oak.

Life is not mechanism. — The phenomena of life are not mechanical; the incessant motion, the countless changes, the perpetual succession of birth, growth, decay, and dissolution, which it exhibits, are events to be accounted for; they are effects, and the only sufficient, or even conceivable, cause to which they can be assigned, is the immediate action of an ever-present and omnipotent God. This is the argument, and you will observe that it is entirely distinct from the reasoning from design, or final cause. This second form of proof will come up afterwards; but for the present, I put it entirely aside. I do not now argue from the peculiarities of certain effects, that they must have been intended or purposed; but from the fact that there *are* effects, which must have a cause. I do not invite you to examine the artistic, the admirable internal structure of some form of vegetable or animal life, as a proof that intelligence, foresight, and benevolence were exerted in producing it; but merely to remember that this individual structure did begin to be; that its existence dates, perhaps, only from yesterday, or from the last hour; that there is a constant motion and change among its constituent parts; and these various beginnings and movements must be attributed to some *efficient* cause which cannot be found in the mere insensate atoms of which the plant or animal is made up, but must be sought for in spirit, or person, the only known source of power. That the plant began to exist, and that it grows, are phenomena to be accounted for in some way, just as much as the curious internal arrangement or organization of that plant.

Among the forms of mere organic life, the birth, development, and subsequent changes of which are to be accounted for by a cause out of themselves, I rank the material framework of my own body, and those merely *vital* movements in it which are not dependent on my own will, and which, consequently, as has been already proved, are truly foreign to myself. Here, then, we bring the only two kinds of efficient or personal power with which we are acquainted, — namely, the human and the Divine, — as it were, into close juxtaposition and virtual coöperation; and thus the point of the argument appears more clearly. *The voluntary movement* of my arm and hand I know to be dependent on myself; I am conscious of willing the movement, and am conscious of making an effort, or exerting my own power, to that end. It is even inconceivable to me, that, within the ordinary sphere of my action, they should move without my agency, or, in other words, should move themselves. Then I say, that *the other motions* in that arm and hand, *which are not voluntary, not mine,* such as the circulation of the blood, the excretions of the skin, the constant flux and change of all the material particles in them, must also be attributed to a cause out of themselves, to a personal agency not inherent in the arm and hand. Even the skeptic will allow me to say, that *the hand does not move itself,* but that I move it; then it seems to me the conclusion is inevitable, that *the blood does not move itself,* and that no physical cause, or mere organization, has any thing to do with its motion, except that it is so constituted as not to interfere with it; but in this case, no less than in that of the planets circling round the sun, the mover is Divine.

Why the phenomena of life appear mysterious. — Of all the mysteries with which we are surrounded, life is thought to be the most inscrutable. The reason of this is, that it cannot even be conceived of as mere mechanism; it refuses to be subject to the ordinary chemical affinities, to computation and law. There is order and uniformity in its manifestations, but it is an order of its own, and one which appears in the midst of infinite variety. The motions of fluids under its influence refuse to submit to the dynamic principles which govern the movements of inorganic substances; the processes which are carried on within its sphere cannot be imitated by the subtlest refinements of chemistry. Endeavor to measure and calculate its action by the aid of what are considered as known laws, and a residuum is always left, which must be attributed to a vital force, a wholly peculiar physical cause, of which we know nothing. In the functions of the living body, *it may be*, that the ordinary laws of chemistry are preserved, and that the elements of carbon, oxygen, hydrogen, and nitrogen combine and separate according to their ordinary affinities, and in no unusual proportions; though this point does not seem to be fully proved. But after death, at any rate, quite a different set of chemical laws come into play, and produce a result which is the very opposite of that before effected. There is no longer any unanimity or coöperation; instead of sustaining or building up the animal tissues, the affinities now in operation tear down, destroy, and resolve them into their ultimate elements, — each part following out its own law of destruction or resolution, irrespectively of the others.

The definitions of life which have been given by the most eminent physiologists, show very clearly their conviction, that the vital processes are neither chemical nor mechanical, but that the principle on which they depend is a mystery inscrutable by the human intellect. Thus, life has been defined by Stahl to be "the condition by which a body resists a natural tendency to chemical changes, such as putrefaction." Humboldt says, that living bodies are "those which, notwithstanding the constant operation of causes tending to change their form, are hindered *by a certain inward power* from undergoing such change." The definition of Kant, who looked at the subject more as a metaphysician than a physiologist, is in truth no definition at all; he says, that "life is *an internal faculty*, producing change, motion, and action." Bichat's definition, that "life is the sum of the functions by which death is resisted," only introduces a correlative mystery into the subject; and as the latter is a negative idea, it would be more correct, as Mr. Whewell suggests, to define death with reference to life, as its cessation, or natural limit. Schmid defines life to be "the activity of matter, according to laws of organization;" and an organized body is said by Kant to be one in which "all the parts are mutually ends and means." * Organization, then, is properly the condition or prerequisite of activity; it is the machine without the moving power. Life is something — we know not what — which keeps

* "It will be observed, that we do not content ourselves with saying, that, in such a whole, all the parts are *mutually dependent*. This might be true even of a mechanical structure; it would be easy to imagine a framework in which each part should be necessary to the support of each of the others; for example, an arch of several stones. But in such a structure, the parts have no properties which they derive from the whole. They are beams or stones when separate; they are no more when joined. But the same is not the case in an organized whole. The limb of an animal, separated from the body, loses the properties of a limb, and soon ceases to retain even its form.

"Nor do we content ourselves with saying that the parts are *mutually causes and effects*. This is the case in machinery. In a clock, the pendulum, by means of the escapement, causes the descent of the weight, the weight by the same escapement keeps up the motion of the pendulum. But things of this kind may happen by accident. Stones slide from a rock down the side of a hill, and cause it to be smooth; the smoothness of the slope causes stones still to slide. Yet no one would call such a slide an organized system. The system is organized, when the effects which take place among the parts are *essential to our conception of the whole;* when the whole would not *be* a whole, nor the parts, parts, except these effects were produced; when the effects not only happen in fact, but are included in the idea of the object; when they are not only seen, but foreseen; not only expected, but intended; in short, when, instead of being causes and effects, they are *ends* and *means*, as they are termed in [Kant's] definition.

"Thus we necessarily include, in our Idea of Organization, the notion of an End, a Purpose, a Design; or, to use another phrase which has been peculiarly appropriated in this case, a *Final Cause*. This idea of a Final Cause is an essential condition in order to the pursuing our researches respecting organized bodies." — Whewell's *Phil. of the Ind. Sciences*, 2d ed. Vol. I. p. 619

the machine in action, and at the same time preserves it from decay, to which it would otherwise be subject at every moment.

Life, then, is *not mere* organization, though most materialists willingly confound the two things; to hear them reason, one would almost suppose that there was no difference between a dead animal and a living one. Organization is subservient to life, ministers to it, manifests it, — supports it, if you please, — but does not constitute it. Life is something added to the organic structure, a new power in action, — or rather, on the true theory, a new and wholly peculiar application of the same power, — not inherent in the parts, the material atoms, nor yet in the complex organism which is made up of those atoms; not compounded of or resulting from the laws of action, or affinities, of the elements of the body, but controlling, overruling, and superseding those affinities, which come into play again only when life departs.

Life overrides or suspends other laws of action. — In whatever manner we contemplate the phenomena of life, the argument seems to me conclusive in favor of the doctrine of immediate Divine agency. If chemical action is mechanical or absolute, if chemical affinities are inherent powers, necessarily belonging to the atoms in which they usually manifest themselves, how are they thus suspended for a season, or during the life of the animal, and then made again to operate after its death? Such intermittent action is not characteristic, is not even conceivable, of a primary and necessary quality, an inherent power; we cannot, for instance, conceive of a material substance as extended at one moment, and not extended the next, or of an atom as impenetrable now, and not impenetrable an instant afterwards; (I refer now, of course, to absolute impenetrability, that quality which matter is conceived to possess of occupying space, and of excluding all other matter from the space so occupied.) And this suspension of the affinities of matter cannot be accounted for by the altered circumstances of the case. An animal, for example, is instantly killed by a blow on the head; but this event does not alter the mutual position and relations to each other of the material particles which form one of its limbs; these remain undisturbed. Yet their action on each other instantly changes, from one that contributed to sustain and build up the organism, to another which carries it by a swift process to dissolution. It is no answer to this argument to remind me, as the chemist will do, of the *allotropic* states even of inorganic substances, in which the same bodies manifest different qualities at successive instants. This is but another instance of the same phenomenon, not an explanation of the phenomenon, or an assignment of its cause, which is admitted to be inscrutable. My point is, that *necessary attributes*, inherent powers, *cannot be allotropic;* if what you call the *action* of the particle changes, this is a proof that the particle is not acting, but is acted upon. Spinoza's doctrine teaches us, that *invariability and uniformity are the characteristics of material and necessary action;* for change, choice, difference, we must go up to the free action of person or mind. The conclusion is inevitable, then, that these chemical affinities, so called, are the results of will and personal power.

The results of mechanical action are perfectly uniform.— Again, these affinities, I say, cannot be necessary and mechanical in their operation, because the phenomena of life do not constantly recur upon the same uniform pattern; they are not only intermittent, they are immeasurably diversified. The life of the organized mass is a free and independent power, as appears from the infinite variety of forms that it assumes. The affinities, or whatever other powers we suppose to inhere in the particles by themselves, do not by their complication and mutual action make up the life, or give rise to the various motions of the organism, or create its numberless outward aspects. For the results of necessary and mechanical action are all alike; either they are perfectly similar to each other, or they change by a fixed law either of deterioration or improvement; while the effects of power controlled by freewill and witnessed by consciousness are multiform, variety being the rule, and perfect resemblance the exception. This is easily illustrated by a comparison of human labor with that of a machine. Of any number of nails made by hand, no two are just alike, while the nail-machine strikes them out in perfect conformity to one pattern; or to take another instance, no handwriting even approaches the uniformity of the engraved or printed letters in many successive copies of the same words. The only difference perceivable in the former case is a regular and gradual one, as the machine or the types slowly wear out. Even these illustrations do not give an adequate idea of the uniformity here in question, as the machine is always controlled or guided, to a certain extent, by human power, and is in itself but an application and direction of the powers of nature, so called, which are really personal and Divine. Active attributes, necessarily resulting from the essence or internal constitution of the thing, are as unchangeable and constant in their operation as the geometrical attributes of space, the immutable and everlasting relations which are studied by the mathematician; and this is precisely the view of the universe, of natural events, which is taken by the logical necessarian, by Fichte and Spinoza.

The results of life are infinitely varied. — Consider, then, the infinite variety of forms and aspects which living nature assumes, and explain these, if you can, on the hypothesis that the universe is a machine. Of the millions of leaves which make up the glorious mass of foliage on a large oak tree, it is said, I believe with truth, that no two can be found exactly alike in outward configuration.* Of all the faces in a large assemblage, or, it may be said, even in the population of a city or a country, not one is the exact counterpart of another. I need not multi-

* "Leibnitz," says De Quincey, "when walking in Kensington Gardens with the Princess of Wales, took occasion, from the beautiful scene about them, to explain in a lively way, and at the same time to illustrate and verify, this favorite thesis, [that amongst the familiar objects of our daily experience, there is no perfect identity.] Turning to a gentleman in attendance upon her Royal Highness, he challenged him to produce two leaves *from any tree or shrub,* which should be exact duplicates or fac-similes of each other in those lines which variegate the surface. The challenge was accepted; but the result justified Leibnitz. It is, in fact, upon this infinite variety, in the superficial lines of the human palm, that *palmistry* is grounded, (or the science of divination by the hieroglyphics written on each man's hand,) and has its *primâ facie* justification."

ply these instances of the unbounded diversity of nature's operations in life; every one's memory will supply a sufficient number of them for the purposes of this argument. The differences allud d to are not those merely which distinguish *races*, but those which mark out *individuals*, separating one generation from another, and giving a peculiar character to each of the offspring of common parents. If we should grant, then, that the simple and uniform effects that are ascribed to gravitation, or even to a more complex cause, chemical affinity, are mechanical, the theory of secondary or automatic causation wholly fails to account for the multifarious phenomena of life. Unity of principle pervading unmeasured and immeasurable variety, is the character of the physical universe; the necessarian may dream that he can account for that unity, by reducing the All to one unchangeable substance; but the variety is to him an inexpliplicable mystery.

Wherever we look in outward nature, then, we behold *proofs* of an ever-present and ever-active Deity. Diversity, change, motion, activity, all ceaseless and endless, show that power is in action; and this *power*, commensurate with the extent and coeval with the duration of the universe, is that of the Infinite One. The *sentiment* which these phenomena inspire, harmonizes with the lesson which they teach to the intellect, and with the logical deductions of the understanding. As surely as our earth, with its sister orbs and companion systems, still rolls in its appointed path, as surely as seed-time and harvest, night and day, return, and life, in countless forms and untiring action, peoples every clod of earth and every drop of water, so surely God liveth.*

---

* Besides the doctrine maintained in this chapter, six different hypotheses have been propounded at various times, to account for the motions and other phenomena of the material universe. I borrow, with much abridgment and some addition, an account of them from Dugald Stewart.

1. The first is that of *materialism*, according to which the phenomena of nature are the result of certain active powers necessarily inherent in matter. In its pure form, this is an atheistic hypothesis; and, in fact, it was the earliest doctrine of atheism, having been taught by Democritus about

450 B. C. It was also the leading feature of the Epicurean philosophy. The powers which are inherent in matter, and which have existed in it from all eternity, are enough, according to this theory, to account for all the phenomena that we witness. From the endless multiplicity of atoms, a fortuitous concourse of them, in an infinite series of years, may assume the appearance of regularity and adaptation; as the chance of order is at least one out of an infinite number of chances of disorder, and therefore must occur at least once during an eternity. The groundwork of this hypothesis is struck away by the proof which has been offered, that *power*, properly so called, cannot even be conceived of as an attribute of brute matter; that *gravity*, in particular, cannot be predicated of matter except by an abuse of words, which confounds the *mode* of action with the *cause* of that action; and that this universe, considered as an organic whole, and as abounding with organic life, is not of indefinite antiquity, but is clearly proved, by geological phenomena, to be of comparatively recent origin.

2. The second hypothesis is theistic, but in nearly every other respect, it agrees with the preceding one, and it is open to the same objections. Its doctrine is, that the phenomena of nature result from certain active powers communicated to matter at its first formation. Except that this theory recognizes a creation and a Creator, it does not account for the phenomena any better than pure materialism; since it is just as difficult to conceive of gravity as a property of matter, whether matter was first endowed with this property many ages ago, or always possessed it. It is inconceivable that matter should act upon matter which is millions of miles distant from it, whether this power of acting is inherent in it, or was first imparted to it at the creation; in either case, we have to meet the difficulty — the contradiction — that something should *act* where it *is not;* in other words, that it should *be* where it *is not.*

3. The third hypothesis is the common one, which ascribes the phenomena of nature to certain *general laws* established by the Deity. We have sufficiently proved that this theory is founded upon a mere abuse of words, so that the proper objection to it is, not that it is false, but that it is meaningless. General laws are merely a classification and description of the phenomena which are to be accounted for; they offer no explanation of these phenomena, and throw no light whatever upon their *efficient* causes. The very purpose of the hypotheses with which we are now concerned, is to account for efficient causation.

4. A fourth supposition is that of Dr. Cudworth, who ascribes the phenomena of the material world to what he calls *a plastic or formative nature,* or (according to his own definition of it) to "a vital and spiritual, but unintelligent and necessary agent, created by the Deity for the execution of his purposes." This mysterious and fanciful doctrine seems to be rather a play of the imagination than a product of the intellect. We can hardly believe that it was propounded seriously. Perceiving the absurdity of the hypothesis, that the Creator endowed brute matter with active properties

Dr. Cudworth preferred to imagine that He first animated it with an indistinct living principle, — a sort of half-life, — so that it became more plastic to His hands, and more obedient to His behest, than it would have been in its original inert and passive state. The supposition is an unnecessary one, as Omnipotence needs no such aid in executing its purposes; and as it is defended by neither argument nor analogy, it may be rejected as a mere dream.

5. Dissatisfied with all these doctrines, Lord Monboddo attempted to revive what he calls *the ancient theory of mind.* Every particle of matter he supposes to be animated with different minds. Thus, there is one, which he calls the elemental mind, that is the source of the cohesion of bodies; another is the cause of their gravitation; and so on. Even in the case of the motion that follows impulse, he holds that the impulse is only the *occasion* of the motion; the *continuance* of the motion is attributable to a mind excited by the impulse, because continued motion implies continued activity. Thus, also, the planets are endowed with minds which guide and impel them in their revolutions round the sun; only these planetary minds are void of intelligence, being mere principles of activity. This theory is open to the same objection as the former one, that it is a mere dream, unsupported even by probability. But both are instructive as showing the difficulty of conceiving principles to be inherent in matter which would account for its phenomena; the agency of mind must, somehow, be called in.

6. The last supposition is that of the philosophers who maintain that the universe is a machine formed and put in motion by the Deity. In this hypothesis, Descartes and Leibnitz agreed, notwithstanding the wide diversity of their systems in other respects. But a machine needs a continuous motive power; it needs the expansive force of steam, the weight of falling water, the elasticity of steel, or some other force; and if this be intermitted, the action stops. A machine is not a contrivance for *creating* power, but only for *using* it, — for applying it in one direction or another, or to one or another purpose. Now, it has been shown that matter has no force of its own. What, then, keeps the machine of the universe in action? It must be the continuous and immediate action of the Deity; and this is the very theory of immediate divine agency which we advocate, except that we throw away the idle and baseless hypothesis, that Omnipotence works through machinery, instead of accomplishing its purposes directly and at once.

CHAPTER VIII.

INFERENCES FROM THE GENERAL CHARACTER OF THE PHENOMENA OF THE PHYSICAL UNIVERSE.

Summary of the last chapter. — In the last chapter, the phenomena of the physical universe, so far as they show change, diversity, and activity, which are not attributable to human power and will, were held to prove the immediate and omnipresent action of the Deity. The argument was, that these phenomena afford incontestable evidence of *power exerted*, or *efficient causation*, and there is no source of such power within our knowledge, and none, in fact, that is conceivable, except in *personal agency;* and in this case, the power being commensurate with the extent and duration of all things, it must be ascribed to the Infinite Creator. This reasoning was carried out in reference to two of the most comprehensive classes of such events, — those, namely, which are ascribed to *gravitation* and to *life;* the phenomena under the former head being the most simple, uniform, and frequent in their occurrence, while those coming under the latter are most complex, varied, and multiform; so that any conclusion established respecting both these classes must hold true of all intermediate ones.

In regard to the former, it was shown that what are called *forces* in mechanical science, are only metaphorical expressions for *the mode* or *order* in which certain events succeed each other, or are mere fictions for the convenience of the mathematician, like the abstractions and hypotheses with which the geometer begins his work; both attraction and the tangential force being, in fact, as imaginary as the eccentrics and epicycles of Hipparchus and Ptolemy. In regard to the latter, the phenomena of *life*, they were shown to be inexplicable and inconceivable as effects of *mechanism*, such effects being necessarily uniform and perfectly similar to each other, or changing only by a regular law of deterioration or improvement; while the numberless aspects, and infinite variations of the activity, of living things, point for their cause to the free volitions of a conscious agent

This form of argument for the being of a God, it was observed, though not so familiar to common minds as the proof from design, — for indeed, it is not fully stated in any work on Natural Theology with which I am acquainted, — is still legitimate and conclusive; and it has this great advantage, that from it we infer immediately his *present* existence, instead of establishing this point by a subsequent process of reasoning. The conclusion to which it leads harmonizes with the natural turn of religious sentiment, or devotion, by referring all events to Divine agency; and thus we avoid the common objection to the doctrine of an overruling and ever-watchful Providence.

Hume's objection to the argument from effect to cause. — A further advantage of this reasoning is, that it is not exposed to the objection urged by Hume, on the ground that the universe is a *singular* effect. The way is paved for this sophism by putting into the mouth of Cleanthes, the character in the Dialogues concerning Natural Religion who plays the part of a rational and consistent theist, a distinct avowal of the mechanical theory of nature. "Look round the world," says Cleanthes; "contemplate the whole and every part of it. You will find it to be nothing but one great machine, subdivided into an infinite number of lesser machines, which again admit of subdivisions to a degree beyond what human senses and faculties can trace and explain." These words, though uttered by an imaginary speaker, convey, I have no doubt, Hume's own opinion; and they certainly leave the door open for the objection that is instantly made by Philo, who supports the character and cause of the atheist.

"When two species of objects," says Philo, "have always been observed to be conjoined together, I can infer, by custom, the existence of one wherever I *see* the existence of the other and this I call an *argument from experience*. But how this argument can have a place, where the objects, as in the present case, are single, individual, without parallel or specific resemblance, may be difficult to explain. And will any man tell me, with a serious countenance, that an orderly *universe* must arise from some thought and art *like the human*, because we have experience of it? To ascertain this reasoning, it were requisite that we had *experience of the origin of worlds;* and it is not sufficient, surely, that we have seen *ships* and *cities* arise from human art and contrivance. Can you pretend to show any similarity between the fabric of a *house* and the generation of a *universe?* Have you ever seen nature in any such situation as resembles the first arrangement of the elements? Have worlds ever been formed under your eye? and have you had leisure to observe the whole progress of the phenomenon, from the first appearance of order to its final consummation? If you have, then cite your experience, and deliver your theory."

This objection confuted. — Now I might answer this sophistry at once, by saying, that although I have not witnessed the fabrication of a universe, I *have* watched the growth of a plant, from the first germination of the seed to the perfection of the blossom; and though I have had no personal experience of the origin of worlds, I yet know, whether from reason or the testimony of others, a fact that Philo himself will not deny, that this *my body*, the material apparatus of limbs and organs in which I live and move, *did begin to be;* and of all its subsequent changes, its growth up to its present state, I have had the most intimate experience. But the admission or assertion of Cleanthes, that the universe is *one great machine*, seemingly bars out this reply, by leading us to infer that the preëxisting machinery in the parent plant or blossom produced the seed, the future development and growth of which are but the subsequent action of the same machinery; so that all which I have actually witnessed or experienced, is not the origin or beginning, but the continuance, of things.

How obvious is the rejoinder, that this phrase, *the universe*, is a mere general expression for the totality of things, having only an ideal and fictitious unity, and being, in truth, nothing but *an abstract conception!* To recur to a former illustration, there is no such thing as an audience, apart from the individual men and women who compose it. Let us not be blinded by mere words. Individual things are the only objects which really exist; as we profess here to argue only from facts, let us not confuse these with mere abstractions and generalities. To talk about explaining the origin of a universe, except this be understood to mean the accounting in succession for each of the real existences which make up a universe, is to deal in nonsense; it is as if, after explaining in due order the motives which brought each of the hearers together, I should still be required to account for the general fact, that there was an audience assembled. And this remark applies, be it observed, not only to the different individuals who *at any one moment* make up a sum total, or class, but to the other individuals who occupied the same spot before these began to be, and to others still, who shall fill their places after these cease to exist. The unity which is attributed by the mind, for the mere convenience of conception and speech, both to successive and contemporaneous individuals, is alike ideal and fictitious.

Individual things cannot have been created by machinery. — Let us see, then, whether this hypothesis of machinery, as the secret of the creation, not of a universe, but of individual things or real existences, is any thing more than a blank assumption. Suppose that two grains of sand, looking just alike, were placed on the floor before us, and, while we were watching them, they should begin to expand, shoot up, alter their forms, take all the aspects and qualities of life, and finally become distinct and recognizable, the one as a giant oak tree, and the other as a living and moving creature. On witnessing so strange a phenomenon, we could not help concluding that *some personal agency had produced it*, some power transcending that of man; after satisfying ourselves that there was no deception or mystification in the matter, we should at once refer it to a supernatural or miraculous cause. Nor would this conclusion be at all less logical, if the phenomenon were a *frequent* one, — if there were a mountain of such sand, from which particular grains being taken at the proper season and carried to the proper place, both time and place being determined by experience, these results invariably followed.

Now, this is a statement but very little disguised, and varying in no *essential* particular, from the description of what is actually and constantly taking place all around us, in living nature. The beginning of all life, and of all tissues, whether animal or vegetable, is in certain primitive cells, or germinal vesicles, perfectly resembling each other in external appearance, and so minute, that they can be discerned only under high powers of the microscope. The germs are alike to the eye; but according to the place which each is taken from, whether from one side or another of the sand heap, it is developed by a regular process into a plant or an animal. If you say that there are specific differences between these microscopic grains, each one veiling some curious and elaborate machinery, peculiar to itself, by which this astonishing result is brought about, I answer, that your assertion is both gratuitous and incredible. It is gratuitous; for certainly we see no such machinery, and have no indication whatever of its existence; we *see* nothing but a little rectangular or circular cell, with a dot in it. It is incredible; for we can no more conceive of the possibility of a machine under such circumstances producing such results, than we can believe that the automaton really plays an admirable game of chess solely by the means of wheels, springs, and cylinders. In both cases, we declare with positive conviction, that intelligence, will, and conscious activity are somewhere at work in this matter, that some *unseen person* is actually causing the phenomenon. "If an animal or a vegetable," says Dugald Stewart, "were brought into being before our eyes, *in an instant of time*, — the event would not be in itself more wonderful than their *slow growth* to maturity from an embryo or from a seed. But on the former supposition, there is no man who would not perceive and acknowledge the immediate agency of an intelligent cause; whereas, according to the actual order of things, the effect steals so insensibly on the observation, that it excites little or no curiosity, excepting in those who possess a sufficient degree of reflection to contrast the present state of the objects around them with their first origin, and with the progressive stages of their existence." Look at the animal when fully grown, moving about and performing all the functions of life, and then believe, if you can, that this creature, in all its parts and powers, is the *necessary* result of machinery and active energy that are underived and naturally inherent in that microscopic cell, that mere grain of sand. Look, further, into your own consciousness,— for you, too, upon this hypothesis, were born from the dust,— and conceive of all your powers of mind and heart, your reasoning, imaginative, and moral faculties, as the mere product of machinery in an infinitesimal germ. The part of the infidel here is really that of outrageous credulity.*

* "The minds of most men are fond of what they call a *principle,* and of the appearance of simplicity in accounting for phenomena. Yet this principle, this simplicity, resides merely in the *name;* which name, after all, comprises, perhaps, under it a diversified, multifarious, or progressive operation, distinguishable into parts. The power in organized bodies, of producing bodies like themselves, is one of these *principles.* Give a philosopher this, and he can get on. But he does not reflect what this mode of production, this *principle* (if such he chooses to call it,) requires; how much it presupposes; what an apparatus of instruments, some of which are strictly mechanical, is necessary to its success; what a train it includes of operations and changes, one succeeding another, one related to another, one ministering to another; all advancing, by intermediate, and frequently by sensible steps, to their ultimate result! Yet because the whole of this complicated action is wrapped up in a single term, *generation,* we are to set it down as an elementary principle; and to suppose, that when we have resolved the things which we see into this principle, we have sufficiently accounted for their origin, without the necessity of a designing, intelligent Creator. The truth is, *generation* is not a *principle,* but a *process.* We might as well call the casting of metals a principle; we might, so far as appears to me, as well call spinning and weaving, principles; and then, referring the texture of cloths, the fabric of muslins and calicoes, the patterns of diapers and damasks, to these, as principles, pretend to dispense with intention, thought, and contrivance, on the part of the artist; or to dispense, indeed, with the necessity of any artist at all, either in the manufacturing of the article, or in the fabrication of the machinery by which the manufacture was carried on."—Paley's *Natural Theology,* Ch. xxiii.

The frequency of the phenomenon does not make it less miraculous. — I say further, that the theological conclusion here is so obvious and reasonable, that all mankind would instantly adopt it without hesitation, just as they do an intuitive truth, if it were not for our familiarity with such results, arising from their *countless number and constant repetition. One* such birth, interrupting the uniformity of living nature, otherwise made up, so far as our knowledge extended, of beings without beginning or end, would instantly convert all men to a recognition of invisible power that is personal and Divine. But the frequency of the phenomenon wears out our wonder; what is not strange, we refuse to consider as miraculous; we look upon it mechanically, and so come to regard it as a mechanical effect.* But can any thing be more illogical or unreasonable, than to alter our conclusion solely *because the evidence is multiplied* on which it rests? Shall *one* birth, one beginning of living existence, prove the being of a Creator, and not a thousand? Yet this is the whole of the atheistic argument: — the phenomena of nature are constantly repeated, therefore the universe is a machine; and not only so, but a machine that made itself, or has existed from eternity.

I have departed here, in some degree, you will perceive, from the strict argument from the effect up to the cause, by entering into some details respecting the peculiar character of certain effects as distinguished from others, so that the reasoning does not depend, as before, exclusively on the mere manifestation of power. This is taking a step towards the argument from design, a mode of proof which seems more conclusive to most persons than any other, on account of its plainness, the numberless illustrations or confirmations of it, and the very direct evidence which it offers of the personality of the Deity.

How the existence of a personal cause is indicated. — It is a

---

* "Sed assiduitate quotidianâ, et consuetudine oculorum, assuescunt animi; neque admirantur, neque requirunt rationes earum rerum quas semper vident; perinde quasi novitas nos magis quam magnitudo rerum debeat ad exquirendas causas excitare." — Cicero, *de Nat. Deor.* II. 38.

step further in the same direction to remark, that the different modes in which Divine power is here manifested, on the theory of immediate creative and sustaining energy, are just such as we might expect from infinite power, wisdom, and beneficence combined in one person, and exerted with entire freedom of will, — exerted also, I may *now* say, with reference to the moral government of intelligent finite beings, like ourselves. We should expect (1.) *constancy in the regular attainment of certain great ends*, and perfect uniformity in the modes of obtaining them; together with (2.) *infinite variety in* what may be called *the details of creation.* The former, *the general laws*, we find in the great recurrent phenomena of the universe, in the laws of *gravitation, heat, light, magnetism, chemical affinity*, and the like; the latter, *the variety*, we find in *the countless differences which distinguish all living forms* from each other, and diversify to an immeasurable extent all the relations of life. With the general laws we are sufficiently acquainted, as it is the peculiar office of science to study them, since they alone serve to guide the conduct of free and intelligent beings, and give all its value to experience. Because the physical inquirer is so exclusively occupied with these, he comes gradually to overlook the endless diversity of form and aspect under which they are manifested; he sees everywhere the action of *law*, and the phenomena of nature appear to him regularly recurrent and mechanical. The botanist, for instance, studies only the specific differences of plants, disregarding the minute varieties of shape and hue which distinguish any two flowers of the same species from each other, and even the occasional freaks of nature, the metamorphosis of organs, the production of a leafy branch from the centre of a flower, or of one flower out of another; or if he considers these abnormal growths at all, it is in a vain attempt to reduce them to the dominion of *law*, by virtue of a theory which represents the universe as incomplete, as an idea not yet realized, a plan not fully carried out. My point here is simply, that *these countless diversities of nature*, which are not studied solely because they are countless, *are as much a part of creation*, a part, so to speak, of the Divine plan, as the general laws themselves. The filaments of order run in every direction through the web of the universe; but they can be discerned only under the surface-pattern, which combines all possible modifications of outline and coloring in measureless profusion.*

Man's conduct shows uniformity united with endless variety. — I say, this regularity in the midst of diversity is precisely what we should expect from the action of a free and intelligent agent; the *order* manifests *intelligence*, the *variety* bears witness to *freedom.* For consider the actions of a finite conscious being, who is a feeble representative, it is true, but the only representative that we have, of Deity, in so far as he unites power with intellect and freewill. So far as the great aims and purposes of life are concerned, according as these are determined by appetite, self-love, habit, or the moral sense, the conduct of man is consistent and uniform, and you may safely predict the future from the past. We may even foresee the results of the combined free activity of great masses of men, from the known motives and the comparative strength of differ-

---

* "Peu de principes, de grands moyens en petit nombre, des phénomènes infinis et variés, voilà le tableau de l'univers." — Baily, *Hist. de l'Astronomie.*

"Nature," says Cuvier, "while confining herself strictly within those limits which the conditions necessary for existence prescribed to her, has yielded to her spontaneous fecundity wherever these conditions did not limit her operations; and without ever passing beyond the small number of combinations, that can be realized in the essential modifications of the important organs, she seems to have given full scope to her fancy, in filling up the subordinate parts. With respect to these, it is not inquired, whether an individual form, whether a particular arrangement, be necessary; it seems often not to have been asked, whether it be even useful, in order to reduce it to practice; it is sufficient that it be possible, that it destroy not the harmony of the whole. Accordingly, as we recede from the principal organs, and approach to those of less importance, the varieties in structure and appearance become more numerous; and when we arrive at the surface of the body, where the parts the least essential, and whose injuries are the least momentous, are necessarily placed, the number of varieties is so great, that the conjoined labors of naturalists have not yet been able to give us an adequate idea of them." — *Leçons d'Anatomie Comparée.*

ent motives which are present to the minds of each one of them. Political Economy is a science wholly made up of such generalizations of the conduct of men as may be made by observing the uniformity of their proceedings in respect to the acquisition of wealth. That competition lowers prices, which are finally adjusted by the ratio of the supply to the demand, is, in truth, a general law of human nature, founded not at all on the nature of the different articles which constitute wealth, but on the dispositions of men. It may be obtained either empirically, by observing the course of trade, or deductively, from the higher laws or generalizations, that all men desire wealth, will buy as cheaply and sell as dearly as possible, and that their intelligence will direct them to the use of similar means for attaining these ends.

Mr. Mill even goes so far as to propose a new science, resting on the same general basis, which he would call Political Ethology, or "the science of the causes which determine the type of character belonging to a people or an age." Here the bias of the Necessarian or Fatalist appears, striving to reduce *all* the complexity and variety of human action under the dominion of *law*, and to calculate it as he would the effects of an ordinary machine. Human conduct, *viewed in the gross*, appears nearly as uniform as the phenomena ascribed to gravitation; but when *viewed in detail*, it is a mass of waverings, inconsistencies, motiveless alterations, and oddities attributed to idiosyncrasies of character, which baffle all computation and foresight. A man seldom walks across a room, greets a visitor, or eats his dinner twice in *precisely* the same manner; the life, the character, of not one individual is the perfect counterpart of that of another. Look at great masses of men only from a distance, at which minute peculiarities are lost in the general effects, (just as the sounds from a distant city are blended into one hollow murmur,) and they appear like machines, or rather the multitude itself seems one great machine. But examine microscopically the conduct of an individual for two successive hours, and the hypothesis of machinery is the very last that you would adopt. How hard it is to reduce one's muscular motions to exact law and method, though each depends on a distinct volition, appears from the difficulty which all find in learning to play on a musical instrument, where the necessities of time and tune require the utmost precision of fingering. Even Mr. Mill is obliged to confess the obstacles to the establishment of his favorite social science, arising from "the idiosyncrasies of organization on the peculiar history of individuals." *

The charge of anthropomorphism considered. — I am aware that this parallel between the providence of God as shown in the physical history of the universe, and the conduct of man considered as depending on intelligence and freewill, may seem to many too bold, and that the doctrine which brings the two together is open to the reproach of anthropomorphism. But we are not to be driven from any wellgrounded conclusions, resting on the testimony of facts or on logical speculation, by any overstrained fastidiousness or a blind horror of an ugly word. This charge of anthropomorphism, or of degrading our conceptions of the Deity by ascribing to him the forms, qualities, and imperfections of finite and dependent creatures, is the favorite resource of the skeptics of the day, directed especially

* "All in external nature," says De Quincey, "proceeds by endless variety. Infinite change, illimitable novelty, inexhaustible difference, these are the foundations upon which nature builds, and ratifies her purpose of *individuality,* — so indispensable amongst a thousand other great uses, to the very elements of social distinctions and social rights. But for the endless circumstances of difference which characterize external objects, the rights of property, for instance, would have stood upon no certain basis, nor admitted of any general or comprehensive guarantee.

"As with external objects, so with human actions; amidst their infinite approximations and affinities, they are separated by circumstances of never-ending diversity. History may furnish her striking correspondences, Biography her splendid parallels, Rome may in certain cases appear but the mirror of Athens, England of Rome; — and yet, after all, no character can be cited, no great transaction, no revolution of 'high-viced cities,' no catastrophe of nations, which, in the midst of its resemblances to distant correspondences in other ages, does not include features of abundant distinction and individualizing characteristics, so many and so important, as to yield its own peculiar matter for philosophical meditation and its own separate moral." — De Quincey's *Essay on Charlemagne.*

against the argument from design, which represents him as using means for the attainment of specific and limited ends; as if the use of any means whatever were a supposition derogatory to Omnipotence. That our knowledge of the Divine character is imperfect at best, and that we are in danger, in seeking to increase it, of passing over to mean and idolatrous conceptions of his attributes, we may frankly confess, as it is a truth attested by the history of all the degrading forms of superstition which have prevailed among ignorant and sinful men. "Canst thou by searching find out God? Canst thou find out the Almighty to perfection? It is high as heaven; what canst thou do? deeper than hell; what canst thou know?" But he has not left us wholly without light; and the indications of his being and attributes that are accessible, whether in the volume of his Word or in that of his works, are to be diligently and reverently studied, without fear lest they should lead our imperfect apprehensions wholly astray. It was the remark of a pagan poet, adopted by a Christian apostle, that "we also are his offspring." And if so, even the weak and bounded faculties of his children, made in his image, when purged of earthly stains and freed from all limitations, may still find their likeness in the attributes of the Infinite One. The charge of anthropomorphism, in the strict meaning of that word, is, of course, a senseless and groundless one, when brought against the doctrine that ascribes *eternal duration*, *omnipotence*, and *omnipresence* to the Deity. And in the higher moral attributes of our own being, if we have no reflection — faint, it is true, but still a reflection — of the Divine nature, — if the highest and purest conception which we can form of *holiness* does not merely come short of, but differs essentially, or in kind, from the Divine exemplar, then indeed are we most miserable, and our knowledge on this subject is worse than utter ignorance. But all intelligence is necessarily of the same order though differing infinitely in degree; and in this respect, we cannot doubt that it is the inspiration of the Almighty that giveth us understanding. To say that the use of means to any end is not consonant with the perfections of an infinite being, is to arrogate to ourselves his absolute wisdom, and to make the creature a judge of the Creator. Besides, the anthropomorphic tendency of our finite conceptions is met by a danger of the opposite character, — by the risk of so far sublimating our notion of Divinity, that nothing shall be left but the undefined shadow of an awful idea, dimly inferred from transcendental musings. Better to sensualize our conceptions, so that the affection due to a Father may enter into them, than to refine them into limitless abstractions.

Order indicates intelligence. — The order that reigns in the works of creation, the uniformity of constantly recurrent phenomena, may be viewed either in itself, as a direct indication of intelligence, or as the fruit of design, and thus indirectly showing the wisdom of the contriver. Order is not necessarily purposed for its own sake; it is the consequence of wisdom in action, constantly tending towards the same ends, pursuing them by the best means, and without variableness or shadow of turning. But it may also be designed, as a part of the scheme for governing those who are left in the main to the guidance of their own wills and understandings, and so need the uniformity of nature's laws for the regulation of their conduct. In the latter respect, then, the consideration of it comes in as one branch of the argument from design; in the former, the point of the reasoning is so well illustrated by an anecdote borrowed by Dugald Stewart from the French, that I translate it from the Notes to his Dissertation on the Progress of Metaphysical, Ethical, and Political Philosophy.

"Among the associates of the Baron d'Holbach [who were all atheists], Diderot one day proposed that they should select an advocate to plead the cause of the Deity; and the Abbé Galiani was chosen. He took his seat, and commenced as follows: —

"'One day at Naples, a certain person in our presence put six dice into a dice-box, and offered a wager that he would throw *sizes* with the whole set. I said, that the chance was possible. He threw the dice in this way twice in succession; and I still observed, that possibly he had succeeded by chance. He put back the dice into the box for the third, fourth and fifth time, and invariably threw *sizes* with the whole set. "By the blood of Bacchus," I exclaimed, "*the dice are loaded;*' and so they were.

"'Philosophers, when I look at the order of nature that is constantly reproduced, its fixed laws, its successive changes, invariably producing the same effect, — when I consider that there is but one chance which can preserve the universe in the orderly state in which we now see it, and that this always happens, in spite of a hundred million of other possible chances of perturbation and destruction, — I cry out, *Surely, Nature's dice are also loaded.*'" *

This argument sound, though not demonstrative. — The argument here is so plain and forcible, and affords so little room for sophistry and cavilling, that we cannot conceive of a person failing to be convinced by it, though he may wish to show his ingenuity in commenting upon it as a piece of reasoning. It is true, that this mode of proof is not, strictly speaking, a demonstration. "The conclusion is not apodictical," says Kant; and this is the only defect which he has to urge against the argu-

---

* "Man is always mending and altering his works; but nature observes the same tenor, because her works are so perfect, that there is no place for amendments, nothing that can be reprehended. The most sagacious men in so many ages have not been able to find any flaw in these divinely contrived and formed machines; no blot or error in this great volume of the world, as if any thing had been an imperfect essay at the first; nothing that can be altered for the better; nothing but if it were altered, would be marred. This could not have been, had man's body been the work of chance, and not counsel and providence. Why should there be constantly the same parts? Why should they retain constantly the same places? Nothing so contrary as constancy and chance. Should I see a man throw the same number a thousand times together upon but three dice, could you persuade me that this were accidental, and that there was no necessary cause for it? How much more incredible then is it, that constancy in such a variety, such a multiplicity of parts, should be the result of chance? Neither yet can these works be the effects of necessity or fate, for then there would be the same constancy observed in the smaller as well as in the larger parts and vessels; whereas there we see nature doth, as it were, sport itself, the minute ramifications of all the vessels, veins, arteries and nerves, infinitely varying in individuals of the same species, so that they are not in any two alike." — Ray's *Wisdom of God in the Creation.*

ment *a posteriori.* But what does such an objection amount to? Suppose that after Franklin had proved the presence of electricity in a thundercloud, by drawing the fluid to the earth, charging a Leyden jar with it, and causing it to manifest all the common electric phenomena, a bystander should still object in this wise to his doctrine and proof: — "You are judging of the presence of a thing only from its effects; the truth of the theory opposed to yours is still conceivable; your facts and arguments do not constitute a chain of reasoning like that which supports a proposition in Euclid." The plain answer would be, that the affirmation is supported by the only evidence of which, in the nature of things, it is susceptible. *A fact can be proved only by other facts;* that which is not perceptible to the senses, can be made known only through its effects. And though the proof be not a demonstration, to reject it would be quite as plain an indication of folly or insanity, as to deny the truth of any theorem in geometry.

Universal skepticism cures itself. — Besides, it is evident, that if we admit the sufficiency of such objections, the whole fabric of physical science, which is founded upon such deductions from facts, must come to the ground. We must reject all that the labors of the last three centuries have accumulated by questioning nature, and sit down contented in hopeless ignorance; for the same considerations which show the unsatisfactory character of what has been done, prove also that nothing more or better can ever be accomplished. As no one can seriously entertain such sweeping disbelief, universal skepticism in fact cures itself, if "its universality is steadily kept in view, and constantly borne in mind. But in practice, it is an armory from which weapons are taken to be employed against *some* opinions, while it is hidden from notice, that the same weapon would equally cut down every other conviction." I repeat it, then, all the common metaphysical objections to the argument from design, and to the other modes of proving the Divine existence which proceed from the peculiarities of the effect to the cause, are equally destructive of our reliance on all history, all physical science, and even on all the ordinary maxims of experience which govern our daily conduct. "Fortunately," says the great skeptic himself, "since reason is incapable of dispelling these clouds, Nature herself suffices for that purpose, and cures me of this philosophical delirium."

"Whatever," says Sir James Mackintosh, "whatever attacks every principle of belief can destroy none. As long as the foundations of knowledge are allowed to remain on the same level (be it called of certainty or uncertainty) with the maxims of life, the whole system of human conviction must continue undisturbed. When the skeptic boasts of having involved the results of experience and the elements of geometry in the same ruin with the doctrines of religion and the principles of philosophy, he may be answered, That no dogmatist ever claimed more than the same degree of certainty for these various convictions and opinions; and that his skepticism, therefore, leaves them in the relative condition in which it found them. No man knew better, or owned more frankly, than Mr. Hume, that to this answer there is no serious reply. Universal skepticism involves a contradiction in terms; *it is a belief that there can be no belief.* It is an attempt of the mind to act without its structure, and by other laws than those to which its nature has subjected its operations. To reason without assenting to the principles on which all reasoning is founded, is not unlike an effort to feel without nerves, or to move without muscles."

The conception of chance analyzed.—The idea of *chance* occurs so frequently in the discussion of the argument from design, that it is of the utmost importance that we should form a distinct conception of what is meant by it, and how the phenomena which common language ascribes to that abstraction are really produced. Now this conception will depend on the peculiar view which we may take of the theory of causation, or of the nature of phenomena in the physical universe. I have said, that there are but two such views or theories which are logical, complete, and consistent; the one, which ascribes all change, all events that take place, to powers necessarily inherent in matter, and which therefore makes out all activity to be necessary and mechanical, and the universe to be one vast machine; the other, which attributes all motion, activity, and change to personal agency, which considers matter as necessarily passive and inert, and hence all phenomena which begin to be as direct results of power directed by intelligence, and accompanied by freewill. Now the word *chance* assumes different meanings according as we adopt one or the other of these theories. Under the former, there is no such thing as chance; the word has absolutely no significance or applicability whatever. We cannot stop short of Spinozism; there is nothing fortuitous; every phenomenon is the invariable and necessary result of its antecedents, the invariable and necessary cause of those which come after it. This truth is so clearly explained and illustrated by Mr. Mill, though certainly without a perception of its logical consequences, that I shall borrow his language.

"*Chance* is usually spoken of," he says, "in direct antithesis to *law;* whatever (it is supposed) cannot be ascribed to any law, is attributed to chance. It is, however, certain, that whatever happens is the result of some law, is an effect of causes, and could have been predicted from a knowledge of the existence of those causes, and from their laws. If I turn up a particular card, that is a consequence of its place in the pack. Its place in the pack was a consequence of the manner in which the cards were shuffled, or of the order in which they were played in the last game; which, again, were the effects of prior causes. At every stage, if we had possessed an accurate knowledge of the causes in existence, it would have been abstractedly possible to foretell the effect. . . . . .

"It is incorrect, then, to say that any phenomenon is *produced* by chance; but we may say that two or more phenomena are *conjoined* by chance, that they coexist or succeed one another only by chance; meaning, that they are in no way related through causation; that they are neither cause and effect, nor effects of the same cause, nor effects of causes between which there subsists any law of coexistence, nor even effects of the same original collocation of primeval causes."

What is denoted, on this theory, by chance. — Obviously, then on this theory, we ascribe the origin of a thing to *chance* only to denote *our ignorance of its true cause, not meaning to affirm that it was not caused at all.* Its antecedents are so numerous and obscure, that we cannot discern the order of their succession, or pick out from among them its latest and invariable forerunner.

> "All nature is but art unknown to thee;
> All *chance*, direction which thou canst not see."

Not knowing the number of times that the dice knock against each other and against the sides of the dice-box, or the exact position in which each one was before it received each blow, we cannot tell which side will fall uppermost; though, if we had this knowledge, from the combined effect of the law of gravitation and of these several impulses, we could foretell the exact position in which they would finally be left. There may be casual *conjunctions* of events, but no casual *origin* of them. Accordingly, on this mechanical theory of the universe, to put *chance* in the place of a *First Cause* is to deal in nonsense; it is not simply an unfounded, but an unmeaning, hypothesis. On this theory, the world had no beginning; nothing ever absolutely began to be.

What chance denotes, on the second theory. — On the other theory, which ascribes all events to immediate personal agency, *chance* has a meaning as the *opposite* or *absence* of design. Whatever is done by a finite being, not for its own sake, but from its subserviency to some other object, is done without regard, if I may so speak, to the whole event, but only with regard to some, perhaps one, of it's relations or effects. If I wish to walk in a certain direction, I may push a stone out of my path, intending only to remove an obstacle, and not caring where the stone may lie, so that it be not in my way; that is, I purpose or design only the removal of an obstruction; I do not purpose its removal to a particular spot. Its falling on a certain spot, then, is said to be, not causeless, — for it had a cause, just as much as any other event, — but *accidental*, that is, *not designed.* On either theory, therefore, to make *chance, a cause,* is simply to talk nonsense. Again, a sculptor removes chips from the marble on which he is at work, intending only to bring out the statue, and not purposing the juxtaposition of these chips and dust as they fall. The form which the heap of refuse matter assumes on the ground is said to be accidental, because it was not designed. Chance, then, is, so to speak, the *residuum* of design; a portion of the event — namely, the form of the chip in part, and its removal from the main block — was effected by design; the remainder of its form, and its position when falling, were not intended, but were casual. Consequently, *chance implies design;* we can attribute only a portion of an effect to it, and in so doing, we admit that the remaining portion was foreseen and desired.

How casual effects may be distinguished from designed effects. — This illustration brings us to the knowledge of a *criterion* by which we may distinguish what is casual from what is intended. If we visited the studio of the artist during his absence, and saw the statue and the heap of chips lying side by side, why do we say that the form of the one was designed, and that of the other was not? Obviously, on account of the regularity of shape and outline of the statue, and from its resemblance to the form of some human being or other creature; for an induction coextensive with our whole experience assures us, that aggregations which were casual, or not purposed, are quite irregular in shape, and bear no likeness to any thing except other aggregations, believed to be as casual as themselves. A skeptic might tell me, it is true, that I could not *demonstrate* the truth of my conclusion; it is certainly conceivable, that the sculptor should have hewed off bits from a block of marble, intending only to make a fantastic or irregular pile of them; and that he happened so to choose the points from which these pieces were taken, that a regular statue was left in the remainder of the block, though he never thought of that remainder. Well, I admit it; this hypothesis *is* conceivable; but is it *credible?* Would you *believe,* under such circumstances, that the sculptor has thus acted, and the statue had thus been produced accidentally, or without being intended?

I am not seeking now to illustrate the main purport of the

argument from design; the instance taken would be poorly chosen for that end. I seek only to expose the true nature of the chief metaphysical objection to that argument, in order that you may see clearly what that objection is worth. My point is, that, in declaring some, if not all, of the phenomena of the physical universe to have been produced by design, we are not making any unfounded assumption, or resting on any intuitive principle of the human intellect; but we are judging from experience, from the largest possible induction of facts, the conclusion being of the same general character with all the ordinary results of physical science; that is, it is supported by evidence of the same kind, though vastly superior in amount. From the experience of our own actions, we know what is the general character of those results which are intended or purposed, and those which are accidental. We know what sort of effects *intelligent* action produces, and what is the general aspect of casual coincidences and aggregations. Judging from this experience, we can tell *where our fellow man has been at work*, and, in the same manner, *where God is at work.* Finite intelligence differs from infinite, not in the general character, but in the extent and excellence, of its operations.*

* Dr. Whewell affirms, that *design* is an intuitive idea, a conception of pure reason, called out and developed, it is true, by experience, but not growing out of that experience. We can hardly believe that he is serious in this assertion. If *design* be considered merely as synonymous with *intention*, or *purpose*, then it is evident, that we can have no knowledge of it until we have had experience of a purpose; that is, until we have intended or designed to perform some act. The origin of the idea is in reflection, or the observation of what passes in our own minds. So we experience a certain emotion, and apply a name to it, in order to distinguish it from other emotions, that differ from it in kind, or are excited by a different class of objects. But it would be very strange to say, that love, or wonder, or pity, was an intuitive idea.

It is very true, that we mean something more than mere *intention*, in speaking of the argument from final causes. But the case here is still stronger against the assertion, which we are now considering. In this case, design is a very complex notion, nearly all the elements of it being drawn from mental experience. They are founded on our observation of ourselves, and are successively elaborated and united into the complex

What is proved by the argument from design. — Strictly speaking, the argument from design does not establish *the existence of a cause*, but only *the character of that cause*, — that it is intelligent, personal, coextensive at least with the universe of existing things, and so Divine. From the reasoning pursued in the two former chapters, we were driven to the necessity of admitting *some cause*, whether personal or not, to account for the events which have taken place, and for those which are constantly going on under our observation; and as the only power, or true cause, with which we are acquainted, is personal, being that of man himself, it was argued that the cause of all things not produced by human agency was also personal. To this it was certainly possible to answer, though the reply is surely a very indefinite and unmeaning one, that, discarding alike the hypothesis of active powers inherent in matter, and of personal agency such as is exerted by man, the phenomena of nature might be attributed to *a cause in general*, of which we

---

notion, which we call design. The idea rests originally on a perception of the relation of means to an end. Having observed, that a particular event followed immediately after another, or several others, and connecting the consequent with these antecedents by an intuitive application of the law of causality, and believing that the course of nature is uniform, or that like effects will follow like causes, and desiring that the consequent event may again occur, — we *act;* that is, we exert our agency to bring about events similar to the former antecedent ones, doing this under the expectation, that a similar consequent event will follow. Thus design implies, — first, *intelligence*, or a knowledge of the laws of causality and uniformity; — secondly, particular *experience* of some one event, A, happening in immediate connection with several others, B and C; — thirdly a *will* to reproduce the event A; — fourthly, *action*, in order to bring about the events B and C, under — (fifthly) an *expectation* that A will immediately follow. Are these five elements *all* of *a priori* origin? Is not action necessarily implied in design? And how can we have an idea of it until we have acted; that is, until we have had experience, and derived knowledge directly from that experience?

It is, indeed, in the complexity of this notion, that the importance of the argument from final causes almost wholly consists. Wherever we find indications of design, there is evidence, to an equal extent, of intelligen e will, activity, and foresight.

can only say that we know nothing, and therefore cannot ascribe to it either intelligence or freewill. This is an appeal to human ignorance, it is true; and it violates that sound rule of inductive logic, which bids us attribute certain effects to any known and sufficient cause, even though no direct connection is traceable between them, provided there is no proved incompatibility of such a cause with these effects, in preference to attributing them simply to some *unknown* cause. But the consideration of the peculiar character of the effect affords a more direct answer to this vague objection, by proving incontestably that the First Cause must unite *intelligence*, *will*, *activity*, and *foresight;* for these are all implied in *design*. The God thus revealed is an individual, self-conscious, and creative being, whose care extends to the minutest part of creation; since his wisdom, activity, and benevolence can be as plainly seen in the structure of a blade of grass, as in a system of revolving satellites and suns.

The argument from design a simple and obvious one. — The argument from design is a simple, obvious, and natural one, which can be assailed only by far-fetched, fine-spun, and metaphysical reasonings; and this, it seems to me, is a strong consideration in favor of its soundness. Common men do not often reason wrongly about simple subjects and matters-of-fact; they are often, indeed, mistaken in their premises; but granting these, they advance from them through a few steps of proof with unerring accuracy to a just conclusion. An uneducated man, of good common sense, is always a better inductive philosopher than a subtile logician, trained in the schools, who often winds himself up in a web of ingenious sophistry, so that he cannot move a step in any direction. The argument has been propounded in nearly all ages of the world, of which we have any distinct record, and even among rude and illiterate tribes of men, to justify that faith which, in the mind of every person, depends upon it to a greater or less degree, though he may not be able to state it in precise language. It was as ably set forth and illustrated by Socrates, twenty-five hundred years ago, as it has been in any recent treatise on natural theology. Paley's celebrated illustration of it by a watch, is almost equalled in beauty and appositeness by Cicero's instance of an ingenious instrument, made by one Posidonius in his day, which accurately represented the motions of the heavenly bodies, as they were then known; the Roman philosopher asks, if this were carried into Scythia or Britain, whether even the barbarous inhabitants of those countries would believe that more intelligence and ingenuity were required to construct this feeble *imitation* of the planetary sphere, than to make and keep in motion the stupendous sphere itself; or that the origin of the poor *copy* must be ascribed to wise design, while the *original* was the product of mere chance. Even the unlettered Greenlander told the Danish missionary, who came to instruct him, that as he knew his *kajak*, or boat, with its tackle and implements, could not be built without much labor and skill, and as the meanest bird required more ingenuity to make it than the best *kajak*, so he had always believed that some being must exist, wiser than the wisest man, who had made all these things.

Statement of the argument from design. — Considering that the existence and eternal duration of a First Cause have been fully proved, both from the beginning and the continuance of the universe of things, the argument from design, in the form least open to cavil, to show that this cause must be intelligent, provident, and benevolent, can be very briefly stated. It is, that *a great number of agents being found to work together by a complex and intricate, yet orderly process, towards the attainment of some end, there must exist an intelligent and active being, who had this end in view, and who made this disposition of the agents as means for its accomplishment.* Orderly coöperation implies intelligent and directing power. And the order may be so perfect, and the number of coöperating agents so great, that this implication becomes, what is called in common discourse, not in logic, absolute certainty. When the material frame of a living thing is so organized and put together, that a great number of motions and effects can be produced with ease and within a small compass, all of them being subservient to the preservation of the animal's existence, and closely adapted to its modes of life, the inference that this animal was fashioned by an intelligent Creator is irresistible. When such instances of joint agency and adaptation are found to be, not few in number, and scattered, as it were, by chance amidst an infinite number of conflicting powers, disorderly arrangements, and nugatory results, but manifestations of a great law that pervades all nature, uniformity being the general rule, and the varieties being strictly suited to the different circumstances, and all the parts, by a visible connection, tending towards and effecting one general result, — namely, the happiness of animal and intelligent life, — then the conclusion, that the whole framework of the universe was designed and executed by one Being of surpassing wisdom and goodness, comes home to the mind with a force and clearness which no prejudice can reject, and no sophistry evade.

Number and perfection of the adaptations found in the physical universe. — The point on which the whole stress of this argument depends, is the proposition, that *adaptation proves design*, or that the concurrence of means to an end, under certain circumstances, must have been intentional; that is, the end was foreseen and desired. All the other points are admitted. It is admitted, for instance, that *design* proves a *designer*, — that there cannot be contrivance unless there was some being who contrived; this is little more than an identical proposition, or an explanation of the meaning of words. So, also, it is admitted that there are wonderful adaptations in the physical universe, countless in number, — grand, complex, and intricate beyond the most elaborate machine of man's device, — delicate, precise, and artistic to a degree exceeding what the finest perception of the senses, aided by the most finished instruments, can discover. I have already spoken of their *number* and *variety*, as they are found in the bodily structure of the animalcules which people with their multitude a drop of water, in the fabric and tissues of all vegetable and animal things, and in the disposition and arrangement of inorganic matter, from a clod of earth up to the wonderful framework and garniture of the heavens; — a system of revolving worlds, whose motions and inequalities are so wonderfully balanced and adjusted, all subject to one law, exerting mutual influence, but never interfering, with the appendage of minor orbs, all working harmoniously with the great scheme "Earum autem perennes cursus, atque perpetui cum admirabili incredibilique constantiâ, declarant in his vim et mentem esse divinam, ut hæc ipsa qui non sentiat deorum vim habere, is nihil omnino sensurus esse videatur." As to their *complexity*, and the subserviency of numerous parts, dissimilar to each other, to one great end, take the most intricate engine that man ever contrived, — a carpet-loom, for instance, or a printing-press moved by steam, which it requires a day's study to take apart and understand; — and yet the anatomist and physiologist will tell you, that this machine is not to be compared, in point of complexity and elaborateness, with your own body, in which the arrangement of means that continue, preserve, and repair it is so curious and intricate, that all the resources of modern science have not yet sufficed to thread the whole labyrinth and show the meaning of the entire structure. As to *nicety of arrangement and perfection of finish*, go into an observatory and examine a chronometer, or a sidereal clock, or a repeating telescope, with its limbs graduated and marked off to the hundredth part of a hair's breadth; and you will have but a faint idea of the delicacy and fine adjustment of the parts in the human eye and ear, through which these organs perform their office, and are preserved from injury or decay.

The whole question is, whether these numerous, complex, and nice adaptations *prove* design.

CHAPTER IX.

THE ARGUMENT FROM DESIGN.

Summary of the last chapter. — Hume's argument, that creation is a *singular* effect, not coming within the range of our experience, and so not to be accounted for by inferences drawn from the phenomena which we now witness, has been answered by showing that the universe is a mere general conception, having but a fictitious unity, and what we are bound to explain is the origin, not of the whole, but of all the parts taken in succession. Adverting, then, to particular phenomena, of which we have experience, I showed that the development of particular plants and animals from microscopic germs, perfectly alike, so far as we can see, is a fact which we cannot help ascribing to some personal agency, some supernatural or miraculous power; for the hypothesis, that it is caused by some invisible machinery in those germs, is both gratuitous and incredible; — gratuitous, because we have no evidence that such machinery exists; incredible, because we cannot conceive of its possibility. I showed, further, that the phenomena of the universe, in so far as they combine unity with diversity, order with boundless variety, general laws with distinctive and peculiar effects not resembling each other, were precisely what we should expect from individual and personal exertion; for these also are the characteristics of human action. The works of intelligence show order in their aggregate, and immeasurable diversity in their details.

An examination of the idea of *chance* proved that it was applicable, not to the origin, but to the conjunctions of phenomena so that to ascribe creation to chance was not merely an unfounded, but an unmeaning hypothesis. On the theory of mechanical action and of powers inherent in matter, no event is fortuitous, but every fact, even the turning up of a card in a pack, or the falling of dice, is the necessary result of immutable law; we *call* it accidental, merely to mark our ignorance of its cause, and not to deny its causation. On the other theory, that of personal agency, chance is simply the opposite, or the *residuum*, of design; it by no means implies absence of causation, but simply that *a portion* of the effect was not intended or cared for by its author.

The criterion by which we distinguish fortuitous from designed effects. — Hence we come, by experience, to the knowledge of a criterion by which we distinguish designed effects from those which are fortuitous, or not designed. *Order, uniformity, resemblance to some object, subserviency to some end,* is this criterion. We have ample experience of both classes of effects; our induction is coextensive with all our observation of our own acts, those of our fellow-beings, and their results; and the difference between the two classes is so striking and obvious, that a child can see it, and read its meaning. We contrast, for instance, the pile of rubbish that a machinist casts out of his workshop with the elaborate, complex, and highly finished engine that he is fabricating within; and if a skeptic should tell us, that *possibly* as much intellect and intention, as much deliberate purpose, went to the formation of that refuse heap as of that engine, or that we had only a contingent, and so an unsatisfactory, assurance that there was any purpose in either, and thus attempt to undermine our belief that there had been any artisan at work there, we should deem either that he was disordered in his wits, or that he was practising upon our credulity.

How many and how curious are the adaptations that are found in nature. — If, with this criterion in hand, we come to examine the phenomena of the universe so far as they do not depend on the agency of man, in order to see if there is any evidence of design in them, the answer which we obtain is decisive beyond all cavilling. We ask not now, whether the several arrangements and results ever began to be, and so ever had a cause, or required power for their production; that point has been considered and determined already; it has been proved that such a cause was, and *is*, — as otherwise the events themselves are inexplicable. The present question is, whether we can find proof that this productive energy was guided by intelligence, was exerted with reference to an end which it proposed and desired to accomplish. The answer is, that the adaptations which we discover in the world are so curious, far-reaching, and important, and moreover so numerous among all the arrangements of matter, — they correspond so perfectly in their general character to the contrivances of man for attaining his objects, though they far transcend such human designs in wisdom, that we are irresistibly led to consider them as intentional. We can conceive that one or two slight adaptations should exist, which were not designed. Among the multitude of stones upon a sea-beach, for instance, we may by long search find one or two that are not only regular in form, but bear some rude resemblance to utensils or implements fashioned by man, so that with some difficulty they may be turned to useful purposes. A rude substitute for a hammer or chisel may thus be discovered. But these are lost among a countless number of shapeless pebbles which can be applied to no use.

Such is not the character of those physical arrangements by or through which animal and vegetable life is sheltered, developed, and continued in being. Here, every thing is artistic; every part, even the minutest, has its use; the whole forms one system, every portion of which is essential to its perfection, as, by the curious disposition of the interior, all the parts act and react upon each other. According to a definition already quoted, *an organism is that of which all the parts are mutually ends and means.* So perfect is this correspondence of the parts with each other and with the whole, that the eye practised in the study of them can, from a minute portion, supply what is lost, and build again the entire system. Give to the comparative anatomist a section of a single tooth, and he will tell you to what animal it belongs; give him one scale of a fish that no longer exists except as imbedded in red sandstone, and he will reconstruct that fish, though he has never seen its entire fossil remains. Which is the worthier of admiration here, — the intellect which infers the shape and organization of the whole structure from so small a remnant of it, or that which so fashioned and ordered all the parts with minute correspondences and relations, that any one of them is a key to all the others? Sagacity and skill, in their highest degrees, were required to find the key to the fabric; and is there no proof of intelligence in the fabric itself, and in the creation of the means by which the discovery was rendered possible? As well might we say that the ability to read a book was indeed a proof of intellect, but not the ability to write it.

Arrangements made for future wants. — Design is necessarily *prospective;* it is the adoption of means to secure *an ena not yet realized,* or which exists only in idea. It implies knowledge and skill, therefore, for the selection of the proper means, and foresight of their mode of operation, and of the nature of the end to be obtained. Now there are certain arrangements in the animal and even in the vegetable kingdom, which, as they at first exist, seem to answer no useful end whatever; but at a subsequent stage in the history of the organism, when new occasions or necessities have sprung up, they are found to be admirably adapted to some essential purposes. These, from their prospective character, seem to afford the required link of proof that the adaptation was intentional or designed. Thus, the human teeth do not grow till they are needed by a change of food consequent on advance in life; and even the first set of teeth, with the alveolar process, or sockets, which contain them, which are suited for the child's use, are displaced or absorbed when the enlargement of the jaws renders them no longer fully competent for their office, and are replaced by a new set, which had long been forming beneath. Can you believe that this arrangement was not *intended* to answer the purpose which it actually does answer?

Other arrangements for contingent wants, or casualties. — Still more strongly indicative of design are the arrangements tc meet certain wants which are not only prospective, but contingent on the intelligence and freewill of another being, s that it is doubtful whether they will ever exist. The *casualties* to which the human frame is subject are, to a great extent, avoidable by human care and forethought; still, they often happen, and there are numerous and beautiful arrangements in the system, or the animal economy, by which their consequences are met and repaired. The broken bone is again united by the matter which exudes from the two extremities, and knits them together even with greater solidity than the limb possessed in that part before, as if to guard against a repetition of the accident. The bruised or diseased flesh is separated by a thickened coating from the sound portion, and then thrown off by suppuration, its place being gradually taken by new and sound tissue. The main artery, which furnishes a limb with its chief supply of blood, being tied up and thus obliterated by the surgeon, in order to avoid the consequences of an accidental enlargement, collateral channels are made or enlarged by the Divine Helper, even the direction of the current in some of them being changed, so that the limb again receives its full supply. Shall we say here, that the surgeon, indeed, *designed* to stop up the main canal, but that there was no purpose or intention in the altered disposition of the other parts, by which the injurious effects of this stoppage were obviated? It is needless to enumerate other instances; the physician or the surgeon will tell you, that the body abounds with such adaptations or contrivances, so that his art is little more than waiting for their operation, and preventing the unwise interference of the patient or his friends. The *vis medicatrix*, the recuperative and repairing force of nature, is that which lends nearly all its efficiency to medical skill.*

Means are varied according to circumstances, but they still conduce to one end. — One other class of illustrations of intentional effects in the physical universe, may be aptly introduced

* "Gaudet corpus vi prorsus mirabili, quâ contra morbos se tueatur; multos arcea; multos jam inchoatos quam optime et citissime solvat; aliosque suo modo ad felicem exitum lentius perducat. Hæc Autocrateia, vis Naturæ medicatrix vocatur; medicis, philosophis notissima et jure celeberrima. Hæc sola ad multos morbos sanandos sufficit, in omnibus fere prodest." — *J. Gregory.*

by a quotation from a medical writer of approved authority. "The intention of nature," he observes, "can nowhere be so well learned as from comparative anatomy; that is, if we would understand physiology, and reason on the functions in the animal economy, we must see how the same end is brought about in other species. We must contemplate the part or organ in different animals, its shape, position, connection with the other parts, etc., and observe what thence arises. If we find *one common effect* constantly produced, though *in a very different way*, then we may safely conclude that this is the *use* or *function* of the part. This reasoning can never betray us, if we are but sure of the facts."

Now, to apply this remark, compare together the eyes of an eagle, a man, a fish, a mole, and lastly consider the case of that singular species of fish which inhabits only the dark waters of a vast cave, and so has no eyes at all; compare them, I say, with reference to *the different circumstances* in which these several animals are placed, and to *the adaptations of the organ to these different circumstances*, and see if it be possible to avoid the inference that the eye was intended to see with. Here we have numerous instances of a concurrence of means to one end; the means being varied just so far as to preserve a constant relation to the several media through which vision takes place, and to the purposes of the animal for which sight is required. The crystalline humor of the eyes of animals living in water, to suit the greater refractive power of the surrounding medium, is made, not plano-convex, as in land animals, but spherical. Means are provided, in the eyelids and tears, for cleaning the human eye from dust; in the fish, this apparatus is unnecessary and is not found; but the mud-crab, which seeks its food in mud and turbid water, and is thus liable to be blinded by slime, has a little brush near the eye, against which the prominent horny eye can be raised and wiped, "with an action as intelligible as that of a man wiping his spectacles." The means for cleaning the eyes should be very abundant and efficacious for birds, as they sweep with great velocity through great spaces of air, and for some quadrupeds whose eyes frequently come in contact

with dust and other floating matter. On this account, their eyes are provided with a peculiar membrane, attached by a slender thread to a muscle placed in the back part of the eye, so as not to obstruct the vision. When this muscle contracts, the membrane is suddenly drawn over the fore part of the eye, sweeping it clean of every particle of dust, and then, by its own elasticity, falling back to its original position. To obtain greater length in a less compass, the cord of this muscle makes an angle, passing through a loop formed by another muscle, and is there inflected, as if bent round a pulley; the second muscle, of course, when it contracts, twitches the first muscle at the point of inflection, and so assists the action designed by both. "Every one," says Sir Charles Bell, "who has ridden a horse on a dusty road, must have been struck with the superior provision in the horse's eye; he never suffers from the dust, because this cartilage, being bedewed with the secretion of a peculiar gland, — not tears, but a matter more glutinous, — sweeps across the eye, and collects and removes every particle of dust."

Such adaptations must have been designed. — Is it credible that this beautiful apparatus, a delicate brush moving by the reciprocal action of a spring and of force applied to a slender cord passing over a pulley, was not contrived for the very purpose of removing injurious foreign matter from the eye, the liability to such intrusion being foreseen, and the machinery being invented with special reference to this contingency? Suppose a laborer, obliged to work amid the thick dust of a coal-mine, were found, on our visit to the pit, though we had never heard of such a contrivance before, to be provided with a compact self-adjusting machine, exactly resembling this *membrana nictitans*, except that it was not permanently attached to his eyes, but was put on and off like a pair of glasses. Suppose the wearer of it should tell us, that it was indeed a very convenient thing for keeping the dust out of his eyes, but that it was not made for this purpose, nor indeed for any purpose whatever, but was the mere freak of an ingenious artisan, who was accustomed to make curious little machines for no object at all, except to amuse himself; and that the laborer, visiting his museum one

day, happened to see this apparatus, and perceiving that it would be useful for the protection of his eyes, had purchased it for this end. Should we believe this extravagant story? I am not caricaturing the matter at all, but supplying what is, on the whole, a *favorable* illustration of the wisdom and justice of that doctrine which denies that *any adaptations whatever*, however complex, delicate, and exactly suited to the end, afford *any* proof of foresight and design. According to the philosophers who entertain this doctrine, all that we are entitled to affirm is the existence of the apparatus with all its parts, and the accomplishment of a certain end by it,—that is, the mode in which it works; for this is all that we see, all that is visible on the very face of the matter. To maintain that *this end was contemplated beforehand, and desired by some other being, who devised these peculiar means for obtaining it*, is to assert a fact of which we have no sensible evidence, and to attribute motives to a cause of whose essence we are wholly ignorant.

Physical inquiry not limited to what can be seen externally.—Is it, then, a received maxim in physical inquiry, that our investigations must be strictly limited to the outside of the phenomena, to a mere description of their external characteristics, and to the law of their succession, so that we are never entitled to infer the existence of any fact which is not directly visible? If so, this criticism is just, and the argument from design is either wholly unfounded and deceptive, or it cannot be classed with the ordinary processes of inductive science whose correctness no one affects to question, and with which it has been my purpose to show that it is entirely coincident. To determine whether this maxim is admitted, I will cite a passage from the latest, and probably the most judicious and profound, writer on inductive logic, who is certainly not biased in favor of any theological argument, and is not thinking of any such argument in the passage in question.

"There is a great difference," says Mr. Mill, "between inventing laws of nature to account for classes of phenomena, and merely endeavoring, in conformity with known laws, to conjecture what collocations, now gone by, may have given birth to individual facts still in existence. The latter is the strictly legitimate operation of inferring, from an observed effect, *the existence, in time past, of a cause similar to that by which we know it to be produced in all cases in which we have had actual experience of its origin.*" Is it possible to give, in abstract language, a more precise description of the case in hand? *We have had actual experience*, both in our own works, and by observing those of our fellow men, of complex contrivances, or designed adaptations to an end; and we have compared or contrasted these with the unintentional collocations of matter which are also attributable to human agency. With the light gained from this comparison, when we come to *observe physical effects and arrangements, perfectly similar* to these designed adaptations, and strongly contrasted with the unintentional groupings, we infer *the existence, in time past, of a cause similar to that which produced the effects of which we have full knowledge,* — that is, an intelligent and designing cause.

Judicial and geological inferences compared with those of natural theology. — I go on now with the extract from Mr. Mill, to show what class of cases he had in view in making this remark, and because these cases are apt illustrations, perfect parallels, of the argument from design. "This, for example," he says, "is the scope of the inquiries of geology; and they are no more illogical or visionary than judicial inquiries, which also aim at discovering a past event by inference from those of its effects which still subsist. As we can ascertain whether a man was murdered, or died a natural death, from the indications exhibited by the corpse, the presence or absence of the signs of struggling on the ground or on the adjacent objects, the marks of blood, the footsteps of the supposed murderers, and so on, proceeding throughout upon uniformities ascertained by a perfect induction without any mixture of hypothesis; so, if we find, on or beneath the surface of our planet, masses exactly similar to deposits from water, or to results of the cooling of matter melted by fire, we may justly conclude that such has been their origin; and if the effects, *though similar in kind, are on a far larger scale than any which are produced now*, we may

rationally, and without hypothesis, conclude that the causes existed formerly with greater intensity." And so, I add, if we find, on the surface of our planet, adaptations exactly similar to arrangements known to be designed by man, we may justly conclude that intelligence was concerned in the formation of both; and if these, *though similar in kind, are on a far larger scale* than any which are produced by man, we may rationally, and without hypothesis, conclude, that the intelligence which produced them was of a higher order than the human understanding.

Mr. Mill further observes, that "in the speculation respecting the igneous origin of trap or granite, the fact does not admit of *direct* proof, that those substances have been actually subjected to intense heat. But the same thing might be said of all judicial inquiries which proceed upon circumstantial evidence. We can conclude that a man was murdered, although it is not proved by the testimony of eyewitnesses that a man who had the intention of murdering him was present on the spot. *It is enough, if no other known cause could have generated the effects shown to have been produced.*" Here, again, the parallel is complete. Certainly we have no direct proof, no testimony of eyewitnesses, that the Deity was present in person before these effects followed, and that he *intended* to produce them. It is enough for us to know, from our own experience and from that of the whole human family, that these effects could not have followed except from intelligent action, from a personal cause; there is no other known cause adequate to their production.

Accumulation of instances not needed; the reasoning strictly logical. — It forms no part of my plan, you will perceive, to enter into a full exposition of the proofs from design, detailing their number and variety, and thus aiming to produce conviction by their cumulative effect. The examples that I have adduced are intended to show only *the nature of the argument, its logical efficiency*, and therefore they have been designedly taken from the most familiar treatises on Natural Theology. Strictly speaking, an accumulation of them is not needed; for if *one* undoubted instance of the designed adaptation of means to ends can be produced, then an intelligent creative Deity must exist. If one fact alone, among all the circumstances enumerated by Mr. Mill, proves incontestably that the man was murdered, the consideration of the other traces of violence may be entirely omitted. Those who wish to enter into the argument in detail may find all that they need in Paley's excellent and unsurpassed exposition of it, two chapters of which, for this purpose, are worth all the Bridgewater Treatises put together. But an undefined impression, a lurking doubt, exists in many minds, fostered, if not created, by some popular metaphysical speculations, that there is a fundamental defect in this reasoning, an illogical assumption, which is carefully suppressed, or winked out of view, by those who are conscious that there is no other mode of getting rid of it. This is skepticism, the more dangerous because it is wavering and indefinite; for the doubt is entertained by many who do not even know what the alleged defect is. It is this vague impression which I have labored to confute, and for this purpose I have entered into a minute and probably tedious examination of the logical structure of the argument, comparing it with the evidence on which all physical science depends. The result is, that it is perfectly coincident with such evidence; it is of the same kind, though vastly superior in degree.

Certain assumptions are necessary in all reasoning. — As to the alleged defect, the supposed assumption which is made, not only in the argument from design, but in all the truths of physical science, and in the regulation of our daily conduct, a very few words will suffice to explain its character. In all these cases, we take it for granted that the human faculties are adequate to their work, that memory is not always confounded with imagination, that from similar effects we may infer the presence of similar causes; and when we have no direct sensible evidence that a certain object exists, or a certain event has taken place, we may still learn the fact from some unquestionable indications of its reality. These are assumptions; and though the skeptic in words may deny them, in action he admits them without hesitation. If the evidence on which the theist relies were multiplied a thousand-fold, it would still be chargeable with the defect which we are now considering, and consistency would require the unbeliever still to reject it. I find this fact so clearly admitted and set forth by the chief of English skeptics, by Hume himself, that it is worth while to quote the passage. In the Dialogues to which I have already referred, after Philo has been arguing for some time, with great subtilty and ingenuity, against these assumptions, Cleanthes breaks out, with some impatience: —

"Your objections, I must freely tell you, are no better than the abstruse cavils of those philosophers who denied motion; and ought to be refuted in the same manner, by illustrations, examples, and instances, rather than by serious argument and philosophy. Suppose, therefore, that an articulate voice were heard in the clouds, much louder and more melodious than any which human art could ever reach: Suppose that this voice were extended in the same instant over all nations, and spoke to each nation in its own language and dialect: Suppose that the words delivered not only contain a just sense and meaning, but convey some instructions altogether worthy of a benevolent being superior to mankind: Could you possibly hesitate a moment concerning the cause of this voice, and must you not instantly ascribe it to some *design* or purpose? Yet I cannot see but all the same objections (if they merit that appellation), which lie against the system of Theism, may also be produced against this inference.

"Might you not say, that all conclusions concerning fact were founded on experience; and that, when we hear an articulate voice in the dark, and thence infer a man, it is only the resemblance of the effects which leads us to conclude that there is a like resemblance in the causes; but that this extraordinary voice, by its loudness, extent, and flexibility to all languages, bears so little analogy to any human voice, that we have no reason to suppose any analogy in their causes; and consequently, that a rational, wise, coherent speech proceeded, you know not whence, from some accidental whistling of the winds, not from any Divine reason or intelligence? You see clearly your own objections in these cavils, and I hope, too, you see clearly, that they cannot possibly have more force in the one case than in the other."

The argument is a simple and obvious one. — The idea that there was a lurking difficulty in the argument, which theologians willingly avoided, seems to have proceeded from the fact, that it appeals to common sense and the plain instincts of our nature, while the objections to it are abstruse, far-fetched, and refined. It needs some study to perceive that they are, at least to an equal extent, shallow and sophistical, as they rest solely on the mistaken notion, that metaphysical reasoning is applicable to matters-of-fact. What would be thought of the wisdom, or even the sanity, of the mathematician who, having found from the calculus what *must be* the form of a body which is to move through a fluid with the least possible resistance, and having ascertained also, (what happens to be true,) that his abstract conclusions are rebutted by simple and decisive experiments, should yet adhere to his results as available for practical purposes, on the ground that they were supported by demonstration, while they were not contradicted except by the evidence of the senses, which is a source only of contingent assurance? The child or the savage knows that *facts are a test of reasoning, and not reasoning of facts.* "Is it not fitting," said a savage of Sumatra to his companion, showing him a watch that had been made in Europe, "that a people such as we should be the slaves of a nation capable of forming such a machine? The sun," he added, "is a machine of the same nature." "And who winds him up?" asked his companion. "Who," replied he, "but Allah." Thus it is, as Paley remarks, that these proofs "are sufficiently open to the views and capacities of the unlearned, at the same time that they acquire new strength and lustre from the discoveries of the learned. If they had been altogether abstruse and recondite, they would not have found their way to the understandings of the mass of mankind; if they had been merely popular, they might have wanted solidity."

Why the Creator works by means and agencies. — But it is said, that the use of means to an end implies the existence of difficulties and obstacles, and so leads to a supposition of defect of power; contrivances are human conceptions to get rid indirectly of obstacles which we are not able immediately to remove by a simple act of the will; therefore they cannot rightly be attributed to Omnipotence, which is always adequate to the direct accomplishment of its ends. Thus, a child must use a lever to raise a weight which the adult lifts at once without effort; the boy must stand in a chair to arrive at an object that is within reach of his parent's arm. It is hardly enough to say, simply, that it has pleased the Almighty to work by means and agencies, instead of directly accomplishing his purposes, unless we can supply some reason for this preference which shall be consistent with infinite wisdom. I answer, then, that we immediately discover such a reason, if we bring in the idea of *the moral government of man*, a creature endowed with intellect and conscience, and left to complete his earthly education and probation by his own freewill. The *ultimate* purpose of all these contrivances, then, is, that the study of them may lead us up to a knowledge of the existence and attributes of their Infinite Author. And further, for the regulation of our daily conduct, in order that we may infer the future from the past, it is necessary that the course of nature, or the action of Deity, should be uniform, or, in other words, that it should be governed by general laws. "It has been said, that the problem of creation was, 'Attraction and matter being given, to make a world out of them.'" How could we act at all, self-guided, unless from reliance on the constantly recurring and uniform phenomena of gravitation, light, heat, chemical affinity, and the like? "These," to quote again from Paley, "are general laws; and when a particular purpose is to be effected, it is not by making a new law, nor by the suspension of the old ones, nor by making them wind, and bend, and yield to the occasion; but it is by the interposition of an apparatus corresponding with these laws, and suited to the exigency which results from them, that the purpose is at length attained." *

The assumption of design a fruitful principle in physical science. — That final causes, or the purposes for which numberless arrangements and adaptations were made, can be discerned in nature, is not only a principle in Natural Theology, but a received doctrine, and a fruitful one, in physical science, especially in the departments of *physiology* and *zoölogy*, in which it has been a guide to the most important discoveries. Thus, Harvey, in 1616, having learned that there were valves in the *veins*, which opened towards the heart, and thus permitted the blood

---

* "Is it nothing more than a lucky accommodation which makes the polarity of the needle to subserve the purposes of the mariner? Or may it not safely be affirmed, both that the magnetic influence (whatever its primary intention may be) had reference to the business of navigation — a reference incalculably important to the spread and improvement of the human race; and that the discovery and the application of this influence arrived at the destined moment in the revolution of human affairs, when, in combination with other events, it would produce the greatest effect? Nor should we scruple to affirm, that the relation between the inclination of the earth's axis and the conspicuous star which, without a near rival, attracts even the eye of the vulgar, and shows the north to the wanderer on the wilderness, or on the ocean, is in like manner a beneficent arrangement. Those who would spurn the supposition that the celestial locality of a sun, immeasurably remote from our system, should have reference to the accommodation of the inhabitants of a planet so inconsiderable as our own, forget *the style of the divine works, which is, to secure some great or principal end, compatibly with ten thousand lesser and remote interests.* Man, if he would secure the greater, must neglect or sacrifice the less: not so the Omnipotent Contriver. It is a fact full of meaning that those astronomical phenomena, (and so others), which offer themselves as available for the purposes of art, — as, for instance, of navigation or geography, — do not fully or effectively yield the aid they promised, until after long and elaborate processes or calculations have disentangled them from variations, disturbing forces, and apparent irregularities. To the rude fact, if so we might designate it, a mass of recondite science must be appended, before it can be brought to bear with precision upon the arts of life. Thus, the polarity of the needle, or the eclipses of Jupiter's moons, are as nothing to the mariner or the geographer, without the voluminous commentary afforded by the mathematics of astronomy." — Taylor's *Introduction to Edwards*, p. cxxxvii.

to pass in this direction, while they would prevent its passage towards the extremities, and that the valves at the exit of the *arteries* from the heart opened in the opposite direction, assumed that these valves must have been *intended* to allow and direct the movement of the blood, and was thus led to the capital discovery of the circulation. To prove the fact, he tied the veins, and found that they swelled on the side nearer the extremities; he tied the arteries, and found that they swelled on the side nearer the heart. It would be easy to show, that nearly all the great discoveries which have been made in physiology since Harvey's time, have proceeded from this same doctrine, — from the assumption, that is, that no part of the body exists without some use, or function, which it was *designed* to fulfil. Observe, that here it is not a knowledge of the adaptation which suggests the purpose, but an assumption of the purpose which leads to a knowledge of the adaptation, or use.*

To show the fruitful application of the same principle in

---

* "In Biology alone," observes Bichat, "have we to contemplate the state of *disease*. Physiology is to the movements of living bodies, what astronomy, dynamics, hydraulics, etc., are to those of inert matter: but these latter sciences have no branches which correspond to them as *pathology* corresponds to physiology. For the same reason, all notion of a *medicament* is repugnant to the physical sciences. A medicament has for its object to bring the properties of the system back to their natural type; but the physical properties never depart from this type, and have no need to be brought back to it; and thus there is nothing in the physical sciences which holds the place of therapeutics in physiology:" "or," Dr. Whewell justly adds, "as we might express it otherwise, of inert forces we have no conception of what they *ought to do*, except what they *do*. The forces of gravity, elasticity, affinity, never act in a *diseased* manner; we never conceive them as failing in their purpose; for we do not conceive them as having any purpose, which is answered by one mode of their action rather than another. But with organical forces, the case is different; they are necessarily conceived as acting for the preservation and development of the system in which they reside. If they do not do this, they fail, they are deranged, diseased. They have for their object to conform the living being to a certain type; and if they cause or allow it to deviate from this type, their action is distorted, morbid, contrary to the ends of nature. And thus this conception of organized beings as suscep-

zoölogical researches, I have only to borrow the language of the illustrious Cuvier, at the commencement of his great work on the Animal Kingdom. "Zoölogy," he says, "has a principle of reasoning which is peculiar to it, and which it employs with advantage on many occasions; this is the principle of *the conditions of existence*, vulgarly called the principle of *final causes*. As nothing can exist, if it do not combine all the conditions which render its existence possible, the different parts of each being must be arranged in such a manner as to render the total being possible, not only in itself, but in its relations to those which surround it; and the analysis of these conditions often leads to general laws, as clearly demonstrated as those which result from calculation or experience." Thus, "If the viscera of an animal are so organized as only to be fitted for the digestion of *recent flesh*, it is also requisite that the jaws should be so constructed as to fit them for devouring prey; the claws must be constructed for seizing and tearing it in pieces; the teeth, for cutting and dividing its flesh; the entire system of the limbs or organs of motion, for pursuing and overtaking it; and the organs of sense, for discovering it at a distance. Nature must also have endowed the brain of the animal with instincts sufficient for concealing itself, and for laying plans to catch its necessary victims." "By such considerations," adds Mr. Whewell, Cuvier "has been able to reconstruct the whole of many animals of which parts only were given; — a positive result, which shows both the reality and the value of the truth on which he wrought."

Natural theology is knowledge; infidelity is ignorance. — Thus it appears that the theological argument from design is not merely coincident in character, and of the same logical force, with the principles of physical science, but it is identical

tible of disease, implies the recognition of a state of health, and of the organs and vital forces as means for preserving this normal condition. The state of health and perpetual development is necessarily contemplated as the Final Cause of the processes and powers with which the different parts of plants and animals are endowed." — *Philosophy of the Ind. Sciences*, Vol I. p. 627.

with many of those principles. It is one and the same maxim, or law of inquiry, which guides the anatomist to a knowledge of many parts of an animal structure that he has never seen, and leads the seeker after religious truth to a recognition of the being, the wisdom, and the beneficence of a God. It furnishes him, also, with an explanation of the mysteries of that universe which he inhabits, with a key to the true purpose and character of those marvellous arrangements and adaptations in the midst of which he lives, and on which, indeed, his existence depends. If the phenomena of nature were not arranged by an all-wise Providence, if this earth does not show the footprints of Divinity, then those phenomena are inexplicable, and the origin and tendency of all things are surrounded by a veil which no human eye can pierce. Our life itself is but "a confused noise between two silences;" we emerge from the darkness at one end, only to find ourselves surrounded with wonders whose meaning we cannot fathom, and then to pass again into the thick gloom whose portal is the grave. Infidelity offers us no compensation or substitute for the light that it extinguishes, for the faith which it destroys; it accounts for nothing, it explains nothing; it is a mere confession of blank, hopeless ignorance. We can find, not a refuge, but a resting-place, either in the appalling system of Spinoza, under the iron rule of fatalism, which deprives us alike of the consciousness of our own personality, and of all motive for action or effort, or in the absolute skepticism of Hume, which is mere negation and darkness, where we have no assurance even of the grounds of disbelief. The doctrine of theism dissipates this gloom; it supplies a reason for exertion, and objects for study; it is a vindication of the possibility of human knowledge. It can be overthrown only by a denial of that possibility.

Theology needed to fill up our knowledge of nature. — What we call *nature* is an assemblage of objects, and a succession of events. These objects are not simple and uniform, but complex, varied, and curiously fashioned, abounding in curious adjustments and nice arrangements of parts. The events do not succeed each other irregularly, or seemingly at random, but in a fixed order, preserving harmonious relations, which enable us to divine the future from the past. In spite of our life-long familiarity with these marvels, and the petrifying influence of such continuous observation upon our feelings of wonder and admiration, we cannot rest contented with the slender knowledge which we gain of them merely from the senses, — that is, with *a record of their occurrence,* and *a description of their successive changes and outward aspects.* An irresistible impulse leads us to inquire into their *origin, meaning,* and *tendency. Whence* are they, and *why* do they exist? Human science alone, without any aid from theology, without any light from above, has no answer to these questions, and, when properly understood, does not even attempt to answer them. It describes the phenomena, as they are seen, with greater or less minuteness, it records the order of their succession, and it assumes the invariability of this order, or its continuance in the future and the past. It describes and classifies facts, and supposes the existence of similar facts; and this is all. With a kind of dim consciousness, indeed, that these results do not exhaust the subject, or satisfy the demands of rational curiosity, it holds up the *laws* of phenomena as substitutes for their *causes,* in a vain attempt to explain their origin. But these *physical causes,* as they are termed, cannot pass for real ones; for the *manner* in which an event takes place does not show the *reason* of its occurrence, or give us any information of the power that produced it.

How our view of nature is affected by a knowledge of its Author. — The great fact of the existence of an omnipresent and ever-active Deity, the author, supporter, and immediate cause of all things, affords the only possible answer to these inquiries, the only key which will open the secrets and the mysteries of the universe. That this doctrine first gives distinctness to our conceptions by explaining the fact of creation, or the origin of things, is an insufficient statement of its importance; it solves the far more difficult problem respecting the continuance, meaning, and tendency of those objects and events which mere human science only observes and records. It answers the questions *why* and *wherefore* for all the phenomena of time and space.

Adaptations now reveal a purpose; nice adjustments show design. We are not limited now to a mere description of the organ, and of the office which it actually performs; we can point to its Creator, and tell *why* it exists, and what object it was intended to answer. We can assume beforehand that every thing, down to the minutest fibre of the humblest organism, has a purpose, or a final cause,* since infinite wisdom does nothing in vain. We can even assume that creation is formed throughout upon one plan, and directed by a single purpose; and we find that this is an intelligible plan, a discoverable purpose. Here is not only a positive enlargement of our knowledge, but a guide and object for our subsequent inquiries. Those who reject the doctrine which furnishes this guide may content themselves, if they can, with those limitations which so eminent a naturalist as Geoffroy St. Hilaire proposed for the bounds of his studies. "I take good care," he says, "not to ascribe any intention to God, for I mistrust the feeble powers of my reason. I observe facts merely, and go no further. I only pretend to the character of the historian of *what is*. I cannot make nature an intelligent being who does nothing in vain." This is the frank avowal

---

* The use of the phrase *final cause*, to express the *end, purpose*, or *intention* for which a thing is made or done, has been so long established by philosophical writers, that it would savor of affectation to renounce it altogether. Yet as Mr. De Morgan remarks, to talk of *final causes* is as unintelligible to most persons as to talk of *final beginnings*.

To understand the phrase, we must remember that the word *cause* was used by the ancients in a very wide sense, corresponding to the *causa* of the Latins, the *cosa* of the Italians, and the *chose* of the French; it signified *the matter or concern which is transacted, spoken, written, or contended about*. To remove the indefiniteness arising from this comprehensive signification, Aristotle properly distinguished four sorts of *causes*, (French, *choses*, English, *things*); he distinguished *material, formal, efficient*, and *final* (Latin, *finis*, English, *end*) *causes*. The *material* cause is the very *matter* out of which a thing is made, considered as the principle of its existence; the *formal* cause is the internal constitution of a thing — that which makes it what it is; the *efficient* cause corresponds to the English use of the word, as it signifies the maker or author of a thing, or that which really produces it; the *final* cause, as we have said, is the *end* or *purpose* for which it was made. To understand the difference between *material* and *formal*

of the skeptic who is willing to remain in his ignorance, even after the brilliant discoveries of Cuvier had shown the fruitfulness of the opposite mode of inquiry.

Physical events, as they appear to the theologian and the skeptic. — Still more striking and important is the change made in our notions of the succession of events, by this doctrine of the constant presence and agency of the Supreme Being. The power that operates in nature is no longer unseen and undiscoverable physical occurrences do not follow each other by any inscrutable mechanism, or by a blind and unconscious fatality. In the countless aspects and ceaseless changes of the world without us, we no longer behold the fortuitous concourse of atoms, self-governed, yet bound one to another by inexorable necessity, and forming an adamantine chain, that is nowhere held up or sustained save by a dim abstraction, — where

> "Chaos umpire sits,
> And by decision more embroils the fray
> By which he reigns: next him, high arbiter,
> Chance governs all."

---

causes, we must attend to the ancient distinction between the *matter* and the *form* of a thing; this is admirably illustrated, as follows, by Mr Thomson, in his *Outline of the Laws of Thought*, page 22.

"A statue may be considered as consisting of two parts, the marble out of which it is hewn, which is its *matter* or stuff, and the *form* which the artist communicates. The latter is essential to the statue, but not the former, since the work might be the same, though the *material* were different; but if the *form* were wanting, we could not even call the work a statue. This notion, of a material susceptible of a certain form, the accession of which shall give it a new nature and name, may be analogically transferred to other natures. Space may be regarded as *matter*, and geometrical figures as the *form* impressed in it. The voice is the *matter* of speech, and articulation the *form*. But as it is the *form* which proximately and obviously makes the thing what it is, (although there can be no *form* without *matter*,) the word *form* came to be interchanged with *essence* and with *nature*."

We may explain the four sorts of causes thus. The *material* cause of the paper on which I am now writing, is the pulp of rags out of which it was made; its *formal* cause is its peculiar texture and other properties, which entitle it to the name of paper; its *efficient* cause is the paper-maker; its *final* cause is to be written upon.

Mind resumes its dominion over the vast expanse, and drives these spectres back to their native realm of ignorance and eldest Night. Every event, from the blossoming of the tiniest flower up to the swift flight of the stars in their courses, becomes as intelligible to man as his own voluntary movements. The contest between mind and matter ceases; spirit animates, moves, and governs all, with a beneficent and discoverable purpose, and with infinite wisdom. The observation of the inherent laws of material atoms now becomes the study of the character, intentions, and will of Him who created the heavens and the earth, and laid the corner-stone thereof.

Theology is the complement and extension of physical science. — The great truths of natural theology, then, not only rest upon the same proofs which support our conclusions in physical science, but they enter into that science as an integral portion of it, as its necessary complement and extension up to the farthest limits which are imposed upon it by the imperfection of our faculties. They are among the facts obtained from our observation of nature, or among the legitimate inferences which are drawn from those facts. They are a portion of the results derived from the strict application of the inductive method to the study of nature, and they are therefore properly recorded with the other conclusions of physical science, among its most valuable contributions to the sum of human knowledge. Certain marks and indentations in red sandstone are held to prove, beyond all question, the existence at some very remote period of a species of birds, of which not one bone or other fragment has ever been discovered, and which must have been wholly unlike any winged creature that now inhabits the earth or air. In like manner, certain arrangements and adaptations in the body of a living animal afford abundant indications of purpose and contrivance, and so prove the wisdom and goodness of the great Cause that brought the animal into being. There is no difference between the inferences drawn in these two cases, except that the latter is the more simple, direct, and unquestionable; it rests upon a more copious induction, and it is certainly more credible that a fortuitous conjunction of other circumstances should have caused certain marks or scratches on a rock, than that an unintelligent and undesigning power should have fashioned so delicate and complex an instrument as the human eye. It is as much the object and duty of science to note and record these indications of intellect and design, as to distinguish fossil remains from the mere inorganic rock in which they are imbedded. The mere description of the object or phenomenon is incomplete without them.*

Physical science stops short of efficient causation. — So, also, if the study of nature, so far as it relates to the course of events, is mainly occupied with distinguishing invariable antecedents from those which are casual and temporary, it is concerned, also, to point out such antecedents as are really causal and necessary, and so invariable. The operation of *efficient* causes is even in a higher degree an object of rational inquiry and effort, than the succession of *physical* causes, provided always that the distinction between them be kept clearly in view, and the one class be not confounded with the other. Our own consciousness gives us a knowledge of one true cause, in the mastery of the human will over the body with which it is connected. As anthropology, or the science of man, would be incomplete without a discussion of this capital fact, so physical

* Dr. Whewell remarks, that even the "physiologists who look with suspicion and dislike upon the introduction of Final Causes into physiology, have still been unable to exclude from their speculations causes of this kind. Thus Bichat, after noting the difference between the organic sensibility, by which the organs are made to perform their offices and the animal sensibility, of which the nervous centre is the seat, says. 'No doubt it will be asked *why*' — that is, as we shall see, for what *end* — 'the organs of internal life have received from nature an inferior degree of sensibility only, and why they do not transmit to the brain those impressions which they receive, while all the acts of the animal life imply this transmission? The reason is simply this, that all the phenomena which establish our connections with surrounding objects *ought to be*, and are in fact, under the influence of the will; while all those which serve the purpose of assimilation only, escape, and *ought* indeed to escape, such influence! The reason here assigned is the Final Cause, which, as Bichat justly says, we cannot help asking for." — *Phil. of the Ind. Sci.* Vol II. p. 626.

science, or the study of nature, is imperfect, and even baseless, if it stops short of the modes of operation of that single Power which sustains, animates, and governs all. The conclusions of the theological inquirer, therefore, in their lower aspect, form a part, a large constituent element, of the great body of scientific truth which man derives from a study of the material and the intellectual universe; in their lower aspect, I say, for this fact would hardly merit notice, except from its relation to my present purpose, which is to show the nature of the evidence upon which these conclusions rest.

The scientific value of theological truths inferior to their moral worth. — Our chief interest in these results does not depend merely on their scientific value, as additions to the sum of human knowledge, but on their religious bearing and their applicability to the government of our hearts and lives. The truths thus far established lead us only to the opening of that great subject which stretches out over the whole field of our duties and hopes as intelligent, moral, and accountable beings. Though the discussion in this work has been strictly confined to the validity of the common argument for the being of a God, so far as this is affected by the metaphysical theories and speculations now most in vogue, and has thus only prepared the way for an inquiry into the whole system of Natural Religion, it has still conducted us to some results which are profitable for reflection and practice. "Of all habits of thinking, the most important to be cultivated is that of referring all the phenomena of nature up to their infinite Creator, and of regarding all events, whether physical or moral, as caused or governed by an ever-watchful and active Providence. To have made this the ruling, the habitual sentiment of our minds, is to have laid the foundation of every thing which is religious. The world thenceforth becomes a temple, and life itself one continued act of adoration." The philosophical doctrine of the immediate agency of the Deity, is that which harmonizes most perfectly with the religious sentiment in man, and gives most satisfaction and support to the devotional spirit. It strengthens the belief in revelation, as the course of all physical events is seen to be directed with a moral purpose; and the blind domain of physical laws and material necessity being broken, a direct interposition of God in the affairs of men becomes not only credible, but natural, and what we should most readily expect from infinite goodness and wisdom combined. We pass on, therefore, from the study of his works to that of his word, not by an abrupt or violent transition, but gradually, and with a distinct recognition of the unity of his character, and of the similarity of plan by which he governs the physical and moral universe, and proclaims his existence and his will to the creatures whom he has made.

SECOND PART.

CHAPTER I.

THE HUMAN DISTINGUISHED FROM THE BRUTE MIND.

Statement of the subject. — We have finished a brief view of the ordinary argument for the being of a God. But the establishment of this truth alone, though it is the central doctrine of Natural Religion, and all the others depend upon it, still leaves us at the threshold of the subject. We have still *to ascertain the character or attributes under which the Deity has manifested himself to mankind*, and to learn if these are such as to create an obligation on our part to conform to his will. Obedience may be yielded either from involuntary awe, or blind submission to absolute and infinite power, or from veneration for perfect wisdom and holiness, and a mingled sentiment of duty, gratitude, and love. The prevalence of one or another of these motives will depend on the views which we may form of the Divine nature; and the peculiarity of the dominant motive will modify and shape the whole religious character.

It is but a part of the same inquiry to ask *what the Divine will is, or what we are required to do, or to refrain from doing*, from a regard to the relations in which we stand to God and to our fellow man Apart from direct revelation, with which at present we have nothing to do, the will of the Deity can be inferred only from a knowledge of his character, and this can be learned in no other way than by the study of his works. His moral attributes, with which we are now chiefly concerned, are made known to us almost exclusively through the constitution of our own moral nature; and accordingly, the study of this nature, or of the ethical constitution of man, must be our chief guide in the present inquiry. As the former Part related mainly to things physical, or to what is taught us of the being and agency of God by the phenomena of the outward universe, so, in the present discussion, *the nature and functions of conscience, and the analysis of our sense of moral obligation*, must enable us to frame our conceptions of religious duty. This will be the principal aim and tendency of the investigation; incidentally, as before, we must seek for illustrations of the will and character of the Deity from the outward and visible things that he has made.

Basis of the inquiry. — What was attempted to be proved in the former discussion will now be taken for granted; and this includes, you will remember, not only the existence of God, but his incessant and omnipresent action in the universe. Both the creation of things and the direction of events are his; the fashioning of our bodies, the constitution of our minds, and the endowment of our moral nature, are alike the effects of his wisdom and appointment; and the reasoning from effect to cause, which was proved to be legitimate in the case already considered, must be applicable in all others. Even the attribute of freewill, in respect to which man alone is created in the likeness of his Maker, is his gift; and the possession of it is an indication of his will that it should be exercised. We are free to choose between the evil and the good; and this freedom presupposes opportunities for choice; it requires that the alternative should be presented to us, or it would be a delusion and a mockery. The promptings of conscience are as clear an indication of the moral judgments of God, as the instincts of animals, the processes of vegetable life, and the structure of the heavens are of his being and his power. In both cases, we reason from the thing that is created and finite to the self-existent and infinite Cause.

The study of human nature is our starting point. Among the works of creation, the study of which leads us up to a knowledge of the being and attributes of God, the foremost place is occupied by man himself. We are ourselves his offspring, creatures whom he has endowed with a peculiar physical, intellectual, and moral organization, the properties and tendencies of which reflect the character and purposes of our Maker. The marvellous structure of our bodies, these tenements of clay which we inhabit for a season, shows his wisdom, his constant agency, his designing care; so also the constitution of our minds, the laws by which our sensations, ideas, and judgments are formed and made to succeed each other, are so many tokens of the Divine will and character. They show what part God intended we should act upon the theatre of the universe. Still further, in our moral nature, or the emotions that are excited in us by the sight of surrounding objects and events, and especially by the contemplation of our own acts, and of those of our fellow beings, we find our only means of knowing what the moral attributes of God are, and what, if any, is his scheme of moral government. Practically speaking, we are concerned to know, not so much what things are in themselves, as the manner in which we are affected by the sight of them, and by living in the midst of them. The fitness of objects to give pleasure to man depends equally on the characteristic qualities of those objects, and on the susceptibility of the human mind to pleasure of one kind rather than another, and indeed on its capacity of being pleased at all.

The true end and aim of man's existence. — We come, therefore, to an examination of the nature and functions of conscience, as the first point of our inquiry. My object will be to show, that *man is not merely an intellectual being, placed here on earth to satisfy his curiosity, and to provide for his own well-being.* This would be a conceivable end of his creation, but it is notoriously not the real end. If he had the intellectual faculties of an archangel, and this earth were a paradise for his habitation, affording every object that could gratify his desires and promote his happiness, — if enjoyment brought no satiety and labor no fatigue, if his birth were only an introduction to active pleasure, and death were nothing but painless extinction, — then we could easily attribute unlimited benevolence to his Creator, and consider that man's only purpose in life was to pass on from one phase of happiness to another. Why is it, that we do not regard this as the actual, or even as a desirable, plan of human existence? It is only an obscure reference to such a scheme which lends any force, or indeed any meaning, to the oft-repeated complaints about the existence of evil under the government of a God of infinite benevolence. Yet when such a plan of life is presented for us to contemplate at once in its entireness, we almost instinctively reject it, as not admitting the existence of those qualities which now constitute the true ornament and dignity of human nature, and as making no provision for their cultivation, even if they did exist. A more authoritative principle than self-love declares to us, that the practice of virtue is higher than the pursuit of enjoyment, that holiness is more desirable than happiness, and that the Divine government, in so far as it shows infinite justice and benevolence combined, and affords scope for progress and effort, as well as for the gratification of desires ending in self, is in truth the noblest conceivable expression of the wisdom and goodness of God.

The contrast between man and the brute. — To prove this point, and to show by contrast the true nature of the moral faculty in man, I propose to go some way back, and to examine *the only case* within the sphere of human observation *where intellectual are not combined with moral qualities, and where, consequently, enjoyment for the time must be regarded as the sole end of existence.* I refer, of course, to the mental constitution of brutes, or of all orders of animated being which are inferior to man. The subject is confessedly an obscure one; but I doubt not that enough of it may be made out with certainty to answer all the purposes of this discussion. If the investigation should lead to the establishment of a broad distinction between man and the brute, so as to show that the mental endowments of the latter differ from those of the former, not in degree only, but in kind, this will be a collateral advantage, which will help us to clear up some other difficulties in our subject.

How far we can know the nature of brutes.—Let me limit the object and extent of the inquiry in the outset. With respect either to the human or the brute mind, we can only ask *what it does;* it would be idle to inquire *what it is,* for we are ignorant of the inward nature, the essential constitution, of both. In the one case, it is true, we have the aid of consciousness, while in the other we are restricted to external observation. But why that unit of being which we call *man*, or *mind*, should have one set of powers and susceptibilities rather than another, is a question which mere physical or metaphysical science does not pretend to answer, otherwise than by saying, that such is the will of his Creator; the moralist or the theologian may here come in, and show the reasonableness of that will, but even he cannot tell how it is carried into effect. In the case of the brute, of course, we can only look at its outward acts, and thence dimly infer its peculiarities of mental organization.

Now there is no action whatever, considered merely as a visible fact, as an exercise of nerves and muscles, which many brutes cannot perform nearly or quite as well as men. They walk, leap, run, and climb; they eat, drink, and continue their species; they weep, cry, and even articulate. From their outward acts alone, then, it seems impossible to deduce the characteristic feature of their mental nature. Luckily, a third question remains to us, the answer to which directly involves the subject of our present inquiry, while it appears to be within the reach of human investigation. In regard either to instinct or intelligence, though we cannot tell *what it is,* we may ascertain *what it is not.* As we affirm confidently that mind is not material, so we may find sure reason to believe that it is radically different from instinct. And to establish this point is my first object.

Instinct is not mechanism.—It is first necessary to determine the meaning of the word *instinct*, or to ascertain what phenomena are properly considered as instinctive. Some writers speak of "physical instincts," among which they class the beating of the heart, the movements of respiration, the peristaltic motion of the intestines, and the like. But as these motions are regular and involuntary, they are more properly regarded as automatic, or mechanical,* and are classed with the phenomena of organic life rather than with those of instinct, especially as operations corresponding to them, or exactly similar, are carried on in vegetables. The touch of an insect alighting on the common flower called Venus's Fly-trap causes its sides to spring forcibly together, so as to catch and hold the intruder, whose struggles only increase the pressure of this self-acting trap. Such movements resemble, not the actions of a bird in building its nest, but the motions of wheels which are dependent on the uncoiling of a spring or the falling of a weight.

Reflex nervous action distinguished from instinct.— Recent discoveries in physiology have established the existence of what is called a *reflex action* in certain nerves, by which, without any sensation being communicated to the brain, and consequently without any effort of the will, an impression made upon the end of a nerve is transmitted to the spinal cord, and is thence sent back again, as it were, along one of the motor nerves to its extremity, producing there a contraction of the muscles, of which the required or appropriate movement of the limb or organ is the consequence. Isolate this pair of nerves entirely, by cutting off its communication, not only with the head, but with the upper and lower portions of the spinal

* To avoid misconception, I may here mention, once for all, that I use the common phraseology that is founded on the mechanical theory of nature's operations, or the doctrine of secondary causes, but without demitting the truth of that theory. In the former Part, I endeavored to prove that all action or change in the purely material creation, must de attributed to the immediate agency of the Creator. Still, for the convenience of speech, to avoid circumlocution and incessant reference to this doctrine, I continue to use the language that is sanctioned by universal custom, though it is derived from what seems to me a wholly unphilosophical and mistaken view of the operations of nature and the sphere of Divine action. It is easy to bear in mind the constant qualification, or protest, under which this phraseology is adopted.

column, reserving only a segment of this column to connect the excitor with the motor nerve, and the reflex movement may still be produced. A decapitated frog remains at rest till it is touched; and then its leg, or even its whole body, is thrown into sudden but momentary action. Cases have occurred in which the spinal cord of a man was so far injured, by disease or accident, that there was no voluntary control of the lower limbs, and not even any sensation in them; but if stimuli were applied to the feet, by tickling or pinching them, or applying a hot plate, the muscles of the leg instantly contracted, and with some violence; and this without the patient having any sensation, either of the cause of the movement, or of the movement itself; in fact, without his knowing it.

Of this nature is the action of swallowing, which is excited by the contact of food or liquid with the back part of the mouth, and then takes place in spite of any effort on our part to prevent it. "Even the respiratory movements," says Dr. Carpenter, "spontaneous as they seem to be, would not continue unless they were excited by the presence of venous blood in the vessels,— especially in those of the lungs. These movements are all *necessarily* linked with the stimulus that excites them; — that is, the same stimulus will always produce the same movement, when the condition of the body is the same. Hence it is evident, that *the judgment or will is not concerned in producing them;* but they may be rather compared to the movements of an automaton, which are produced by touching certain springs." *

* As the reflex action of the nerves had not been discovered, I believe, when Dugald Stewart published (1826) the third volume of his Elements of the Philosophy of the Human Mind, he has some excuse for maintaining that the operations, not only of suction and swallowing, but of respiration, must be ascribed to instinct. But his doctrine now appears even less plausible than that of Dr. Darwin, who gravely supposes that the fœtus learns to swallow by its experience *in utero*. Stewart mentions the fact, that thirty pairs of muscles must be employed in every draught, and seems to believe that a distinct volition is required for the movement of each pair; though the well-known facts respecting the catenation of the

The object of all such mechanical and involuntary motions is to supply the imperative wants of the body, and to preserve it from the injuries to which it is most frequently exposed. The watchfulness of the animal is not sufficient for its own preservation; the want of care, quickness, and decision in the control of the will is thus compensated by a mechanical contrivance, a spontaneous movement, which repels the danger, or satisfies the want, before we are conscious of its existence. A beautiful instance of this is the instantaneous and automatic movement of the eyelids, by which so delicate an organ as the eye is preserved from sudden injury. The slightest stimulus causes them to close, even the flash of powder having this effect before the flame can reach the eyeball. It would be an abuse of language to apply the same name to a contrivance like this, and to the marvellous instinct that guides the migrating bird, at the proper season, in its long flight to its winter home.

Instinct distinguished from the appetites. — Besides these mechanical operations, or organic functions of life, which are common to the animal and vegetable kingdom, though they are more numerous and more complex in the former, I exclude the simple appetites and passions from the class of instincts properly so called. These appetites have been called instinctive, because they seek their own gratification without the aid of reason, and often in spite of it. They are common to man and the brute; but they differ, at least in one important respect, from those instincts of the lower animals which are usually contrasted with human reason. *The objects* towards which they are directed *are prized for their own sake;* they are sought as *ends,* while

---

muscular actions might have convinced him of the absurdity of such a theory. His *naïve* astonishment, that an infant, as soon as it comes into the world, should know how to "perform *with the most perfect success* the function of respiration, — a function which requires the alternate contraction and relaxation of certain muscles in a regular order and succession," — is certainly an amusing instance of this weakness. He might just as well have been surprised that it should know how to keep up the circulation of the blood in its tender limbs; for the will of the infant has certainly as much to do in this case as in that of respiration.

instinct teaches brutes to do many things which are needed only as *means* for the attainment of some ulterior purpose. Thus, *instinct* enables a spider to *entrap* his prey, while *appetite* only leads him to *devour* it while in his possession. Nay, the two impulses often act in opposition to each other, as when the bird restrains its own hunger for the sake of feeding its young. Appetite is blind and affords a motive, but no guidance, for effort; instinct, on the other hand, often supplies an object for action, though it is more frequently indebted for this to appetite, and always points out the course for its attainment. It is true, that appetite sometimes appears to direct the choice; yet so far only as the absence or presence of it leads the animal to reject unsuitable food, and to devour that which is adapted to its physical constitution. That a dog will not eat hay, nor a horse swallow raw meat, is no more a proof of instinct than the corresponding fact in man, that sweet things are pleasant to the taste, while bitter are disagreeable, is an indication of reason.

It is evident that the appetites have been called instinctive, only because they are *not acquired by experience or instruction;* they are innate. But this is far from being the only characteristic of what are usually termed the instincts of the lower animals, which often lead to complex and prolonged tasks, involving a constant sacrifice of their natural desires and inclinations. Instinct is marvellous and inscrutable in its operations, as much so as reason itself. But that the appetites have their appropriate objects, and reject all others, is no special cause for wonder, any more than the fact, that glass transmits light, while it is impervious to air. Such is its original constitution.

Definition of instinct. — How may we define instinct, then, as distinguished from appetite on the one hand, and from reason on the other, as all three are motives or guides to action? It is *an impulse conceived without instruction, and prior to all experience, to perform certain acts which are not needed for the immediate gratification of the agent, which in fact are often opposed to it, and are useful only as means for the attainment of some ulterior object; and this object is usually one of preëminent utility or necessity,* either for the preservation of the ani mal's own life, or for the continuance of its species. The former quality separates it from *intelligence*, properly so called, which proceeds only by experience or instruction; and the latter is its peculiar trait as distinguished from *appetite*, which, in strictness, uses no *means* at all, but looks only to *ends*.*

In the remainder of what I have to offer, it will be my object to show, *first*, that instinct is distinguishable from reason by many other peculiarities, which are so obvious and striking, that we must admit the difference between the two attributes to be radical or essential, — a difference not in degree, but in kind; *secondly*, that all animals inferior to man are guided in a greater or less degree, if not entirely, by instinct, while man is never subject to it, but is governed exclusively by reason, — the effects of mechanical contrivances, and of mere appetites, or blind desires and inclinations, which are confessedly common to man and the brute, having been set aside for reasons already mentioned; and *thirdly*, that the lower animals, because their highest attribute is instinct, have no moral character whatever, and consequently do not merit praise or blame, — so that their actions, and the scheme or plan of their existence, show us what

* "All those acts of animals are instinctive which, though performed voluntarily, do not depend primarily on the mere will of the animal; they have an object according with the wants of the organism, but this object is unknown to the animal; the hidden cause incites the brute to the necessary acts, by presenting to it the 'theme' of the voluntary movements to be executed in detail by the influence of the will. We are ourselves conscious only of feelings and impulses to determinate acts. The number of instinctive acts is great in animals in proportion to their incapability of accomplishing by their own mental powers the design for which their species was created." — Muller's *Physiology*, p. 946.

Hence, as Dr. Holland remarks, the two great faculties of reason and instinct exist in an inverse ratio to each other. "In man, instincts, properly so called, form the *minimum* in relation to reason. They multiply continually, and become more distinct in character, as we descend in the scale; their completeness in reference to the life of the individual, increasing in the same ratio as the intelligence becomes less." He adds, "as a further proof of the inverse perfection of intellect and instinct, tha the class of insects, in whom these instinctive functions are most strikingly manifested, appears to rank very low in the scale of intelligence."

man would be, if he was deprived of the ethical part of his nature, and thus, in the higher meaning of the phrase, not subject to the moral government of God. *The general conclusion will be*, that the animal as well as the vegetable creation, like inorganic things, and the course of merely physical events, are not *ends* in the Divine government, but *means*, the leading purpose of all being the moral education and government of man.

Instinct acts without instruction or experience. — And first, it will not be necessary to use many words to prove that instinct, unlike reason, acts without instruction or experience. Chickens hatched by steam, which have never seen any older birds of the same species, perform all the duties of incubation and feeding their young as perfectly as if they had been the constant objects of Dame Partlet's care in their own callow infancy. Insects born only after the death of their parents still run the little cycle of their appointed tasks, and make provision for their own future progeny, which they are never to see, with as much labor and foresight as were exercised in preparing and storing their own cradles. The moth, with great care, collects food of a kind which it never uses for itself, as a provision for its young when in a transition state. Certain insects, governing for the moment their own appetites, which would lead them to devour their food as soon as found, store up in subterranean cells a provision for the coming winter, though as yet, in their short life, they have experienced only the warmth and abundance of summer and autumn. In all these cases, there is no opportunity for experience, and no source of instruction; and the end attained is one that is essential for the preservation of the species.

"Who bid the stork, Columbus-like, explore
Heavens not his own, and worlds not known before?
Who calls the councils, states the certain day?
Who forms the phalanx, and who points the way?"

Instinct not susceptible of improvement. — The next peculiarity of instinct, a necessary consequence of the one already noticed, is, that it is not susceptible of improvement or education. It is complete from the beginning; it makes no progress either in the individual or the race. The bee, as soon after its disclosure from the pupa as its body is dried and its wings expanded, takes its part in the labors of the little commonwealth with as much apparent activity and efficiency as its elders. It collects honey and builds a cell as adroitly in the first, as in the last, hour of its existence. And so it is with the species; the internal economy of a hive was just as marvellous in the days of Aristotle and Virgil, as in those of Huber. The reported cases of greater docility shown by the offspring of trained animals, than by the young of the same species when in their wild state, can all be explained from the fact, that most quadrupeds and birds are more or less prone to imitate the habits of those around them, so that they become more teachable by observing, from the moment of birth, the movements of the elder animals.

Instinct within its sphere transcends reason. — It is important to observe that the power of instinct, in many cases, quite transcends that of reason; if it differs from human intelligence, not in kind, but in degree only, it is undoubtedly the superior. Man may go to school to the dog, the swallow, and the bee, but he can never equal his teacher. Let him attempt, for instance, without the aid of any tools or machinery, and with the utmost economy of space and material, to construct a symmetrical hexagonal cell, closed at one end by a trihedral pyramid, each side of which is a rhombus, with its obtuse angles measuring precisely 109° 28′, and its acute angles 70° 32′. Without instruments or a pattern, he probably could not cut out such a rhombus with perfect accuracy after a thousand trials. But the bee does this before it is a day old. And in this statement of the task, the greatest difficulty of all is left out of it; we have solved the most abstruse problem in it, in order to make the performance more easy. In order to make the cell with as little wax and space as possible, it is necessary that the angles of the rhombus should have precisely these dimensions, and no other. It was only after the invention of the integral calculus that man was able to determine the angles required for this purpose, or, in other words, to discover how far the wisdom of the bee transcends his own. In Virgil's time, the bee was wiser than the greatest human mathematician of its day.

Those who are familiar with the habits of animals can produce a multitude of other instances to show the vast superiority of instinct, in its proper and limited sphere, over the best efforts of human reason; especially when we make the proper qualification, that the animal usually works without instruments of any kind, except those furnished in its own body, which affords nothing to be compared, in point of convenience, with the human hand. But I give one other case, which needs not this qualification; it is found in the explanation of the proverbial phrase, "a bee line." Remove a man blindfold several miles from his home, by a route with which he is entirely unacquainted, and require him to return to his own door by a mathematically straight line. The bee will do so; but a man's path under such circumstances would probably be rather crooked. And the difference between them cannot be explained on the supposition of the insect's greater sharpness of vision, or by the greater elevation at which it flies; let the hive be in the midst of a forest, so that the intervening trees hide it when one is a rod off in any direction, and the bee still flies straight to its home.

> "'But honest Instinct comes, a volunteer,'
> Sure never to o'ershoot, but just to hit;
> While still too wide, or short, is human wit."

Instinct works in a narrow sphere. — The consideration of this manifest preëminence of instinct, *in its limited sphere*, over reason, was necessary, in order to put in a proper light the next peculiarity of it which I have to notice, and which certainly divides it by a very broad line from any thing in the mental constitution of man. *Instinct is limited to a very few ends*, mostly to those which are essential to the preservation of the animal itself, or of its species. It works in a prescribed and narrow path, to accomplish these purposes and no others; its methods are invariable, or nearly so, its power of adapting itself to circumstances being confined within a very narrow range Take the animal out of its sphere, and its mental endowments cease to be even comparable with those of man. It falls infinitely far below him. The bee, which in certain tasks seems wiser than a Euclid or an Arkwright, is, when compelled to labor for any other purpose than that for which nature has specifically adapted it, more stupid than an idiot. If one accidentally flies into a room through the lower half of an open window, and, seeking to return, happens to strike against the glass above, it will continue buzzing about and knocking its head against the same pane oftentimes for an hour, though it would find free egress a few inches below.

Instinct does not adapt itself to circumstances. — Again, the instinct often continues to act *when the occasion for its exercise has ceased*, so that its operations are unmeaning and purposeless. Thus, a squirrel, imprisoned in a wire cage, if it has received more nuts than its appetite craves for the moment, will scratch diligently at the bottom of its cage, and then place a nut upon the spot; — in this way showing the continuance of the instinct which was needed only in its wild state, and its utter ignorance of the effect of a change of circumstances. A still more curious instance is that of the beaver, whose instincts seem more closely than those of any other animal to simulate human reason. "The building instinct," says Dr. Carpenter, "shows itself even when the beaver is in captivity, and in circumstances in which it can be of no use. A half-domesticated individual, in the possession of Mr. Broderip, began to build as soon as it was let out of its cage, and materials were placed in its way. Even when it was only half-grown, it would drag along a large sweeping-brush, or warming-pan, grasping the handle with its teeth, so that the load came over its shoulder; and would endeavor to lay this with other materials, in the mode employed by the beaver when in a state of nature. The long and large materials were always taken first; and two of the longest were generally laid crosswise, with one of the ends of each touching the wall, and the other ends projecting out into the room. The area formed by the cross brushes and the wall he would fill up with boots, books, sticks, dried turf, or any thing portable. He would often, after laying on one of his building materials, sit up over against it, appearing to consider his work, or, as the country people say, to 'judge it'; this pause was sometimes followed by changing the material judged, and sometimes it was left in its place. After he had piled up his materials in one part of the room, for he generally chose the same place, he proceeded to wall up the space between the feet of a chest of drawers which stood at a little distance from it, high enough on its legs to make the bottom a roof for him; using for this purpose dried turf and sticks, which he laid very even, and filling up the interstices with bits of coal, hay, cloth, or any thing he could pick up. This last place he seemed to appropriate for his dwelling; the former work seemed to be intended for a dam."

"Other animals are, in like manner, occasionally conducted by their instincts to the performance of actions equally irrational, and quite incapable of answering the purpose which the particular instinct is destined to serve." In all that goes beyond the sensations of the present moment, in every thing that relates to the future, and therefore requires the use of means, which in a human being would imply sagacity and foresight, the several classes of brutes do *one thing in only one way*. Following that narrow path, they appear like prodigies of wisdom; remove them ever so little from it, and they again become — brutes. In this respect, the parallel between the human and the brute mind fails entirely; instinct is no longer to be compared with reason, but with a machine. The analogy here is perfect; a jenny or a mule can spin yarn much better than man could with the aid only of his fingers; but it cannot card, weave, or dress; it can do nothing but spin. A machine performs a single task, usually with wonderful speed, neatness, and precision; but its utility is limited to this single purpose. So a bee constructs its combs with admirable art; but it cannot build a hive, or house for these combs. It cannot fashion a *paper* house, like the wasp, or dig subterranean chambers for its home, like the ant. But the pliability of the human mind, its power of adapting itself to circumstances, is one of its most marvellous attributes. Sagacity shown in one case is a good test of general ability for all occasions. Increased facility in performing particular tasks is acquired by habit; but the mind is master also of its habits, forming or destroying them at pleasure.

Instinct capable of a few adjustments. — I do not say that instinct *is* the action of a machine, but only that it *resembles* this action more nearly than it does the curious, flexible, and far-reaching operations of reason. In one respect, it is like a cunningly devised engine which admits of several adjustments, so that, though it still performs but one kind of work, it allows of a few variations in its pattern and fabric. These variations are limited in extent, and never amount to a change of the main objects in view; but if accident, or man's device, interferes with the animal's *ordinary* mode of attaining that object, it will often *slightly modify* the operation, so as to get rid of the difficulty.*

* Sometimes it is essential for the purpose which the particular instinct is designed to answer, that there should be a certain degree of flexibility in that instinct. Thus, a certain kind of spider always spins a circular web, and must therefore have the power of affixing threads of different lengths to different portions of the circumference, wherewith to attach the web to the variously shaped openings in a wall, or among the branches of a tree or shrub, within which the web is to be supported. The marvellous power of instinct is often strikingly shown in the different expedients which this spider uses, to attach the web to the supports in its neighborhood with the greatest economy of labor and material. I once saw such a web, not more than six inches in diameter, which the spider had placed in one of the upper corners of an opening, about three feet long and two feet high, in the wall of a shed. Half of the circumference, it was obvious, was easily supported by prolonging a few of the radii a short distance, till they met the two nearest sides of the opening in the angle of which the web hung. But how was the opposite semi-circumference held up, without extending its radii two or three feet, to meet the two further sides of the opening? Single threads of this great length would be very apt to be broken, and could hardly be hauled taut enough to give the requisite stiffness to the fabric. On looking nearer to the web, however, I found that the instinct of the spider had hit upon an expedient which had not at first occurred to me. It had spun a stout thread diagonally across the angle within which the web was hung, in the direction of a tangent to the outer semi-circumference, and distant only an inch or two from the nearest point of that circumference. Two or three *guys*, also, were attached to different points of this diagonal thread, whence being carried to the adjacent sides

Though walking in a narrow path, it can still turn aside a little to the right or the left, so as to avoid an obstruction in the way. Honey-bees can alter their work just enough to avoid what may be termed the *ordinary* casualties of the hive. When extraordinary disorders in the combs take place, Huber tells us that they pull the grubs out of the cells to perish, demolish the structure, and begin anew.*

Instinct compared with habit.—Instincts have sometimes been called *innate habits*, and the parallel thus indicated appears a very just and striking one. Cuvier long ago remarked, that animals guided by instinct appear, like a man in a dream,

---

of the opening, and hauled taut, they served to stiffen that diagonal. Thus the circular web was inscribed in a triangle of the most convenient size, two sides of which were formed by the angle of the opening in the wall, while this ingeniously stiffened diagonal thread formed the third side. Any observer, by examining closely some of these circular webs, which he may find in any garden or neglected outhouse, will find various and equally ingenious expedients adopted to fasten it firmly, and with the greatest economy of material, to the nearest supports.

We have here, also, a good illustration both of an instinct's pliability within a certain range, and of its fixedness for every thing which lies beyond that range. The expedients for supporting a *circular* web must be almost infinitely varied, according to the exigencies of the locality where it is placed. But why does not this spider ever spin a *triangular* web, or one of any other form, as other spiders do, and thus avoid all trouble in suspending it in any place?

* "Bees cemented their combs, when becoming heavy, to the top of the hive with mitys, in the time of Aristotle and Pliny, as they do now; and there is every reason to believe that then, as now, they occasionally varied their procedures, by securing them with wax or with propolis only, either added to the upper range of cells, or disposed in braces and ties to the adjoining combs. But if, in thus proceeding, they were guided by reason, why not, under certain circumstances, adopt *other* modes of strengthening their combs? Why not, when wax and propolis are scarce, employ *mud*, which they might see the martin avail herself of so successfully? Or why should it not come into the head of some hoary denizen of the hive, that a little of the *mortar* with which his careful master plasters the crevices between his habitation and its stand, might answer the end of mitys? '*Si seulement ils élevoient une fois des câbanes quarrées*,' says Bonnet, when speaking as to what faculty the works of the beaver are to be referred; '*mais ce sont éternellement des câbanes rondes ou ovales.*'"—*Kirby and Spence.*

to be haunted by one idea, or, like a somnambulist, to perform a very difficult task without being conscious of it. In the human mind, frequent repetition appears to unite the parts of a long and complex mental process into one whole, so that the several required volitions follow each other with as much order and facility as if they were links of the same chain. There is no delay in order to dwell on any part of the operation, and consider what is to be done next. The needful step is suggested precisely at the right moment, and instantly performed, so that no effort of the will seems to have been necessary, and we say that the whole was done unconsciously. Thus, an absent-minded man may undertake a long walk by a familiar path, his mind being occupied all the while with some knotty subject of thought, which has nothing to do with the cause of his excursion; and he arrives safely at the desired point, without being aware of the bodily exertion he has made, or of having attended to any object on the road, or to a single incident of the journey. There may have been several diverging routes, and he always selected the right path, without being aware that he exercised a choice. At each step, a distinct volition was required to lift his foot from the ground; but he was not conscious of any exertion either of the will or the body. It seems as if there was a latent idea in his mind, never rising into the sphere of consciousness, which still governed every motion of the will, and brought out the desired result at last, though the man himself was as ignorant of the process as if he had been a mere machine.*

---

* "The effect of habit," says Dr. Holland, "in giving an automatic character, almost like an instinct, to certain groups of muscular actions — as in speaking, walking, and the other numerous and complex movements of the limbs — is absolutely necessary to human existence, and admirably suited to this necessity." In comparing Habits with Instincts, he afterwards observes, an essential point is their respective relation to the Will. Instinct at first is independent of the Will, though afterwards often modified by it; on the other hand, the actions which were at first entirely controlled by the Will, as they become habitual, gradually lose this dependence, and at last seem wholly involuntary. "It is well worthy of note,

Instinct is unconscious of the ends it subserves. — Now the bee, in constructing a comb, works like a somnambulist, or like this person laboring under absence of mind. It reflects not upon the object of its labors; for having had the experience but of one season, or perhaps of one day, it knows not what that object is. Foresight it has not, unless it be the foresight of a god rather than a man; for human foresight is nothing but the reflection of past scenes upon the mirror of the future.

> "The lamb thy riot dooms to bleed to-day,
> Had he thy reason, would he skip and play?
> Pleased to the last, he crops the flowery food,
> And licks the hand just raised to shed his blood."

It is not conscious of design or contrivance; for this implies preconceived ideas of ends not yet realized, and such ideas, we have seen, it cannot possess. The bee toils on just as unconsciously as the man moves his limbs in that dreamy walk; *there is a purpose, a useful end, to be obtained by the exertion; but neither of them is aware of it at the moment.* In the man, indeed, the purpose was preconceived, and will come back to his mind at the end of the walk. The bee knows nothing of a purpose, but toils on as an humble instrument in the hands of another. Its vocation is that only of the common laborer, to bring bricks and mortar for the construction of those wonderful cells whose real Maker and Architect is Divine, and who appears, in this instance at least, if not in every other, constantly superintending and controlling his own works.

> "Esse apibus partem divinæ mentis, et haustus
> Ætherios, dixêre; deum namquė ire per omnes
> Terrasque, tractusque maris, cœlumque profundum:
> Hinc pecudes, armenta, viros, genus omne ferarum,
> Quemque sibi tenues nascentem arcessere vitas."

---

how closely the results continually approach to each other, though thus remote, and even opposite, in their source." "The closest approximation of Habits and Instincts is undoubtedly shown in the tendency of the former to become hereditary — a fact variously proved both as to bodily and mental habits; and equally curious and important in reference to the whole economy of animal life." — *Mental Physiology*, pp. 223, 224.

And here we see an obvious reason why the instincts of animals are not susceptible of education or improvement. The operation that is continued from the mere force of habit, will never be improved. If the pedestrian suddenly quickens or slackens his pace, it is a sure sign that he has begun to think about the object of his journey. So a practised musician may play a familiar tune, without appearing to bestow any attention upon it, — merely from habit. But he will make no progress in his art by *such* exercise. In order to improve, he must pause and dwell upon the process, note the defects in his execution, and by distinct and conscious effort try to remove them. The brutes, also, acting under their instincts, as men do when guided only by habit, ignorant of the objects of their toil, and therefore never reflecting upon the best means of obtaining those objects, perform their last labor precisely like their first. Their physical powers improve as they grow to maturity; but their *modes* of operation are never altered.

Instinctive distinguished from imitative acts. — I say nothing of the feats which animals may be trained by man to accomplish, because these may all be traced to the blind and unconscious faculty of imitation or mimicry, and to the continued association of reward or punishment with certain actions. An animal blindly repeats some movement which a man performs only from a perception of its true meaning and purpose; we must not therefore attribute such a perception to the brute. Parrots may be taught to articulate; but they do not thereby learn to talk. A monkey, in a painter's studio, will seize his brush, and cover the walls of the room with unmeaning scrawls; it imitates the physical act of the painter, but without any glimpse of its intention and real character. The teachableness of the different classes of animals seems to depend on the comparative strength of this imitative propensity; and as many of the exhibitions of this propensity, even in man, are blind and purposeless, we may reasonably conclude that they are always so in the brute.

The acquired habits of *domesticated* animals mostly override and conceal their natural inclinations, so that they do not seem o possess as many or as striking instincts, as some *wild* brutes which are certainly inferior to them in the scale of being. Many of these instincts, also, are of a social character, and therefore can be manifested only when the individual is in the wild herd with its fellows. But, *in one degree or another, instinct is displayed by all the animals inferior to man.* We find the plainest marks of it precisely where we should expect, among the means provided for the continuation of the species. What directs the young colt, or the calf, at once, to the only proper source of its nourishment? or why does it not attempt to crop the herbage for food, like its dam? The stratagems used by wild beasts to ensnare their prey must all be attributed to instinct, as each species uses but one or two forms of such artifice, and shows little or no power of adapting them to circumstances. How many other instincts are naturally conjoined with these, it is impossible to tell, as they are freely manifested only in the wild state, and are concealed by artificial habits when they are subject to the care and observation of man.*

Instinct teaches the brutes how to see. — In one respect, indeed, all animals are admirably fitted for the exigencies of their situation immediately after birth, while the human infant is left to the slow inductions of experience under the guidance of its elders. Man's first step in education is to acquire the use of his own eyes, or to learn how to *see.* It is a fact now firmly established, both by *a priori* reasoning and observation, that the eye directly sees nothing but colors, and cannot perceive immediately either distance, figure, dimension, or situation. Colors

* "Wherever there is organization, even under the simplest form, there we are sure to find instinctive action, more or less in amount, destined to give the appropriate effect to it. This is true throughout every part of the animal series, from Man and the Quadrumana down to the lowest forms of infusorial life. When we consider how vast this scale is — crowded with more than a hundred thousand recognized species, exclusively of those which fossil geology has disclosed to us — we may well be amazed by this profuse variety of instinctive action, as multiplied in kind as are the organic forms with which it is associated, and all derived from one common Power." — Holland's *Mental Physiology*, p. 206.

are the only visible things, just as sounds alone are audible experience teaches us, from slight variations or peculiarities of these, to *infer* the distance, magnitude, and other tangible qualities of the objects which possess or emit them. This fact has been demonstrated by experiments on persons born blind and subsequently restored to sight, and may be confirmed by watching the movements of an infant soon after birth. Place some bright or gayly colored toy before its eyes, and its looks and movements instantly betray its desire to grasp it; and if the object be actually placed in its hands, it will hold it firmly, and seem unwilling to relinquish it; but hold it a little way off, and the hands grope for it seemingly at random, or so as to show the infant's entire ignorance of its true distance and position. If its bungling attempts be attributed in part to ignorance of the right mode of using its arms and limbs, this only places in a stronger light its inferiority for the time to the young brute. In a beautiful experiment made by Galen, a kid, just snatched from the matrix of its dead mother, used its limbs at once with perfect facility and success, and with the characteristic movements of its species. Like the newly born colt or calf, also, it walked with freedom, inspected objects near at hand, and avoided those which were in its way, — not, as in the case of man, with an acquired judgment, but from an instinctive knowledge of their true position.

Man has no instincts properly so called. — Now, if in so important a respect as the use of his eyes, on which man is dependent for safety at almost every moment of his existence, while by their aid alone his other faculties attain their full development, — if on this cardinal point, man is left entirely to the slow deductions of experience, we may well believe that, in no other respect, with him, is instinct made to supersede the use of reason. We are led to conclude, then, not only that all the lower animals are copiously endowed with instincts, but that man is absolutely devoid of them, and is left to be guided by reason alone. The utter helplessness of the human infant, when compared with the young of other animals, appears in nothing so strongly as in its inability to see, even when the eyes are opened, and their physical structure is perfect. In fact, there is no instance commonly adduced to prove that man is ever governed by instinct, except the first mode in which he receives food; and even this is admitted to be, at most, but a *transient* instinct, given to provide for his safety in the first helpless hours of his existence. It is very doubtful, however, whether even this temporary impulse can properly be called instinctive. Recurring to the definition already given, is it certain that this is an instance of action not pleasurable in itself alone, but useful only as a means for some ulterior object? That mere muscular exertion is pleasant in itself, is evident enough to one who observes the uneasiness of infants, and the strange gymnastic experiments of children of a little larger growth. If a small object be placed in the hand of an infant, its little fingers readily close around it, apparently from the mere pleasure of calling the muscles into activity. The sphincter muscle of the mouth may do the same, when any object comes within its grasp; and then the child needs but a single inspiration, which automatically recurs at every instant, in order to have its first pleasant experience of the gratification of appetite. When this pleasure has been a few times repeated, the habit, aided by the uneasiness of hunger, becomes so strong, though at the same time so blind, because the intellect is as yet not at all developed, that the infant eagerly sucks every object presented to its mouth. It is this eagerness, manifested at so early a period, which has led most observers to consider the action as instinctive. But Dr. Carpenter, an eminent physiologist, expressly refers this act of suction to the reflex function of the nerves, thus considering it to be as mechanical as the shutting of the eyelid, or the beating of the heart; for infants that have been born destitute of brain, and have lived for some hours, and other animals' young whose brain had been removed, have readily sucked a moistened finger, when introduced between their lips. Dr. Henry Holland, also, who is high authority on such a subject, observes that "the first sucking of the infant is probably a simple reflex action, following an impression on the nerves of sense."

It has now been conclusively shown, if I mistake not, that a class of phenomena are manifested by the lower animals, which may be as sharply distinguished from the effects of human reason, on the one hand, as from those of appetite and natural desire, on the other; and these phenomena are attributed to a power which we call *instinct*. Give it any other name, and it will answer the purpose equally well. All the lower animals manifest it; man never does; — these are the only propositions with which we are now concerned. All the actions of man, which have been loosely considered or described as instinctive, may be referred either to the powers of organic life, — that is, to mechanical forces, — or to the teachings of experience, or to the class of appetites. Human nature shows no trace whatever of that marvellous power which governs the bee in the construction of its cell, and guides the migrating bird to its winter home. But man is the only being who is not under its influence; every other animal, from the noblest quadruped to the humblest insect, gives frequent indications of its presence and control.

Instinct probably never united with reason. — So numerous and striking, indeed, are the manifestations of it by every species, that there appears good reason to doubt whether it is ever mingled, even in them, with what is properly called *intellect;* whether all the reputed cases of sagacity and intelligence in the higher animals may not be referred, after all, into a mere blind propensity *to imitate actions, the meaning and purpose of which they cannot understand,* or into an instinct *more flexible and varied,* indeed, than that of the lower tribes, but which is still seen to be radically different from reason. Without entering into this difficult discussion, I will merely allude to the striking improbability of the lower animals being endowed with reason, which they need to exercise *only on infrequent and extraordinary emergencies,* while all the *ordinary* occasions of their being — their wants, dangers, and the continuation of their species — are provided for by the lower attributes with which they are specially endowed. These certainly suffice for the most wonderful works that are performed by them; the whole insect tribe unquestionably knows no other guide than instinct and if this power be enough to account for the actions of the ant and the bee, we hardly need seek any other key to the supposed sagacity of the dog and the elephant, as they also possess it, and it governs nearly all their conduct.

But the negative on the other side is more easily supported, and by direct evidence. However it may be with the brute, reason is not united with instinct (properly so called) in man. The human intellect is pure and unmixed. It may be obscured by appetite, or stormed by passion; habit may render its operations so swift and easy, that we cannot note and remember their succession. But when free from these disturbing forces, it acts always with a full perception of the end in view, and by a deliberate choice of means aims at its accomplishment. We have the immediate testimony of consciousness, that we never select means until experience has informed us of their efficacy, and never use them but with a full knowledge of their relation to the end.

Summary of the characteristics of instinct.—Each of the qualities of instinct on which I have remarked, is a peculiarity of it in respect to reason, and serves more or less to distinguish it from that faculty; while the aggregate of these peculiarities shows conclusively that the difference between the two is fundamental. This will appear more clearly from a summary of the several points that have been considered. It has been shown, then, that instinct exists before experience, and is wholly independent of instruction; that it is not susceptible of education or improvement of any kind, either in the individual or the race; that it works successfully towards important and remote ends by the use of complex and laborious means, yet without any apparent consciousness of the difference between means and ends; that it acts, in truth, by impulse, and not through reflection,—at least, as much so as the man who has gained by habit the power of performing a long operation without reflecting on any part of it; that it is limited to a few objects, and out of the narrow sphere of work required for these objects it is altogether useless; and that, consequently, it appears in the same animal, and at the same time, both as the most brutish stupidity and as the highest wisdom, for some of its creations shame the greatest ingenuity of man.* As we are confessedly ignorant of the internal constitution of both faculties, reason and instinct, and are compelled to judge of them exclusively by their outward manifestations, it is difficult to conceive of two powers which should appear more unlike.

Beings guided by instinct are not moral beings. — It is vain to form conjectures respecting the inward essence, or ultimate cause, of a faculty which appears to human reason so anomalous. Yet one or two points, perhaps, may be satisfactorily made out respecting the mental constitution of brutes, which will afford us a glimpse of the final end of their being. Whether instinct be the mere action of a curious machine, or the effect of the constant agency and promptings of the Deity, or the working of some still more secret principle which is nowhere manifested but in animal life, it is not a free and conscious power of the animal itself in which it appears and works. It is, if I may so speak, a foreign agency, which enters not into the individuality of the brute. The animal appears subject to it, controlled and guided by it, but not to possess and apply it by its own will for its own chosen purposes. We cannot conceive of wisdom apart from reflection and consciousness; there is an absurdity in the very terms of such a statement. The skill and ingenuity, then, which appear in the works of the lower animals are not referable to the animals themselves, but must proceed from some higher power, working above the sphere of their consciousness. This assistance is meted out to them for specific and limited ends, and has no effect on the rest of their conduct, which is governed by their own individuality. In its highest functions, the brute appears only as the blind and passive instrument of a will which is not its own.

---

* "The absolute hereditary nature of instincts, — their instant or speedy perfection, prior to all experience or memory, — their provision for the future without prescience of it, — the preciseness of their objects, extent, and limitation, — and the distinctness and permanence of their character for each species, — these are the more general facts on which our definition must be founded." — Holland's *Mental Physiology*, p. 201.

"And Reason raise o'er Instinct as you can,
In this 'tis God directs, in that 'tis man."

The power is granted to it for a time, but is not susceptible of improvement by practice while in its keeping, is invariably applied in the same way, and with perfect success, and is withdrawn as soon as the purposes for which it was given are answered. No moral character is attributable to a faculty which is unconsciously exerted, and no moral aim can exist where progress or change is impossible. When deprived of this extraneous power, or viewed apart from it, the brute appears in its true light, as the creature of a day, born not for purposes connected with its own being, but as an humble instrument, or a fragmentary part, in the great circle of animated nature, which, as a whole, is subservient to higher ends.*

---

* I hardly need observe how much the phenomena considered in this chapter tend to confirm the doctrine of immediate divine agency. This was the opinion of Sir Isaac Newton, who, in the famous 31st Query, or General Scholium to his "Optics," says, "the instinct of brutes and insects can be nothing else than the wisdom and skill of a powerful, ever-living Agent, who, being in all places, is more able by his will to move the bodies within his boundless uniform sensorium, and thereby to form and reform the parts of the universe, than we are by our will to move the parts of our bodies." Even Müller, the physiologist, says, "The cause of instinct appears to be the same power as that on which the first production of the animal, and the perfection of its organization, depend. The instinctive acts of animals show us that this power, which thus forms the whole organization with reference to a determinate purpose and in accordance with an unchanging law, has moreover an action beyond this; they prove that it influences the voluntary movements. That which is effected by the instinctive movements is equally in accordance with a determinate purpose, and as necessary for the existence of the species as the organization itself; but while, in the case of the organization of the being, the object attained formed part of the organism, in the case of the instinctive movements, it is something in the exterior world; the mental power of the animal is incited by the organic creative force to the conception and attempt to attain some special object."

Again, "it is further to be remarked that the realization of the ideas, images, and impulses, thus developed in the sensorium, is admirably facilitated by the organization of the animals. Both the internal impulse

CHAPTER II.

THE PRINCIPLES OF ACTIVITY IN HUMAN NATURE.

Summary of the last chapter. — The object of the last chapter was, by a brief inquiry into the mental constitution of the animals inferior to man, to bring out into a stronger light those peculiarities of human nature which show what is the purpose of our being in this life, and what are the leading features in the scheme of Divine Providence for the government of man. I do not forget that our first object is to show what are the moral attributes of God, and to ascertain if there is sufficient evidence to justify us in imputing to him those qualities of infinite wisdom and benevolence, of perfect justice and holiness which the religious sentiment within us instinctively requires in the person towards whom it is directed. But these qualities can be manifested to our eyes only in his works and ways; and it is by studying these, that is, by ascertaining what human nature is, how it is endowed, and what is the part which it has to perform in this stage of existence, that we can arrive at any certain and precise knowledge of the Divine nature. Now we are so much accustomed to take for granted a knowledge of the human constitution, both intellectual and moral, it is so much easier to

---

and the external organization being dependent on the same original cause, the form of the animal appears in complete unison with its impulses to action; it wills to do nothing which its organs do not enable it to do; and its organs are not such as to prompt to any act to which it is not impelled by an instinct." Thus, the indistinct sight of the mole, arising from the smallness of its eyes, which are also shielded by thick hairs, and the shape of its claws and feet, are admirably adapted to the subterranean life which its instincts impel it to lead. The instinct of the sloth urges it to climb trees and live in them, a mode of existence for which it is perfectly well fitted by the shape of its extremities, which allow it to walk on the ground only with great difficulty and awkwardness.

use our faculties in the study of external objects than of the mind itself, that, without some object of comparison or contrast, it is difficult to understand, or, at any rate, to have a clear and lively sense of, those endowments by which we are distinguished among God's creatures, and of the purposes for which these distinguishing attributes were granted to us. We see the work that is accomplished by brutes, and how they are fitted for its performance. We are conscious of the possession of higher faculties than theirs, and we seek to know how our task and our destiny differ from theirs; or whether, in truth, we have any task set to us, or any great end to obtain. The character and intentions of the Deity must appear most clearly from a comparative examination of the two higher orders of animated being which he has made.

One point I may now assume, as sufficiently established in the First Part of this discussion. It is inconsistent, — I do not say with *infinite* wisdom, for perhaps we are not justified at this stage of the argument in considering any of the attributes of God, except his duration, as infinite, — but it is inconsistent with the transcendent wisdom which is everywhere visible in the works of creation, to suppose that any thing was created in vain, or that a difference is established between two orders of being without any reason for that difference. To act with reference to improper or ill-chosen ends, is the part of imperfect intelligence; but to act without any end at all, is mere brutishness, or a sign of the absolute want of understanding. We cannot believe that the creation of man, or the constitution of his being in any respect, is as meaningless as seems the direction of the clouds that float athwart a summer's sky.

Discipline and self-development are the ends of human life. — A comparison of the human with the brute mind shows, first, that self-development is one of the great ends of our being here, and that the fulfilment of this purpose is left in a great degree to our own freewill. It is not enough that the intellect should be competent for its task; the work of preparation, or the act of rendering it competent, is itself the first object for which we are urged to any kind of exertion. Discipline and progress, not mere possession or enjoyment, is the great purpose of human life. The workings of instinct, if we look only at the importance and difficulty of the results obtained, often surpass the most strenuous efforts of the conscious mind. Man, as I have said, may go to school to the ant and the bee; in fact, there is hardly one of the inferior animals whose habits he may not study with a well founded hope of obtaining direction for his own labors. Why, then, is he not led, unconsciously and passively, as the brutes are, by the wisest and most effective means, selected without any effort of his own judgment and ingenuity, to the immediate accomplishment of far more brilliant results than he has ever yet worked out by the natural exercise of the faculties with which he is at present endowed? Why, for instance, after all his bitter experience in the matters of government and social institutions, and after the wisdom of thirty centuries has been exhausted in pondering upon the several problems of social philosophy, is he still unable to form a society which, in point of orderly arrangement, harmony, and effective coöperation for the general good, shall even approach the excellence of a community of bees? His faculties, his powers, both of body and mind, are unquestionably higher than theirs; the gregarious appetite or passion with him is as strong; and his happiness, if not his safety, is consequently as dependent as theirs on the perfection of the arrangements which may be made for living and working in company with his fellows. Why, then, has not the same Almighty Guide, who condescends to order and sustain the economy of a hive, placed man also, without any effort of his own, in a perfect social state, thus saving him from the disorder, contention, anarchy, and misrule, the long and painful recital and description of which now constitute the history of the human race? It were surely as easy to do this for man as for an insect; and why, then, is it not equally desirable in the two cases?

There can be but one answer to this question. It is, that an improved condition of society, *bestowed at once by the free gift of the Creator, instead of being attained by human trial and effort, is not an end so desirable as that very unassisted trial and effort*, however costly these may seem in respect to human happiness or mere enjoyment. He who complains of the necessity of this labor, and thinks it an impeachment of the goodness of God that the object cannot be acquired without it, really envies the condition of an insect, who is led blindfold, but in absolute security, to the fulfilment of the conditions of his existence. Will he consent to change places with it? I do not *yet* say that the lot of human beings, with all this necessity for toil, with all their liability to repeated mistakes and failures, and consequent sufferings, is still infinitely higher and happier than that of the lower orders of animal life, who walk darkling, but in safety; who have no liberty of choice, and so never mistake; who are God-guided, and therefore never fail of the end that is placed before them. The question of the comparative desirableness of the two situations, or the two schemes of life, as they may be termed, will depend on the result of our subsequent inquiry into the comparative value of discipline and enjoyment; of a character self-formed, and a nature endowed and wholly controlled, however happily, by another; of virtue united with freewill, and happiness enjoyed of necessity. But it is important here to understand the radical difference of the two situations, and the consequences which necessarily follow from the different endowments of man and the brute, and the dissimilar parts which they have to play upon the theatre of creation.

Why physical laws are permanent and uniform. — The plan of Divine Providence in the government of the universe must be studied as a whole. We cannot understand the economy of one of the parts without contrasting it with that of the others, and seeing how, in the several cases, different ends are obtained by different means, and one end, again, made subservient to another and higher one, so that all work together for good. Man is not the only denizen of the earth, nor is his happiness the single purpose, or even the highest purpose, of creation. His improvement, the perfecting of his moral character by his own choice and effort, may be this purpose; but this is the point to be established by our present inquiry. We have seen that the course of merely physical events, or the succession of what are called cause and effect in the material universe, is sustained and guided by the immediate agency of the Deity, and in every part it affords sufficient evidence of his wisdom and power. These events do not succeed each other at random, but according to what we term *natural law;* that is, in a fixed and orderly succession, similar antecedents being always followed by similar consequents. There must be some reason for this order and harmony, some purpose to be accomplished by it; for as each event is caused immediately, or without the intervention of secondary causes, its character is in nowise *necessarily* determined by the event which preceded it, but its occurrence, if the Deity had so willed, might have been marked by wholly unprecedented circumstances. I say that there must be some reason or purpose for this preservation of natural law, because all physical arrangements and adaptations, all the organisms of nature, as we have seen, reveal design; and it is inconsistent with the Divine wisdom that is evinced by this fact, to suppose that any thing is, or takes place, in vain, or without a purpose.

Permanency of law not needed for the brutes.— Now, this regularity of succession, or permanency of natural law, is not needed for any object connected with the animal kingdom, which is inferior to man. Brutes, as far as we can see, make no selection of means, and seem wholly ignorant, indeed, of the difference between means and ends. Every act performed by them appears to be done from immediate impulse, or desire relating to that act alone; they are literally slaves of the appetite of the present moment. Of the subserviency of the action to some result which is to take place hereafter, of its fitness to satisfy some future want, or to make provision for satisfying it, they have no knowledge. They profit not by experience, and indulge in no anticipations; or, at any rate, they never conform their conduct to anticipations of the future. The resemblance, then, of the present and future to the past, the fact that similar events may be expected under similar circumstances, is not needed for their guidance. Order and harmony are not for those who are incapable of comparing them with confusion and discord, and who could not profit by their continuance. Limited in its desires and feelings to the present moment, looking neither before nor behind, and so incapable, as we may suppose, of any purely intellectual exercise, the animal creation, excluding man, is still susceptible of enjoyment, and its pleasures, as they are evidently not of its own procuring, afford the clearest evidence of the benevolence of the Deity. The exigencies of their situation, the wants of their nature, and especially the continuance of their species, are all provided for, without any tax on their own skill or energy, by the same power and wisdom which ordained their existence.

Moral purpose of physical law. — The predominance of *law*, then, in the course of nature is intended for the guidance of man; we can imagine no other purpose for it. It is a portion of the scheme of Providence for the government of a being endowed with freewill, furnished with motives or inducements to action, supplied with a capacity for knowledge and means of instruction, and then left by his own effort to form his character and shape his destiny. There must be some object in such a plan of government beyond the mere production of happiness; that end, as has been shown, is sufficiently answered in the case of the lower animals by simpler means, by a less complex constitution of mind, and fewer adaptations to it of external circumstances. There must be some higher and more desirable attainment than the mere sense of pleasure or enjoyment for the time; and therefore, the subordination of the lower end to the higher, the occasional sacrifice of human happiness for the promotion of a worthier object, is perfectly consistent with the infinite benevolence of the Creator. Man, as has been shown, has no instincts whatever; appetites, desires, and affections, relating to objects immediately before him, he has in common with the brutes; and, like these, he is susceptible of pleasure from the gratification of them. But he has no means of foreseeing the exigencies of his situation, and, of course, no power of providing for his future wants, or of aspiring to any thing higher than this merely sensual pleasure, except from what his reason teaches him respecting the course of nature, and the laws which govern the succession of events. Reason proceeds only by experience ; and the lessons of experience would be of no worth, they would be mere reminiscences of past events, without any inferences deducible from them, unless the course of nature were uniform, and similar circumstances were always attended with similar results.

This doctrine, that the fixed laws even of material nature have a moral purpose, will appear to most persons, I am well aware, as a bold and fanciful speculation. The prevailing opinion, though it be not often openly avowed, is, that these laws have no object but to uphold the beauty and order, the stupendous mechanism, of the outward universe, one being subordinated to another, or included in it, and all working together in grand and complex harmony to keep up the perpetual cycle of events, and sustain the unity of the system of created things. This, I am sorry to believe, is the prevailing and increasing tendency of the physical science of the present day, — to reduce the study of nature to the determination of its laws or regularities of succession and arrangement, to maintain that any one of these principles has no object or function but its subserviency to a higher one, and that the widest generalization of them is the highest truth attainable by the human faculties.* According-

* One great cause of infidelity at the present day is the want of consistency, the apparent contradiction, between most persons' religious views and their scientific opinions, or their ideas of the course of nature and the operation of physical causes. The doctrine of an immediately superintending Providence, ordering all events for the moral instruction and government of man, cannot be reconciled with the idea of a chain of events, each link of which is determined by an inherent necessity, growing out of its relations to those which precede and follow it in the succession.

Religion requires us to consider ourselves as the objects of a Divine Providence, of an infinite superintending care, which orders all events for good. This doctrine is a necessary consequence of a belief in the benevolence and justice of the Deity, and in his moral government of the world. A devout mind recognizes it almost instinctively as such, and considers all events, especially those which concern one's personal welfare or happiness, as dispensations which are required for his instruction or improvement. It discerns *a moral purpose in all things*, believing that they *were specially*

ing to this view, either the material creation had no purpose beyond itself, or that purpose is not discoverable by man; we must look upon it, indeed, as a grand and marvellous work; but

---

designed to produce a certain effect on the character and heart. It subordinates the physical to the moral; regarding the former as means, and the latter as an end. Life is a gift and a trust, to be exercised for certain purposes; death is a warning, and a token that, in a particular case, these purposes are accomplished. Every cause of affliction or rejoicing has an errand and a meaning, and it is our duty to consider it as such, to try to read its lesson, and apply it for the regulation of our hearts and lives. This is the view which the believer takes, in profession at least, of the affairs of this world, and of its moral government by the Almighty; it is the view which religion *requires* him to take, if it be not reduced to a mere speculative belief in the existence of a God, who is no further concerned with the lot of mankind than as he originally created them, endowed them with certain faculties, and placed them upon the earth to determine their destiny by their own wisdom and their observation of the workings of nature.

But in practical life and the management of their daily concerns, as well as in scientific investigations, most persons act upon a theory which is the very opposite of this religious doctrine. They look upon the course of events as *inevitably determined,* from the beginning, *by the inherent constitution of things* and by the relations of objects and circumstances to each other, *without reference to the merit or demerit of accountable beings, and without regard to any moral lesson or purpose whatsoever.* Every occurrence in the outward universe is an efficient cause, which is necessarily followed by an effect exactly proportioned to it; and this effect, again, being causal in its nature as to the events which follow it, inevitably acts upon them all, and has a share in determining their character, so that its consequences might be traced, — if we had the power of distinguishing them from the similar operating causes with which they are mingled, — in an ever-widening stream, through all time. Life and death, motion and rest, health and disease, growth, progress, decay, and restoration, are all necessarily determined by each other and by attendant circumstances, and follow each other in perpetual succession; moral good or evil having, at most, a power too small to be appreciated in checking the current or altering its direction. Man himself, though his freewill be admitted as *one* of the causes which affect his lot, is still operated upon by so many other and more powerful ones, that he seems like a leaf floating upon the stream, and hurried away by it, he knows not whither. His birth and death, to recur to a former illustration, were both determined ages before by the altered position of a grain of sand. He is for ever complaining that he is the sport of circum-

after we have explored all its recesses and fathomed its lowest depths, the only impression left on the mind is a vague feeling of wonder and admiration. A more profound philosophy shows

---

stances, be his efforts and merits what they may. Even his character, if we may believe his murmurings, is formed rather *for* him than *by* him, through the accident of his birth in one or another country, in a higher or lower position of life, and through the circumstances which surrounded his infancy and childhood, before either body or mind had strength enough to contend against external influences. Who can discern, he asks, in moments of despondency, the watchfulness and justice of an ever-ruling Providence, or any moral intention whatsoever, amid this chaos of blind and conflicting forces? When in such a mood, the highest virtue within his reach, or the one most essential to his well-being, seems to be the Stoicism which teaches insensibility to hardship and wrong, and the stifling of all generous aspirations.

Do I exaggerate the inconsistency, then, between what may be called the religious and the practical view of life? Is it possible for the two to coexist in the same mind, without the individual becoming conscious at times that they are wholly irreconcilable with each other, so that he is reduced to the sad necessity of choosing between them? Either God governs the world, or the blind fatality of physical causes, operating through the powers inherent in every atom of brute matter, governs it; there is no other alternative. In his closet, or while listening to a sermon, or under the affliction caused by a recent bereavement, or in near view of approaching death, man accepts the former doctrine, and thinks that he believes it, though he has made no examination of the grounds on which it rests. But he goes out into the world, his mind, as he supposes, recovers its tone, he watches the course of events, judges of the future by the past, prepares to resist the force of circumstances or to yield to them, and acts altogether on the supposition that these events and circumstances depend on natural causes, which operate irresistibly, and were not designed or directed by a conscious being with any moral or spiritual purpose whatever.

And here, I apprehend, is the reason why scientific pursuits have not, of late, always tended to confirm the religious faith of those who were engaged in them. It is the business of the man of science to discover the invariable connections and sequences of facts and events, and to separate these from the casual, temporary, and irregular combinations which throw no light upon the nature of the phenomena. This attempt has been crowned of late years with the most brilliant success, the dominion of law, as it is called, having been everywhere established in the midst of what seemed to be the greatest variety and confusion. The laws of nature, we are told, admit of no exceptions; seeming anomalies and contradictions,

us that the object of God's works is *not merely to astonish but to teach*. To borrow the eloquent words of Dr. Channing "Mind is God's first end. The great purpose, for which an

---

when further studied, are found to exemplify a higher law, or to come from the mingled operation of two or more principles, so that the apparent exception confirms the rule. But the moral effect or tendency of a phenomenon is not found to be one of its invariable characteristics, and so, even when observed, it is considered only as a fortuitous coincidence, which indicates nothing as to the fixed relations of events, and therefore comes not within the field which the student of nature endeavors to survey. The mere separation of the moral from the physical sciences, and the division of labor which assigns one class of men exclusively to the study of the latter, necessarily draw off their attention from those observations and inquiries which give a meaning and a purpose to natural phenomena, and which lead us from the study of this fabric of the universe up to the character and intentions of its Almighty Architect. If this search after the necessary and immutable relations of things, in which the followers of physical science are wholly absorbed, has led many of them to doubt whether man's own nature be not subject to a like inevitable control with that which governs the fall of an atom and the courses of the planets, and so to reduce the human will to a phenomenon of the same class with gravitation, all the effects of which may be predicted beforehand from its known laws, why should we wonder that most of them practically regard external nature as mere mechanism, which has no motive power save two or three inherent and inexplicable forces, and is strictly limited to the production of mechanical results.

In opposition to this view, I have endeavored, in the First Part of this work, to prove that *physical laws* are no causes at all, but are mere expressions of the order and uniformity of physical phenomena, so that to attribute efficient causation to them is, in fact, an abuse of words, or a meaningless statement; and that all the phenomena are directly produced by the immediate action of the Deity. In this Second Part, I proceed to show, *first*, that the physical laws themselves, or the order and uniformity of events in nature, have a *general* and exclusively moral purpose, being intended solely for the guidance of man; and, *secondly*, that they have a *specific* moral purpose, many or all of them being intended to enforce upon man the observance of the moral law or the commands of God. Having proved before, that God works immediately in nature, we now show that the effects of his agency are not merely physical, but moral. Not only order and uniformity, but justice and benevolence, are the laws of his creation. The lessons which the universe teaches are addressed to the conscience, no less than to the intellect, of man.

order of nature is fixed, is plainly the formation of mind. In a creation without order, where events would follow without any regular succession, it is obvious that mind must be kept in perpetual infancy; for in such a universe, there could be no reasoning from effects to causes, no induction to establish general truths, no adaptation of means to ends; that is, no science relating to God, or matter, or mind; no action, no virtue."

Analysis of the principles of human action. — As we are compelled to admit, then, that there is a higher purpose in the Divine government than the mere promotion of happiness, that end being sufficiently provided for in the constitution of the lower animals, we come to an examination of what Dugald Stewart calls "the active and moral powers of man," as our means of discovering what that purpose is. The first fact that strikes us here is, that most of *the lower incitements to action* — all the *appetites*, and most of the *desires* and *affections* — *are common to the human and the brute mind.* They involve no exercise of reason; they are blind, but unerring, in their operation, and they supply a stimulus for exertion, which is either constant, or recurs at frequent intervals. Their indulgence brings with it certain consequences of good or evil, according as their proper limits have been observed or transgressed; but *the perception of such consequences is not necessary to their vitality or efficiency as motives to action.* This will be readily admitted in regard to the appetites, such as those of hunger and thirst, for instance. They first manifest themselves by a sense of uneasiness, which subsides, and is followed by a feeling of enjoyment, as soon as they are gratified. Afterwards, indeed, the recollection of this enjoyment will be associated with the primitive craving, and may lead us to stimulate or provoke it with a view to the pleasure which is to come from its indulgence. But this association was not needed to excite the appetites at first; and though it may heighten, it certainly does not wholly create, the pleasure which they subsequently afford.

Final cause of the lower impulses to action. — The only other remark needed as to these original impulses is, that their adaptation to the necessities of the body, their graduated and periodically recurring influence, is in itself a beautiful instance of design. Life is preserved by coupling with that which is necessary for its preservation an imperative, but blind *desire*, which is *not subject to the will*, and is thus guarded against the effects of inattention or carelessness. The uncertainty of the voluntary action of mind, the intermittent and fitful character of attention and reason, is not permitted to hazard the performance of those acts on which our continued existence depends. The appetites are aided by other propensities, tending either to action or repose, which are equally blind, and go to keep up that salutary medium between sluggishness and undue exertion, which is necessary for the health both of body and mind.

Purpose and function of the affections and desires. — The desires and affections, which I come next to consider, are distinguished from the appetites in so far as they do not take their rise from the body, nor operate periodically; but they agree with them in being *independent of reflection and calculation*, and in *tending directly towards specific objects as their ultimate ends.* We can give no further account of them, nor explain their preference of one object over another, otherwise than by saying, that such is the constitution of our being. Jouffroy calls them the primitive and instinctive tendencies of human nature, which show themselves in man almost from the first moment of his existence, and develop and strengthen themselves with every step that he takes towards maturer years. Among these original desires may be mentioned the love of *knowledge*, of *society*, of *approbation*, of *power*, and many other things, the number of which will depend on the fineness of our analysis of the several objects, or on our principles of classification. Why we should desire these things rather than their opposites, is a question that we are no more able to answer, than we are to tell why certain odors are pleasant, and others offensive, or why glass is transparent, and metal opaque. The desires exist in greater or less strength in different minds, but *in some degree, they are common to all minds;* for without them, man would sink into a state of entire inaction and repose, or rather, he would never have risen out of such a condition. He would still be capable of inert contemplation and reverie; a perpetual succession of loosely connected images and ideas might float for ever before the mind, and with these might be coupled a consciousness of existence, — all without the will ever being called into activity. But *to live and to think are not the only ends of our creation.* Action is necessary for our improvement and our happiness, and the necessary stimulus to action is supplied by these several desires, the number and variety of which open a wide field for effort, and permit many to labor side by side with less risk of interference.

These desires are among the earliest manifestations of the infant mind. They do not wait for the development of the intelligence, nor are the teachings of experience or the instructions of our fellow-beings needed to call them forth, or to keep them in exercise. The infant shows the love of society and of approbation almost as soon as the appetite of hunger. "Attend only," says a distinguished naturalist, "to the eyes, the features, and the gestures of a child on the breast when another child is presented to it; — both instantly, previous to the possibility of instruction or habit, exhibit the most evident expressions of joy. Their eyes sparkle, and their features and gestures demonstrate, in the most unequivocal manner, a mutual attachment. When further advanced, children who are strangers to each other, though their social appetite be equally strong, discover a mutual shyness of approach, which, however, is soon conquered by the more powerful instinct of association."

The desires are unselfish. — But a stronger proof of the primitive and unreflecting character of these desires is the fact, that most, if not all, of them are shown in various degrees of intensity by the lower animals. Emulation is the prevailing trait in the disposition of a horse, as the love of approbation is in that of a dog, and the desire for society in that of all the gregarious animals. In these cases, certainly, it is not the utility of the several objects that are aimed at, or the pleasure which they are capable of imparting, that is the foundation of the desire; for this pleasure is made known only by experience, the utility is discoverable by reason alone; and brutes are incapable of profiting by the one or the other. It is a proof of the goodness of God, that these animals and human beings are so organized, their sensibilities are such, that the gratification of these desires is generally accompanied by a pleasurable feeling, or a sense of enjoyment. But this is not a necessary accompaniment; we can easily conceive of a sensibility so constituted, that the fulfilment of the desire should be attended with pain instead of pleasure; and yet the desire would be not the less real, not the less a stimulus to action. In fact, under certain circumstances, in certain states of body or mind, the satisfaction of our longings does become a source of torment, instead of happiness; Heaven punishes us by granting our guilty prayers; and though this result be foreseen, though we have a moral certainty that more pain than pleasure will be the consequence of the accomplishment of our wishes, we persist in the effort. The vehemence of the desire conquers every thing, — even our regard for our own happiness.

The affections are original tendencies of our nature. — I have dwelt the longer on the uncalculating, and therefore, in one sense of the term, unselfish, nature of the original appetites and desires, in order to prepare the way for a similar conclusion (where it is more important) in regard to the last class of these primitive impulses which we have to consider, — namely, the affections. These are usually divided into *two* classes, according as their object is the communication of *enjoyment* or of *suffering* to our fellow-beings. In the first class are reckoned the affections of *kindred*, of *friendship*, *patriotism*, *pity*, *gratitude*, and the like; in the second are comprised *hatred*, *jealousy*, *envy*, and *revenge*, all of which, however, are more properly considered as modifications of the single principle of *resentment*. What benevolent purposes are answered by ingrafting these principles in the human constitution, is a point for subsequent consideration. My only present aim is to show that these affections, like the simple appetites and desires, are original tendencies of our nature, and point towards their several objects simply from an instinctive liking for those objects, and without any regard to the pleasure or pain which may attend the exercise of the affections themselves on the part of those who feel them; in other words, that there is such a thing as benevolent affection, original and unmixed. There is pleasure consequent on their entertainment, but a desire to receive that pleasure is not the reason why we entertain them. We do this because we cannot help it. Under certain circumstances, we are affected with love, pity, gratitude, or resentment, whether we will or no; we admit these feelings as necessarily as the understanding yields assent on the presentation of sufficient evidence. We act in accordance with them, not from any selfish desire of the pleasure or profit which such action will occasion to ourselves, but because the affection itself prompts us to act; and this prompting would be felt, though injury or death should be the consequence of yielding to it. Why has it ever been supposed that it was otherwise?

Origin of prudence or self-love. — To answer this question, I must explain the origin of the feeling of *self-love*, and the nature of *the selfish system* in morals, as it is called, which attempts to reduce all motives, and refer all conduct, to this single principle. As every appetite, desire, and affection, when gratified, brings with it a sense of enjoyment, *the sum of these several enjoyments constitutes our idea of happiness*. Experience of pleasure, of course, brings with it a desire of its recurrence; and as we wish that this pleasure should be as extensive and varied as possible, we are led to study the art of so combining and regulating our motives and actions, that one shall not interfere with another, and that the general result shall be the maximum of enjoyment. Reason teaches us often to sacrifice a less pleasure for a greater, or to postpone a momentary indulgence for a larger and more permanent good to be obtained hereafter. To borrow the language of a great moralist, "any condition may be denominated happy, in which the amount or aggregate of pleasure exceeds that of pain, and the degree of happiness depends upon the quantity of this excess." Reason, guided by experience, that is, by the materials afforded by the gratification of the several desires, decides upon the course of conduct which will raise this excess of pleasure over pain to the highest attainable point; and *to act from this rational and calculating regard for our own interest, is said to be the dictate of self-love.*

Prudence first distinguishes man from the brutes. — Here, first, in the active part of his nature, does man show his superiority over the brute. The latter, unable to profit by experience, and incapable of foresight, cannot regulate its actions by *a system, or plan of life,* but necessarily follows *the impulse or desire of the moment.* The complex and abstract idea of happiness lies beyond its power of conception. It cannot foresee even the enjoyment which will follow the gratification of its present appetite, but it acts under the immediate pressure of that appetite, almost as mechanically as a machine moves from the impulse given to it by a spring. *For all the lower animals, prudence is an impossible virtue; but with man, it is the dawning of his intellectual and moral life,* the first step which he takes as a rational and self-improving being. He *can* restrain the impulse of the moment, be it appetite, affection, or desire, till he can study the consequences of yielding to it, till he can remember what was the effect of a former gratification of it, till he can ascertain if there be not other objects which he desires more earnestly, while the attainment of them will be hindered or rendered impossible by the present indulgence. To act thus deliberately, with reflection and foresight, is the part of prudence; this is *the lowest* in the scale of virtues, for it ends in self; but it is also *the first,* for, *without it, the practice of any other virtue would seldom be possible.* By the exercise of it man first rises above the condition of the brutes, and manifests, not, indeed, a moral nature, properly so called, but the capacity of receiving such a nature, and of acting up to its dictates. Here, also, *where morality first becomes practicable,* was placed, as you will remember, *the decisive evidence of human freewill,* — in man's power of governing and restraining for a time the operation of motives, till he could consider and select from them a fitting principle of action.

How far self-love is legitimate. — *Prudence,* which I here use as synonymous with *self-love,* is only a well-considered and dispassionate regard for our own future welfare; and, as such, it is perfectly legitimate, and even commendable, when it interferes not with higher obligations. Its function is supervisory, and its sphere embraces all the lower incitements to action, which we have already considered. It is a governor and a judge among the appetites, affections, and desires; restraining, regulating, or indulging them, at the bidding of the sovereign reason. If it abdicates its throne, man becomes a mere brute, — that is, a slave to the impulses and passions of the instant. If it rules too absolutely, usurping or disregarding the authority of a higher faculty, namely, the conscience, then man becomes, not a brute, but a demon, or an utterly selfish being. There is much less danger of this perversion of the faculty than of the former one, for men yield far more readily to their immediate passions than to calculations of their future interest. "A regard to our own general happiness," says Sir James Mackintosh, the safest and most philosophical of all modern commentators upon the theory of ethics, "is not a vice, but in itself an excellent quality. It were well, if it prevailed more generally over craving and shortsighted appetites. The weakness of the social affections, and the strength of the private desires, properly constitute *selfishness*; — a vice utterly at variance with the happiness of him who harbors it, and as such condemned by self-love."

Explanation of the selfish system. — But the fact, that the lower incitements to action are under the government of prudence, and are directed with reference to our future welfare, has given rise to the monstrous theory in morals, that *man's whole conduct is determined by the love of self*, and that he is *incapable of disinterested action.* He seeks only his own interest, says Hobbes, and virtue, consequently, is but a name. The benevolent affections are placed on the same level with the private desires, such as those of emulation and revenge; because pleasure, or some ulterior advantage, follows the gratification of them, we are said to yield to them only from a view to our own happiness. The passions to which we give separate names differ from each other, according to Hobbes, only in their outward aspect, — that is, with reference to the different objects towards which they are turned; at bottom, they are but modifications of *the only true passion of which human nature is susceptible, — the love of self.* If we *honor* or *reverence* another being, he says, it is only because we are aware of his superior power, and we desire to conciliate his good-will. *Ridicule* is only an intense conception of our own superiority to the person who is laughed at. *Love*, even that of a mother for her child, is but prudent forecast, a lively anticipation of the services which may be hereafter rendered us by the loved object. *Pity* is the imagination of evil which may happen to ourselves, excited by contemplating the misfortunes of another. *To be charitable* is only to be proudly conscious of having power enough not merely to create our own happiness, but to promote the happiness of another. Thus, because the goodness of God has so ordered the course of events, and so formed our hearts and minds, that every kindly and noble feeling is its own reward, and every generous and virtuous action redounds even to the temporal advantage of the agent, does the perverse ingenuity of the theorist twist all these feelings into forms of selfishness, and represent the action as only simulating the virtues of which human nature is really incapable. Because honesty in the long run is the best policy, we are said to be honest only because we are politic, and dread the consequences of detected knavery.

Refutation of this system. — This repulsive and degrading theory could never have obtained the notice which it has received, if it had not been urged with great ability by Hobbes, a reasoner of singular acuteness, and one of the greatest masters of prose style in the English language. The refutation of it has already been laid before you, in the obvious fact, that *the primitive passions and desires all seek their several ends irrespective of the consequences of their gratification.* We claim no more for the social *desires* than for the *appetites.* A man drinks because he is thirsty, and not in order to preserve life, though death would be the consequence of an utter privation of liquids; just so, he seeks society because he is gregarious by nature, and not on account of the advantages he may derive from the coöperation of his fellows, signal as these advantages are found to be. In fact, he never could have known that society would be useful to him except from experience; and he could certainly have had no experience till a society was first formed. Men were first brought together, then, without a possibility of being acquainted with the only motives which, according to the selfish system, could ever bring them together.

Again, man is at one time benevolent or compassionate, just as he is revengeful at another, without regard in either case to the effect which giving way to the emotion may have upon his own well-being. When stung by a keen sense of wrong, he will often prosecute his revenge to the utter destruction of what are called his worldly prospects, and knowing all the while that he is rushing upon his ruin. So, if his pity is strongly excited, he will attempt to relieve the distress in a manner which a moment's reflection would have assured him would do great injury to himself and to society, without materially benefiting the object of compassion. It is plain, therefore, that *the benevolent affections are just as uncalculating and disinterested as their opposites, or those which tend to the harm of others, — and no more so.* In truth, a theory which represents the affection of a mother, when hanging over the cradle of her child, as dictated only by a selfish regard for the comfort and advantage which that child may hereafter afford to her declining years, hardly merits refutation. Why, the brute feels this affection, if we may judge from appearances, quite as strongly as the human being; and we know that the brute is incapable of calculating consequences.

The affections are not virtues. — I have dwelt thus long upon the selfish system, only to bring out into a stronger light the unreflecting and irrational character of all the direct incentives to action, including the affections and sentiments, as well as the appetites, and so to justify the arrangement of them under so low an attribute even as prudence or self-love; the sphere of conscience, or the proper domain of morality, being as yet hardly in sight. Our natural affections, as Dugald Stewart observes, "cannot be exalted into *virtues;* for in so far as they arise from original constitution, they confer no merit whatever on the individual, any more than his appetites or desires; — at the same time, there is a manifest gradation in the sentiments of respect with which we regard these different constituents of character. Our desires, although not virtuous in themselves, are manly and respectable, and plainly of greater dignity than our animal appetites. In like manner, it may be remarked, that our benevolent affections, although not *meritorious*, are highly *amiable*."

To follow the blind impulse of a sentiment or emotion which is not controlled or sanctioned by any higher faculty, is conduct little worthy of a rational being. Yet human nature is far more prone to this fault, than to the opposite excess of listening to the cautious whisperings of self-love, which looks not only to present gratification, but to future and permanent well-being. There is an exaltation in fine sentiment, a nobleness in the generous affections, which hurries away the will, before consequences can be estimated, or the claims even of justice can obtain a hearing. But such enthusiasm is usually barren of good results, and however amiable it may appear in the eyes of the unthinking, it must not arrogate to itself the rewards of self-sacrificing virtue. In such conduct, indeed, there is no abnegation of self; for without reflection and forethought, there can be no consciousness of any advantage that is resigned, or any enjoyment that is sacrificed. To act thus is the part rather of reckless and short-sighted selfishness, which covets the brief pleasure that always follows the immediate gratification of the impulse of the moment, whether that impulse tends to the welfare or the injury of our fellow-beings. It cannot be amiss to determine, as I have attempted to do, the true moral character of these original incitements to action, since it is part of the philosophy of the day, so called, to yield them implicit obedience. But I pass on.

Self-love subservient to conscience. — Prudence, or self-love, is distinguished from its rightful superior, the moral faculty, in this, — that it has regard only to the *outward* consequences of actions. It governs and directs the desires and affections with a view to the effects, whether near or remote, which their indulgence will have upon our future welfare. Its functions, therefore, are *rational*, but not properly *moral;* while the motives that it governs, as has been shown, are animal, for they are common to man and the brute. Prudence never considers the nature of the motive in itself, before it passes into action, but only questions whether it may be indulged to advantage in respect to the events which will follow its indulgence. It is the servant of conscience, then, which never looks beyond the inner man, and never speaks but with absolute authority.

The affections evince benevolent design. — Before considering the nature and functions of *conscience,* which is the only point wanting to complete our survey of the moral nature of man, it remains to be seen whether the affections are so constituted as to afford any indications of the goodness and the will of the Deity. As they are primitive in their character, or parts of the original constitution of our being, whatever adaptations may be found in them to the situation and wants of man are just as much proofs of design, as the most curious and useful contrivances in our animal frame. If they are found to work together, so that the ends toward which one is impelled by them severally do not conflict, but harmonize, and the general result is conduct which tends to the good both of the individual and the race, the arrangement certainly shows the wisdom and benevolence of the Designer even more clearly than these are seen in the material universe. If a finer analysis should show that some of the feelings in question are not original, but acquired, — that is, that they are not implanted at first in the infant mind, but necessarily spring up afterwards, under the influences to which that mind is always exposed, — this will make no difference as to the force or relevancy of the argument. It is enough for our purpose, that the affection is necessarily developed sooner or later, and that it tends to good. It may be, for instance, that many of the kindly sentiments which are usually distinguished by different names spring from the same root, and are, in truth, but various forms of one primitive feeling; their subsequent divergence may be accounted for by the association of ideas, or that law of our nature which often transfers attachment from the end to the means. As the miser loves gold at first only for the pleasures that it will purchase, but finally for its own sake, so it may be, that friendship is but the transfer to persons of the feelings of complacency and enjoyment first produced by the sense of mutual obligation, and by the wish for their recurrence. Thus there may be a selfish element in the emotion at first; but it purifies itself by indulgence and habit, and is not perfected till it amounts to self-sacrifice.

It is obvious enough, that *the affections of kindred*, especially those of parent and child, are chiefly useful for the preservation of the race; and this we may suppose to be the leading purpose of their creation. But observe, further, how *they coöperate with the social feeling*, and first make *society* possible, by affording a type of it in the *family*. Submission to paternal authority paves the way for obedience to a political head; and the love of kindred needs but little expansion to become a love of country. Since the affections weaken as they expand, the most general of all, *philanthropy or universal benevolence*, is quickened and made intense by *sympathy*, a principle which is as unquestionably primitive or innate as the love of offspring, and is so universal and salutary in its operation, that an eminent moralist has taken it to be the foundation of our ethical nature, or the fountain of all the virtues. It is the proper antagonist or corrective of *selfishness*, as under its impulse we instinctively make the sorrows and pleasures of others our own, and in turn feel our own joys heightened, and sufferings diminished, through the consciousness that they are shared by our neighbors. The endowment of the human mind with this principle alone, peculiar and striking as its effects are seen to be when we reflect upon them, seems to me as plain an indication of the benevolence of the Deity, and of his will that men should cultivate kindness and affection for each other, as the explicit enunciation of the same truths in Scripture.

Respective claims of the different affections. — All the relations in which we stand to our fellow-beings have separate affections corresponding to them; and our sense of the duties which are incumbent upon us in each case, is developed and confirmed by this association. *The strength of the affection may generally be taken as a safe measure of the duty. Parental love* is stronger than *friendship; sympathy with distress* is more vivid than *sympathy with enjoyment; the love of family* is more powerful than *the love of country;* and *the love of country,* again, is more urgent than *universal benevolence.* Few will deny, that the scale of duties exactly corresponds to this gradation; so that, even if reason did not operate to show the comparative utility of the performance of these duties, we should have what might be called an instinctive appreciation of their relative importance. Theorists, it is true, have often tried to invert this natural order of the virtues; but, as might be expected, with small success. Thus, circumstances led the ancients to exaggerate the merits of *patriotism;* and even Plato held the opinion, that the indulgence of the domestic affections unfitted men for the discharge of their political duties; he went so far as to propose, on this account, that children should be separated from their parents immediately after birth, and brought up at the public expense. The enthusiasm of modern times has taken a somewhat different course; *universal philanthropy* is now the fashionable virtue, and it is preached up to an extent that throws all the most private affections into the shade, even if it does not menace their extinction. But the duties which lie within the narrowest circle are most frequent in their recurrence, and so tend to keep up the habit of virtue; while the benevolent feeling which can take in no less an object than the whole human race, for want of striking occasions on which to manifest itself, is apt to be wasted in speculation and magnificent professions. There is deep meaning in the language of our Saviour, when he inculcates *love to all mankind* under the figure of *love to our neighbor.*

Lofty and abstract principles not needed for every-day guidance. — Be not always eager, then, to direct your course only by some lofty, abstract, and distant principles, to the disregard of the humbler and more practical rules of morals which shine directly around and near our daily life. This is the folly of attempting to steer always by the stars, though the coast be near at hand, and the low, familiar beacons on it, if we will only heed them, will guide us safely into port. And do not, if you get into difficulty by acting in this manner, lay all the blame upon the stars; they shine in their proper places, but we have no instruments nice enough to take their precise bearings, where a very slight error might lead to fatal consequences. *High principles are always right;* but we make egregious mistakes in *attempting to act upon them on slight and familiar occasions,* when there are less ambitious, but safer, rules of guidance at hand, if we will only heed them. These lofty maxims come into play but seldom, — on great occasions; and even then, they serve only as *comprehensive precepts for the general formation of our hearts and characters, and not as precise rules of conduct,* that are serviceable on particular emergencies. We look to the stars for pilotage when we are in the midst of a broad and trackless ocean, and no landmarks are in sight; and they show us only the general direction in which we ought to steer. When the breakers are close around us, it is no time to look aloft. Goethe gives good advice: — If perplexed by the many calls that are made upon us, and by conflicting rules of life, let us always do first *the nearest duty;* when this is finished, the others will already have become clearer.

The affections indicate their objects. — The affections, like the desires, create a feeling of uneasiness and discontent in the absence of their respective objects, and prompt to exertion for the supply of the deficiency. The love of friends is a craving which makes itself more or less distinctly known according to the experience which we have had of companionship. "As the lamb," says an able writer, "when it strikes with the forehead while yet unarmed, proves that it is not its weapons which determine its instincts, but that it has preëxistent instincts suited to its weapons, so, when we see an animal deprived of the sight of its fellows cling to a stranger, or disarm by its caresses the rage of an enemy, we perceive the workings of a social instinct, not only not superinduced by external circumstances, but manifesting itself in spite of circumstances which are adverse to its operation. The same remark may be extended to man; when in solitude he languishes, and, by making companions of the lower animals, or by attaching himself to inanimate objects, strives to fill up the void of which he is conscious." *The feeling is blind, indeed;* instinct in animals, and reason in man, alone can supply the means of satisfying the want; *but we know that there is a want,* and that the uneasiness will remain till it is gratified.

A still more striking instance of this truth may be found in *the religious sentiment,* to which I have already often alluded. Man is created with a capacity and inclination for worship, with a deep feeling of veneration, which finds no appropriate object on which to expend itself among the persons and things with whom he is associated on earth, but constantly seeks for such an object, and usually finds it, in the conception of some spiritual existence higher and holier than any created being. From this fact alone can we explain the endless variety of religious systems which have obtained in the world, no nation or race having ever been discovered, which had no form of religious worship. The savage makes his idol of a block or stone. The half-enlightened barbarian finds a Divinity all around him, and peoples the mountains, the streams, and the forests with their attendant deities. When more cultivated, his thirst for knowledge leads him to study the heavens, and the sun, moon, and stars become his gods. Finally, whether as the last triumph of the unaided intellect or by special revelation, the sublime doctrine of monotheism is preached to the world, and calls forth the purest form and highest degree of reverence of which the human heart is capable.

CHAPTER III.

THE NATURE AND FUNCTIONS OF CONSCIENCE.

Summary of the last chapter. — I endeavored to show, in the last chapter, from a comparison of the human faculties with those of the brutes, that *discipline*, or *self-development*, is the great end of our existence upon earth; *mere enjoyment*, or *the conscious gratification of desire*, being only *a secondary* aim. The prevalence of *law*, or *the uniformity of causation*, in the material universe, is not intended merely to uphold and continue this universe, — an object which might be accomplished far more easily and directly, — but to operate as a means for this education of man; that is, to guide the conduct of a being who is not, like the brutes, conducted blindfold and unconsciously to the performance of every work that is necessary for the continuation and welfare of his species, but is rendered capable, through freewill, judgment, and forethought, of acting for himself. An examination of the lower motive powers of the human mind — the *appetites*, *affections*, and *desires*, — was intended to prove that they are mere blind impulses, or springs of activity, differing from each other in strength, but *having regard only to their own immediate gratification;* the objects of them being sought invariably as *ends*, not as *means*. So far as man is under their guidance, he has no superiority over the other orders of the animal creation. Prudence, or self-love, is the first element of his intellectual being; the office of this faculty is to restrain the primitive impulses and desires, to ascertain the relative importance of the ends towards which they are directed, and thus to subject the lower to the higher, and to make all of them conduce to the working out of that scheme of happiness, or general well-being, which has been devised by the intellect.

Man as a rational and prudent being. — Here, then, man first appears in his distinctive character as a rational being. He is not yet a moral one. His own happiness is the highest end that is yet in view, and all things are judged or estimated by their relative fitness to promote this single object. They are compared with each other, not as *good or evil*, but as *expedient or injurious*. The desires and affections are not considered in themselves, or with reference to their inherent character, but are viewed only *indirectly, through the outward consequences* which will result from their indulgence. There is room enough for the exercise of freewill, even if we look only to these external results. The immediate impulse, or passion of the moment, which always determines the action of the brute, is checked or restrained by man, till he can see the probable effect of giving way to it. At least, this is what he is capable of doing, and what he must do, if he would exercise those prerogatives of his nature through which alone he is placed at the head of the animal creation.

Man as a moral being. — But is this all? Have we completed the description of human nature, when man is made to appear as a being endowed with reason and foresight, free to act, and able to learn through experience what actions will most effectually promote his present and future happiness? The consciousness of every individual will answer, that it is not all; — that *there is an element of our nature, which excels prudence, more than prudence excels animal instinct or passion.* This principle extends its jurisdiction over our whole being, claiming authority to control and subdue the promptings of self-love as absolutely as it overrules the appetites and desires. By the side of *prudence*, or above it, it introduces the novel conception of *duty*, or moral obligation; over *personal happiness*, as an object of effort and a guide to action, it places the idea of *absolute right.* Putting aside the consideration of external things, it erects its throne in the soul of man, and judges, *not the outward act, but the motives and intentions* which lead to it and constitute its moral character. *Dealing thus exclusively with conceptions of the intellect, or pure ideas, all contingency or uncertainty disappears from its decisions,* and the sentence which it pronounces is as unchangeable as the purposes of the Almighty.

It supplies the medium and the standard of judgment through which we regard our own conduct and that of our fellow-beings, and form our notions of the attributes of God. Here, then, is the proper foundation of Natural Religion. Natural *Theology*, which is the product of the intellect, makes us acquainted with the being and the natural attributes of the Deity, such as his infinite duration, power, and wisdom, *merely as facts of science, or truths for contemplation.* Natural *Religion*, proceeding from conscience, makes known to us his moral nature, his purposes and will, and so *terminates, not in knowledge, but in action.*

It is difficult to explain the nature and functions of conscience, without seeming to dwell on mere truisms, or to adopt an abstruse and technical phraseology, which will tend rather to confuse than to rectify our notions of the subject. The terms expressive of moral distinctions, and of our feelings in regard to them, *have so passed into common use as an integral part of all languages*, and we have so frequent occasion for them both in writing and conversation, that it is not an easy task to call attention to the fundamental facts in our constitution which they signify, or to imagine what the nature of man would be, or how it would appear, if it were suddenly deprived of the moral faculty altogether, so that these words and phrases should no longer convey any intelligible meaning. Yet this is what is necessary to be done, before we can gain a clear conception of the office of *conscience*, or of the nature of the addition which it makes to the merely animal and the merely intellectual part of our being. To analyze, or otherwise describe, the ideas of *right* and *wrong*, is quite as difficult as to furnish correct and lucid definitions of *the particles*, or connecting links of speech, which we learn to apply, through long experience, with great precision, though their very commonness makes it hard to show what is their exact meaning. The particles themselves enter into every definition we can form of them. So *we cannot show what the dictates of conscience are, without presupposing that every one has a conscience*, and can listen to its voice. My object is, to show the importance and the distinctive character of this ethical element in the human constitution; that it is not blended with, or made up from, our other faculties, but is original and peculiar; that it makes a large addition to the stock of our ideas derived from other sources, and in fact modifies and controls the whole nature of man.

Increase of knowledge by the addition of a new sense. — It is not easy, perhaps, to imagine how our perceptions of external objects would be affected, if the number of the senses were suddenly increased, and, through the addition of another organ, we were enabled to look into the internal constitution of things, of which we have now only a superficial knowledge. We may form some idea, however, of the change that would thus be produced, by considering the case of a person born blind, and remaining so for many years. To him, the word *color* has absolutely no meaning, and no combination of words, no illustrations drawn from the ideas furnished by the other senses, could ever give him even the remotest conception of what the word signifies. It is said, that such a person, being once asked what idea he had of an object colored red, answered, that he thought it must resemble the sound of a trumpet; and this reply, extravagant as it seems, really comes as near the truth as any which the most gifted intellect, under such circumstances, ever has given, or ever can give. Now suppose, that from a human being who has long labored under this awful privation, the veil should in one moment be removed, that the scales should fall from his eyes, and for the first time in his life, he should be able *to see.* For the first time, upon his aching and astonished sense, bursts the glorious prospect of this green earth, its hills, plains, woods, and waters, with their thousand hues, and, bending over all, the blue arch of heaven, relieved only by vast folds of white cloud, lit up by the intolerable splendor of a noonday sun, or, at eve, "thick inlaid with patines of bright gold." The rush of overwhelming sensations that would oppress and burden his spirit under such circumstances, could be adequately described only in the poet's inspired language: —

"He looked;
Ocean and earth, the solid frame of earth,
And ocean's liquid mass beneath him lay,

In gladness and deep joy. . . . . . Sound needed none,
Nor any voice of joy; his spirit drank
The spectacle; sensation, soul, and form
All melted into him. . . . . . In such high hour
Of visitation from the living God,
Thought was not; in enjoyment it expired."

The addition to his stock of knowledge would not cease with the first view of this grand spectacle, or be limited to ideas of color alone. How long, it has been asked, would it take, for a person born blind, to acquire, by the unaided sense of touch, a complete idea of the front of a large Gothic cathedral, with its profusion of ornament and minuteness of tracery? The power of vision would increase a thousand-fold the aptitude of this other sense to convey the information that is really peculiar to it, though it is now so quickly suggested by visual sensations, that it seems to us attributable to the eye alone. Strictly speaking, as I explained in a former chapter, we *see* nothing but color; the ideas of distance, magnitude, and shape, which seem to be derived immediately from sight, being in truth first communicated to us through touch, or what has been called the muscular sense, and are afterwards suggested to the eye through the varieties of tint, of light and shade, with which they are found to be invariably associated. Then, as the education of the newly acquired sense was gradually perfected, it would become the constantly enlarging inlet of new ideas, till all the knowledge previously acquired from other sources should seem as nothing, when compared with the flood of information thus swiftly, and without effort, conveyed to the mind by a new organ of perception. It will hardly be deemed too fanciful to add, that if, in a future state of being, our power of acquiring knowledge is to be immeasurably increased, we can imagine no more direct mode of effecting this end, than by the endowment of the soul with new organs of sense; or rather, by stripping it entirely of the opaque and perishable covering of clay that now limits its perceptions and veils its glories, and in which the senses that we now possess are but narrow loopholes, through which we catch faint glimpses of the universe that God has made.

The addition of conscience equivalent to the creation of a new sense. — To apply this illustration to the subject before us, I say that the situation of the intellect which had never known the eye for its minister, or as an inlet of knowledge, would be but a faint parallel of the condition of the soul, or the whole man, on whom the light of conscience never beamed, and who, consequently, has no moral ideas whatever, but is as ignorant of the meaning of *right* and *wrong*, *duty* and *obligation*, as the man born blind is of color. The ideas, conceptions, or feelings, — call them what you may, — which come to us through this source, are *as peculiar and distinctive, as impossible to be derived from any other fountain* than that which actually does furnish them, *as are the sensations of vision.* They enter into and influence all our deliberations; they mould our judgments of our fellow-beings and of ourselves; they furnish a new guide to conduct; they lend a new aspect to life. I do not speak now only of those over whose actions and thoughts they habitually exercise a strong influence. I do not speak only of *good* men, or of any class of men, as distinguished from others; I speak of all human beings, of man himself, and of that which makes him what he is, — a man, and not a brute. Human nature is essentially moral, and we can no more put off, or lay aside, even for a time, this attribute of our being, than we can discard reason and take instinct in its place. There are *im*moral men, who hear the voice of conscience, but heed it not; but there is no such thing as an *un*moral man, to whom conscience speaks not at all. At any rate, no such being can be found out of a madhouse; and even there, what we see is not so much the absolute privation of the rational and moral faculties, as the awful spectacle of reason and conscience alike in ruins.

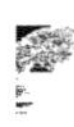

Instances of ideas and distinctions perceived by conscience alone. — Let me try to illustrate this point; though, for the reason already mentioned, it is hard to put it in a clear light for those who are not accustomed to abstractions, without seeming to dwell upon facts which are too obvious for notice. Suppose, then, that two persons, in whom we are equally interested, receive each an injury of the same magnitude, and attended with precisely similar results; let the two cases, in fine, be entirely parallel, except in this single particular, that in the one, the injury done was wilful, wanton, and unprovoked, while in the other, it was wholly accidental. Observe that *the supposed distinction* between the two cases *rests upon no outward fact*, — *upon nothing visible to sense*, but upon the secret motives and intentions of the authors of the deed, — upon what was passing in their minds before the blows were struck. Yet all mankind acknowledge this difference to be real and vitally important; they allow it to exercise entire control over their judgment of the two transactions, over the opinions which they form and express of them, and over their subsequent feelings towards the agents of the mischief. In every language that is spoken upon the earth, there are words to express the difference between simple *harm* and positive *wrong*. We can easily imagine a person wicked and brutal enough to commit the injury in the causeless manner first mentioned; but we cannot imagine any human being either bad or stupid enough to be affected in precisely the same manner in the two cases, and to see only equal cause for blame and praise in them. An animal grazing in the field might turn an equally careless eye upon the outward tokens of the harm done in both instances; and if we could suppose its instinct to be so far supplanted by reason that it could know the one deed to be intentional, and the other accidental, we should still believe that it would retain its indifference, unless, by a further change in its nature, the gift of moral, should be added to that of intellectual perception. My point is, that *conscience differs as widely from reason, as reason does from instinct.*

We may take another instance from the affection of *general benevolence*, or the desire of doing good to mankind. This is a primitive or natural impulse, somewhat strengthened by *sympathy*, which seeks its own end without regard to any ulterior gratification, and, when pure and unmixed, without reference to any higher law or motive. The private relations between the two parties, the giver and receiver of the benefit, do not increase or diminish the addition that is made to the stock of human happiness. We sympathize involuntarily with happiness conferred; we rejoice at the opening of new avenues to human enjoyment. Now, suppose that the means of pleasure thus bestowed were not the rightful property of the donor, that they were not his to give. He had them only in trust from one to whom they properly belonged, and who would very certainly have made a bad use of them, — have devoted them only to selfish purposes, or perhaps to doing evil instead of good to his fellow-men, if they had remained in his possession. No matter; *justice* requires that they should have been restored to him, to be squandered or misused as he saw fit. Here, then, the feelings of justice and benevolence are in conflict; and what human being hesitates to admit that the claims of the former are superior? I have intentionally taken an instance which proves that *mere philanthropy*, or the desire of promoting the happiness of others, though it is the most estimable of the affections, *is not the whole duty of man;* and, consequently, that the affections alone, being impulsive and irrational in their nature, are an insufficient guide to conduct. There are many, perhaps, who, in the case supposed, would sacrifice justice to benevolence; but they would still be conscious — if not at the moment, at any rate, after time had come for reflection — that they had acted wrong.

Conscience the sole voucher of its own authority. — What is this sentiment or idea of *moral wrong*, which arises not merely in the two instances I have mentioned, but so frequently in every healthy mind as to influence our conduct in all the relations of life? It surely is not conveyed to us through *the senses;* nor is it the offspring of the affections or desires, the impulsive part of our nature, to which it is frequently set in opposition. Is it the product of *intellect*, then? The office of this faculty, we know, is to discover truth, to discern the fitness of means to ends, to perceive the relation of premises to conclusions. It has nothing to do with action, but is limited entirely to contemplation. In the first case mentioned, reason might inform us of the fact, that the one deed was purposed, and the other casual; this truth would be learned by inference from certain outward circumstances that enable us to judge of the intentions of the parties. The intellect stops here; the judgment subsequently passed, the idea of guilt or innocence that supervenes, is not related to the knowledge thus obtained, as an inference is to its premises, or as an end to means employed. Why is intentional harm done to a fellow-being a wrong? We cannot tell. Why are the claims of justice superior to those of benevolence? We cannot tell. But we know that it is so, not only in the judgment of men, but in the councils of God.

And further, the idea of *retribution* or *punishment* arises after that of acknowledged wrong, even when the injured person is beyond the reach of reparation, and when we are not looking to the reformation of the guilty. Human legislation, indeed, is properly confined to these two ends, and to the protection of society. Human laws aim to provide for the redress of injuries, the reformation of the criminal, and the welfare of all classes; but they seek to accomplish these ends at the expense of the offender. It is just, it is right, that the wrongdoer should suffer: — we admit this principle intuitively, though it is directly opposed to the dictates of sympathy and natural benevolence, which aim to prevent all suffering. The decisions of conscience, then, are authoritative and supreme. It overlooks and controls the lower motives to action, even those which are most amiable or excellent; its voice is never heard but in tones of absolute command. "If it had might, as it has right, it would govern the world."

Conscience infallible within its proper sphere. — This brings me to the next characteristic of the moral faculty in its proper sphere, — the *absolute certainty* of its decisions. I say "in its proper sphere," because, as we had occasion to remark in the former Part, the undue extension of the commands of conscience beyond their proper subjects, *the motives and intentions* of men, to *the external acts or occurrences* through which those intentions are manifested, often creates doubts, and gives opportunity to question its absolute veracity. But in its own domain, in the sanctuary of the soul, where all thoughts and motives are judged, it is an undoubted sovereign. The certainty of its decisions is like that which belongs to the convictions of the understanding in regard to abstract truth. *Right and wrong are not interchangeable even in idea;* we cannot imagine, we cannot even conceive, of any instance in which the one should be substituted for the other. As it is not within the power even of Omnipotence to reverse the abstract laws of number and space, so it is not his to alter the moral relations of thoughts and acts, and our judgments of them, through which we look up reverently to his throne, and form our conceptions of infinite holiness, justice, and truth personified in him. This is only saying, that it is impossible for the Divine nature to act contrary to itself. The sublime exclamation of Pythagoras, when contemplating the immutable relations of space, "God himself geometrizes," expresses but feebly the absolute trust with which the soul reposes on those intuitions of eternal and necessary truth, which are vouchsafed to us as the foundations of our moral and intellectual being.

Conscience contrasted with taste in respect to the immutability of its decisions. — We may gain a clearer idea of the infallibility of conscience, by comparing it with the other capacities of our nature, with which, at first sight, it seems most nearly allied. Take the emotions of taste, for instance. The contemplation of an exquisite work of art, or of grand and striking scenery in nature, affects us with a lively and agreeable feeling, which we call the perception of beauty or sublimity. All men are subject to it, though in different degrees, depending on the cultivation of the taste. But there is nothing absolute or immutable in our ideas of the qualities which call it forth. The child is delighted with that which appears to the adult as gaudy, puerile, or unnatural. Nay, there is a "want of agreement as to the presence and existence of beauty in particular objects among men whose organization is perfect, and who are plainly possessed of the faculty, whatever it may be, by which beauty is discerned. One man sees it perpetually, where to another it is quite invisible, or even where its reverse seems to be conspicuous Nor is this owing to the insensibility of either of the parties; for the same contrariety exists where both are keenly alive to the influences of the beauty they respectively discern. The gardens, the furniture, the dress, which appeared beautiful in the eyes of our grandfathers, are odious and ridiculous in ours. Nay, the difference of rank, education, or employments, gives rise to the same diversity of sensation." And even if all men could be brought to unanimity upon this point, we could still *conceive* of such an alteration in their capacity of discerning beauty, that what is now most pleasing to them should become disagreeable, and the reverse. In fine, the beauty or sublimity which we discern is in our own minds; and we do not *know*, that is, we cannot be sure, that there is any thing corresponding to them in the world without, or in the intrinsic nature of things.

But it is not so with our perceptions of moral good and evil. Try to imagine that the relations of right and wrong are reversed, — that it is just to deceive, or to withhold from another his own, — that it is commendable to inflict a wanton injury upon a fellow-being, — and that falsehood is more praiseworthy than truth. *You cannot do it.* The principles which forbid such a reversal of judgment are erected, whether you will or no, whether your conduct conforms to them or not, into absolute standards in your own minds, to which you refer every motive and action for approbation or censure. The ideas of right, of duty, of moral obligation, are inwrought with our inmost being, and we can no more conceive that they are subjective only, or without a basis in the essential nature of things, than we can imagine the annihilation of time and space. It is conceivable, indeed, though the supposition is a violent one, that the constitution of our minds should be altered far enough for us to see these things reversed, and to imagine that injustice and falsehood were meritorious. *Just so we admit the possibility of insanity.* But we cannot admit that such a change would be in the direction of the truth, or that, when it had taken place, we should not be laboring under a fatal error. Right and duty, *as we now perceive them*, are absolute conceptions, and must exist as they are, wholly irrespective of the manner in which they are viewed by different minds.

Moral obligation universally admitted to be supreme.—The correctness and the unanimity of men's moral *judgments* must be clearly distinguished from their universal acknowledgment of the supremacy of moral obligation. There is considerable diversity of opinion in the former respect, in the estimate which we may form of the moral character of certain actions, and especially of the relative importance of certain duties; though men's ideas on this subject usually converge, just in proportion as they become enlightened, and inform their minds by reflection and experience. Savages may deem it right to plunder and to kill; the Spartans taught their children to steal; the ancients generally held that falsehood and deceit were justifiable, if practised for the public good, and not for one's individual advantage. But none of these doubted that the right, as they esteemed it, was obligatory; they acknowledged with one voice, that they were bound to practise it. The words *duty* and *law* had as much meaning and force in their ears, as they have among the most enlightened and most Christian communities of our own times. It is this sense of *obligation,* this recognition of an act as something which *ought* to be done, or to be left undone, which is the capital fact in our moral being; it is the foundation and superstructure of our moral nature. It is not an idea furnished by the senses, or in any way suggested by sensation. Men may differ in applying this idea of duty; they may consider one or another act as binding upon them; but they never fail to recognize *obligation* somewhere, to acknowledge its rightful supremacy, and to distinguish it clearly from the feeling of *compulsion,* or restraint. And the instances even of mistaken application of the idea of duty are so few and unimportant, that they may properly be viewed as perversions of the moral faculty, rather than as proofs of its original incapacity or blindness. Morality, as a general rule, needs not to be taught, but to be guarded against the effects of wrong teaching. The unperverted conscience of a child shrinks from the act which its fanatical parents attempt to impose as a duty.

Attempts to account for the supremacy of conscience. — Butler and Mackintosh, with other writers upon the theory of ethics, have been much exercised in the attempt to find a basis for the supremacy of conscience, or a reason for the despotic authority which it claims over the other principles and motives of our nature. They thought it necessary to justify the overruling and despotic influence, which the moral faculty claims over the whole man, but does not always succeed in enforcing, since the lower propensities often exceed it in strength. I have an impulse, it is true, to be just to my fellow man; but I have also an impulse to gratify my anger, to pamper my appetites, to secure the means of selfish enjoyment, and even to assist the unfortunate with the property which happens to be in my hands, though it really belongs to another. These two impulses often clash, and the latter, which is rightfully the inferior one, frequently gets the upperhand. Why, then, do I believe that it is rightfully inferior, or why do I feel compunction after it has triumphed? If the sentiment of duty comes in conflict with a feeling so powerful as self-love, or so amiable as benevolence, though I have a distinct consciousness that the former *ought* to prevail, it is well to see if there are any good grounds for this assumed superiority, and thus to fortify the demands of conscience by satisfying the reason.

Sir James Mackintosh thought that he had found a basis for this claim of supreme authority in the fact, that *conscience acts directly upon the inner man*, having its throne within the soul, *while all the other impulses and desires point to outward objects.* The sense of duty governs the motives, intentions, and dispositions of men. Hence it is *universal*, or it regulates the *whole* conduct and character; while the objects of the other propensities are *particular*, as well as *external.* If I yield to anger, for instance, while all my other passions and appetites are restrained by the law of conscience, the act of resentment is perceived to violate the harmony of the system; it is an act of disorder, which will be recognized as such when the temporary excitement subsides. Again, the objects of the passions and desires being external, I must use *means* for their gratification. I may not be able to gratify my appetite, because I cannot find the means of doing so. But I can always satisfy my conscience, because here no means are needed; the will, the intention, is enough; duty asks nothing more. The failure of the intention may cause sorrow, but cannot produce remorse. Hence, *conscience is independent*, or *sufficient unto itself;* while the gratification of every other impulse depends on outward circumstances. Passion often defeats itself; the desires remain unsatisfied; appetite cannot obtain its appropriate food; self-love not infrequently brings its own punishment. But the sense of duty never fails, and yielding to it is at once success and enjoyment.

Futility of these attempts. — These suggestions of an accomplished moralist, though they illustrate the general subject, do not seem to me to throw much light upon the particular inquiry in which we are now engaged. It is true, that conscience is universal and independent, as well as supreme; but it does not appear very clearly how the latter attribute is a consequence of the two former ones. *Though I am independent, it does not follow that I am entitled to command;* though not subject to control, I may not be permitted to exercise it. Moreover, *prudence*, or an enlightened self-love, seems to have quite as wide a domain as the moral sense; it *also is universal*, for it often assumes to regulate the whole conduct and character, with a view only to the individual's own future happiness. Yet no one thinks of saying that it is supreme. I need not dwell upon attempts less ingenious and plausible than that of Mackintosh to solve this problem, since all occasion for them disappears when we come to examine the subject more closely.

The supremacy of conscience an ultimate fact. — A full analysis of our moral perceptions will show, if I mistake not, that the supremacy of conscience is an ultimate fact, and that we cannot go behind it, or give a reason for it, without reasoning in a circle, or virtually denying the very point we attempt to prove. To ask *why* I ought to obey the law of right, is, in truth, *to suppose that there is some obligation of greater moment than the sense of duty*, some consideration which needs to be alleged in its support, *and thus to take for granted that it is not supreme.*

We might as well ask a reason for our belief that every event must have a cause.

Moral taste explained. — Certain motives and actions are made known to me, and recognized by conscience, as good and right. I may simply contemplate them with complacency and approbation, just as I am gratified with the view of a beautiful landscape, or struck with awe at the sight of the starry heavens. A kind of *moral taste* is thus formed, which is productive of as much enjoyment, when properly cultivated, as our sensibility to the other emotions of taste, or our capacity of receiving pleasure through the senses. Though I were incapable of action myself, and therefore should never have occasion to apply the epithets to my own conduct, I should still derive pleasure from awarding them to others, and from reflecting on their deeds which merit to be so distinguished. We see an obvious illustration of this fact in the pleasure that we derive from fictitious representations of life, which call all our moral sentiments into play, though we are perfectly conscious at the time, that the incidents are imaginary. In reading a novel, or seeing a theatrical performance, we are pained and disappointed, if the rules of "poetical justice," as it is termed, are not observed. It is a noble characteristic of the taste and conscience of man, that they require in art a closer adherence to the principles of the beautiful, the just, and the right, than we can reasonably expect to be exemplified in nature and life. The *beau-ideal* is not found in the world; poetical justice is confessedly unreal; it does not follow merit and demerit in this stage of existence. But the restraint of circumstances is not felt in the province of invention; and where man is the creator, he becomes responsible for the whole work. He is bound to "submit the shows of things to the desires of the mind." If he cannot embody in his work that perfect beauty and absolute right, of which we dream, and to which we are constantly reaching forward, he is under an obligation, at least, not to allow the virtuous to go finally unrewarded, nor the wicked to triumph.

Moral taste shown to be insufficient. — But we shall have a most imperfect view of the action of the moral faculty, if we stop here. This merely intellectual view of right and wrong, this cool survey of motives and conduct in their ethical aspect, this feast of the moral sensibilities at the table of fiction, will be almost as profitless in its consequences, as it is meagre and unsatisfactory in point of scientific truth. We must go back to the origin of these distinctions, to the primal revelations of conscience, and see where it is that the ideas of moral good and evil have their birth. What is most peculiar and original in the action of this faculty, and from which, indeed, all the other moral facts of our nature are but inferences and generalizations, is the impulse of duty, or the feeling of moral obligation. *I am bound* to act with justice and benevolence; *I ought* to do right and to follow after truth. This sense of obligation, this recognition of an absolute and rightful command, having reference only to conduct, is what we call conscience, in its simplest and primitive meaning. The words *right* and *wrong* have no significance, except as convenient appellations afterwards given by the intellect to those deeds which I am thus bound to perform or abstain from. *Merit* and *demerit* signify only the feelings which arise in my mind according as this command has been obeyed or violated. We cannot analyze this feeling or idea of duty, for, being simple, it does not admit of resolution into parts, or explanation by any more obvious terms. To have it is to recognize its authority, for positive obligation is supreme in its very nature; nothing can come in conflict with it but desire, which is no obligation at all.

There is a confusion of speech, then, in asking why we are bound to comply with the requisitions of conscience; it is requiring one to tell *why it is a duty to perform a duty*, — thus indicating *a doubt whether there is any such thing as original and necessary obligation.* Whatever answer is given, it is evident that *the question may be continually repeated.* If it be said, for instance, that I must obey conscience because it is expedient, or because it is conformable to the fitness of things, or to reason, or because it is the will of God, the question instantly recurs, Why am I obliged to do what is expedient, or to conform to reason or the fitness of things, or to obey the will of

God? The higher reason of man never thus returns in a circle upon itself, for ever seeking without coming to a knowledge of the truth. What we mean by asking in reference to any particular action, *Why* is it a duty? — *why* ought I to perform it? is no more than this: — Prove to me that it *is* a duty; only place it before me in so clear a light that my conscience shall recognize and approve it, and I ask for no higher sanction. The absolute obligation of the deed is then revealed to me.

Right implies obligation. — This doctrine is very clearly and forcibly stated by Dr. Adams, a moralist of Oxford. "*Right,*' says he, "implies *duty* in its idea. To perceive an action to be right, is to see a reason for doing it in the action itself, abstracted from all other considerations whatever; and this perception, this acknowledged rectitude in the action, is the very essence of obligation, — that which commands the approbation and choice, and binds the conscience of every rational human being Nothing can bring us under an obligation to do what appears to our moral judgment *wrong*. It may be supposed our interest to do this, but it cannot be supposed our duty. For, I ask, if some power, which we are unable to resist, should assume the command over us, and give us laws which are unrighteous and unjust, should we be under an *obligation* to obey him? Should we not rather be obliged to shake off the yoke, and to resist such usurpation, if it were in our power? However, then, we might be swayed by hope or fear, it is plain that we are under an obligation to *right*, which is antecedent, and in order and nature superior, to all other. Power may compel, interest may bribe, pleasure may persuade, but reason [conscience] only can oblige. This is the only authority which rational beings can own, and to which they owe obedience."

All lesser obligations are resolvable into this primal idea of duty, and are, in truth, but the various forms which this idea assumes, when it is applied to the various relations and circumstances of life. Thus, the state, the society, or the family, to which one belongs, is said to have authority over him, and he is bound to render obedience to that authority, and to its expressed will in the form of law. But so far as this obedience is not the effect of compulsion or of the persuasion of interest, it is rendered only because reason brings the acts which are preservative of such associations within the sphere of conscience, and this faculty makes them *obligatory*, in the proper sense of that word. *Law* itself, whether human or Divine, is but *a generalization of the commands of conscience*, and has no proper authority but what is derived from this source, however it may be surrounded with rewards and punishments, which are intended to act upon our prudence or self-love. It is this wide compass and ceaseless application of the primitive sense of duty, which lends all its force to Wordsworth's magnificent exaggeration of the idea, in his Ode to this "stern daughter of the voice of God."

> "Thou dost preserve the Stars from wrong,
> And the most ancient Heavens, through Thee, are fresh and strong."

Why law is applied metaphorically to physical events. — We see, then, how violent is the metaphor by which we apply the term *law* to the uninterrupted, or causal, succession of events in the physical world. We speak, for instance, of the constant movements of the planets in their courses as the consequence of the *law* of gravitation, — finding no figure more appropriate to express the immutable order of their motions, than to represent these vast orbs as voluntary agents, hearkening to the stern monitor within the breast, following its dictates with implicit obedience, and thus preserving the eternal harmony of the universe. The awful supremacy of conscience is thus extended, though by a figure of speech, over the material creation; and we mark our sense of the absolute character of moral obligation by applying it to what is most fixed and unchangeable among the works of God.

Even bad men acknowledge conscience to be supreme. — I draw one other illustration of this subject from Dugald Stewart, in his fine remark, that "the supreme authority of conscience is felt and tacitly acknowledged by the worst, no less than by the best, of men; for even they who have thrown off all hypocrisy with the world, are at pains to conceal their real character from their own eyes. No man ever, in soliloquy or private meditation, avowed to himself that he was a villain; nor do I believe that such a character as Joseph Surface, in the School for Scandal, (who is introduced as reflecting coolly on his own knavery and baseness, without any uneasiness but what arises from the dread of detection,) ever existed in the world. Such men probably impose on themselves fully as much as they do upon others. Hence the various artifices of self-deceit, which Butler has so well described in his discourses on that subject."

"We may defend villany," says Lord Shaftesbury, as quoted by Dugald Stewart, "and cry up folly before the world. But to appear fools, madmen, or varlets *to ourselves*, and prove it to our own faces that we are really such, is insupportable. For so true a reverence has every one for himself, when he comes clearly to appear before his close companion, that he had rather profess the vilest things of himself in open company, than hear his character privately from his own mouth. So that we may readily from hence conclude, that the chief interest of ambition, avarice, corruption, and every sly insinuating vice, is to prevent this interview and familiarity of discourse, which is consequent upon close retirement and inward recess."

The Moral distinguished from the Physical Sciences. — The metaphorical application of words, the frequent interchange of terms between the Moral and the Physical Sciences, has tended greatly to obscure and perplex the subject of which we are now treating, and to cover up some essential differences which would otherwise appear in the clearest light to the understanding. A statement of these differences and distinctions may serve to elucidate the theory of human nature, and to show how we are related to the natural world, at the same time that we are subjects of a moral government. The object of the physical sciences, and of the intellect generally in its searches after truth, is to answer the question, *What is?* All degrees of probability or certainty attend our answers to this inquiry, and serve only to mark how successful we have been in the undertaking. We endeavor not only to ascertain facts, but to arrange and classify them with a view to their mutual relations; and the use of general terms enables us to make comprehensive statements of the results of our study, and to store them up in a form convenient for future reference. Such statements are often called *laws*, and are said to *govern* all the cases which are merely included under them. From the idea of *government*, we pass naturally to that of *influence and production*, or *causation;* and the *law*, or general statement, is then said to *cause* all the particular facts which it comprehends. Unable to find the true cause, we assign a fictitious one, which is at first recognized by the understanding to be fictitious, but which comes at last to claim as its own the character which it had only borrowed.

The object of ethical science, and of the moral faculty generally, is quite distinct from this; here we ask, *What ought to be?* — our aim being, not so much to satisfy our curiosity, as to regulate our conduct. We seek to ascertain "the rules which *ought* to govern voluntary action, and to which those habitual dispositions of mind which are the source of voluntary actions *ought* to be adapted." The conception of duty, and of absolute right, which then comes before the mind, corresponds to nothing physical, and has no archetype in the external universe. We enter a new world here; we may ask for the cause of a fact, an event; but it is irrelevant and absurd to inquire after the cause of an obligation. *Duty is not caused, for it never began to be;* it has existed from eternity. We cannot even conceive of a period when justice was not, or will not be, obligatory upon every being capable of understanding what justice requires. Upon the idea or feeling expressed by the word *ought* the whole science of morals depends. It differs not in degree, but in kind, from desire and appetite, so that these can never really come in competition with it. In truth, *it does not admit of degrees*, for there are no half-way obligations; conscience either speaks absolutely, or not at all. I am obliged either to cultivate a certain disposition of mind, or to repress it, if it be not indifferent, in a moral point of view, whether it be cultivated or not. The desires, on the other hand, exist in all conceivable degrees, from the faintest shade of inclination up to the strong passion which takes the reason prisoner.

Source of uncertainty or skepticism in morals. — It is only when the dictates of conscience are drawn out into the form of propositions, and stated as general laws, that any question *can* arise as to their certainty. Even then, the question would not be hard to answer. The intellect, we know, must begin with propositions which it cannot prove, because nothing more evident or certain can be found on which to rest the argument. That which is self-evident is not, surely, to be deemed inferior to that which requires to be supported by other evidence, before we can receive and act upon it. He who can seriously distrust the evidence of his senses, or doubt his own identity, or deny that every event must have a cause, must be permitted, also, to exercise his skepticism as to the grounds of morality, and to maintain that he sees no reason why we should sometimes be obliged to sacrifice ourselves for others, or to submit our compassionate or benevolent impulses to the sense of duty and justice. It would avail nothing, if we were to hold up general expediency, or the command of God, as such a reason. He who cannot recognize the independent nature and entire supremacy of moral obligation, *as such*, will never yield to considerations like these, which have in fact no weight, unless a sense of duty be taken for granted. *We cannot argue with those who will not first admit the principles upon which all reasoning is founded.*

But, fortunately for the world, skepticism in morals can never be any thing more than a diversion or a whim. The matter is exclusively a practical one. We are not concerned here about the truth of propositions, and therefore cannot be perplexed by the artifices of the logician and the sophist. Whether we know the meaning of words or not, we cannot but be conscious that we are urged to do and to refrain from doing certain things by a principle which is not coincident with self-love, but often runs counter to it, and assumes to moderate and restrain it with absolute authority. Call this principle what we may, its existence is a fact attested by consciousness; and whether we submit to its guidance or not, we cannot but be conscious that it puts forth a higher claim to our obedience than all other motives and springs of action united. No one had a clearer perception of this fact, or avowed it more frankly, than Hume himself.

"Those," says he, "who have denied the reality of moral distinctions may be ranked among the disingenuous disputants; nor is it conceivable, that any human creature could ever seriously believe that all characters and actions were alike entitled to the regard and affection of every one.

"Let a man's insensibility be ever so great, he must often be touched with the images of *right* and *wrong;* and let his prejudices be ever so obstinate, he must observe that others are susceptible of like impressions. The only way, therefore, of convincing an antagonist of this kind, is to leave him to himself. For, finding that nobody keeps up the controversy with him, it is probable he will at last, of himself, from mere weariness, come over to the side of common sense and reason."

CHAPTER IV

THE NATURE OF MORAL GOVERNMENT.

Summary of the last chapter. — The object of the last chapter was to explain the nature and operations of that faculty, by the possession of which, even more than by the gift of reason, man is raised above all the other orders of created being with which we are acquainted. Conscience, I endeavored to show, is the inlet of a new set of ideas, which differ as widely from those which are furnished by the intellect, as the perceptions of vision do from those of touch and hearing. The object of the intellect is truth; that of conscience is duty. The former teaches us *what is;* the latter shows us *what ought to be.* The moral faculty is universal; for the most depraved and wicked person that ever lived, is not ignorant of what the words *ought* and *duty* mean, though he may not heed them in his conduct. The uninstructed or perverted understanding may apply them wrongfully; but, however applied, their obligatory or binding character is always recognized. The idea of duty or moral obligation is simple or uncompounded; it does not admit of definition, because it is not susceptible of analysis, or of division into parts. Hence, it is not communicable by instruction; if it did not already exist in the infant mind, all the teaching in the world could never place it there, — any more than mere words could inform a man what the color *yellow* is, if he had never seen a yellow object. In the latter case, indeed, the senses give us the necessary information; having once seen the unclouded sky, or the distant hills, or the deep ocean, I can afterwards form a conception of them, and can then learn what the word *blue* signifies, or the objects to which it is applicable. Not so in the moral world; sense renders no aid here. The primary application of the words *right* and *wrong* is not to visible or tangible things, or even to any outward act, but to the secret purposes of the heart; for however strange or mischievous the deed may appear, as soon as we ascertain that it was unintentional, or that it proceeded from the best motives, we immediately relieve the doer from any moral blame. Just as the understanding discerns resemblance or contrariety between two ideas, does the moral faculty pronounce that truth-telling is right, and falsehood wrong; the only distinction between the two cases is, that, in the former one, the mental act terminates when the judgment is formed, truth or knowledge being the only end in view; while, in the latter, the conception of duty or moral obligation immediately rises, the judgment pointing directly to action. It is not properly a *judgment*, then, but a precept or command. I not only know that falsehood is wrong, but I feel that veracity is a duty, — that I am bound, on all occasions, to tell the truth. More properly speaking, indeed, the conception of duty is involved in the judgment of right, and forms a part of it; to perceive the motive to be sinful, and to recognize the obligation to repress it, is one and the same act.

It was remarked, further, that *the paramount character of moral obligation* over all other motives or incentives to conduct, *is involved in the very idea of obligation.* It is an impertinence to ask for a foundation for the supremacy of conscience. He who commands, indeed, assumes that he has authority; and we often reasonably doubt the fact, and require him to show his commission. But in so doing, we virtually acknowledge that there is authority somewhere, that a higher power exists, whom we are bound to obey, and who is capable of delegating his right to command. Now it is only by a metaphor, though an apt and natural one, that we speak of the *commands*, or the *voice*, of conscience. It is the office of this faculty to create that primitive and simple feeling of obligation which is expressed by the word *ought*, and which alone gives to duty and authority any proper meaning. There is a common confusion of thought here. With regard to a particular act or duty, it is reasonable to inquire if I am under a moral obligation to perform or to cherish it; but when this point is ascertained, to seek a reason for that obligation, is to ask, why it is a duty to perform a duty, — which is nonsense. It is demonstrable that no answer can be given to the question which will prevent it from being instantly repeated. That what is *right*, is of higher authority than what is merely *expedient*, is evident from the simple fact, that *right and obligation are correlative terms, or merely two aspects of the same idea;* while obligation does not enter at all into the meaning of the word *expedient.*

Obligation distinguished from constraint. — It is with great diffidence that I venture to differ on this point from so eminent an authority in ethical science as Sir James Mackintosh. But what he has here attempted to add to the theory of ethics as expounded by Bishop Butler, seems to me a violation of the simplicity and truth of the whole scheme, and, instead of furnishing a basis for the authoritative claims of conscience, to deprive this faculty of that original and supreme authority which is its most striking characteristic. There is a fundamental difference between the ideas of *obligation* and *compulsion*, which, though often lost sight of in the metaphorical use of language, is essential to any proper understanding of the subject. A subordinate officer may say, that he is *obliged* to obey the commands of his superior; but this is *constraint*, not *duty;* because he knows, that if need were, a file of soldiers would enforce the command. On the other hand, the dictates of conscience are enforced by no power whatever. Any one may disobey them who will. But, even in the moment of disobedience, he is conscious that he is violating an obligation, properly so called, which is in its very nature supreme.* We do not do right because God commands it, but God commands it because it is right. The idea of moral obligation, then, — I speak it reverently, — lies behind the authority of the Almighty, and is the only buttress of his throne. As for the other supports that have been devised for the sense of duty, — that the action is obligatory because it is expedient, or because it is conformable to reason, to order, or to the fitness of things, — they hardly merit notice.

Abstract arguments a priori cannot prove the moral government of God. — And here I rest what I had to say upon the moral nature of man, as preparatory to the further inquiry

* The word *ought* is the only one in our language which means, exclusively and unambiguously, *to be held or bound in moral obligation, through the consciousness of a law of paramount authority.* This also is the primary meaning of the word *oblige;* but unfortunately, this word has come to have a secondary meaning, corresponding very nearly with *must,* and indicating *physical necessity or compulsion;* as when we say that the commander of a besieged fortress is *obliged* to surrender when his means of defence are exhausted, or that the captain of a ship is obliged by adverse winds to move in a wrong direction. In all languages, words are found corresponding with *ought,* and with the primary meaning of *oblige;* this may not be their sole meaning, but it is always one of their recognized significations. This fact indicates that the sense of *moral obligation,* wholly distinct from *persuasion* or *desire* on the one hand, and from *physical necessity* on the other, is a part of the universal consciousness of men; it is always recognized, though it is not always obeyed. As it is a simple idea, we cannot analyze it; and as it is an ultimate principle in human nature, we cannot explain or account for it.

into the attributes of the Deity, and into that manifestation of them which calls for the religious homage of the whole human family. The question now is, — Have we satisfactory assurance, even from the light of nature, that God does indeed govern the earth? and if so, by what rule does he govern it? The doctrine of uninterrupted Divine agency, which was considered at length, and, as I think, established, in the former Part, teaches us, indeed, that all events are of his disposal; but the doctrine was then viewed chiefly in relation to *physical* occurrences, or to what are called the laws of the *outward* world. Is the *moral* world equally under his guidance and dominion? and does conscience, in its purity and supremacy, only mirror to us the light of his countenance? Is man, also, *in his intellectual and moral nature*, subject to laws as inflexible as those which govern the planets in their courses? and as the latter manifest to us the wisdom and power of the Lawgiver, so do the former evince to us his justice, benevolence, and holiness?

The answer of these questions in the affirmative, upon satisfactory grounds, you perceive, will afford evidence *a posteriori* of the moral character of the Deity, and, as a necessary consequence, of the religious duties of man. It is customary with writers upon this subject, I am well aware, to proceed entirely upon abstract reasoning, and to deduce the moral attributes from the natural ones, the whole doctrine resting upon arguments *a priori*. Thus, the doctrine of the *omniscience* of the Divine Being is upheld, as "a necessary inference from that of a *universal Creator*. He who made all creatures and things — that is to say, who gave them their being and properties — cannot but know the being and properties which himself has given, and the ways in which they will be developed and will operate." Again, the infinite *benevolence* and *holiness* of God are deduced immediately from a consideration of his *omniscience* and *infinite power* and *wisdom*.

Now I am far from denying the validity of such reasoning as this, and there is unquestionably a certain class of minds so peculiarly constituted that it is more satisfactory to them than any other. But it seems to me to be chargeable with this great defect,—that unless it can be supported by the evidence of facts, that is, by observation and experience, it leaves the inquirer in a worse condition than he was before he began the study of the subject. Of what use is it to demonstrate to him by abstract reasoning, that the Almighty *must* govern in holiness the world which he has made, when, from his knowledge of history, from the mode in which he has been accustomed to look upon natural occurrences and the conduct of mankind, and from his personal experience, he is compelled to doubt whether the world is governed at all? Perplexed by this contradiction between reason and experience, he will be tempted to reject the doctrine and the argument along with it,—not that he can detect any flaw in the latter, but because he is obliged to distrust the power of the human mind ever to arrive at any truth. Prove to him, that an omniscient God must necessarily be infinitely benevolent and holy, and at the same time allow him to believe, that the history of mankind is one long record of wretchedness and sin, and what conclusion can he draw, except that the doctrine of a superintending Providence is either an inexplicable mystery or a delusion, or that reasoning which seems to be demonstrative is, in truth, wholly treacherous and unsound? The adoption of the latter alternative only adds *skepticism in philosophy* to *disbelief in religion*. If we were concerned with the truths of theology only as we are with the principles of *abstract science*, then this mode of evolving them one from the other in logical succession, as it would add to the symmetry and elegance of the theory, and lead to no consequences that would be practically injurious, might well be adopted, if for no other reason, yet as a diversion of the intellect.* But as matters of immediate and momentous interest,

* In the exact sciences, too much regard cannot be paid to method, to the systematic evolution of principles in their natural order, each step being the natural consequence of its immediate predecessor, and the natural preparation for the one which is to follow it. Geometry and Mechanics owe much of their beauty, as well as their intelligibleness, to this rigid observance of method in the evolution of their principles. They are as perfect examples of synthesis as the composition of stones that

it behooves us to study them in such a manner as to leave clear and deeply rooted convictions in the soul. They relate not merely to faith, but to practice; and experience is therefore our surest guide in the investigation, and the safest teacher in conduct. By approaching the subject in this manner, we remove the difficulties alleged by the skeptic before laying the founda-

---

constitutes an arch. But in the moral sciences, it may be doubted whether the love of system has not been carried too far, whether the desire to round off one's speculations into a complete theory has not led, on the one hand, to a suppression or imperfect statement of some important truths, and on the other, to a needless repetition and an exaggerated estimate of some principles which are really of secondary importance. Both in Politics and Political Economy, the system which professes to be deduced in an exact method from a single principle, is very apt to be a false system. These sciences are based upon human nature, and therefore must be conformed to the manifold diversities and inconsistencies of that nature. Mr. Mill derives the whole theory of Government from the single assumed fact, that every man pursues his interest when he knows it; to which Sir James Mackintosh acutely objects, that "a nation, as much as an individual, and sometimes more, may not only mistake its interest, but, perceiving it clearly, may prefer the gratification of a strong passion to it. The whole fabric of Mill's political reasoning seems to be overthrown by this single observation; and instead of attempting to explain the immense variety of political facts by the simple principle of a contest of interests, we are reduced to the necessity of once more referring them to that variety of passions, habits, opinions, and prejudices, which we discover only by experience."

In Political Economy, hardly can any one topic be adequately developed and explained, without taking for granted a general knowledge of all the other topics, or entering into a provisional explanation of them. Wealth, Exchange, Value, Money, Cost, Profits, Wages, — all are connected with each other like the threads of a continuous network inclosing a sphere. It matters little where we begin; whatever part we first take up will be found to involve a consideration of nearly all the other parts of the system. In such cases, we best preserve the essentials of method, by sacrificing its outward forms. Logic must give way temporarily to rhetoric; that view of the subject which most readily presents itself to an inquiring mind, ignorant as yet of the elements of the science, should be preferred to the more comprehensive and exact development of it, which can be understood and appreciated only by the proficient who has carefully examined the whole ground. A picture is better than a map for some purposes.

tions of our religious belief, and then proceed to erect the structure with a firmer assurance, that "the gates of hell shall not prevail against it."

Constraint distinguished from government. — I go back, therefore, to the question as I first propounded it: — Looking at the world only as the theatre of human experience, is there sufficient evidence that it is constantly under the government of its Creator, who directs the conduct, and takes an interest in the welfare, of the beings whom he has made? The inanimate universe and the inferior orders of living creatures, as we have seen, depend immediately, and in all their movements, upon the constant care and agency of the Supreme Being. The same power which brought them into existence, sustains and guides them, whether in motion or at rest. Every event, every change in their condition, from the falling of an atom up to the revolutions of a system of worlds, is attributable directly to the agency of God. But this agency here is immediate and exclusive; it is the direct exercise of power, not coöperating with or modified by any power inherent in the bodies themselves, but negativing the existence of such secondary power; it is constraint, not government. But man is a free agent; in one sense, and to a certain extent, he governs himself. Endowed with freewill, and left to choose among many motives of action, his obedience, if rendered at all, is voluntary, not mechanical. Is such obedience claimed of him? Is man, also, under Divine government, — the will of his Creator being signified to him in language that he cannot mistake, and *enforced, not indeed by the iron law of necessity, which is incompatible with his whole moral nature,* but by such considerations as may influence the conduct of a free and rational being?

Butler's argument for the moral government of God. — To this question it is usual to answer, as Bishop Butler has done, that the pleasures and pains of our mortal existence are properly considered as rewards and punishments, the distribution of which was intended to influence our conduct. They mark out the course in which it was designed that we should walk, and serve at once to indicate the will of the Ruler of the universe, and to supply strong motives for compliance with his commands. "All which we enjoy, and a great part of what we suffer, is put in our own power. For pleasure and pain are the consequences of our actions, and we are endowed by the Author of our nature with capacities of foreseeing these consequences. . . . . . It is certain matter of universal experience, that the general method of Divine administration is, forewarning us, or giving us capacities to foresee, with more or less clearness, that if we act so and so, we shall have such enjoyments, and if so and so, such sufferings; and giving us those enjoyments, and making us feel those sufferings, in consequence of our actions."

It is hardly necessary to adduce examples to illustrate this mode of government, as every human being has daily experience of its operation. Imprudence, negligence, or feebleness in the management of our ordinary concerns, is sure to be followed by mischievous consequences, which form its appropriate punishment. If I transgress the known laws of physiology, I am sure to suffer for it by bodily weakness or disease; and if the transgression becomes extreme, sickness ends in death. The health of the mind is equally cared for; we are admonished, in very significant language, that mental cultivation, exertion, and repose are appointed to us, each in its season and proper degree, and the evils of neglect, delay, or excess, are the sharp penalties that enforce the law. As yet, I intentionally pass over all instances relating to the breach of moral laws; these will be considered hereafter, in a different connection.

It is no objection to this view of the matter to say, that *these assumed penalties are but the inevitable results of the natural constitution of things*, the necessary effects of known physical causes. The constitution of things is the appointment of the Creator, and what is called *physical causation* is *the constant working of Divine power.* When we speak of the laws of nature as invariable, and of the consequences of a failure to comply with them as inevitable, we only mark our sense of *the constancy and stability of his administration.** The govern-

* "'But all this is to be ascribed to the general course of nature.' True. This is the very thing which I am observing. It is to be ascribed to the

ment under which we live never fluctuates, wavers, or sleeps; its care extends to the regulation even of our minutest concerns, and the offence against it which is committed in secret bears its penalty as surely as that which was flagrant and avowed in the face of day.

Obedience required irrespective of consequences. — But I go much further. From the analysis of our moral nature, which has just occupied our attention, it appears that obedience to law is demanded of us for its own sake, *irrespective of the consequences that will follow transgression.* Prior to all experience, in the mind of every human being, arises spontaneously the idea or sense of obligation, of duty as such, of submission to authority which is recognized as supreme, and obeyed without compulsion or reference to the consequences of disobedience upon our personal welfare. This idea is the one that lies at the root of all government, and without which, in fact, no government is possible, except that of despotism supported by irresistible power. *Authority can have no other title but that of might,* or of *right.* In the former case, *obedience, being compulsory, is,* properly speaking, *no obedience at all.* It is but a mechanical yielding to superior force. An offender who is actu-

general course of nature: *i. e.* not surely to the words or ideas, *course of nature;* but to him who appointed it, and put things into it; or to a course of operation, from its uniformity or constancy, called natural; and which necessarily implies an operating agent. For when men find themselves necessitated to confess an Author of Nature, or that God is the natural governor of the world, they must not deny this again, because his government is uniform; they must not deny that he does things at all, because he does them constantly; because the effects of his acting are permanent, whether his acting be so or not; though there is no reason to think it is not. In short, every man, in every thing he does, naturally acts upon the forethought and apprehension of avoiding evil or obtaining good: and if the natural course of things be the appointment of God, and our natural faculties of knowledge and experience are given us by him, then the good and bad consequences which follow our actions, are his appointment, and our foresight of those consequences is a warning given us by him, how we are to act.' — Butler's *Analogy,* Part I. Chap 2.

ally in the grasp of the officers of the law, and is dragged away by them to punishment, may be said to *obey* their motions; but in no other sense than as a ship is said to obey the impulse of the winds. There is no will, no proper volition, in the case; and therefore no proper submission or obedience. Even if violence is not actually applied, but *only threatened*, there being a moral certainty that the threat will be executed, the individual may be said to yield, but he does not properly obey, or recognize the authority which thus constrains him against his will. He is still, either in expectation or reality, moved by brute force, — *not governed.*

A mere system of rewards and punishments is not government. — Perhaps it will not be deemed refining too far, if I add, that a mere system for influencing the conduct of others through rewards and penalties, without reference to an assumed legitimate authority, or right to command, is not government, but persuasion. Thus, *I may determine the conduct of my neighbor by making sufficiently liberal appeals to his interest;* I may induce him to give up to me his house and land, or even to sell his services. *Still, he is not governed;* there being no assumption of authority, no claim of right, on either side. He only governs whose commands are obeyed from a sense of moral obligation; and the fruits of disobedience are properly considered as punishment, only after it is admitted that the disobedience is a moral wrong. Hence, no one is justified in violating the law simply because he is willing to suffer the penalty attached to that infraction, nor does the suffering expiate the guilt which he has incurred. Penalties are means of enforcing obedience which are but one degree less violent than the direct application of superior strength.

I do not say that a system of rewards and punishments is so inconsistent with the nature of moral government that the two cannot exist together, or that the one cannot be a supplement of the other, operating to make it more universal and effective. On the contrary, I shall attempt to show hereafter, that such a system, very complete and admirable in its arrangements, is an actual adjunct of the Divine government, which, without it, would be quite too limited in its effects upon human conduct. But my present point is, that *the government itself*, or the pronunciation of a law and the recognition of its authority and binding power, *is perfectly distinct from the means and appliances by which it is made effective, and men are brought under its control;* the *promulgation* of a law is one thing, and *the apparatus for its enforcement* is another. We can conceive of a community so virtuous, that rewards and penalties should not be needed or known among them, but obedience should be spontaneous and universal; their state, then, would not be the absence of government, but its perfection. With less compliant dispositions, some means of enforcing the law are needed, till obedience becomes a habit, and the yoke, as in the former case, is easily borne. Thus, in the scheme of Divine Providence, *rewards and punishments are our schoolmasters; by them we are educated into obedience*, and become willing subjects of the reign of God upon the earth.

"Lord, with what care hast thou begirt us round!
  Parents first season us; then schoolmasters
Deliver us to laws; they send us bound
  To rules of reason, holy messengers,
Pulpits and Sundays, sorrow dogging sin,
  Afflictions sorted, anguish of all sizes,
Fine nets and stratagems to catch us in,
  Bibles laid open, millions of surprises,
Blessings beforehand, ties of gratefulness,
  The sound of glory ringing in our ears;
Without our shame, within our consciences;
  Angels and grace, eternal hopes and fears.
Yet all these forces, and their whole array,
One cunning bosom-sin blows quite away."

How obedience, at first selfishly rendered, becomes pure.— That beautiful law of our mental constitution, which accounts for the formation of what are called "secondary desires," affords a means for the purification of the motive, and for a passage from the selfish to the disinterested stage of moral progress.

The process is a simple one, being merely *a transference of the affections from the end to the means.* By the association of ideas, that which was at first loved or practised only as an *instrument*, becomes the leading idea and the *chief object* of pursuit. Thus, in the downward course, *money*, at first desired only as a means of gratifying the appetites, or of answering some higher ends, becomes itself "an appetite and a passion," and the vicious habit of avarice is formed. And so, in our upward progress, the *honesty* which was first practised only because it was the best policy, the worship of God which was first paid only as the price of heaven, become at last the unbought and unselfish homage of the soul to uprightness, holiness, and truth. *Virtue* deserves its name only when, by long practice, it has become *a fixed habit;* for then only is it freed from the stain of selfishness. The terrors of the law are proclaimed to the sinner only that he may be able to overcome the first shock of the transition from sin to holiness; its promises are reserved for those only who, by patient continuance in well-doing, have become alike indifferent to the debasing fear and the debasing hope.

Conscience proves the moral government of God. — But to return to the leading branch of our subject; — I do not see that there is any possibility of regarding the most prominent fact in the moral constitution of man in any other light, than as a direct proof of the government which the Deity exercises over him, and of the constant submission and obedience which are required of him, even at the expense, if necessary, of his temporal interests. His consciousness informs him, that *the authority* thus exercised *is absolute, or supreme;* all considerations of interest, all earthly authority, must give way to it. At the same time, this subject of the Divine government *remains a free agent;* he may, he often does, act in opposition to the law within the heart, and braves the consequences of the violation. What those consequences are, or how the moral law is upheld by corresponding arrangements in the physical universe, or the general constitution of things, I do not now consider; nor is it necessary for our present purpose to ask what the commands are which are promulgated under this awful authority. It is enough at present to show, that *a claim to supreme authority, for commands of whatever nature, is actually set up and universally recognized;* for this is sufficient proof that the affairs of the moral universe are under the constant direction and government of its Creator. The Epicurean theory, that God exists, but does not govern, is not a whit less improbable and absurd than the hypothesis of the atheist.

Objection refuted. — To this argument it may be objected, that, according to the view already taken of the theory of ethics, *the obligation* of the moral law *does not in anywise depend upon the will of the Deity,* but exists anterior to all command, and forms, in truth, the only ground upon which we can impute holiness to him, or justice to his dealings with men. Certainly, this law does not appear to us as arbitrary, or dependent upon mere will; if it did, we could not recognize its absolute and inherent obligation. But *it may properly be regarded as his law through whose agency alone it is made known to us; he who promulgates and sanctions a law, may be regarded as the author of it* by those whom he addresses. He has so constituted our minds, that we cannot escape a knowledge of the law, and frequent monitions of its paramount claims to obedience. The endowment of conscience is as plain an indication of his will in this respect, as the curious structure of the eye is of his intention that we should see. Compliance with the law of conscience, then, is obedience to God.

Argument from design founded on our intellectual and moral nature. — The extraordinary number, obviousness, and beauty of those illustrations of the argument from design, which are drawn from the physical universe, arrest and detain the attention with so strong a grasp, that it is difficult to give due prominence and effect to the other branch of the same argument, which rests upon the intellectual and moral nature of man. If we were not accustomed to dwell so exclusively upon the former, attracted by the copious and interesting details which it brings to our notice, I think every one would acknowledge, that the latter was really even more direct, logical, and convincing The marks of contrivance in the arrangements of matter which fill earth, sea, and skies, the effects that are constantly reproduced, all working together harmoniously, often by long and complex processes, for the production of specific and useful results, compel us to believe, not only that God exists, but that he is constantly present in his material creation, sustaining, vivifying, acting with ceaseless energy; the objects themselves, and all the changes and movements which take place in them, affording equally striking proofs of his immediate agency and universal Providence. But minds which are compelled to admit this conclusion without hesitancy, are so much perplexed by the history of man upon the earth, by the long and gloomy record of human folly, ignorance, passion, wilfulness, suffering, and sin, that they are half disposed to make our race the only exceptions to the universality of Divine care and forethought, and to believe that man alone is left to himself in this world, free to work out his own inventions, and to endure their consequences. A belief in the absolute freedom of the human will seems, at first sight, almost necessarily to lead to this doctrine. *How can man*, they ask, *be both free and governed, self-directed and subject to another's will and power,— at the some moment a sovereign, and an automaton or a slave?* And the result, the effects that are actually produced, appear to corroborate this opinion, to which we have been led by the antecedent view of the case. If man be governed at all by Supreme Power, his history seems to prove that he is very ill-governed. To recur to a former illustration, the economy of a hive of bees puts to shame the most orderly society that the wit of man ever framed and maintained. No wonder that the doctrine of the original and total depravity of the human race has obtained so ready an acceptance with most theologians, even on grounds apart from Scripture. The history of the civilized portion of the race, to say nothing of the earlier ages of the world, or of the great majority of its present inhabitants still sunk in barbarism and all the evils of savage life, seem to sustain and also to demonstrate it.

Beauty of the contrivance by which this problem is solved. — I admit the difficulty to its full extent, and have endeavored to make the statement of it as full and forcible as possible, so as to give no room for the imputation of evading the real knot and perplexity in the argument. But it is on account of the greatness of the difficulty, — because we see that human *reason* alone, unaided by *conscience*, could not reconcile the contradiction which is here presented to it, — that we are so much struck by the display of infinite wisdom which has solved the problem so completely, that not a shadow remains from it upon the faith of the believer. *To reconcile absolute government with perfect freewill on the part of the governed,* and to account for the existence of moral and physical evil without imputing either carelessness or malevolence to the ruler, *is the problem to be solved.* The instinct of brutes, which is a power acting above their individual nature and the sphere of their consciousness, shows us how man *might* be guided to the highest and noblest ends, so that all the lower purposes of his being should be answered, and his happiness provided for in full measure, without any moral endowment whatever, and of course, without any responsibility on his part, or any possibility of sin. But merit and demerit would then be words without meaning, as *compulsory virtue* is a contradiction in terms. Man, then, must be self-guided, but must still act under the consciousness of a law which he acknowledges to be supreme, and to which he owes implicit obedience. The point is, that he should be able to recognize the supremacy of this law, and still be free to obey it or not. Admitting his freedom, and the full force of the instinctive passions and appetites by which he is swayed or impelled, how can he remain a subject of the Divine government?

Solution of the problem. — Suppose, then, that a voice from heaven should proclaim to him distinctly, at every hour and minute of the day, the will of an infinitely superior being as to the regulation of his conduct, — the voice being accompanied by such manifest and imposing tokens of the majesty and omnipotence of the source whence it came, that even the natural sentiment of awe, not supported by any direct reference to conse quences, would incline him to submit implicitly to the command. Suppose that the purport of the order thus supernaturally communicated to him was to restrict his natural impulses and desires, and to set before him a rule of conduct more perfect even than a chastised and rational regard for his own happiness, so that a self-guided will should submit to the sacrifice of self. Still it might be said, that *his awe-struck faculties were terrified into submission*, so that in truth, compliance was no longer free. And so, if man were endowed only with appetite and intellect, must every other attempt fail to get rid of the difficulty in question, and to remove what seems, in the eye of reason alone, the absolute inconsistency between the ideas of subjection and freedom.

Now change the supposition a little, but enough to conform it to the real state of the case. Imagine, that, instead of a voice from heaven thus constantly proclaiming to us the will of the Supreme Being, enforced by all the outward terrors of the law given from Sinai, the injunction should constantly be repeated within the mind itself, in a manner far more impressive than if it were accompanied by the thunder and the earthquake from without. Imagine that the order thus made known is attended by a conception — that of *duty* — which the intellect alone could never frame, and which alone can reconcile the idea of *law* with that of *liberty*, of absolute *obligation* with perfect *freedom*. Yet this imagining is but a plain statement of the functions of conscience, — of the miracle, so to speak, which is constantly wrought within us, in order that we may perceive that our moral freedom is compatible with our subjection to the Divine government. Remember how numerous are the occasions on which this idea rises, and the variety of applications of which it is susceptible. It colors nearly every action of our lives, and modifies every judgment that we can form of the conduct of our fellow-beings. By introducing the idea of a law of paramount obligation, and, at the same time, removing all show of compulsion or even of terror, and speaking without reference either to rewards or punishments, it first makes the conception of virtue possible. Far from negativing the freedom of the will, *it pre-*

supposes freedom, — *it is not compatible with any condition but that of freedom,* — and therefore we cannot even conceive of its application to brutes.

Moral good implies the possibility of moral evil. — All virtue is conformity to the rule thus made known to us, and all vice is departure from it. It is demonstrable, then, that moral good flows from the same fountain as moral evil, and that the one cannot exist without the possibility of the other. Why is it that we are so painfully affected, on reviewing the history of mankind, or examining into their present condition? It is because the requisitions of conscience are so high and pure, and in judging of the conduct of *others,* at least, it is so natural to apply them, that we almost involuntarily dwell upon the examples of transgression, upon the amount of sin and consequent woe which is in the world, and which operates to divert our attention from the moral good of which these evils are the necessary price, and by which they are accompanied and redeemed. It is only to this one-sided view that the prospect seems dark, and God's scheme of government of the human family appears one of doubtful wisdom or benevolence. Why not dwell rather upon the virtues that are practised, the amount of good that is actually done, and then admire the perfection of the scheme which renders such excellence attainable by man? It is true that *moral excellence is not usually so prominent,* or so likely to arrest the attention of the observer, *as moral delinquency;* for great crimes usually announce themselves with startling effect, and are attended by a long train of disastrous consequences, which extend and deepen the impression; while the virtues love the shade, and the good which flows from the observance of them is a noiseless stream. But if we judge men by their intentions rather than their outward conduct, — and this is obviously the only correct judgment, — I am inclined to believe that the law of conscience is far more frequently obeyed than violated. The worst man that ever lived is still conscious at times of noble and virtuous impulses, and in his own view of the matter, at any rate, if not in that of his neighbors, his conduct often conforms to them. A conscious transgression of the most obvious principles of rectitude is too unnatural and too painful an act to be wantonly or frequently repeated. Certainly, a whole life of crime, of gratuitous violence and wrong, relieved by no compunctions, and unvaried by any act of mercy, truthfulness, or justice, is so monstrous a conception, that no one ever expects to see it realized.

Why evil appears prominent in history. — "How small," says Stewart, "is the number of individuals who draw the attention of the world by their crimes, when compared with the millions who pass their days in inoffensive obscurity! Of this it is scarcely necessary to produce any other proof, than the fact which is commonly urged on the other side of the argument, — the catalogue of crimes and calamities which sully the history of past ages. For whence is the interest we take in historical reading, but from the *singularity* of the events it records, and from the contrast which its glaring colors present to the uniformity and repose of private life? Even in those unhappy periods which have furnished the most ample materials to the historian, the storm has spent its rage in general on a comparatively small number of men, placed in the more conspicuous stations of society by their birth, by their talents, by their ambition, or by an heroical sense of duty; while the unobserved multitude saw it pass over their head, or only heard its noise at a distance. Nor must we pronounce all those to have been unhappy who are commonly styled the unfortunate. The mind suits itself to the part it is destined to act, and, when great and worthy objects are before it, exults in those moments of hazard and alarm, which, even while they threaten life and freedom, leave us in the possession of every thing that constitutes the glory and the perfection of our nature."

It is *the sensitiveness of our moral constitution*, alive to the slightest appearance of wrong, and painfully affected by any manifestation of it on a large scale, which leads us, on a speculative view of the subject, to exaggerate the amount of moral evil in the world. Far from being a defect, this sensitiveness should be accounted an excellence in our moral being, as it shows how strong is our appreciation of the authority of conscience, how wide a field in our view is covered by its commands, and how quick is our perception of any case in which these commands are violated. Thus, as Butler finely remarks, the judgments which men form of each other tend to carry out the purposes of the Almighty, by constituting a part of the punishment which he has appointed for every transgression. They enter into the scheme of Divine government, which, even as manifested in the history of our race, is far more direct, comprehensive, and searching than most persons imagine. A little reflection will convince them, that they have greatly underrated the number and minuteness of the occasions in which the moral faculty is called into exercise, and really determines the conduct even of the worst of men.

The incessant and universal activity of conscience. — The institution of *property*, for instance, is founded entirely on our sense of justice, which is correctly defined to be "the constant intention to give to every man that which is rightfully his own." He who voluntarily deprives himself of any thing which seems to him at all valuable or desirable, for the mere purpose of restoring it to another who has a better claim to it, or who even abstains from the attempt to seize and appropriate it when it is in the possession of its rightful owner, is so far actuated by the feeling of justice, or is obedient to that injunction of the Almighty which is manifested through the conscience. Now, *no nation has ever been discovered on the earth, so low and brutal in their inclinations and habits,* so destitute of any idea of right, *that the institution of property,* to a greater or less extent, *does not exist among them.* The right of the savage to the tools and weapons which his own hand has fashioned, and to the game which he has caught, is universally respected by his fellows; or if this original title is ever violated, it is from some rude notion of government, or authority in the head of the tribe, or punishment inflicted for some offence, at the bottom of which notion, also, lies the feeling of right, as distinct as in the case of original ownership. That the property *continues* in the possession of the owner, is owing only to a *constant* exercise of self-denial on the part of those who have it not and still desire it; thus showing that the sense of rectitude is, to this extent at least, a permanent and effective rule of conduct. The familiar proverb, that there is honesty even among thieves, at any rate in their treatment of their fellows, proves that this remark holds true even of those who are commonly supposed to live in open defiance of every law, both human and Divine. Now a single instance of robbery on a great scale, by the general indignation that it creates, occupies a larger space in the minds and memories of men, than all this continuous observance of the rule.

If any doubt remains as to the entire dependence of this institution on our primitive and habitual regard for law, it will be removed by a glance at the brute creation. The lower animals have not even an instinct which leads to restitution; the power of the strongest is, with them, the only law. The hungry mastiff wrests the bone from his feebler companion, and blind appetite or fear alone guides the more ferocious beasts in the appropriation of their food. The mother-bird, indeed, stints its own appetite for the benefit of its young; but this is only from the strong impulse of natural affection, which is as blind and unreasoning in the brute as in the human heart. The constant respect for property, then, proves the universality and ceaseless operation of the moral nature of man.

Distinction between absolute and relative right. — It is obvious that this argument for the constancy and immediateness of the moral government of God applies with the greater force, in proportion to the culture which our moral perceptions have received. I have already hinted, that bad men are not so bad as they seem; and one reason why they are not, is, that they look at their own conduct from a different point of view from that which is taken by the bystanders. A good deal of the disorder and injustice which we see, does not demonstrate any ill intention on the part of its authors; nay, it often proceeds from an uncultivated or misdirected sense of duty, and is so far meritorious. We must distinguish carefully between absolute and relative right. "An action is said to be absolutely right," says Dugald Stewart, "when it is in every respect suitable to the circumstances in which the agent is placed; or, in other words, when it is such as, with perfectly good intentions, under the guidance of an enlightened and well-informed understanding, he would have performed. An action is said to be relatively right, when the intentions of the agent are sincerely good, whether his conduct be suitable to his circumstances or not. According to these definitions, it is evident, that an action may be *right* in one sense, and *wrong* in another; and it is no less evident, that it is the *relative* rectitude alone of an action, which determines the moral desert of the agent in the sight of God and of his own conscience."

Conscience gives us the conception of duty, or feeling of obligation, but does not apply this feeling to outward conduct. Its sphere of action is wholly internal, motives and intentions being its only subjects; what course of conduct will best carry out these intentions, is a question, not for the moral faculty, but for the intellect, to answer; and the uninformed or perverted understanding may answer it very ill. Thus, conscience approves and enjoins *justice*, *benevolence*, *veracity*, which is a form of *justice*, and *patriotism*, which is a department of *benevolence;* it even pronounces upon the relative claims of these virtues to observance, though not so distinctly, affirming that *justice* is of higher obligation than *benevolence*. But what conduct, what outward acts, will be truly just, or truly benevolent, or whether a patriotic intention will justify cunning words or harsh deeds, are doubts of which it furnishes no solution. Reason must here be our guide. The train of consequences, some of them very remote, which every action carries with it, must be foreseen and estimated, — a work for the understanding, — before these questions can be answered. Our moral sense, which is infallible in its sphere, only declares that an action *is* just *to him who intends it for justice;* and to him who thinks a certain deed is benevolent, to him it shall be accounted for benevolence. Apply these principles to history, and to our common observation of mankind, and much of what we are accustomed to consider as evidence of the depravity and wickedness of the human race disappears altogether; nay, if fully considered, it affords proof of the existence of high virtues among men, for the action, in the case considered, becomes not only innocent, but meritorious.

This distinction illustrated. — Take *war*, for instance. To one who reads history in a proper spirit, there is probably nothing so painful as the almost continuous record which it affords of the bloodshed, misery, and corruption caused by this brutal and detestable practice. War is, indeed, "the garment of vengeance with which the Deity arrays himself, when he comes forth to punish the inhabitants of the earth." Looking at it from a distance, in the light of a calm philosophy, no less than of a pure morality, we are tempted to believe that it must be waged by demons rather than by men, and that its motives are as bad as its consequences are afflicting. The language of Robert Hall seems hardly exaggerated, when he says, that "the plague of a widely extended war possesses, in fact, a sort of omnipresence, by which it makes itself everywhere felt; for while it gives up myriads to slaughter in one part of the globe, it is busily employed in scattering over countries exempt from its immediate desolations the seeds of famine, pestilence, and death. . . . . . While the philanthropist is devising means to mitigate the evils and augment the happiness of the world, a fellow-worker together with God, in exploring and giving effect to the benevolent tendencies of nature, the warrior is revolving, in the gloomy recesses of his capacious mind, plans of future devastation and ruin. Prisons crowded with captives, cities emptied of their inhabitants, fields desolate and waste, are among his proudest trophies. The fabric of his fame is cemented with tears and blood; and if his name is wafted to the ends of the earth, it is in the shrill cry of suffering humanity, in the curses and imprecations of those whom his sword has reduced to despair."

The picture is indeed a terrible one, though but few will think it is overdrawn. Yet the truth, I suppose, unquestionably is, that *almost every person concerned in war, whether an originator of the strife or an actor in it, is either actuated, or, what amounts to the same thing in the light in which we are now viewing the matter, believes himself to be actuated, by the highest and holiest motives.* The statesman thinks that the welfare and honor of his country are at stake, and that it is his stern duty to stifle his feelings of compassion for the multitude, and to punish aggression, arrogance, and injustice, even at the expense of a long and bloody conflict. The military chieftain feels that the safety and honor of his troops depend upon his courage and conduct, and that he acts under an awful responsibility to the rightful government of his country, which has confided this awful mission to his hands; it may be, that he goes to a hopeless contest, and then the feelings which support the martyr at the stake are hardly superior to his. Hence the strange contradiction, as it seems, of which history affords more than one instance, that a commander, on the morning after he had achieved a great victory, should be found weeping like a child over the spectacle that the field afforded of suffering and death which his own hand had caused. Lord Collingwood was one of the most high-minded, pure, affectionate, and strictly moral men of whom the British peerage can boast; yet this man commanded the ship which fired the first English gun in the sanguinary naval conflict of Trafalgar. The common soldier is ignorant and brutal, most likely; but he, too, in the moment of action, has learned to suppress all other feelings at the mandate of duty, — the duty on which every thing then depends, that of implicit submission to his superiors. It would be a strange paradox to say, that a camp is a nursery of lofty and stern virtues; yet it certainly does foster a chivalrous exaltation of feeling, which reason, indeed, condemns, as an impure mixture of false sentiment with an austere regard for duty, but which has so much of the moral element in it, that it cannot be harshly reprobated.

I am not palliating the evils of war; God forbid that I should say one word, to make any human being look upon the practice of it with less horror and detestation than he now feels! I am only suggesting some reasons why it should not make us think so badly of our fellow beings, as to doubt whether they are under the moral government of God. If the distinctions here suggested do not tend at all to abate the severity of our condemnation of immoral practices, but only to render our feelings more charitable and just towards those who are engaged in them, they may well be kept in mind even by the professed philanthropists. The spirit of our religion certainly requires us to hate sin, but holds up the sinner to us as an object of compassion, kindness, and love.

Conclusions respecting the moral government of God. — I have not intended in this chapter even to approach the great problem of the origin of evil; that remains for subsequent consideration. I have only wished to show, that, in the moral constitution of man, there is the plainest proof, not only that we live under the immediate government of God, but that this government is effectual, the results produced being commensurate with the means employed. Not only is the will of God made known to us, at every moment of our lives, as the absolute rule of our conduct, the supreme law; but the announcement of this law is made compatible with human freedom, and the law itself is practically recognized and observed, to a greater or less extent, by every human being. Human government, the direction and control of organized societies of men, rest upon this Divine government, and would not be practicable without it. Property, as we have seen, is supported in the same manner. The law of God, promulgated through the conscience, and acknowledged both by the savage and by civilized man as supreme, exerts an influence that no man can measure over the life of every individual; it forms the basis of those institutions which are essential to the very existence of society; it sways the councils of nations; it governs the course of human affairs.

And the means by which these great ends are accomplished — especially the manner in which we are perpetually reminded of the Divine command, as if by a voice from heaven, and the mode of reconciling liberty with law — are as beautiful instances of contrivance, they furnish quite as striking indications of Divine wisdom and goodness, as any which the material universe affords.

CHAPTER V.

THE CONTENTS OF THE MORAL LAW A REVELATION OF THE CHARACTER OF THE DEITY: THE ENFORCEMENT OF THE MORAL LAW.

Summary of the last chapter. — I attempted to prove, in the last chapter, that the moral constitution of man affords direct and irrefragable evidence, that he is under the constant and immediate government of God. That the pleasures and pains which we experience in this life, and which proceed from regular and determinable causes, and therefore may be foreseen by us, may properly be regarded as rewards and punishments, indicating to us the will of the Deity that we should perform certain actions and abstain from others, is another argument tending to the same conclusion; but it does not seem to me so complete and satisfactory as the former one. Conscience announces to us a law of absolute authority for the guidance of our hearts and lives; its monitions are frequent, if not incessant, and the obligation which it imposes is recognized, whether we will or no, to be supreme. At the same time, it does not compel or force obedience, so that the liberty of the will is not infringed, but government is made compatible with freedom. This idea of pure and absolute obligation, or the sense of duty *as such*, as distinguished from *compulsion* on the one hand, and from a perfectly unregulated and ungoverned will on the other, is one which the intellect alone could never frame, and it does away with the apparent contradiction between liberty and law. Here, I observed, is contrivance, the indication of purpose, in the moral nature of man, just as visible as in the curious physical apparatus by which we see, and just as clearly indicative of the intention of the Creator. The law thus revealed to us is *His* law who reveals it. If the fashioning of our bodies —

these wonderful but perishable tenements of clay that we inhabit for a season — shows the wisdom and the purposes of Him who made them, how much more does the framework of our intellectual and moral being testify to the same effect! This is equally His contrivance, His work. It is not more evident that the ear was made to hear with, or the organs of voice to speak, or the lungs to breathe, than that the law proclaimed by conscience should be obeyed as His will; otherwise, the moral faculty is constituted in vain, and exists for no conceivable purpose.

This scheme of government, I remarked, is both comprehensive and minute; it assumes to regulate every purpose of the heart, and to mould the whole life and character. And it is effectual; the purpose which is indicated by this endowment of the mind with the power of distinguishing right from wrong, is carried out and realized to the fullest extent that is consistent with individual liberty. The conduct even of the vicious and the profligate, of the savage as well as the civilized man, is daily and hourly influenced by the law written on the heart. Society itself could not exist without it, as its most important institutions, government and property, recognize it, and are, in fact, supported by it. Through the sensitiveness of our moral nature, I endeavored to show, we are prone to exaggerate the moral disorder and depravity which are in the world and are revealed in history. If we judge men by their intentions, instead of their outward conduct, — and it is the former alone which the plan of Divine government assumes directly to regulate, — much of their seeming lawlessness and wickedness disappears. Even war, that great scourge of the human family, is carried on, by most of those who are engaged in it, with a high moral purpose, — misdirected, it is true, but pure. I am well aware that this explanation leaves the ignorance of men, and the blinding power of their passions, as evils still to be accounted for; these remain for subsequent discussion. At present, I am only concerned to show, that *there is a Divine government, — not that it is a perfect government.*

The contents of the moral law. — So we have not considered as yet, except incidentally, the purport or contents of the law which is revealed in the conscience; the mere existence of such a law, and its claim of absolute supremacy, with the fact that it is recognized and acted upon, being the only points upon which stress has been laid. We have now to consider what the law enjoins. The very brief answer may be given, that it requires of us *a pure heart and a virtuous life;* all that is comprehended under these phrases being entitled to the name of purity or virtue, only because it *is* required by conscience. *Disinterestedness* is included; for the most obvious characteristic of the voice of conscience is, that it is to be obeyed at all hazards. *The obligation is perfect;* no matter by what sacrifice, I *must* render to another that which is his own, and my word *must* be kept. And as no fear or hope with regard to the consequences of the act upon my own welfare should tempt me to wrong-doing, so they ought not to be my reasons for following the right. *Virtue must be cultivated for its own sake;* otherwise, it is not virtue, but selfishness. It is hardly necessary to say, that the law is so watchful and exacting, that it descends to the secrets of the heart, and declares what the purpose shall be, before that purpose is realized in the act; this is the primary function of the conscience. The immediate object of the law, as already observed, is *not conduct, but the intention which regulates the conduct.* And all these points in the law are rendered so plain and familiar, even to the uninstructed, that in enlarging upon them, I must appear to you to be dwelling upon mere truisms. It is only when we come to reflect upon the marvellous constitution of our bodies and minds, considered as the work of the Almighty, and as indicating his will, that these worn truths reassume freshness and interest. At other times, we take them for granted, and *intend* to act upon them.

Why virtue is enjoined. — The question may now be asked, Why is it that we are enjoined to cultivate such dispositions of mind, or to act upon such intentions, in preference to all others? In one sense, the answer has been already given; it is because we have an intuitive knowledge, that virtue is of paramount obligation, or absolutely binding for its own sake, so that to inquire, *why* it is obligatory, is just as much an impertinence as it would be to ask, *why* two and two make four. The axioms of morals stand on the same basis with the axioms of mathematics; they cannot be proved because they need no proof; they are self-evident. But as we are here considering the subject in reference to the Divine government and the character of God, I put the question in a little different form:—*Why has the Deity so constituted our minds that we must perceive the supreme obligation of virtue?* If it was not His will alone which established the moral law, it was certainly His will which gave us the power or faculty of perceiving that law and its absolute obligation, and thereby of distinguishing right from wrong. He might have constituted us like the lower animals, who have no knowledge of it whatever. Why did he impart that knowledge to us? or, in other words, why has he given to man a conscience?

Conscience not needed for the preservation of life. — Certainly, not for the same reason for which we are endowed with appetites; these were intended to stimulate us to the exertions that are requisite before the wants of the body can be supplied. Without hunger, we should forget or neglect to eat, just as we now omit many precautions and exercises which are really important for the preservation of health, though not, like food, absolutely essential to life. But conscience is not essential for the preservation of animal life; like the brutes, we might get along without it; that is, we might preserve a merely animal existence. So one use of intellect—a lower use, but yet a sufficient reason for implanting the faculty in man—is to direct those exertions to which we are stimulated by the appetites and desires, or to discover appropriate means for those ends which are pointed out to us by our physical constitution. In this respect, *reason* takes the place in man of *instinct* in the brute creation. But a sense of duty is not needed for the performance of this office, so that we still ask, why we were gifted with this sense. The manifold arrangements and beautiful contrivances, with which the purely material universe abounds, all subserve important ends, and in these ends we read the purposes of their Contriver. Each has its part to play in upholding the fabric of that universe of which it is a portion, and we know that it was *designed* to fill that part. But the law of right, with the consciousness of it which animates every human breast, has no such function to perform. Earth's base is not built upon it; nor does it form the pillars which support the material firmament. The outer world might exist without it, as the geologists tell us it did, for ages before it was tenanted by man. The laws of gravitation, chemical affinity, and the like, — if I may adopt for a moment the phraseology of a theory which I repudiate, — all work to visible and highly useful ends; — Does the law of morality alone answer no purpose in the universe which God has made?

Conscience overrules all considerations of utility. — The question becomes still more striking, when we remember that conscience not only is not needed for any of the offices which we have thus far considered, but that it absolutely precludes all reference to them, when their performance would come in conflict with any of its own absolute commands. The call of duty must be obeyed, though the appetites should remain without their appropriate food, and the desires should languish, and the intellect should forget its cunning; the demands of justice must be satisfied, though the body should perish, and even though the heavens should fall. And this peculiarity in the law of conscience enables us to prove, that one beneficial result, which actually is accomplished by implanting this faculty in man, still does not reveal the reason or purpose for which it was so implanted. The law *does* conduce to *the welfare of society*, which probably could not even exist without it. That state of things which Hobbes imagined and described with so much graphic power, as the natural state of man, unquestionably would be his natural state, if, as Hobbes supposed, his desires and actions were not controlled by any innate sense of right. Every man would be the natural enemy of his fellow, the passions and appetites stimulating him to grasp at every thing which pleased his senses, or promised future enjoyment, without regard to any principle of ownership, and without consciousness of any law, whether human or Divine, which forbade robbery or unpro-

28

voked aggression. Man would be a solitary and purely selfish animal, never meeting even his nearest relative except in a struggle to wrest from him any valuable which his strength or ingenuity had created. There could be "no arts, no letters, no society; and the life of man [would be] solitary, poor, nasty, brutish, and short."

But conscience furnishes that restraining and regulating force which Hobbes could find only in a wise despotism. The feeling of moral obligation introduces order into this chaos. The individual voluntarily submits to the ordinances of society decreed and enforced for the common good, because the sense of duty, the idea of submission to law and right, is inwoven in his constitution. He becomes capable of human government, because Divine government is established in his own bosom. And as society in this way first becomes practicable, so its welfare is promoted just in proportion to the prevalence of the sense of right among its members. If the practice of virtue were universal, if men acted up to their own convictions of duty, there would be no need of human legislation, or of any external apparatus for the government of man.

Virtue not enjoined for the sake of its outward beneficial consequences. — Still, I say, the great good thus effected is not the object for which the practice of virtue is enjoined. Conscience itself informs us that it is not; far from laying down the rule because its observance would be beneficial to society, it erects the rule itself into a standard to which our regard for the welfare, the material well-being, of the community must conform. Justice must be enforced, though the commonwealth should suffer for it. Though the pride of the state should be humiliated, and its power be diminished, and its prosperity should receive a real or a seeming check, the law of right must be obeyed. It must have absolute sway and masterdom, for in this light alone it is revealed to us. *Virtue is an end, never a means;* and, of course, the end can never become subservient to the means. Instead of saying, therefore, that the moral law was enacted for the benefit of society, in order that men might live peaceably and profitably together, it would be more proper to affirm, that, so far as we can see into the designs of Providence, *society itself was intended to be only the occasion and the theatre for the display and development of this law*, in order that the virtues which it enjoins might have scope and objects on which they might be exercised. The good which the community reaps from the cultivation of virtue, is, therefore, an incidental advantage of the law, not the great purpose for which it was ordained.

The law of conscience reveals the character of the Creator. — Finding, then, that no object or purpose, inferior in dignity and excellence to the law of rectitude itself, affords any sufficient reason why that law was engraved on the human soul, we are compelled to admit, that *the contents of the law are simply a revelation of the character of the Creator.* Absolute rectitude or holiness is His will, because it is His nature, and the law which requires it is a reflection of that nature. In its purity and comprehensiveness, in its primary reference to character rather than conduct, in governing the affections and motives whence the acts proceed, rather than the acts themselves, and in its claim to absolute dominion and supremacy, excluding even the idea of subserviency to lower ends, the law images to us the perfections of Him from whom we received it.

Thus, by the way of observation and experience, we arrive at that conclusion respecting the moral attributes of the Almighty, which is usually obtained deductively, or by necessary inference from his eternal and uncaused duration. This course is most satisfactory to my own mind, because it does not leave us to reconcile as we may the unlimited conclusions of *à priori* reasoning with the subsequent lessons of experience; but the doctrine carries its own justification along with it, and harmonizes with all which we have previously learned from the study of external nature, and of our own intellectual and moral being.

Conscience requires perfection. — It is unnecessary here to carry out the reasoning in detail, and deduce the moral attributes of God, one by one, from the requisitions of our moral nature. This application of the argument is sufficiently easy and obvious. We need only remark, that *these requisitions are unlimited.* Every virtue, every trait of character, that is to be cultivated at all, is enjoined to its utmost extent, perfection being the only standard that is placed before us. It is not a certain measure of justice that we are required to render towards our fellow-beings, but absolute justice, to all men, and on all occasions. We have proof, then, that the moral attributes of the Almighty exist each in its perfection; in Him are *absolute* justice, purity, truth, and love.

How far the natural course of events enforces the law of right. — It only remains to inquire, if the evidence from without tends to strengthen and confirm that belief in the moral government of God, which is founded primarily upon the internal constitution of our faculties; — in other words, if the natural course of things in the external world, the ordinary tendencies of human affairs, harmonize with and enforce those laws which are set up in the conscience. As both the inner and the outer world are under the guidance of the same wise and omnipotent Being, we naturally expect that the testimonies of the two will coincide, or that the principles established in the one will be, to a great extent, or in all their main features, carried out in the other. I say, "to a great extent;" because we do not look, in the current of human fortunes, *for that immediate and invariable enforcement of the moral law, which would either deprive man of his free agency, or reduce his virtue to a mere selfish regard for his own happiness.* If, for instance, honesty were the best policy, not merely as a general principle, and in the long run, but always, instantly, and plainly, there would be great danger that men would altogether cease to be honest, in the proper sense of the term, and would be only politic. So weak are human purposes, that we cannot often be certain of ourselves, until an emergency arises in which we are required to be virtuous at some apparent cost, or by some sacrifice. God's justice will be sufficiently vindicated, if it shall at length appear, that the cost is only apparent, and that the sacrifice is ultimately repaid a hundred fold.

How happiness is distributed in this world. — What we observe of the distribution of happiness in this world between the virtuous and the wicked, has been so clearly and fully stated by Adam Smith, in his Theory of Moral Sentiments, that I borrow his language. "If we consider," he says, "the general rules by which external prosperity and adversity are commonly distributed in this life, we shall find, that notwithstanding the disorder in which all things appear to be in this world, yet even here, every virtue naturally meets with its proper reward, with the recompense which is most fit to encourage and promote it; and this, too, so surely, that it requires a very extraordinary concurrence of circumstances entirely to disappoint it. What is the reward most proper for encouraging industry, prudence, and circumspection? Success in every sort of business. And is it possible, that, in the whole of life, these virtues should fail of attaining it? Wealth and external honors are their proper recompense, and the recompense which they can seldom fail of acquiring. What reward is most proper for promoting the practice of truth, justice, and humanity? The confidence, the esteem and love, of those we live with. Humanity does not desire to be great, but to be beloved. It is not in being rich that truth and justice would rejoice, but in being trusted and believed, — recompenses which those virtues must almost always acquire.

"By some very extraordinary and unlucky circumstance, a good man may come to be suspected of a crime, of which he was altogether incapable, and upon that account, be most unjustly exposed, for the remaining part of his life, to the horror and aversion of mankind. By an accident of this kind, he may be said to lose his all, notwithstanding his integrity and justice; in the same manner as a cautious man, notwithstanding his utmost circumspection, may be ruined by an earthquake or an inundation. Accidents of the first kind, however, are perhaps still more rare, and still more contrary to the common course of things, than those of the second; and it still remains true, that the practice of truth, justice, and humanity is a certain and almost infallible method of acquiring what those virtues chiefly aim at, the confidence and love of those we live with. A person may be very easily misrepresented with regard to a particular action; but it is scarce possible that he should be so with regard to the general tenor of his conduct. An innocent man may be believed to have done wrong; this, however, will rarely happen. On the contrary, the established opinion of the innocence of his manners will often lead us to absolve him where he has really been in fault, notwithstanding very strong presumptions. A knave, in the same manner, may escape censure, or even meet with applause, for a particular knavery in which his conduct is not understood. But no man was ever habitually such, without being almost universally known to be so, and without being even frequently suspected of guilt when he was in reality perfectly innocent. And so far as vice and virtue can be either punished or rewarded by the sentiments and opinions of mankind, they both, according to the common course of things, meet, even here, with something more than exact and impartial justice."

The connection between virtue and happiness admitted by all men. — But my point is, perhaps, sufficiently established by a general reference to the fact, that nearly all writers upon the theory of ethics, some of whom have written *against* the evidences of religion, have yet traced a close connection between virtue and happiness; many of them going so far as to maintain, that virtue is obligatory only *because* it is useful; * and

---

* Hume, in his Principles of Morals, adopts the Selfish System to its full extent, maintaining that the virtues are obligatory upon us only because they are pleasing and amiable, and because they conduce to our own welfare and to the welfare of those around us, in whom we are interested by sympathy. According to this System, self-denial is not a virtue; a sacrifice of happiness can never be a duty, since an action becomes obligatory only so far as it conduces to happiness. "Are not justice, fidelity, honor, veracity, allegiance, chastity," he inquires, "esteemed *solely on account of their tendency to promote the good of society?*" Speaking of industry, discretion, frugality, etc., he asks, "can it be doubted, that the tendency of these qualities to promote the interest and happiness of their possessor, is *the sole foundation of their merit?*" He had previously declared, that "*personal merit* consists altogether in the possession of mental qualities useful or agreeable to the person himself, or to others." On this

others, more trustworthy, holding up utility as the only safe *criterion* or test of right conduct; so that, when we are in doubt whether a certain action is morally right or wrong, the

---

ground, such pleasing personal qualities as wit, good-manners, affability, liveliness, etc., are elevated by him to the rank of virtues; while self-denial, humility, and the like, are transferred to "the opposite column," and placed "in the catalogue of vices."

In answer to this sophistry, it is enough to say, that conscience requires us to act justly, even to the extent, if necessary, of abridging our own means of happiness, and injuring the welfare of the community in which we live. It is not necessary to prove, that an act of justice may sometimes require such a sacrifice. It is enough that the agent *believes* he is resigning some personal good, or is perilling his own welfare, by following the dictates of conscience. There may be a compensation to him in the long run; but if he does not foresee that compensation, does not believe that he will obtain it, and acts altogether without reference to it, then, in the view of all the spectators of his conduct, his merit is enhanced by his disinterestedness. According to Hume, this very disinterestedness renders the action blamable instead of praiseworthy. If an apparently benevolent action is found to have a taint of selfishness in it, if the agent was really consulting his own good while he appeared to be acting solely for others, he actually forfeits all claim to the approbation of other persons or of his own conscience; but, according to Hume, his merit would be enhanced by such a motive. In respect to the definitions of virtue and personal merit which lead Hume to confound *talents* with *virtues*, Dugald Stewart justly remarks, "nothing can be plainer than that the words *virtue* and *vice* are applicable only to those parts of our character and conduct which depend on our own voluntary exertions. Sensibility, gayety, liveliness, good-humor, natural affection, are a source of pleasure to every beholder, and, wherever they are to be found, entitle the possessor to the appellation of *amiable;* but in so far as they result from original constitution, or from external circumstances over which he had no control, they certainly do not render him an object of moral approbation."

Still, the testimony of such a moralist as Hume upon the point considered in the text, — the intimate connection between virtue and happiness, — is valuable, for it is the testimony of an opponent of all religion. The following passage is the conclusion of his "Inquiry concerning the Principles of Morals."

"Let a man suppose that he has full power of modelling his own disposition, and let him deliberate what appetite or desire he would choose for the foundation of his happiness and enjoyment. Every affection, he would observe, when gratified by success, gives a satisfaction propor-

only mode of resolving that doubt is to inquire, whether the action is, on the whole, beneficial or injurious to the agent, to society, and to mankind. There may be a few moralists who

---

tioned to its force and violence: but besides this advantage, common to all, the immediate feeling of benevolence and friendship, humanity and kindness, is sweet, smooth, tender, and agreeable, independent of all fortune and accidents. These virtues are, besides, attended with a pleasing consciousness or remembrance, and keep us in humor with ourselves as well as others; while we retain the agreeable reflection of having done our part towards mankind and society. And though all men show a jealousy of our success in the pursuits of avarice and ambition; yet are we almost sure of their good-will and good wishes, so long as we persevere in the paths of virtue, and employ ourselves in the execution of generous plans and purposes. What other passion is there where we shall find so many advantages united; an agreeable sentiment, a pleasing consciousness, a good reputation? But of these truths, we may observe, men are of themselves pretty much convinced; nor are they deficient in their duty to society, because they would not wish to be generous, friendly, and humane, but because they do not feel themselves such.

"Treating vice with the greatest candor, and making it all possible concessions, we must acknowledge that there is not, in any instance, the smallest pretext for giving it the preference above virtue, with a view to self-interest; except, perhaps, in the case of justice, where a man, taking things in a certain light, may often seem to be a loser by his integrity. And though it is allowed that, without a regard to property, no society could subsist, yet, according to the imperfect way in which human affairs are conducted, a sensible knave, in particular incidents, may think that an act of iniquity or infidelity will make considerable addition to his fortune, without causing any considerable breach in the social union and confederacy. That *honesty is the best policy* may be a good general rule, but is liable to many exceptions. And he, it may perhaps be thought, conducts himself with most wisdom, who observes the general rule, and takes advantage of all the exceptions.

"I must confess, that if a man think that this reasoning much requires an answer, it will be a little difficult to find any which will to him appear satisfactory and convincing. If his heart rebel not against such pernicious maxims, if he feel no reluctance to the thoughts of villany or baseness, he has indeed lost a considerable motive to virtue; and we may expect that his practice will be answerable to his speculation. But in all ingenuous natures, the antipathy to treachery and roguery is too strong to be counterbalanced by any views of profit or pecuniary advantage. Inward peace of mind, consciousness of integrity, a satisfactory review of our own

would not accept either of these doctrines in so broad and unqualified a manner as I have stated them; but I never heard of one who was bold enough to maintain, that vice, on the whole, was the best policy for the individual, or most likely to promote the interests of society; the common sense of mankind would instantly reject so monstrous a paradox. For the truth on this subject is held not merely by instructed and reflecting men, by those who are inclined to speculative pursuits, or who have made ethics a favorite study, but it is embodied in a multitude of those proverbs and axiomatic sayings, which are the repositories of the wisdom and the experience of the bulk of mankind. Poor Richard's morality is a mere string of such sayings, all going to show the invariable connection between integrity, sobriety, and industry on the one hand, and health, peace of mind, reputation, and riches on the other. The indignation or sorrow which we feel, when one of these virtues fails to meet its appropriate reward, or when, in solitary instances, knavery or indo-

---

conduct, these are circumstances very requisite to happiness, and will be cherished and cultivated by every honest man who feels the importance of them.

"Such a one has, besides, the frequent satisfaction of seeing knaves, with all their pretended cunning and abilities, betrayed by their own maxims; and while they purpose to cheat with moderation and secrecy, a tempting incident occurs, nature is frail, and they give into the snare; whence they can never extricate themselves, without a total loss of reputation, and the forfeiture of all future trust and confidence with mankind.

"But were they ever so secret and successful, the honest man, if he has any tincture of philosophy, or even common observation and reflection, will discover that they themselves are, in the end, the greatest dupes, and have sacrificed the invaluable enjoyment of a character, with themselves at least, for the acquisition of worthless toys and gewgaws. How little is requisite to supply the *necessities* of nature? And in a view to *pleasure*, what comparison between the unbought satisfaction of conversation, society, study, even health and the common beauties of nature, but above all, the peaceful reflection on one's own conduct, — what comparison, I say, between these, and the feverish, empty amusements of luxury and expense? These natural pleasures, indeed, are really without price; both because they are below all price in their attainment, and above it in their enjoyment."

lence seems for a time to prosper, is always mingled with surprise at an occurrence so unlooked for; and the prominence which the case at once assumes, the frequency of the allusions to it, shows both that our moral constitution is very sensitive in this respect, and that the vast majority of examples turn the other way.

Pleasures and pains are intended to urge us to right conduct. — There are many pleasures and pains which follow so closely upon the virtuous and vicious actions of which they are the legitimate consequences, or have so obvious and intimate a connection with them, that even the most unthinking or immoral persons are obliged to admit, that these consequences are proper rewards and punishments, which were *intended* both to guide and to urge us to right conduct. Take the effects upon the bodily health, for instance. It is notorious, that vice enfeebles, corrupts, poisons, and destroys the physical constitution, while virtue invigorates and preserves it, retards the approach of disease, or mitigates its virulence when it comes, sweetens life and prolongs it. *The laws of hygiene, when well understood, are but interpretations of the laws of morals.* The physician will tell you, that he who desires the greatest of all earthly blessings — a sound mind in a sound body — has no shorter course for obtaining it than by making himself a thoroughly good man. The unhappy consequences of intemperance and debauchery, of riotous and malevolent passions, are so many beacons erected along the roadside, to warn the traveller against even occasional deviations from the path of rectitude. Debility, consumption, fever, insanity, and nearly all the other ills that flesh is heir to, when traced to their sources, are usually seen to be the results of imprudence or sin; and even if apparently transmitted by inheritance, so that the immediate sufferer under them is guiltless, the warning which they utter is only the more impressive, as they show that the sins of the fathers are visited upon the children, and the natural affections are thus more strongly enlisted on the side of virtue. Can any one even imagine, that this direct connection between right conduct and bodily health, is accidental or meaningless? Ought we not rather to consider it but as one feature, and that not the most prominent one, in the broad scheme of Divine government, all the parts of which are consistent with each other, and all visibly tend to the upholding of that law which is written upon the heart?

The tendencies of virtue and vice. — We have still further proof that virtue is advantageous both to the virtuous man and to society, if we look not only to its direct *consequences*, but to its *tendencies*. There are many hindrances here below to what may be called the natural operation of things. Take away these impediments; give time, scope, and opportunity for each cause to work separately, and produce its appropriate results, unobstructed by the action of other causes, and we shall more easily discern its true nature and peculiar effects. Virtue and vice, for instance, are commingled among men, and even in the same person; the beneficial effects of the one are hidden or neutralized by the unhappy consequences of the other; the merit of a good action is obscured by the misconduct that follows it. An upright man suffers from the crimes of his ancestors or his neighbors; even in this case, we see that crime is punished, or has injurious tendencies; only merit does not seem to receive its due. In fact, it *is* rewarded, for the suffering which flows from the crimes of others would be enhanced, if the sufferer himself were also guilty. As it is, his innocence mitigates the blow, the consciousness of integrity, under any circumstances being one of the greatest delights the mind can experience. *Isolate each case, consider how virtue and vice would work, if they were not brought in contact with each other, and their respective tendencies*, or the true character of their effects, *will be revealed.*

Suppose, for example, as Bishop Butler has done, the existence of a republic or society of men, perfectly virtuous, during a succession of ages. Selfishness, fraud, or treachery, would have no part in their councils; they would deliberate only about the best means of effecting good, and no force would be needed in order to carry their decisions into effect. Envy having no place among them, the direction of affairs would readily be conceded to those who had the most intelligence and capacity; and hese would covet the post only from the superior advantages it afforded for carrying out their benevolent schemes or projects for advancing the common welfare. As all would be equally industrious, poverty with its long train of ills would be unknown; almshouses would be no more needed than prisons. Health and long life would reward their temperance and the restraint of their passions, and death would be only the painless sequel of old age, when one was satiated with living. The neighboring communities, revering their virtues or admiring their prosperity, would hasten to place themselves under their dominion; and their peaceful victories would far exceed all that have ever been gained by the sword.

I know that this supposition could never be realized, except by a change miraculously effected in the hearts of men; but improbable as it seems, is it any thing more than a faithful delineation of what the consequences of virtue would be, if it were possible to separate them from the effects of vice? Grant that such characters are possible, and even from what we now see of the current of this world's affairs, is it not certain that such conduct and such prosperity would be the result? If so, the intentions of the Almighty are apparent even in the present and actual constitution of things. Virtue, *as such*, is rewarded, and vice, *as such*, is punished, in spite of the seeming confusion that results from both these classes of effects being visible at the same time.

The inward delights of virtue. — However the outward advantages of right conduct may be hidden for a time, the inward delights which it produces are constant and of vast importance; and as these result from the general constitution of our minds, apart from the moral faculty itself, they are properly ranked among the incentives to and rewards of virtue. It is well observed by Sir James Mackintosh, that although there may be immortal acts which, in some sense, or for a season, appear to be advantageous to the actor, "the whole sagacity and ingenuity of the world may be safely challenged to point out a case, in which virtuous dispositions, habits, and feelings are not conducive in the highest degree to the happiness of the individual; or to maintain that he is not the happiest, whose moral sentiments and affections are such as to prevent the possibility of the prospect of advantage, through unlawful means, from presenting itself to his mind. It would, indeed, have been impossible to prove to Regulus, that it was his interest [voluntarily] to return to a death of torture in Africa, [merely because he had plighted his word that he would return]. But what if the proof had been easy? The most thorough conviction on such a point would not have enabled him to set this example, if he had not been supported by his own integrity and generosity, by love of his country, and reverence for his pledged faith. What could the conviction add to that greatness of soul, and to these glorious attributes? With such virtues, he could not act otherwise than he did. Would a father, affectionately interested in a son's happiness, of very lukewarm feelings of morality, but of good sense enough to weigh gratifications and sufferings exactly, be really desirous that his son should have these virtues in a less degree than Regulus, merely because they might expose him to the fate which Regulus chose? On the coldest calculation, he would surely perceive, that the high and glowing feelings of such a mind during life, altogether throw into the shade a few hours of agony in leaving it. And if he himself were so unfortunate, that no more generous sentiment arose in his mind to silence such calculations, would it not be a reproach to his understanding not to discover, that though, in one case out of millions, such a character might lead a Regulus to torture, yet, in the common course of nature, it is the source not only of happiness in life, but of quiet and honor in death? A case so extreme as that of Regulus will not perplex, if we bear in mind, that, though we cannot prove the *act* of heroic virtue to be conducive to the interest of the hero, yet we may perceive at once, that nothing is so conducive to his interest as to have a mind so formed that it could not shrink from it, but must rather embrace it with gladness and triumph."

This case is not so singular as we are apt to imagine. *Every prisoner of war who observes his parol*, though the consequence to himself is a long and irksome captivity, acts from the same motives which guided the conduct of the Roman hero, and at a sacrifice, which, though less than his, is still considerable. But in the estimate not only of his comrades, with their peculiar notions of honor, but of all mankind, this sacrifice is so far from being unaccompanied by a full recompense in the high and pleasurable feelings which attend it, that, if he fails to make it, he becomes an object of universal pity and contempt.

Human government is but one form of Divine government. — That many of the rewards and punishments which wait upon the observance or infraction of the Divine law, are dispensed at human tribunals, or through the agency of men in society, is no proof that they are not divinely appointed. Human government is but one form or manifestation of Heaven's direction and control, — rendered somewhat less upright and sure, it is true, by passing through man's hands, but yet created in all its essential features by what are called the necessities of the case; — that is, arranged with reference to the wants and interests of society, these wants and interests being determined by the general constitution of things, or by the ordinary current of human affairs, which is formed and guided by the wisdom and power of the Deity. *Crime*, for instance, is punished by men, *not so much because it is disobedience to God, as because it is prejudicial to society; but then it is God's appointment that it should be thus prejudicial to society*, and that men should thereby be urged to punish it. Now the prevailing tone and direction of human law, in all countries and all ages, is coincident with the dictates of conscience. *Virtue is rewarded, and vice is punished, by society.* Examine all the codes of law that have ever been framed, and you will find that their chief purpose and tendency are to repress immoral conduct, and to encourage and protect the innocent and the virtuous. That government is a bad one, which fails to carry out these purposes with sufficient vigor, promptness, and effect, or which mingles up with them more or less of unholy ambition and arrogant self-will; but no government was ever wicked enough to reverse these purposes, and to aim directly and avowedly at the encouragement of vice, the distress of innocence, and the punishment of goodness. Even an

Asiatic despotism professes, and probably intends, to punish theft, perjury, fraud, and unprovoked injury, in all cases where its own interest is not immediately concerned; that is, of course, in the vast majority of cases that arise among its subjects. It may omit all the forms and precautions that civilized nations have come to observe, as the safeguards of innocence and preservatives against unintentional wrong; it may administer wild justice, but justice is its aim; it wields the sword against crime, and often with terrible effect. Even the law which regulates the intercourse of nations with each other, and which, probably, is the most imperfect of human codes, still founds most of its provisions on the natural sense of right, and most of the actions which it forbids are decidedly immoral and injurious.

It is an obvious remark, that a *system* or *scheme* of government should be distinguished from a number of *single, unconnected acts* of distributive justice and goodness. Now the instances already adduced, are surely enough to show, that if there be such a system or general plan, it is favorable to virtue, and was designed to encourage men in right conduct. All that can be urged on the other side amounts to a gleaning of disconnected facts, in regard to which, it may be difficult to see that the law of equity, of righteous retribution, has been observed; it is not pretended that these facts are numerous or grave enough to afford a presumption, either that the government is favorable to vice, or else that there is no government at all, — pleasure and pain, prosperity and adversity, being allotted at random. Thus much is admitted on all hands; — *that the virtuous man is prosperous is the rule; that the vicious sometimes succeed, is the exception. We have a right, then, to appeal to our ignorance and shortsightedness, to our limited means of observation, in order to explain away even these few exceptions.* We cannot trace all the consequences of another's act; those which are near may be injurious, those which are remote may be beneficial, and far more numerous and important. We cannot enter into the mind of the agent, and discern what secret satisfaction is there, which far outweighs the external harm. Above all, we may be mistaken in the character of the act itself, and lose sight of the distinction between absolute and relative rectitude. A seemingly meritorious deed may have had its origin in selfishness; another, wrongful in its outward aspect, may have proceeded from the highest and holiest intentions. We are not, then, lightly to suppose that the moral government of God is at fault, even in isolated cases.

The moral world subject to general laws, as well as the physical world.—We conclude, then, from an abundance of testimony, that the sense of moral obligation, which rises spontaneously in the mind of every human being, and is as much a part of his constitution as his reason or his senses, is supported and enforced by arrangements in the world without, and by the course of events in the external history of man. The law has been traced up to the Lawgiver, and in the contents of the law we have found a delineation of the character of its Author. We now learn, that, as the Creator and Governor of the universe, he has established a harmony between the requisitions of that law which he has imprinted on the conscience, and the external fortunes of men, or the current of this world's affairs. The moral world, or the history of mankind, is no more an unregulated chaos, or a fortuitous combination and succession of dissimilar and characterless events, than is the physical universe. In both, we discern, not merely the filaments of order, but a closely woven web covered with a uniform and glorious pattern. General laws, as they are called, — literally in the former case, metaphorically in the latter, — are found to pervade the whole fabric. It is not more certain, that the forms and changes of aggregations of matter are determined according to the principles of gravitation, affinity, definite proportions, and the like, than it is that the consequences of human action and the annals of human life accord with the fixed principles of morals and the stern demands of distributive justice. To the uninstructed mind, not trained in habits of scientific observation, and unskilful in finding the key which converts an apparent maze into an harmonious and well proportioned plan, there are not only many anomalies, but seeming lawlessness and confusion in both.

Apparent exceptions really prove the general rule. — If the child or the savage, for instance, should begin to trace the yearly paths of the planets among the stars, as they actually appear to the observer from the earth, should combine and compare such observations for successive years, and thus come to know the alternate direct and retrograde motions of these bodies, recurring at irregular intervals, the quickening and retarding of their pace, their occasional stops, and the strange curves which they describe on the nightly skies, he would certainly conclude, that their seemingly fantastic movements could neither be traced to any fixed cause working uniformly, nor reduced to any plain and symmetrical system. He would rather class them with the arbitrary turns, the inconstant swaying, rising, and falling of a single feather left to float at random in the wind. But the man of science places before you the simple diagram of the solar system, explains each illusion that arises from the position of the observer on the earth, deduces every movement that takes place from the single principle of gravitation, by the aid of which he can predict the very point of space which either of the orbs will occupy at any future moment, and thus shows, in truth, that the simplicity of the scheme, and the harmony of all its parts with each other, are its most striking features. He will even find harmony and law in the capricious movements of the feather, and show that all its gyrations may be traced to the same law of gravitation which directs the planets, and which operates as regularly and absolutely in this case, as in guiding those vast bodies in their swift flight around the sun.

Just so the moral world, the history of the individual, of nations, and of the race, to the unreflecting or careless mind, seems to present a mere jumble of events, — the blind goddess of fortune distributing the parts, and allotting at random to each performer the measure of good and evil in this life which he is fated to receive. But study this maze by the aid of the eternal principles of right and wrong which are enthroned in every heart, strive to go behind the external trappings of prosperity and adversity, to count the hours of real, not merely seeming, enjoyment, or, in other words, to *explore the private history of every man, as well as the story of his outer and public life,* and this confusion will clear away almost as fully as in the case of the physical universe. I say "*almost* as fully;" for it cannot be denied, that the problem is more complicated in its very nature; — the material universe, in all its large features, presents to us exclusively the picture of God's doings; the moral world, so far as it is visible to our eyes, shows the union of man's action with that of his Maker. God still governs, and that absolutely; but through moral, not mechanical means. Human freewill is allowed a large theatre on which to develop itself, and the results are necessarily more complex and intricate than when Divine agency alone is exerted. Still, the government prevails, order reigns, eternal laws are prescribed and enforced, and the purposes of the Almighty are carried out. In the distribution of bodily and mental health and disease; in the conditions of what is called success in life; in the secret contentment and joy which wait on the unostentatious fulfilment of ordinary duties, and in the glow and exaltation of feeling which accompany and reward a great apparent sacrifice for the right; in the institutions of society and the sympathies of mankind, which aim directly to encourage the good and to punish the evil-doer; — in these and many other circumstances, I see all the grand features of a comprehensive plan, wisely contrived and efficiently carried out, to win men to the practice of virtue and to punish every violation of the moral law. If, in a few cases, I behold apparent exceptions to the rule, or am not able to trace the workings of the plan, I do but follow the ordinary principles of scientific method and inductive logic in maintaining, with full-assured belief, that a more complete knowledge of the circumstances would show that the scheme operates even here, the seeming anomalies being in truth its most beautiful exemplifications. If a planet on the outer verge of our system shows perturbations for which, according to our present knowledge of that system, the law of gravity will not account, I do not therefore conclude that the law is suspended in this single case, but rather wait with firm trust for the progress of discovery to point out some still exterior orb, as yet invisible to mortal eyes, the action of which will explain the seeming disturbance, and make the law appear as universal as it is wise.

The general rule should not be sought for in isolated cases. — The argument for the moral government, the justice and benevolence of the Deity in his ways with men, has, I think, suffered somewhat by the injudicious course of those who have treated it, in dwelling at too great length upon these *isolated cases and seeming anomalies*, as if at least a probable explanation of every one of them was needed before we could believe in the system; or *as if there could be no government at all, unless*, with our present imperfect means of information, *we could plainly see that it was a perfect government.* But the man of science will tell you, that the principle which really holds throughout a class is to be sought for, not among the few scattered members of that class which are least known, but in the vast majority of those cases which are most directly exposed to observation. Look away from these specks and anomalies, and contemplate the broad features of the case. He who, on the evidence thus presented, will still doubt, whether the general and widely prevailing tendency of this world's affairs is really to uphold the law of conscience by a system of rewards and punishments graduated to that end, and actually intended by the Disposer of all things so to influence the conduct of men, is not a person to be reasoned with, but to be pitied.

How anomalous facts in history are to be explained. — The history of distant countries and past ages affords some perplexities in this view of the subject, precisely because it is a very imperfect description of men and events that are little known. *We are prone to consider nations as individuals, morally responsible, and having a continuous life;* and hence to require that their external fortunes should be adjusted to their deserts, and thus the justice of God be vindicated on a large scale. Why, then, we ask, for instance, were the Northern barbarians allowed to overrun what was then the only enlightened portion of the globe, and to tread out all but the last spark of learning and civilization, as it seemed, for centuries to come? I answer, first, that the researches of modern historians and philosophical inquirers have fully established the point, that this seeming deluge of barbarism actually renovated a soil that had become effete, and planted in it the fresh seeds of knowledge and progress, which afterwards shot up in such luxuriance at the Revival of Letters. If a stranger, wholly unacquainted with the circumstances of the case, should happen to visit Egypt at the season when all its cultivated fields are under water, and the inhabitants are compelled to move about in boats, he would probably conclude that the inundation of the Nile was a judgment upon the people for their sins. I answer, secondly, that *a nation has only a fictitious unity and personality, individuals being the only actual subjects of the Divine government.* Now history teaches us but very little about individuals, except of the few who occupy thrones or other prominent stations in the state, and who, from the very peculiarity of their position, afford us no safe rule by which we can estimate the characters and fortunes of the multitude. If, therefore, when we trace the fortunes of nations, the operation of the law is not very manifest, this is precisely what we might expect. Let the inquirer take the history of a single person, — especially his own history, the only one that he can know thoroughly, — and the fact that he lives under the Divine government becomes far more obvious. Let him inquire whether *his own* situation and experience furnish greater inducements for the practice of virtue or vice, and there is little fear that he will arrive at a false conclusion.

It is true, then, in the moral as well as the physical sense, that God governs the earth, — governs it, too, in both cases, not by secondary causes or vicarious means, but by the direct and constant exertion of his own wisdom and power. The belief of the pious heart is also the conclusion of the enlightened understanding, that the will of the Almighty determines all events, and disposes them for good. Science adopts and sanctions the theory of religion in regard to an overruling Providence ; — the theory which discerns a moral purpose in all things, maintaining that they were specially designed to produce a certain effect on the character and the conduct; which subordinates the physical to the moral, considering the former as means, and the latter as an end; which regards life as a gift and a trust, to be exercised for certain purposes, and death as a warning and a token that, in a particular case, these purposes have been accomplished.

CHAPTER VI.

THE GOODNESS OF GOD.

Summary of the last chapter. — The brief examination, in the last chapter, of the contents of the law imprinted upon the conscience, of the nature of the precepts which it issues for our observance, was intended to prove, that these injunctions reveal to us the character and attributes, as well as the purposes, of the Almighty. They do so, because *they answer no lower purpose, they are not subservient as means to any end but this.* They were not required to stimulate the body or mind to exertion, or to direct that exertion, or to preserve and uphold the arrangements and the workings of the material universe. They are of absolute obligation, so that the advantages which the observance of them actually procures are to be considered as their guards and enforcers, not as their purpose or final cause. Consequently, they are, to the human mind which receives them, a revelation of pure will, or a manifestation of the Divine nature and glory, irrespective of any purposes which may be answered by the display. Requiring perfection, or unlimited obedience, they show the perfections of their Author.

The scheme of Divine government, I attempted to show, includes a system of rewards and punishments, which follow immediately upon the observance or transgression of the law. Human life presents so many instances of these as to make the conclusion irresistible, that the current of this world's affairs, the natural course of events, is superintended and directed with a view to moral retribution. The object of the pains and pleasures which we experience, whether they grow out of our connection with the body, appearing as health or disease; or out of the relations which bind men together in society, then taking the form of success or failure in life, and of the honors and penalties which society has to bestow; or out of the constitution of the mind itself, in the various forms and degrees of remorse or inward gratification and the consciousness of merit; — the object, I say, in all these cases, is to uphold and enforce the law of right. That the incidents of life are distributed with a view to this end is the general rule; the apparent instances of an unequal or fortuitous distribution of them are only apparent, and they are the exceptions. There are a few seeming anomalies, which are most apt to present themselves in the consideration of those cases of which we know the least, — for instance, of historical personages and events, — while they very seldom trouble one's retrospect of his own experience; here, knowing all, he knows that the law is carried out completely. And the proper conclusion, from the presence of such anomalies as we cannot explain, is, not that the doctrine of a superintending Providence must be given up altogether, that doctrine being supported by the vast majority of cases, but that we do not always know how such a Providence acts. It is certain that we are under a scheme of government; but we are not able to follow all the workings of that scheme, or to assure ourselves, from direct observation, that it is perfect. The belief of the pious mind is hereby amply confirmed, that all events which affect our personal welfare, are dispensations of almighty wisdom and justice.

The infliction of pain not inconsistent with benevolence. — It has not been without design, that I have placed the argument for the moral government of God by a system of rewards and punishments *before* the consideration of the evidences of the Divine benevolence, though this is reversing the order usually adopted by writers upon the subject. But it is certain that the claims of *justice* are superior to those of mere *benevolence.*

We are required to do good to our fellow-beings so far as we can without violating other and higher obligations; we ought not to deprive another of that which is rightfully his own, or to utter an untruth, or to break our pledged faith, even for the sake of benefiting millions, while the wrong would be felt only by an individual. Nay, as the appointed ministers of justice, it may often be our duty to inflict suffering, and to stifle the emotions of sympathy and compassion which prompt us only to increase his happiness. What is done from such motives is no imputation upon the benevolence of the individual; his heart may be overflowing with love to his neighbor, at the very moment when he is doing him harm, or is the minister of the law to him for a righteous retribution. And generally, we may say, that the measure of immediate happiness or pain which is dispensed by any being is a very imperfect criterion of the real goodness of his disposition. The surgeon, for instance, is not necessarily a hardhearted man, though he passes his life in causing pain to others; he intends, indeed, to benefit them ultimately; but the benefit is remote and contingent, while the suffering caused by the operation is immediate and certain. In like manner, it may be better for the criminal himself, it may be more for his highest and most permanent interest, that he should be punished for his present offence, than that he should be permitted to sin with impunity. Yet men have argued as if the presence of any pain, the existence of any suffering, in the moral universe, was a fact irreconcilable with the infinite benevolence of the Creator.

Punishment for wrong-doing is consistent with benevolence. — I do not dwell upon this consideration now, as a better occasion will arise for developing it afterwards. I have alluded to it here only to remind you, that, as the obligation to promote the happiness of others, is always secondary to the demands of justice, we may at once, in estimating the proofs of the benevolence of the Deity, leave out of the account entirely all the pain which is evidently produced for the punishment and repression of sin. And how great is the deduction that will thus be made from the amount of suffering in the world! How large a portion of the evils borne both by individuals and communities are attributable directly to their own misconduct, to their wilful disregard of the monitions of conscience! The bodily frame, which is now languid from inaction or enfeebled by disease, might have been active and vigorous, prompt to second every wish of its owner, and ministering to his enjoyment through every sense, joint, and limb. The community which is now torn with civil dissensions, or prostrated in an unequal strife with its rivals, might have been peaceful, affluent, and flourishing, if its rulers and their subjects had heeded the stern calls of duty, instead of blindly following their own tumultuous passions. Once admit the great truth, that *virtue, not happiness, is man's highest interest,* and most of the pains of this life indicate the goodness of God quite as clearly as its pleasures. Consider, further, that virtue must be spontaneous or self-cultivated, since what is compulsory or mechanical can afford no ground either for praise or blame, and most of the problems which would otherwise perplex us in a view of this world's affairs admit of an easy solution.

Proofs of a preponderance of happiness. — But our present object is to inquire, whether there be not, on the whole, a vast preponderance of enjoyment in the world, from which, without troubling ourselves yet about the presence of evil in a few cases, we may directly infer the kindness and benignity of the Supreme Being. It is hardly possible to add any thing to Paley's admirable summary of the argument upon this point, nor can the heads of it be more forcibly or succinctly stated than in his language. The first proposition is, "That in a vast plurality of instances in which contrivance is perceived, the design of the contrivance is beneficial;" the second, "That the Deity has superadded pleasure to animal sensations beyond what was necessary to any other purpose, or when the purpose, so far as it was necessary, might have been effected by the operation of pain."

His assertion, however, that evil is never the object of contrivance, needs to be explained and limited, before we can admit it. *Evil* here does not mean *mere pain,* for this, I believe, is often intended and provided for, both to punish wrong, and to warn us against danger. But the distribution of this pain indicates pure benevolence united with perfect justice. It is never placed where it is not needed for some higher purpose; and therefore it is never the *ultimate* object of contrivance.* It is needed, for instance, to discourage and repress wrong-doing,—the moral education of man being here the final aim of the arrangement. So the physiologists tell us, that the parts of the body which are most delicate and most exposed to injury from without, are rendered most acutely sensitive; while those which are guarded in the main by their position, are not liable to pain. A mote, a grain of dust, in the eye, causes an intolerable smart; while the deeply seated muscles and tendons may be cut or torn almost without the consciousness of suffering. There are good reasons to believe, that the sensibility of the lower animals to pain is very slight, a warning of danger being comparatively useless to them, who have not reason and foresight to take

* As an apology for venturing to criticize this masterly argument by Paley, I quote the whole of it, since it is unrivalled for vigor, simplicity, and conclusiveness.

"Contrivance proves design; and the predominant tendency of the contrivance indicates the disposition of the designer. The world abounds with contrivances; and all the contrivances which we are acquainted with, are directed to beneficial purposes. Evil, no doubt. exists; but is never, that we can perceive, the object of contrivance, Teeth are contrived to eat, not to ache; their aching now and then is incidental to the contrivance, perhaps inseparable from it; or even, if you will, let it be called a defect in the contrivance; but it is not the *object* of it. This is a distinction which well deserves to be attended to. In describing implements of husbandry, you would hardly say of the sickle, that it is made to cut the reaper's fingers, though, from the construction of the instrument, and the manner of using it, this mischief often happens. But if you had occasion to describe instruments of torture or execution,—this engine, you would say, is to extend the sinews; this to dislocate the joints; this to break the bones; this to scorch the soles of the feet. Here, pain and misery are the very *objects* of the contrivance. Now, nothing of this sort is to be found in the works of nature. We never discover a train of contrivance to bring about an evil purpose. No anatomist ever discovered a system of organization calculated to produce pain and disease; or, in explaining the parts of the human body, ever said, This is to irritate;

measures to avert it. The horse and the cow, when shockingly wounded in the lower extremities, have been observed to move about, even upon their bloody stumps, and to graze with apparent unconcern. The head of a dragon-fly will eat after it is severed from the body; and Mr. Kirby saw a cockchafer walking with no show of uneasiness, after a bird had almost wholly deprived its body of the viscera. The noted saying, that

> " the poor beetle which we tread upon,
> In corporal sufferance, feels a pang as great
> As when a giant dies,"

however calculated to extend the range of our sympathies, certainly contains more poetry than truth.

Enjoyment is the rule, pain is only the exception. — But we are more concerned now to observe, that in unnumbered instances throughout God's creation, the production of happiness is the *sole* object of the contrivance. The *natural* operation of all the senses, organs, and faculties is a source of pleasure.

---

this to inflame; this duct is to convey the gravel to the kidneys; this gland to secrete the humor which forms the gout: if by chance he comes at a part of which he knows not the use, the most he can say is, that it is useless; no one ever suspects that it is put there to incommode, to annoy, or to torment. Since, then, God has called forth his consummate wisdom to contrive and provide for our happiness, and the world appears to be constituted with this design at first; so long as this constitution is upholden by him, we must in reason suppose the same design to continue.

"The contemplation of universal nature rather bewilders the mind than affects it. There is always a bright spot in the prospect, upon which the eye rests; a single example, perhaps, by which each man finds himself more *convinced* than by all others put together. I seem, for my own part, to see the benevolence of the Deity more clearly in the pleasures of very young children, than in any thing in the world. The pleasures of grown persons may be reckoned partly of their own procuring; especially if there has been any industry or contrivance or pursuit to come at them; or if they are founded, like music, painting, etc., upon any qualification of their own acquiring. But the pleasures of a healthy infant are so manifestly provided for it by *another*, and the benevolence of the provision is so unquestionable, that every child I see at its sport, affords to my mind a kind of sensible evidence of the finger of God, and of the disposition which directs it."

It is sweet to see, to hear, to eat, to breathe, to perform any of the ordinary functions of life, when the body is in its normal state. There is just enough of uneasiness, recurring at intervals, to remind us of the work that must be done in order to keep the body in this healthy condition. Even the consciousness of living, of continued existence, under common circumstances, is agreeable; for those who are most apt to complain of the burden of existence would resent the proposal, if you should offer immediately to rid them of it. It is finely observed by Abraham Tucker, that our "pleasures spring from steady, permanent causes, as the vigor of health, the due returns of appetite, and calls of nature to exercise or rest; but pains proceed from accidents which happen rarely, or diseases which are either slight or temporary." "Even our troubles come attended with their alleviations; we have remedies and assistance in diseases, comfort in distresses, and hope lies ready as a salve for every sore; nor are there any in so forlorn a condition, but may find something to thank God for, if they will look about to seek it. Epicurus, though disposed to find all the faults he could in the system of nature, yet made it one among his collection of Maxims, 'That pain, if grievous, was short; if long, it was light.'"

Happiness is so far the normal condition of existence, that we are hardly conscious of the extent and the perpetual succession of our enjoyments, till something occurs to interrupt them. Thus, we mourn the loss of friends, though their departure ought to remind us of the length of years through which we have had the comfort of their society. *Most of our sorrows are of a negative character;* they are not so much positive pains, as occasional privations of blessings to which we have been long accustomed. "The rays of happiness," a poet tells us, "like those of light, are colorless when unbroken." It is no paradox, then, to say, that pains, when not too frequent or too violent, contribute directly to increase our conscious enjoyments, which could not be perpetually renewed without them. An attack of illness, if not too severe, is generally more than compensated by the pleasure of returning health, that comes with a glow and freshness, of which one who has never been an invalid can have no conception. But these pains, because they are infrequent, stand out like landmarks in our remembrance, while the wide expanse of happiness which they diversify is unnoticed or forgotten. Probably the happiest portion of our existence, is that which leaves the least impression on the memory; and the happiest man, is he whose life affords the fewest incidents for the biographer.

The adaptation of external nature to the mind of man, its fitness to excite pleasurable emotion, is another proof of the beneficence of the Creator. The beauty of the vegetable creation, from the tiniest flower up to the moss-grown oak, its almost endless variety of form and hue, the delicacy and high finish of its minutest parts, with the luxuriance and grandeur of its aggregated masses, are enough to stir the most sluggish soul to admiration and gratitude. The useful functions of plants in the economy of nature, — their effects, for instance, in purifying the air and elaborating food for the animal kingdom, — might all be performed without this richness of embellishment. *Their beauty is something superadded*, for no conceivable purpose but that of imparting pleasure. And the ear is gratified as well as the eye. All natural sounds, — the song of birds, the hum of insects, the breaking of waves on the shore, the murmuring of the wind amid the branches of a forest, even the sullen plunge of the cataract, and "the bass of heaven's great organ," — are harmonious; the operations of man alone jar the delicate sense,

"Straining harsh discords and unpleasing sharps."

"The necessary purposes of hearing," as Paley observes, "might have been answered without harmony; of smell, without fragrance; of vision, without beauty. The properties given to the necessaries of life themselves, by which they contribute to pleasure as well as preservation, show a further design than that of giving existence." It is so with the chief articles of food, eating being certainly necessary for the continuance of animal life; but "why add pleasure to the act of eating, — sweetness and relish to food? why a new and appropriate sense for the perception of the pleasure? That this pleasure depends, not only upon our being in possession of the sense of taste, which is different from every other, but upon a particular state of the organ in which it resides, a felicitous adaptation of the organ to the object, will be confessed by any one who may happen to have experienced that vitiation of taste which frequently occurs in fevers, when every taste is irregular, and every one bad." And if this pleasure forms but a small and rather ignoble item among the enjoyments of man, let it be remembered that it is spread over a large portion of the existence of brutes, especially of the ruminating animals.

The pleasures of taste intended solely to promote happiness. — It matters not at all, for the purposes of this argument, whether the beauty of forms, colors, sounds, and the like, is something intrinsic, inherent in the nature of the things themselves, or is superadded by our modes of perception; — whether, to speak technically, the beauty be *objective* or *subjective*. It is indifferent whether we say, that objects are so constituted as to impart pleasure to the mind, or that the mind is so constituted as to receive pleasure from them, when our only object is to prove, that the pleasure itself is actual and abundant. In truth, I can see no reason why the emotions of beauty and sublimity were added to our mental faculties, except the mere purpose of enlarging the sphere of our enjoyments. They do not conduce to the preservation of life, they are not needed to keep up society, or to influence our conduct. They often stimulate to action, it is true; for when we have once experienced the pleasure that they afford, we desire its repetition, and seek the objects which occasion them. But this is only their secondary effect; and it is neither certain nor necessary, the stimulus to activity which is otherwise provided being stronger and quite sufficient. They are copious sources of delight, which is often vivid and intense, and is shared in a greater or less degree by all; this is the only important part which they play in the economy of our being, and is the obvious purpose for which they were created.

These pleasures adapted to all ages and conditions. — Acknowledged differences of taste form no argument against the reality and abundance of the pleasure which every person receives from this endowment of his nature, however mistaken his notions may be as to the beauty or sublimity of particular objects. A child's delight in a daub of bright colors, or an unmeaning jingle of sounds, is as real and hearty as the connoisseur's appreciation of the merits of a Raphael or a Mozart. Indeed, I count the flexibility of these emotions, the numberless occasions on which they rise, their adaptation to all ages and conditions of life, and the rapid changes which cultivation effects in them, among the perfections of their contrivance, when regarded as a means of enlarging human happiness. We have thus a greater range and variety in our pleasures, every stage in our existence and education having its own peculiar stock of them, every day contributing some new occasion on which they are felt, and the effect of familiarity and repetition in dulling the sense of enjoyment being thus completely obviated. We see here a reason for that infinite variety in the details of the material universe, amidst which, as I remarked on a former occasion, we trace the threads of uniformity and the prevalence of law. In the glorious mass of foliage which crowns an oak, it was then observed, there are no two leaves which perfectly resemble each other; and I may now add, that there is not one of them which is not graceful. Objects are seen under different and very dissimilar aspects, and under all, contribute largely, if not equally, to the pleasure of the beholder. No two sunsets are exactly alike, nor is there one mass of white cloud on the blue sky which is the very pattern of another. The changes of the seasons are continually altering the appearance of the landscape; every month in the year it images a new feeling, but never lapses into ugliness.

Variety and wide diffusion of these pleasures. — I have dwelt thus long upon the pleasures of taste, because the capacity for them, more than any other part of our constitution, seems to have been created for the *sole* purpose of increasing the store of human happiness. Let it not be thought, on account of their gentle and unobtrusive character, and the trifling value which we put upon them in moments of excitement, or when we think that great.r interests are at stake, that they form an insignificant addition to that store. They are diffused, so to speak, over the whole plain of human existence, making up, by their variety, their duration, and their constant recurrence, for their lack of intensity, and the slightness of their hold when the stronger passions assert their power. The pleasures of ambition, pomp, and power visit us only in lightning flashes, as brief as they are vivid; they are often purchased, also, at a heavy sacrifice; they are crossed by the pains of failure and disappointment; and even the happiness which they are thought to constitute, is more properly ascribed to the toil and effort which we expend in their pursuit. But the enjoyments procured by the faculty of taste are unmingled with losses and sacrifices, and, for the most part, are unbought. They come to cheer the intervals of exertion, and to speed the long hours which are not filled with grave cares or enterprises of great pith and moment. They form the relaxation alike of the monarch on his throne and of the peasant in his hut; the social instinct prompts each to seek companionship, and the conversation which turns not upon business or causes of anxiety, is prolonged merely for pleasure into an idle chat. A company of laborers, talking around the fire after the day's work is ended, experience this delight quite as strongly as the crowd which fills the apartments of the fashionable and the learned. "It is a happy world after all." In spite of all the labors, cares, and troubles of life, we still spend a considerable portion of our time merely in amusing ourselves.

The capacity of happiness adapted to all beings and all conditions of life.—The wide diffusion of these simple pleasures suggests another arrangement in nature, which affords still stronger proof of the benevolence of the Deity;—I mean the adaptation of the capacity of happiness to all orders of being and to all conditions of life. Considered in reference to its sources and occasions, *happiness* is not an absolute, but *a relative term.* When we say, that any creature is as happy as it is capable of being, we express its *perfect* enjoyment; the lowness of the capacity does not lessen this perfection. The causes and nature of the enjoyment may make it very unsuitable for a being of a different order, or for one of the same order, but of different pursuits and tastes. Still, it is real and perfect, and in this argument, therefore, is entitled to just as much weight as pleasure of a higher character. But we are all prone to erect our own ideas upon this subject into an absolute standard, and to pity all who do not come up to our peculiar notions of happiness; we do not always remember, that, very likely, the objects of our compassion are, at the same moment, pitying us. This propensity leads us greatly to overrate the amount of misery that there is in the world, when, if we would but reflect upon it, the propensity itself is an additional indication of the goodness of God; each individual supposes that his own happiness is the highest possible happiness, and his enjoyment is naturally enhanced by this belief. Ideas of what constitute pleasure and pain vary more widely than we are apt to imagine, especially if we include the lower animals in the survey. To take the strongest instance that I can think of; — the sight of a wild beast eagerly tearing and devouring the prey that it has just seized, makes us shudder; yet the animal is then experiencing the keenest enjoyment that it is capable of, and if, as is generally the case, the prey is instantly killed by its captor, so that there is little or no suffering on either side, the spectacle, apart from its effect on our involuntary sympathies, ought rather to make us rejoice. We look upon the condition of a tribe of savages with similar feelings, and, so far as mere happiness is concerned, we almost equally misjudge the case. Pity them, if you will, for not being able to appreciate your refined and elevated pleasures, but for nothing else, since they are not only unconscious of suffering, but, for most of the time, they are enjoying themselves. We are shocked by the ignorance of great multitudes of men, and the feeling is a proper one in regard to their future, as the want of instruction frequently leads to crime; but in connection with our present topic, we ought to remember that ignorance is often bliss. Information on many points would only breed discontent.

Tucker on the distribution of happiness. — These considerations seem to me to have so much weight, that I cannot regard

Abraham Tucker's animated picture of the distribution of happiness as at all exaggerated. "We should cease," he says, "to measure others' satisfaction by our own standard, and to think nothing desirable to them which we would not choose for ourselves; we shall then discern a variety of tastes adapted to the several conditions wherein men are placed, and things which are irksome at first, becoming pleasant by custom. We may see that children have their plays; the vulgar their amusements, coarse jokes, and May-games; even folly does not exclude pleasure, nor poverty banish contentment. There is as much mirth in the kitchen as the parlor, and as great diversion in a country fair or a cricket-match, as at a card assembly or a ridotto. The cobbler whistles at his stall; the dairy-maid sings while she is milking; the ploughman munches his mouldy crusts with as good a relish as the rich man eats his dainties with, for he has that best of sauces, hunger, to season his victuals. Labor purifies the blood, invigorates the limbs, strengthens the digestion, insures quiet sleep, and renders the body proof against changes and inclemencies of weather; all which are considerable articles in the enjoyment of life, nor can their loss be compensated by any enjoyment of family, fortune, learning, and politeness. Nor is the lowest herdsman incapable of that sincerest of pleasures, the consciousness of acting right; for rectitude does not consist in extensiveness of knowledge, but in doing the best according to the lights afforded; and many artisans, servants, and laborers, find as much satisfaction in fulfilling the duties of their station, as the philosopher in his researches into nature. Nor need we stop at the human species; for the brute creation, too, exhibits scenes agreeable for the good-natured man to look upon; he may rejoice to see the cattle sporting in the fields, to hear the birds singing and chirping out their joys, to behold the swallow building nests to hatch her young, the ant laying in stores of provision for her future accommodation, the flies, in a summer evening, dancing together in wanton mazes, the little pucerons in water frisking nimbly about, as if delighted with their existence. Whoever has a heart to enjoy such contemplations, will be apt to pursue them until he has satisfied himself, that there is a much greater quantity of enjoyment than suffering upon earth."

Why there is no absolute standard of happiness. — Suppose that the belief which every individual is prone to entertain on this subject, were well founded; suppose that there were an absolute standard of happiness, as there is of virtue. Is it not obvious, in the first case, that all the lower orders of being, differing fundamentally in their endowments and constitutions from man, would be as incapable of enjoyment as they now are of rectitude? Deprived of all access to refined and elevated pleasures by the coarseness of their organization, and the ruder delights of eating and mere bodily activity being struck out of the scale, what would remain to them but the life (if we may call it by that name) of a machine, or, in other words, mere senselessness and the incapacity either of joy or woe? Again, unless all the differences of character and variety of talents and occupations, which now distinguish men from each other, were done away, the establishment in their minds of but one standard of happiness would deprive all but an insignificant fraction of their number of any experience of pleasure. If this standard were accommodated to man's character, the child could not rise to it; if it were suited only to the cultivated mind, the savage would have no compensation for the evils of his lot; if it had regard to difference of sex, one half of the human family would be joyless. If it were made known to all, in the absoluteness of its conditions, just as the standard of rectitude is, even the few could have but partial enjoyment; for perfection in happiness would be as unattainable as perfection in morals. There must be such a standard, for absolute happiness alone can express the condition of an omnipotent and omniscient Being; but in his mercy, it is not revealed to man in this stage of existence, nor to any of the creatures which He has made. Yet such a revelation would be consistent with mere justice; for the pleasures of virtue alone would satisfy all the requisitions of the moral sense. Men might be made happy only in proportion as they were good. Now, indeed, their pleasures are enhanced by the consciousness of rectitude; but they are not wholly destroyed by the recollection of sin. God sendeth his rain alike on the just and the unjust, his government being one not merely of absolute rectitude, but of perfect love.

The kind affections prove the benevolence of God. — I shall allude to but one other proof of the benevolence of God, and that is, the endowment of the mind with benevolent affections, care being thus shown for the happiness of all, by rendering men the guardians and partakers of the happiness of each other. We are not left in this respect to the monitions of conscience alone, though the general obligation to relieve the distressed and to do good to all is recognized, and even strongly inculcated, by that faculty. But the social and kind affections also, which stand foremost among our primary impulses, and which are prompt to act before reason can come into play or the voice of conscience be heard, are so many ever-watchful sentinels to increase the joys and lessen the sorrows of our mortal lot. So quick and powerful is their operation, that the action which proceeds from them seems involuntary. The sight of distress prompts an instant attempt to relieve it, no matter who may be the sufferer. Imminent peril hanging over the head of another, causes a shuddering in all our limbs, as if our own lives were menaced; and often the sharp cry of warning is uttered, before reason can teach us that the distance is too great for the voice to be heard. We rejoice in the happiness of others, though the difference of taste, situation, or character makes their standard of enjoyment the farthest possible from our own. The aged are always the most ready to encourage the sports of childhood, to join in the shout that follows their success, and to please the infant with a rattle or a straw. The affections of kindred are indestructible while life and sense remain; they often overbear all regard for our own comfort, and a painful death becomes a pleasant one, if suffered for their sake. Disinterestedness is so prominent a trait in them, that even the suggestion of their being alloyed by the hope of compensation is resented as an affront. They often rise to enthusiasm, so as to need the curb of reflection and a sense of duty to keep them from a harmful excess. So exquisite is the pleasure of their indulgence, and so easily are they brought into play, that, when real occasions to call them forth are wanting, we seek fictitious ones, and grieve over the sorrows, or sympathize in the joys, of imaginary beings. What direct interest has the spectator at the theatre, or the reader of a romance, in the characters represented, his sympathy with whom is attested by his emotion and his tears?

> "What's Hecuba to him, or he to Hecuba,
> That he should weep for her?"

We can explain this effect only by admitting, that our affections and sympathies are more speedy and overpowering than the action of the intellect, which would teach us, if it had time or could gain an audience, that we were weeping over shadows and airy fancies.

Distribution of the affections. — Consider, now, the human mind, figuratively, with its complex and delicate network of faculties and springs of action, as a machine or a contrivance, the problem being, how to constitute it so as to take the greatest possible security for the happiness of the race. What more effectual means could be devised for this end, than to endow men first with the social or gregarious instinct, which keeps them always near to each other, and then to knit their hearts together with so many of these kindly affections, that not a chord of joy or sorrow can be touched in one, without finding an instant response in many others? Observe, too, how these affections are distributed in regard to their objects, the strongest always uniting those who live nearest and most familiarly with each other, and who consequently stand most in need of mutual aid, the assistance that is most readily offered being thus also always the nearest at hand; while the other feelings weaken, indeed, as they expand, but continually take in a larger number, till that of general benevolence includes the whole human race. The love, for instance, which surpasses all others, is that of a mother for her child, these two being for months and years inseparable, and the latter being wholly dependent on another's care.

Indeed, the bodily constitution of the human infant, when compared with that of the young of other animals, shows that it is trusted for protection and support almost exclusively to maternal affection; and the trust is not in vain. "One animal," says Mr. Stewart, "is armed with the horn, another with the tusk, a third with the paw; most of them are covered with furs, or with skins of a sufficient thickness to protect them from the inclemencies of the seasons; and all of them are directed by instinct in what manner they may choose or construct the most convenient habitation for securing themselves from danger, and for rearing their offspring. The human infant alone enters the world naked and unarmed; exposed without a covering to the fury of the elements; surrounded with enemies who far surpass him in strength or agility; and totally ignorant in what way he is to procure the comforts or even the necessaries of life." A being formed for tears, says Pliny, but soon to exercise dominion over all the other creatures that God has made;—*Flens animal, cæteris imperaturum.*

That it is the living constantly together, and not some hidden virtue in mere kindred blood, which forms the groundwork of the family affections, seems to me to be proved by the fact, that long separation greatly weakens these natural ties, while the factitious unions of marriage and friendship put others in their place which are equally effective. Wherever we are placed, then, however far our journeyings may be, these kindly feelings spring up around us in a natural growth, the Divinely appointed guardians of our happiness; a removal separates us from one class of them, but the loss is soon repaired by others. It is hardly possible for man to occupy a position so isolated, that he shall not be joined by one or more of these peculiar bonds to a portion of his fellows, to whom he may look for especial sympathy, consolation, and aid. Even if all others should drop away, the last and most comprehensive of all, which must remain, the tie of a common origin and a common nature, that makes a brotherhood of all mankind, is one of no mean force. When a fit occasion arises, its strength is manifested. If, for instance, the cry of famine or pestilence is heard, though it comes from the uttermost isles of the sea, from a people with whom we have no relationship or common interest, the sympathies of all are excited, and the means of relief, if possible, are sent. The same feeling, trained into a custom and guarded by religious sanctions, protects the wandering stranger among the robber tribes of the desert; the head even of the fugitive from justice is sacred, when he has once tasted of the salt at the chieftain's board. The rights of hospitality are more or less respected all over the globe, merely from a recognition of the common humanity of the host and the guest.

The kind affections support each other. — Observe, also, how these feelings intertwine and support each other. Compassion is met by gratitude, the latter often rising into heroism, and the charge of a want of it, next to the accusation of falsehood, being the bitterest reproach that can be uttered. An interchange of kind offices strengthens the benevolent purposes of either party. Maternal love is repaid by filial affection, friendship by its like, and every kindly emotion has its counterpart and reward in the mind of him who is its object. It is justly observed by Mr. Stewart, that "the peculiar sentiment of approbation with which we regard the virtue of beneficence in others, and the peculiar satisfaction with which we reflect on such of our actions as have contributed to the happiness of mankind, to which we may add the exquisite pleasure accompanying the exercise of all the kind affections, naturally lead us to consider benevolence or goodness as the supreme attribute of God. It is difficult, indeed, to conceive what other motive could have induced a Being, completely and independently happy, to call his creatures into existence." Indeed, the experience of our own day has shown, that general philanthropy can become a profession and a fascinating pursuit. There is so much luxury in the indulgence of feelings which point to the general improvement and moral elevation of the race, that they have sometimes thrown off the yoke of reason and justice, to which they are rightfully subject. We respect or reverence men for the sterner virtues which they exhibit, but we *love* them for their benevolence, although the objects of their kindness are persons for whom we entertain no peculiar esteem. The memory of John Howard, for instance, is as sacred to us as if we had personally known, esteemed, and loved every one of the wretched beings to the improvement of whose lot his life was devoted. Considering, then, how much our daily comforts and enjoyments depend upon our fellow beings, especially upon those with whom we constantly associate, it may well be doubted, whether any other arrangement of Providence to secure our happiness is so effectual, as that which animates us all with the spirit of active love and kindness towards each other.

Even the selfishness of men contributes to the general welfare. — Still further; as men are dependent upon their fellow beings not merely for sympathy and additional means of enjoyment, but for necessaries — for the active coöperation without which life could not be supported — not only are mutual kindly affections implanted in them, but *their interests* are so interwoven, that even the cupidity and selfishness of individuals are made to conduce to the general good. What may be called the economical laws of human nature, (the principles of Political Economy,) in their general effects upon the well-being of society, manifest the contrivance, wisdom, and beneficence of the Deity just as clearly, as do the marvellous arrangements of the material universe, or the natural means provided for the enforcement of the moral law and the punishment of crime. The lowest passions of mankind, ostentation and ambition, petty rivalry, the love of saving and the love of gain, while they bring their own penalty upon the individual who indulges them, are still overruled for good in their operation upon the interests of society; — nay, they are made the most efficient means of guarding it from harm and advancing its welfare. In the vast round of employments in civilized society, there is hardly one in which a person can profitably exert himself, without at the same time profiting the community in which he lives, and lending aid to thousands of human beings whom he never saw. We are all servants of one another without wishing it, and even without knowing it; we are all coöperating with each other as busily and effectively as the bees in a hive, and most of us with as little perception as the bees have, that each individual effort is essential to the common defence and general prosperity. "This dependence and combination," says McCulloch, "is not found only or principally in the mechanical employments; it extends to the labors of the head as well as those of the hands, and pervades and binds together all classes and degrees of society."

"The great Author of nature," says Barrow, (second sermon on Industry,) "hath so distributed the ranks and offices of men, in order to mutual benefit and comfort, that one man should plough, another thrash, another grind, another labor at the forge, another knit or weave, another sail, another trade, another supervise all these, laboring to keep them all in order and peace; that one should work with his hands and feet, another with his head and tongue; all conspiring to one common end, the welfare of the whole, and the supply of what is useful to each particular member; every man so reciprocally obliging and being obliged, the prince being obliged to the husbandman for his bread, to the weaver for his clothes, to the mason for his palace, to the smith for his sword; those being all obliged to him for his vigilant care in protecting them, for their security in pursuing the work, and enjoying the fruit of their industry.*"

---

* For a more specific illustration of this truth, I borrow a passage from Adam Smith.

"The interests of the inland dealer [in corn,] and that of the great body of the people, how opposite soever they may at first sight appear, are, even in years of the greatest scarcity, exactly the same. It is his interest to raise the price of his corn as high as the real scarcity of the season requires, and it can never be his interest to raise it higher. By raising the price, he discourages the consumption, and puts everybody, more or less, but particularly the inferior ranks of people, upon thrift and good management. If, by raising it too high, he discourages the consumption so much that the supply of the season is likely to go beyond the consumption of the season, and to last for some time after the next crop begins to come in, he runs the hazard, not only of losing a considerable part of his corn by natural causes, but of being obliged to sell what remains of it for much less than what he might have had for it several months before. If, by not raising the price high enough, he discourages the consumption so little, that the supply of the season is likely to fall short of the consumption of

Broad conclusions from this argument. — It is unnecessary to carry these illustrations any further, though any exposition of this broad theme, the benevolence of God as displayed in the material and moral universe, must necessarily seem imperfect. It is important to mark the breadth of the conclusion at which we have now arrived. It is proved, not only that good predominates to a vast extent, but that, secondary only to the support and enforcement of the law of right, the production of happiness is the chief purpose in the creation and government of the world. Strike out the pains which were intended to vindicate the law of primary obligation, and to show that virtue was of more importance than mere enjoyment, and happiness is seen to be the normal condition of mankind, — happiness which was contrived, and which is the sole object of the contrivance, — happiness which fills up so large a portion of the hours of existence, that hardship and suffering are restricted in comparison to minutes. Evil exists, undoubtedly; but it is the exception, and not the rule. It is never designed for its own sake; it is nowhere the ultimate object of the contrivance.

No difficulty appears till the idea of infinity is brought in. — There is, then, sufficient, even abundant, proof of the benevolence of the Creator. And this benevolence is not scanty or

---

the season, he not only loses a part of the profit which he might otherwise have made, but he exposes the people to suffer before the end of the season, instead of the hardships of a dearth, the dreadful horrors of a famine. It is the interest of the people that their daily, weekly, and monthly consumption should be proportioned as exactly as possible to the supply of the season. The interest of the inland corn dealer is the same. By supplying them, as nearly as he can judge, in this proportion, he is likely to sell all his corn for the highest price, and with the greatest profit; and his knowledge of the state of the crop, and of his daily, weekly, and monthly sales, enables him to judge, with more or less accuracy, how far they really are supplied in this manner. Without intending the interest of the people, he is necessarily led, by a regard to his own interest, to treat them, even in years of scarcity, pretty much in the same manner as the prudent master of a vessel is sometimes obliged to treat his crew. When he foresees that provisions are likely to run short, he puts them upon short allowance." — Smith's *Wealth of Nations*, p. 233.

parsimonious in its character; its arrangements are vast, imposing, commensurate with the scale on which the universe is made. The whole difficulty which is presented to us, in the problem respecting the origin and continuance of evil, relates *to the infinity* of Divine benevolence. That there is some evil in the world, is an apparent indication that the deity is not *infinitely* benevolent; but it is no indication whatever that he is not benevolent at all. It affords no presumption even against the doctrine that he is largely benevolent, — bountiful and gracious to man, far beyond the measure of his absolute wants or rightful claims. This conclusion, therefore, — that God wishes the happiness, not the misery, of his creatures, and has made rich provision to this end, — remains to us unshaken, whatever may be our success in the subsequent part of the inquiry.

I insist strongly upon this point, because the nature of the difficulty occasioned by the presence of *any* evil in the world has been greatly misunderstood. Nearly all writers upon the subject have argued the matter, as if the existence of sin and suffering in any degree, however small, or however overbalanced by virtue and happiness, afforded a presumption that the Deity was not benevolent at all, — nay, that he was malevolent, that he intended the misery of his creatures. But not so. It is one thing to prove that God is wise, powerful, and good; and another and quite a different thing, to prove that he is infinitely wise, infinitely powerful, and infinitely good. The difference between these two lines of proof has sometimes (and very properly) been made a topic for discussion by itself; the infinity of the Divine attributes is to be made out by reasoning somewhat different from that which establishes the reality of the attributes themselves. Infinity is a metaphysical idea; our notion of it is confessedly inadequate. We have but a negative idea of it; it implies that certain qualities exist in an *unknown* perfection. To prove that the attributes are infinite, then, may be desirable for philosophical purposes, for the completeness of theory, and for rounding out with entireness a system of theology; but it is not essential either for religious faith or practice. For these latter purposes, it is enough to show that the qualities exist unlimited by the attributes of any other known being or thing, and in a degree which challenges our wonder and adoration. This has been already done, and religious faith, properly so called, is sufficiently vindicated. It is proved that God exists, and that he governs the world in righteousness and with mercy, at once upholding the law which he has revealed through the conscience, and showing by manifold provisions his care for the happiness of his creatures.

Our idea of infinity necessarily inadequate.—It is observable, in the next place, that there are difficulties in the very conception of infinite goodness united with infinite power, which ought to warn us that the imperfection, after all, is more apt to be in our limited modes of thought, than in the constituted nature of things. I borrow on this point the very clear and precise statement of Abraham Tucker.

"God," he observes, "is completely happy in himself, nor can his happiness receive increase or diminution from any thing befalling his creatures; wherefore his goodness is pure, disinterested bounty, without any return of joy or satisfaction to himself. Therefore it is no wonder we have imperfect notions of a quality whereof we have no experience in our own nature; for *we* know of no other love than inclination, which prompts us to gratify it in the same manner as our other inclinations. In the next place, let us examine our idea of infinite goodness taken in the abstract, before we inquire whether God be good or no,—and we shall find it incompatible with that of infinite power; for infinite goodness, according to our apprehension, requires that it should exhaust omnipotence, that it should give capacities of enjoyment, and confer blessings, until there were no more to be conferred; but our idea of omnipotence requires that it should be inexhaustible, that nothing should limit its operations so that it could do no more than it has done. Therefore it is much easier to conceive of an imperfect creature completely good, than of a perfect being; for if he pursues invariably all opportunities of doing good to the utmost of his power and knowledge, he deserves that character; and if there are any injuries sustained which he cannot redress, any distress unrelieved which he knows not of, his weakness and ignorance are a full excuse for his omission. But where there is almighty power, unlimited knowledge, and perfect wisdom, we can neither conceive that infinite goodness should extend to the utmost bounds of that which has no bounds, nor yet that it should stop until it can proceed no further. Since, then, we find our understanding incapable of comprehending infinite goodness joined with infinite power, we need not be surprised at finding our thoughts perplexed concerning them; for no other can be expected in matters above our reach; and we may presume the obscurity rises from something wrong in our ideas, not from any inconsistencies in the subjects themselves." In short, here as elsewhere, whenever we apply a purely metaphysical idea to matters-of-fact, we end in a contradiction or an absurdity.

The proof of the Divine benevolence is complete in itself.— You will not understand me, by these remarks, as holding forth the opinion, that the problem respecting the origin of evil is insoluble, or as evading the difficulty of solving it. On the contrary, I believe, and I shall attempt to show, that all events are ordered for the best, and that the supposed evils which we suffer are parts of a great system conducted by almighty power, under the direction of unlimited wisdom and goodness. I adopt the opinion, maintained in all ages by the best and wisest philosophers, that the creation of beings endowed with freewill, and consequently liable to moral delinquency, and the government of the world by general laws, from which occasional supposed evils must result, furnish no solid objection to the perfection of the universe. This, I admit, is a system of optimism; but it is not the optimism of Leibnitz, grounded upon a denial of man's free agency, and as such justly ridiculed by Voltaire. And the general doctrine of the benevolence of God, is in nowise accountable for, or dependent upon, the sufficiency of the argument in defence of this metaphysical system. That doctrine rests upon its own proofs, which are abundant, undisputed, and irrefragable. This question respecting the presence of *any* evil in the world, is a collateral affair, which must be considered, indeed, before we can complete a scheme of theology, and about which theologians and metaphysicians may differ. But the religious man has no concern with it, and his faith, whether derived from the teachings of nature, or from express revelation, is not burdened with its doubts and intricacies. It is enough for him, that he can trace everywhere the footprints of a wise, just, and benevolent Ruler of the universe.

CHAPTER VII.

THE ORIGIN OF EVIL.

Summary of the last chapter. — The argument in the last chapter for the benevolence of God, was not founded upon metaphysical reasoning, or upon any consideration *a priori* of the Divine nature, but upon observation and the results of experience. It is because human life, on the whole, is a happy one, because its pleasures far exceed its pains, and because these pleasures were evidently designed, while the pains are only incidental or secondary to some great object, that we are enabled to pronounce with confidence, that the Deity wishes the happiness of his creatures. The sufferings which are the immediate consequence and punishment of vice, it was remarked, are properly left out of the account, since these evince the goodness of God no less than the happiness resulting from virtue, the object in both cases being to advance man's highest interests by the improvement of his moral character; just so the affectionate parent rewards the obedience and punishes the faults of his child, love equally constraining him to adopt either course. Now, these sufferings constitute so large a portion of the misery that is in the world, that, when they are deducted, the balance inclines altogether on the side of happiness. Our enjoyments, also, proceed from steady and permanent causes the performance of all the ordinary functions of life, when the body is in its normal state, being a source of pleasure. Sickness is an accident and an exception; health is the intended and usual condition.

The pleasures of taste arise from an adaptation of external nature to the mind of man, which must have had for its *sole* purpose the increase of our happiness; and these pleasures are so various, recur so frequently, and occupy so many hours of our existence, as to give a smiling aspect to the whole. Happiness, it was also observed, is accommodated to all beings and conditions; there is no absolute standard of it, which would necessarily limit its distribution. The pleasures of the child, the savage, and the brute, are as real and hearty, as complete in their way, as those of the mature and cultivated mind. All have the means of enjoyment provided for them, suited to their peculiar sphere, adapted to their organizations and their tastes. Lastly, the endowment of the mind with the benevolent affections, is a most effectual security for our happiness, by making us all the guardians of the happiness of each other. It is not only the duty, but one of the primitive impulses, of man, acting spontaneously, and for the time irrationally, to aid, protect, and sympathize with his neighbor. These affections profit not only the objects of them, but him who cherishes them; the luxury of their indulgence being so great, that when real occasions to call them forth are wanting, we seek fictitious ones, and spend them upon imaginary beings.

The occasional presence of evil does not disprove the goodness of God. — These facts, I observed, show *a vast predominance of happiness* in our condition, and so, notwithstanding the occasional presence of evil, amply vindicate the benevolence of the Creator. What remains is a point of curiosity and theory, rather than of substantive importance, for the religious inquirer Insist as we may upon the existence of sin and suffering in the world, these, in the amount in which they are visible to us, do not disprove, do not even cast a doubt upon, the goodness of God; they affect only the doctrine of the *infinity* of his benevolence, a subject with which we, his finite creatures, with our limited intelligence, have little or no concern. It is probable, it is even certain, that the whole difficulty consists, not in the nature of the facts themselves, but in the imperfect comprehension of our minds, which cannot unite the conceptions of infinite power and infinite goodness without stumbling upon a contradiction and an absurdity. After this explanation, we approach the deep and dark problem of the origin of evil without anxiety.

Proper statement of the question. — The question in its simplest form is, How can there be *any* evil in the world, if it was created and is governed by an all-powerful and all-gracious God? The difficulty disappears, and the problem is solved, if we can prove that the existence of any amount, *however small,* of sin and suffering, is compatible with a belief in the omnipotence and infinite benevolence of the Deity; for, in the first place, it was shown in the last chapter, that the amount is actually small, when compared with the happiness and virtue for which provision is made, and which are really experienced or exercised; and, secondly, if *any* evil, *however slight,* can be satisfactorily accounted for, without bringing the infinite power and goodness of God into doubt, the question respecting *the magnitude* of this necessary evil can be determined by infinite wisdom alone. It is not competent for us to settle *this* question; nor is it desirable, for the answer to it does not at all affect our belief in the moral attributes of the Supreme Being, and is obviously beyond the reach of the human faculties. We might as well assume to determine how many stars there ought to be in the sky, as to say how much or how little of any quality or thing ought to be permitted under God's government, when we have once clearly seen that its presence in some degree is essential. Only an Alphonso of Castile could be guilty of such folly. He alone who knows the whole, and governs the whole, of the universe of which we form but an infinitesimal part, — our time in it being but a moment, and our space a dot, — can tell *how much* is essential, when we know that *some* is essential. Our ideas of quantity and magnitude are wholly relative; however great the sum may appear to us, no one can affirm, that, in the eye of Infinite Wisdom, it is not a *minimum*. Nay, after the proofs already advanced of the Divine benevolence, the presumption is inevitable, that it *is* a *minimum*.

Exaggerated statements of the amount of evil in the world. — I place stress upon this point, because, both by the friends and the opponents of religion, the problem respecting the origin of evil has been unnecessarily darkened and rendered formidable by declamatory and exaggerated statements of the *amount* of sin and woe which sadden the annals of mankind. Thus, Bayle, the most acute and sarcastic of modern infidels, after quoting Cicero's pathetic account of his voyage home from Asia, at one point in which he beheld around him the deserted ruins of so many cities, once renowned for their power and splendor, goes on to say, — "History is, properly speaking, only a record of the crimes and the misfortunes of the human race. . . . . . If man is the creation of a single being, who is supremely good, supremely holy, and supremely powerful, how can he be exposed to disease, to cold, to heat, to hunger, to thirst, to pain, to sorrow? How can he have so many wicked inclinations? How can he commit so many crimes? Can infinite holiness create a wicked being? Can infinite goodness create an unhappy being? Will not sovereign power, joined with infinite benevolence, overwhelm its creature with benefits, and remove far from him all that can offend or sadden?"

The following picture, by Abraham Tucker, though well intended, is quite as exaggerated and unnecessary. "That there are innumerable evils," he says, "the phenomena of nature sufficiently assures us: storms and tempests, earthquakes and inundations, lay fields and cities desolate with all their produce and inhabitants; blighting winds and pestilential vapors wither up and destroy, ravenous beasts devour, villains assassinate, thieves break through and steal, tyrants oppress, diseases torment, cross accidents vex, old age debilitates, our necessary employments fatigue, our wants interfere, our very pleasures cloy, and man is born to sorrow as the sparks fly upward. We are necessitated to destroy vermin that would overrun us, to slay our fe'low-creatures for our sustenance, to weary them out with toil and labor for our uses, to press one another into wars and sea-services for our preservation. Nay, evil is so interwoven into our nature, that the business of mankind would stagnate without it; most of our cares being employed in delivering ourselves from troubles we lie under, or warding off those that threaten."

The fallacy of these sweeping statements exposed. — It is hardly necessary to say, that such statements as these are one-sided and exaggerated, and that the general impression which they leave on the mind is wholly unfounded. The great but covert fallacy in this general impression, is, that *the whole human race is regarded but as one individual,* whose existence extends through all ages and over all parts of the earth, so that his single experience comprises all the woes and crimes which are actually distributed among countless millions of beings. Now it is the veriest truism to say, that happiness or misery is experienced *only by individuals;* that *there is no such thing as the suffering of the race in general;* that any one man would be considered as marked out for sorrow, as a special object of compassion, who should be afflicted by any *one* of the great evils above mentioned; that it is impossible, in the nature of things, for any one to suffer from all of them; and that the occurrence even of one would occupy but a small portion of the experience of an individual, all the rest of which might be almost unmingled enjoyment. How many of those who read this page have been plagued by famines, inundations, earthquakes, the assassination of friends, robbery, ravenous beasts, tyranny, the necessity of slaying a fellow-creature for sustenance, or the like? And if, which is very improbable, there be an individual who has experienced one of these calamities, *how small a portion of his whole existence has been immediately saddened by the event, and how many compensating hours has he had* of amusement, indifference, or positive happiness? How idle is it, then, to make out a catalogue of all the calamities and crimes of which there is any mention in history, and to speak of *human life* as vexed by them, thus conveying the impression, though it is not a logical inference, that it is *the life of an individual* which is thus spoken of! For when happiness or misery is the topic of discussion, if it be not an individual existence that is referred to, this enumeration, this adding of one woe to another, and one crime to another, is meaningless and impertinent. To take a particular instance, — it was a misfortune and a wrong that Socrates should drink the hemlock. But how many, with the same virtues and the same genius, have suffered the same fate as the Grecian sage? and how great or how long was this suffering even for him, when compared with the many and bright hours of instruction and happiness which constituted the remainder of his individual experience? If we were wise, we should thank God that Socrates lived and taught as he did, rather than grieve or murmur because he died a felon's death.

The real problem stated as a dilemma. — Putting aside, then, these rhetorical exaggerations of human wretchedness, we come to the real problem, — how to reconcile the presence of any pain or wrong, however slight, with the infinite power and goodness of the Governor of all things. The whole difficulty here is well stated in the form of a dilemma by Lactantius, who professes to have taken it directly from Epicurus, into whose philosophy it entered as a proof of his doctrine, that the Deity existed indeed, but that he exercised no oversight or government of the affairs of this world. "The Deity," he says, "is either willing to take away all evil, but is not able to do so, in which case he is not omnipotent; or he is able to remove the evil, but is not willing, in which case, he is not benevolent; or he is neither willing nor able, which is a denial of the Divine perfections; or he is both able and willing to do away with the evil, and yet it exists." Now it is obvious, in the first place, that this dilemma is made to cover too much ground; for while *inability* to remove the evil is rightly held to disprove the *infinite power* of God, his *unwillingness* to remove it is held to prove, not that his benevolence is *imperfect,* which would be a just conclusion, *but that he is not benevolent at all,* or rather that he is *malignant,* the evil being intentional, and not incidental. The facts, certainly, support no such conclusion. We may suppose, if we will, that the Deity has a general intention to provide for the happiness of his creatures, and, in the long run, or as a general rule, has taken measures to secure it; but that he is not watchful in every case, and has not provided for all emergencies, thinking it best, perhaps, that, on a few occasions, slight evils should be endured. Such is often the conduct of an earthly parent, who would never be accused of a want of love for his offspring. But this is not general enough to be considered as a satisfactory solution of the problem, nor do I propose it as such.

Metaphysical impossibilities do not disprove omnipotence. — We shall gain a clearer idea of the true purport of the question, by examining more closely the meaning of the words employed. *Omnipotence* and *benevolence* are apparently very simple and very comprehensive terms, though few are more vaguely used. The former means a power *to do every thing;* but this does not include the ability *to do two contradictory things at the same moment*, or to accomplish any metaphysical impossibility. Thus, the Deity cannot cause two and two to make five, nor place two hills near each other without leaving a valley between them. The impossibility in such cases does not argue *a defect of power, but an absurdity in the statement of the case* to which the power is to be applied. A statement which involves a contradiction in terms does not express a limitation of ability, because, in truth, it expresses nothing at all; the affirmation and the denial, uttered in the same breath, cancel each other, and no meaning remains. All metaphysical impossibilities can be reduced to the formula, that *it is impossible for the same thing to be and not to be at the same moment*, as this would be an absurdity, — that is, an absurd or meaningless statement. Thus, *virtue cannot exist without free agency*, because a free choice between good and evil is involved in the idea of *virtue*, so that the proposition means no more than this, — that what contains freedom cannot be without freedom. Compulsion is a denial of freedom; therefore, the phrase *compulsory virtue* does not so much express an impossibility, as an absurdity; it is nonsense. We cannot choose between good and evil, unless good and evil are both placed before us, — that is, unless we know what these words mean; and we cannot express our choice in action, unless we are able to act,—that is, unless we have the power of doing either good or evil. In the dilemma quoted from Epicurus, a contradiction in terms is held to prove a defect of power, or to disprove Omnipotence; the dilemma, therefore, is a mere logical puzzle, like the celebrated one of Achilles and the tortoise. The only difficulty is, how to lay bare the fallacy, or expose the contradiction, since it is very skilfully covered up by the language employed.

Outward acts do not disprove benevolent intentions.—The meaning of *benevolence* appears simple enough; but it is often difficult to tell whether a certain *act* was or was not prompted by kind *intentions*. Strictly speaking, of course, *benevolence is a quality of mind*,—that is, of will (bene *volo*) or intention,—*not of outward conduct.* An *action* is said to be benevolent only by a metaphor; it is so called, because we infer from it, with great positiveness, that the agent must have had benevolent intentions. We think that the motives are indicated by the act; but we may be mistaken. He who gives food to the hungry poor would be esteemed benevolent; but he may do it with a view to poison them. To strike for the avowed purpose of causing pain, usually argues ill-will or a malignant design; but the blow may come from the kindest heart in the world, for the express purpose of benefiting him who receives it. In the present argument, Epicurus assumes that the presence of evil, that is, *the outward fact*, is enough to prove *a want of benevolence*, or even a malignant design, on the part of him who might have prevented it. But if, by evil, is here meant mere pain or suffering, whether proceeding from bodily or mental causes, we may boldly deny the inference. If pleasure or mere enjoyment is not the greatest good, if sometimes it is even inconsistent with the possession of a higher blessing, then a denial of it may be a proof of goodness instead of malice. The problem respecting the existence of evil is really solved by the single proposition, that *virtue, not happiness, is man's highest interest.* Not only mere harm or suffering, but the liberty to do wrong, is essential for the existence of virtue.

The presence of evil does not impeach the perfections of God. — I cannot admit, then, on general grounds, that the presence either of moral or physical evil in the world throws any doubt whatever upon the perfections of the Deity, or offers any argument against the doctrine of an ever-watchful and ever-gracious Providence. It is demonstrable, that there could be no such thing as holiness, if sin were not possible; that happiness is not man's greatest good; and that occasional privation of it, or positive suffering, may be essential for our education in virtue. We cannot always trace the immediate connection between the evil that we now endure, or which we compassionate in others, and the moral purpose that it is designed to further, or the benevolent intention of which it is the index. But we can discern all the great features of the scheme, and see that what is hard to bear, or painful to look upon, in a particular case, may be a necessary part of a system of government contrived by infinite wisdom, and executed with almighty power and perfect love. But as it is not the general argument, in the somewhat abstruse and technical form that I have here given to it, which usually perplexes our ideas of Divine Providence, but rather the hardship and the wrong in particular cases, which, we are prone to think, might have been prevented by the goodness of God, without altering, in any material respect, the broad features of his administration of human affairs, it may be worth while to develop and apply these principles with some minuteness.

Progress, not mere attainment, is the law of our being. — All that we know of the human mind and of the history of this world's affairs, with the intimations that these respectively afford of the designs of Providence, leads us to conclude, that *moral discipline, or the formation of character by our own efforts,* aided, indeed, but not determined, by power from on high, is the great end of our being here below. Not mere attainment, but progress, is the law of our finite condition, — progress desired, planned, and accomplished by ourselves, assisted by means that are placed within our reach, though we are free to use them or not. Trial and effort, mistakes committed and rectified by increased effort, temptations to be met and vanquished, and difficulties to be overborne, are essential parts of such a scheme. Our progress is to be measured, or, in other words, *our merit is to be determined, by the quantity of ground that we have passed over*, not by the absolute distance of the point that we have reached from the termini of the course. Therefore, all start fair in the race, though their points of departure may be far apart. Mere happiness, however elevated and unalloyed, is not the grand object; for *happiness is a state or fixed point*, implying neither movement nor effort; the desire of happiness is implanted in us only as a principle of activity, to stimulate, never to be fully satisfied. *Virtue*, on the other hand, *is not a state, but an action;* it is *not being, but doing.* All advancement made in it conveys increased power of progress, the motive constantly elevating itself and becoming purer, obstacles vanishing, and temptations losing their force, as we go on. Mere enjoyment, on the other hand, satiates and cloys; a fresh struggle with difficulties is soon required, or the cup loses all its sweetness. Repose is pleasant, but continued idleness is intolerable.

Difference in this respect between instinct and reason.— There cannot be a better illustration and proof of the correctness of this view of life than is afforded by the contrast, which I have already placed before you, between *instinct* and *reason.* The safety and comfort of the lower animals are provided for, and all the ends of their being are obtained, under an unerring guide acting above the sphere of their consciousness. They reverse the law of human condition; *enjoyment, not progress, is their highest good.* Results, which, if brought about by man, would imply great sagacity and inventive power, would tax the loftiest intellect and the most profound study, are accomplished by them without effort, without education, and without liability to error. Their faculties, if we may call them theirs, are not susceptible of any discipline or improvement whatever; at the dawn of their existence, they begin their allotted tasks, and finish them as perfectly as at its close. Having no foresight, they have no foretaste of evil. With little, if any, sensibility to suffering, their enjoyment, such as it is, appears always com plete. Death which cannot be foreseen has no terrors; for them, it is simply ceasing to live, and is therefore no more an evil, than their non-existence was during all time anterior to their birth.

Contrast their situation with man's, who is born helpless, ignorant, and unprotected, save by the affection of his own kind. He is left to himself; his will is free, and his reason must be developed by its own efforts, through constant trials and mistakes, and frequent pain. With all his boasted learning and ingenuity, so slowly and laboriously acquired, he cannot build so perfect a cell, he cannot form so perfect a society, as the bee; because the construction of a house or a society, however faultless, is not the object of his being. The purpose for which he was created is, *that he may fit himself* for these and greater tasks; *the education thus self-acquired being the great end in view*, and not the mere accomplishment of the task, which is comparatively of little moment. We are constantly mistaking means for ends, the importance of the supposed ends being exaggerated in our view, in order that we may be induced to use the supposed means; in this use or application, in this effort and the consequent improvement, lies the real end. Most of the ends which men pursue, are pointed out to them by the passions and the appetites, — that is, by the lower part of their nature; the strain of the faculties in this pursuit is counted as a necessity and a hardship, but is submitted to as the condition of success. Reason and conscience, if properly developed, are continually admonishing us, it is true, that we mistake in this matter; that the end first in view is not the real end, or of substantive importance; that the formation of character, the development of intellectual and moral power by our own efforts, is the true object; — but their voice can scarcely be heard amid the din of the passions.

The increase of happiness is not the greatest good. — I do but take the most general instance under these remarks, when I say, that the love of happiness itself is but one of these lower desires, and as such, is rightfully restrained by the conscience, which declares to us with an authority that we cannot but recognize, though our actions are too seldom directed by it, that mere enjoyment is not the greatest good. How, then, is it an impeachment of the goodness of the Creator, that the happiness of man, though carefully provided for within certain limits, is still made secondary to his moral improvement? As the idea of virtue includes trial, temptation, suffering, and the liability to sin, *it is a contradiction in terms, to ask that progress in virtue should be made compatible with the non-existence of evil.* All improvement presupposes a lower state as a point of departure; all merit presupposes that the improvement is voluntary, and is due to one's own exertions.

It may be disputed, perhaps, that the happiness of the brute creation is complete; but we have a right to imagine that it is so, and then to compare our own condition with theirs, supposing all drawbacks to their enjoyment to be taken away. Is there a human being, whatever may have been his individual experience, or however large may be his estimate of the sin and misery which darken the lot of mankind, who will not exclaim, "God be thanked that he has not made me a happy brute, or a senseless machine?" Is not our lot, with all our experience of pain and wrong, vastly preferable to theirs, even with their supposed immunity from physical suffering? Sin, of course, they are not capable of. Or can we imagine any possible constitution of the human mind, or any government of this world's affairs, which shall effectually exclude evil without reducing man to the situation of an animal or a machine? If not, *if no better system in this respect is even conceivable*, to say nothing of its possibility, *then is the present one the best possible*, and both the justice and the benevolence of its Author are amply vindicated. Our inability to conceive of a better one cannot be referred to the limitation of our faculties, since we are not called upon to devise a scheme, but are enabled to see that any improvement of the present one, in respect generally of the presence of evil, would involve a contradiction or an absurdity.

General laws are necessary to guide beings who are endowed with freewill. — In order to apply this *general* solution of the problem to *particular instances* of misfortune and wrong, we must rememb(r that the scheme of Divine government is to be taken as a whole. *Whatever is essential to carry out any part of the plan, must be regarded as a necessary feature of the system, and we must accept all its consequences along with it.* The education of man, both moral and intellectual, by his own effort, being the object to be gained, it becomes necessary that the course of events should be governed by *general laws;* or, in other words, that the action and government of the Deity should be uniform, so that events should not appear to us to succeed each other confusedly or at random, but in a fixed relation of antecedence and consequence. If reason is to take the place of instinct, that is, if man is to be self-taught, instead of being directly moved, like an automaton, by superior wisdom and power, then the means and appliances must be provided through which alone reason can act. As a guide to conduct, reason would be useless without foresight. We could not shape our actions beforehand, without some knowledge of the future which they are to affect; nor could this knowledge be gained, without such a clew as is afforded by the uniformity of nature. Experience, the great teacher of reason, derives all its efficacy from our belief, that the future will resemble the past, that bodies will always retain their properties, that food will continue to nourish, fire to burn, and poison to kill, and that different motives will retain generally the efficiency they have often shown in swaying the conduct of others. A rational being could not move a step, except at random, but for this confidence in the permanency of natural causes, as they are called. We have a right to say, then, that *the preservation of general laws is an essential feature of that scheme of Divine government* which we have tried to develop, — that, without them, man could not be self-taught, would not be capable of progress, could not be a free agent or a moral being. It is no paradox to say, that the continuance, the inflexibility, of the law of gravitation, is essential to the support of the law of morality, is vital to the existence of virtue itself.

General laws cannot be suspended in particular cases. — Then we must accept all the necessary consequences of general laws along with them. In the vast majority of instances, we may presume that they will work for good, tending equally to guide the conduct, satisfy the wants, and promote the happiness of man; and this presumption, as we have seen, is amply sustained by experience. But in particular cases, their very inflexibility occasions their doing apparent harm; and these are the instances of evil which most frequently incline men to murmur against Divine Providence. They are called "accidents," "misfortunes," and even the believer sometimes repines because the good are not protected against them. But it has been proved that there is no such thing as chance, or accident, or fortune. The position even of a grain of sand, the waving of a leaf in the wind, is determined, not indeed by the blind and mechanical coöperation of the properties of matter, but by the same wisdom and goodness which made human nature capable of virtue, and which dispose all events for the guidance and the moral improvement of the human family. Unless the course of these events were uniform and inflexible, the whole effect of the lesson would be lost. It seems a light thing for the sufferer under a particular calamity to ask that the law of order may be suspended in his case, at least for this time, — that the tempest may not wreck his vessel, or the fire consume his dwelling, or the blight visit his fields, — that the hand of the oppressor may be stayed, and the wicked may cease to triumph. But as *millions have equal reason to ask for the same indulgence,* if the prayers of all were granted, general disorder and confusion would ensue. We could no longer profit by the past, or prepare for the future. Prudence would be a word without meaning, and foresight an impossible attainment. The study of nature, which now, in a greater or less degree, taxes and improves the intellect of every human being, would be a profitless collection of individual and isolated cases, from which no instruction could be gleaned; and, as such, it would be abandoned. Having no means of divining the future, man could only stumble onward in the dark, or be led by the hand at every step, like a blind child, through the palace of God's works.

"If we attempt," says Dr. Ferguson, "to conceive such a

scene as some skeptics would require to evince the wisdom and goodness of God, a scene in which every desire were at once gratified without delay, difficulty, or trouble, it is evident, that, on such a supposition, the end of every active pursuit would be anticipated; exertion would be prevented, every faculty remain unemployed, and mind itself would be no more than a consciousness of languor under an oppression of weariness, such as satiety and continued inoccupation are known to produce. On this supposition, all the active powers which distinguish human nature would be superfluous, and only serve to disturb our peace, or sour the taste of those inferior pleasures which appear to be consistent with indolence and sloth."

Suspension of the law would work greater evils. — But you ask that the law may be suspended *only in this instance,* and still be allowed to prevail elsewhere, so that, here, signal virtue may be rewarded or saved from suffering, while the uniformity of Providence may be maintained as a guide to man on all other occasions. Passing over the difficulty already adverted to, that the number of equally just applications for interference would so far balance the number of cases in which the law held good, as to destroy all confidence in the uniformity of nature, it is important to consider how far the consequences of any one interference might extend. If the wind is not to blow, in order that the hopes of one righteous man may not be wrecked, the atmosphere may stagnate and corrupt over large regions of space, bringing pestilence and death to thousands. The inundation that sweeps away one house, may fertilize a whole district.

"Think we, like some weak prince, the Eternal Cause,
Prone for his favorites to reverse his laws?
When the loose mountain trembles from on high,
Shall gravitation cease, if you go by?
Or some old temple, nodding to its fall,
For Chartres' head reserve the hanging wall?"

Besides, in order that the good may improve in goodness, *there must be something contingent and uncertain in the rewards of virtue.* Constituted as we are in other respects, and general laws still holding good in the majority of cases, the invariable visible connection of virtue with happiness would destroy the whole foundation of disinterested conduct. Moreover, the mischance, as we call it, affects only the outward advantages of rectitude; its inward rewards are always sure, and these are a sufficient compensation for the hardship or loss.

> "What nothing earthly gives, or can destroy,
> The soul's calm sunshine and the heartfelt joy,
> Is virtue's prize; a better would you fix,
> Then give Humility a coach and six,
> Justice a conqueror's sword, or Truth a gown,
> Or Public Spirit its great cure, a crown."

Each particular virtue presupposes the existence of its opposite. — And this suggests the next consideration, that, if we examine separately the requisitions of the moral law, we shall find that each individual virtue presupposes the existence either of misfortune or wrong. Thus, *courage* would not be possible without *danger*, nor *fortitude* without *pain*. There could be no *temperance*, but for *the liability to excess*, and no *benevolence*, unless there were *wants to satisfy, or sufferings to relieve.* Even *justice* would lose the greater part of its merit, if there was *no self-denial* in satisfying its demands. *Prudence* could not be exercised, if *recklessness* could not suffer; and even *veracity* would be no virtue, if one *could not help* telling the truth. He who *could not* do harm or wrong, might still be *innocent*, it is true; but there would be no *merit* in his innocence. In short, merit consists in withstanding temptation, alleviating pain, and opposing wrong; so that, *without the presence of evil, there would be nothing to praise, and nothing to blame.* These reasons, be it observed, account not only for the permission of the crimes, whether of omission or commission, which men are guilty of, but for the physical evils which befall us from the unalterable course of external nature, or are only so far connected with mind, that we must assume the existence of a sentient being before the mischief can be felt.

Evil has always a compensating good. — That there is no evil, dependent on natural causes alone, which has not its compensating good, is a truth which has been so much insisted u] on)y writers on this subject, that I need not dwell upon it here.* The difficulty of finding out what this compensation is, in some cases, shows the imperfection of our faculties, but certainly does not accuse the benevolence of God. The most obvious reason for this difficulty, is the vast compass of the system, of which each individual being constitutes so small a part. "Imagine only," says Shaftesbury, "some person entirely a stranger to navigation, and ignorant of the nature of sea or waters: How great his astonishment, when, finding himself on board some vessel anchored at sea, remote from all land prospect, whilst it was yet a calm, he viewed the ponderous machine, firm and motionless in the midst of the smooth ocean, and considered its foundation beneath, together with its cordage, masts, and sails above, — how easily would he see the whole one regular structure, all things depending on each other; the uses of the rooms below, the lodgements, and the conveniences of men and stores! But being ignorant of the intent and design of all above, would he pronounce the masts and cordage to be useless and cumbersome, and for this reason condemn the frame and despise the architect? O, my friend, let us not thus betray our ignorance, but consider where we are, and in what a universe! Think of the many parts of the vast machine, in which we have so little insight, and of which it is impossible that we should know the ends and uses: when, instead of seeing to the highest pendants, we see only some lower deck, and are

* "Thus, for example, poverty, or the want of riches, is generally compensated by having more hopes, and fewer fears, by a greater share of health, and a more exquisite relish of the smallest enjoyments, than those who possess them are usually blessed with. The want of taste and genius, with all the pleasures that arise from them, are commonly recompensed by a more useful kind of common sense, together with a wonderful delight, as well as success, in the busy pursuits of a scrambling world. The sufferings of the sick are greatly relieved by many trifling gratifications imperceptible to others, and sometimes almost repaid by the inconceivable transports occasioned by the return of health and vigor. Folly cannot be very grievous, because imperceptible; and I doubt not but there is some truth in that rant of a mad poet, That there is a pleasure in being mad, which none but madmen know." — *Soame Jenyns.*

in this dark case of flesh confined, even to the hold and meanest station of the vessel."

General laws, on the whole, promote order and happiness. — Every discovery in science, all progress in the knowledge of nature, goes to illustrate and confirm the truth, that the tendency of the general laws which prevail in the universe is favorable, on the whole, to order and to happiness. Time is necessary, that this truth may become known. An observer of vegetable life, whose knowledge was confined to a single year, would consider the approach of winter as an irreparable calamity. The falling of the foliage, the death of annual plants, the earth sealed up by frosts, and the skies darkened by storms, would appear to him not merely as unredeemed evils, but as tokens of a universal cessation of life, if not of a dissolution of all things. But so familiar to us is the fact, that the decay of plants is necessary to keep up the fertility of the ground, and that the powers of vegetation, suspended during the winter, burst forth with additional luxuriance in the spring, that we hardly think of reckoning the end of the glories of autumn among the evils of nature. The most poisonous plants, when administered with skill and in moderate doses, have been found to possess the most valuable medicinal qualities. The pain which follows cutting or otherwise wounding the flesh, and generally the great sensitiveness of the outer surface of the body, were thought, till very recently, to be unmitigated evils; but it is now ascertained, from the distribution of this sensitiveness, that its purpose is unquestionably one of pure benevolence, its office being to warn us against the approach of bodily harm, since those parts which are not liable to injury are not rendered sensitive. But the skeptic will ask, *If Omnipotence could not guard us against such harm, without the use of means that involve suffering?* Certainly it could, just as it does, in the case of *the lower animals, by leading us blindfold away from the harm,* compelling us to take precautions against it without our being conscious that they are precautions. But then *where would be human reason, forethought, and free-will?* or how would mental and moral discipline, or self-education, be possible? Consistently with the preservation of these great ends, which we have seen to be paramount in importance over all others for man's own good, we may confidently say, that the means actually adopted in man's case are the wisest, kindest, and best.

Special provision against pain. — But the progress of discovery within a year or two has added another and still more striking illustration of the truth here referred to. To the perfection of the plan just described, for warding off bodily harm, it might have been objected, that surgical operations sometimes become necessary for removing a deeply seated injury, and that the pain which the surgeon is then obliged to inflict, being useless for its original purpose of warning us against danger, is an evil without compensation. This objection, I say, might have been made, though it would not have seemed a very reasonable one; for it amounts to asking, that, under a system of which the preservation of general laws is an essential part, precisely the same thing — namely, the cutting of the flesh — should be attended with pain, if done accidentally, but should be free from pain, if done intentionally, and with a benevolent purpose. This would seem to be a contradiction. But who shall prescribe bounds to the wisdom and goodness of God? Certain substances in nature have been endowed with such properties, that when administered to the patient, without causing any harm to his bodily constitution, his sensibility to pain, for a time, is entirely destroyed, and the surgeon may do his most formidable office upon him, while he is enjoying the happiest of dreams. Will even the skeptic dare affirm, that the marvellous anæsthetic properties of ether and chloroform were not added to these substances for the express *purpose* which they have recently been discovered to answer, or that the discovery itself, so unexpectedly made, was not *intended* both to reward and stimulate man's researches in science with a view of doing good to his fellows, so that it is comprehended under that vast scheme of self-education which is the great object of man's earthly existence? In reference only to this discovery and its immediate results, it is not going too far to apply the remark first made in regard to the astronomer, and to say that the undevout surgeon is mad.

Increase of knowledge would explain away other evils. — Self-improvement, both of the individual and of the race, seems to be the leading purpose of the Deity in the government of mankind. The several parts of man's nature are developed through their influence on each other, and in due proportion. The cultivation of his intellect, and the stores of knowledge thereby amassed, are continually adding to the safeguards of conscience and to the evidences of religion, — continually doing away with those objections to the providence of God, which, in the infancy of the race, perhaps, can be met by the humility and the power of Faith alone. Who can say how many of the apparent individual evils of man's condition upon earth, now inexplicable, except from the general consideration that the possibility of suffering and sin is absolutely essential to any progress in happiness and virtue, will be directly explained away by the future triumphs of science, which has recently shed so much light upon the beneficent constitution of the body in regard to pain? *

* In the argument from design, as Lord Brougham remarks, we infer that contrivance is universal, because we are able to trace and comprehend it in the great majority of instances; the number of exceptions to the rule continually diminishing as our knowledge of nature increases, we have a right to conclude, with respect to every natural arrangement in which we cannot yet detect a purpose, that the fault is only in our imperfect information, — that the purpose exists, though we have not yet discovered it, and that the Deity really does nothing in vain, though man may not be able, in every case, to read His designs.

The same form of reasoning may be employed, when we would account for the origin of evil. Many things were considered by the ancients to be unmitigated evils, which, as the progress of modern science has shown, ought rather to be considered as unmingled good. The instance given in the text is a fair example. We can now see, that the liability to pain never exists except where it answers a useful purpose, — that of warning us against danger; and that means are placed within our reach to effect a temporary suspension of the pain even in these cases, if any necessity arises for performing a surgical operation. Modern investigations have brought to light so many instances of this sort, that a fair induction from them enables us to conclude, that all the remaining specks will disappear, as soon as scientific research is carried far enough. We may even discern a reason why they are still allowed to dim the prospect; it is that we may

That the general laws of the universe are favorable to order and to happiness, is an observation, says Mr. Stewart, which "I am persuaded will appear, upon an accurate examination, to hold without any exception whatever; and it is one of the noblest employments of philosophy to verify and illustrate its universality, by investigating the beneficent purposes to which the laws of nature are subservient. Now, it is evidently *from these general laws alone*, that *the ultimate ends of Providence can be judged of*, and not from their accidental collisions with the partial interests of individuals; — collisions, too, which so often arise from an abuse of their moral liberty. It is the great error of the vulgar (who are incapable of comprehensive views) to attempt to read the ways of Providence in particular events,

---

be incited to make the requisite efforts for the attainment of that knowledge in whose light they will finally disappear.

"The problem has been solved by mathematicians, Sir Isaac Newton having first investigated it, of finding the form of a symmetrical solid, or solid of revolution, which in moving through a fluid shall experience the least possible resistance; in other words, of finding the form which must be impressed upon any given bulk of matter, so that it shall move more easily through a surrounding fluid than if it had any other conceivable form whatever, with a breadth or a length also given. The figure bears a striking resemblance to that of a fish. Now suppose a fish were formed exactly in this shape, and that some animal endowed with reason were placed upon a portion of its surface, and able to trace its form for only a limited extent, say at the narrow part, where the broad portion or end of the moving body was opposed, or seemed as if it were opposed, to the surrounding fluid when the fish moved; — the reasoner would at once conclude, that the contrivance of the fish's form was very inconvenient and artificial, and that nothing could be worse adapted for expeditious or easy movement through the waters. Yet it is certain, that, upon being afterwards permitted to view THE WHOLE body of the fish, what had seemed a defect and an evil, not only would appear plainly to be none at all, but it would appear manifest, that this seeming evil or defect was a part of the most perfect and excellent structure which it was possible even for Omnipotence and Omniscience to have adopted, and that no other conceivable arrangement could by possibility have produced so much advantage, or tended so much to fulfil the design in view." — Brougham's *Supplementary Dissertations to Paley.*

and to judge favorably or unfavorably of the order of the universe from its accidental effects with respect to themselves or their friends. Perhaps, indeed, this disposition is inseparable, in some degree, from the weakness of humanity. But surely *it is* a weakness, which we ought to strive to correct; and the more we *do* correct it, the more pleasing our conceptions of the universe become. Accidental inconveniences disappear, when compared with the magnitude of the advantages which it is the object of the general laws to secure: 'or,' as one author has expressed it, 'scattered evils are lost in the blaze of superabundant goodness, as the spots on the disk of the sun are lost in the splendor of his rays.'"

Merit determined by progress, not by attainment. — That *progress* in knowledge, happiness, and virtue, effected through our own exertions, and not the mere *attainment* of any fixed point or degree in either, is the main purpose of our being here below, and really our greatest good, is a doctrine which immediately explains away all those supposed evils in human condition, which are usually classed under the heads of *inequality and imperfection. All conditions are alike in this respect,* inasmuch as all admit of advance and improvement; the progress of each individual being measured from his own starting point, all have an equal chance of winning the prize, though the lot of some be cast in the early ages of hoar antiquity, and others are seemingly favored by the intelligence, the arts, and the morals of civilized nations and modern times. The happiness of each, as we have seen, is computed by his own standard of happiness, whatever that may be; and his merit, also, is determined by the measure of his moral *improvement,* and not by the refinement of those ideas of virtue which he may finally attain. It is, then, so far from an impeachment of the goodness of the Creator that he has made us finite beings, finite in our existence, our capacities, our virtues, and our enjoyments, that we see at once, *infinity or perfection is the only point from which progress is impossible.* Death alone, or in itself considered, apart from the antecedent dread of it, and from the injury to the feelings of the survivors, is not even an apparent evil, any more than the fact of our non-existence through antecedent ages.* It is matter of the commonest observation, also, that it is not the possession of any given quantity of the means of enjoyment, however great, but the *increase* of that quantity, whether the original sum were a unit or a million, which makes a man happy. To adopt Paley's illustration, "It is not the income which any man possesses, but the increase of income that affords the pleasure."

Virtue and happiness determined only by reference to capacity. — How unphilosophical, then, as well as ungrateful, is that frame of mind which looks with a jaundiced eye over creation, intent only on spying out its evils and imperfections; which pities the oyster, because it is inferior to the vertebrated animal, the quadruped, because it is not equal to man, and man, because his finite capacities are far below the perfections of the Infinite One! Yet it is only such reasoning as this, which has

* There is so much truth, as well as beauty, in the following remarks by Soame Jenyns, that I quote the whole passage, though some of the particular statements and arguments in it are open to criticism.

"Death, the last and most dreadful of all evils, is so far from being one, that it is the infallible cure of all others.

To die is landing on some silent shore,
Where billows never beat, nor tempests roar;
Ere well we feel the friendly stroke, 't is o'er.

For, abstracted from the sickness and sufferings usually attending it, it is no more than the expiration of that term of life God was pleased to bestow on us, without any claim or merit on our part. But was it an evil ever so great, it could not be remedied but by one much greater, which is by living for ever; by which means, our wickedness, unrestrained by the prospect of a future state, would grow so insupportable, our sufferings so intolerable by perseverance, and our pleasures so tiresome by repetition, that no being in the universe could be so completely miserable as a species of immortal men. We have no reason, therefore, to look upon death as an evil, or to fear it as a punishment, even without any supposition of a future life: but if we consider it as a passage to a more perfect state, or a remove only in an eternal succession of still improving states, (for which we have the strongest reasons), it will then appear a new favor from the divine munificence; and a man must be as absurd to repine at dying, as a traveller would be, who proposed to himself a delightful tour through

made the problem respecting the origin of evil to appear insoluble. However great the good which is actually provided may be, the skeptic fancies that he may always ask, Why is it not greater? If mankind are happy, why were they not created earlier, or why do they not now exist in greater numbers? Here is the error of supposing that virtue and happiness are tangible products, instead of abstract ideas, — are quantities which may be weighed or measured, the goodness of the Creator being estimated by the magnitude of the aggregate. But it is not so; each can be determined only in reference to the capacities of the individual, whose cup of enjoyment, whatever its dimensions may be, being full, or whose merit being positive from the moral improvement that he has made, no matter where he began or where he leaves off, the equity of the Divine government, in his respect, is sufficiently vindicated. Hence the justice as well as the beauty of the solemn affirmation of our

---

various unknown countries, to lament that he cannot take up his residence at the first dirty inn which he baits at on the road.

"The instability of human life, or the hasty changes of its successive periods, of which we so frequently complain, are no more than the necessary progress of it to this necessary conclusion; and are so far from being evils deserving these complaints, that they are the source of our greatest pleasures, as they are the source of all novelty, from which our greatest pleasures are ever derived. The continual succession of seasons in the human life, by daily presenting to us new scenes, render it agreeable, and like those of the year, afford us delights by their change, which the choicest of them could not give us by their continuance. In the spring of life, the gilding of the sunshine, the verdure of the fields, and the variegated paintings of the sky, are so exquisite in the eyes of infants at their first looking abroad into a new world, as nothing perhaps afterwards can equal. The heat and vigor of the succeeding summer of youth ripens for us new pleasures, the blooming maid, the nightly revel, and the jovial chase: the serene autumn of complete manhood feasts us with the golden harvests of our worldly pursuits: nor is the hoary winter of old age destitute of its peculiar comforts and enjoyments, of which the recollection and relation of those past are perhaps none of the least; and at last, death opens to us a new prospect, from whence we shall probably look back upon the diversions and occupations of this world with the same contempt we do now on our tops, and hobby-horses, and with the same surprise, that they could ever so much entertain or engage us." — *Soame Jenyns.*

Saviour, that "There is more joy in heaven over one sinner that repenteth, than over ninety and nine just persons who need no repentance." A German writer has expressed the same general truth in a forcible, perhaps hyperbolical, manner. "If," says Lessing, "God should hold all truths inclosed in his right hand, and in his left, only the ever-active impulse to the pursuit of truth, although with the condition that I should always and for ever err, and should say to me, Choose! — I should fall with submission upon his left hand, and say, Father, give! Pure Truth is for Thee alone."

CHAPTER VIII.

THE UNITY OF GOD.

Summary of the last chapter. — It was remarked in the last chapter, in reference to the problem respecting the origin of evil, that we need not consider *how much* evil there is in the world; for the problem is solved, when we can account for the existence of *any* evil, however small, and show that it is reconcilable with a belief in the infinite goodness and almighty power of the Creator. Now, omnipotence does not include the power to accomplish a metaphysical impossibility, the statement of which always involves a contradiction, or, in other words, is an absurd and meaningless statement. It is just as contradictory to suppose that virtue can exist without a free choice between good and evil, as that four is not equal to twice two; for freedom is involved in the idea of virtue, just as twice two is involved in the idea of four. The phrase *compulsory* or *enforced virtue*, is quite as absurd as that of a *virtuous machine*. Sin and suffering, therefore, must be possible, if virtue is to be possible; and if virtue is man's highest interest, which both reason and conscience loudly declare, then it is not only compatible with infinite benevolence, but essential to it, that pain and wrong should be permitted. The balance is consequently on the side of good, or a greater good is accomplished than would otherwise be possible. Benevolence does not consist simply in preventing pain, but in bestowing the largest amount, or balance, of pleasure; just as a man with an income of a thousand a year, but who is in debt for a hundred, is still richer than one with an annual revenue of five hundred, which is wholly unincumbered. It was shown that no exemption from evil was possible, or even conceivable, which would not reduce man to the condition of a brute or a machine; and as his state, at the worst, is immeasurably preferable to theirs, his state is, in fact, the best possible; for we cannot even conceive of a better one, — that is, we cannot point out any defect in it.

In applying this solution to *particular cases* of evil, it was remarked, that education self-acquired, or progress in virtue and happiness through one's own efforts, is our greatest good, and the final end of our being here below. It is essential for such progress that the universe should be governed by *general laws;* that is, that the course of nature, or the action of the Deity, should be uniform; — reason would otherwise be inferior to instinct, and could not operate as a guide to conduct. We may expect that the general tendency of these laws will promote order and happiness; but, for the very reason that they are general and inflexible, they must sometimes conflict with the interests of individuals. The weakness of human nature is prone to magnify the importance of these collisions, and to complain of them as defects in the order of Providence. In a broader view, they are seen to be necessary parts of a system devised by infinite wisdom and benevolence for the highest interests of mankind. Some good always results from them; none are without compensation, in respect either of outward advantages or of inward enjoyment. The imperfections and inequalities of human condition cease to appear as evils, when self-improvement, or an advance in knowledge, virtue, and happiness, is regarded as the principal aim of our existence; upon this theory, all start alike, and we no longer regret that absolute perfection is unattainable, when we remember that it is the only state in which progress is impossible. As science advances, and we learn more of the secrets of nature and the purposes of the Deity, these apparent evils lessen in number and gradually fade away. Bodily pain, which ranks first among them in the estimation of the vulgar, has been shown by recent discoveries to be a purely beneficent institution; and as our horizon enlarges and our vision improves, there is every reason to hope, that all the other ills of our lot will appear either imaginary, or such as would in no way interfere with the enjoyment of a wise and good man. The specks that are apparent in the administration of this world's affairs will be lost in the unutterable splendors of Divine justice, mercy, and love.

The doctrine of the Manichæans. — Among the most remarkable theories to which the discussions respecting the origin of evil have given rise, is the doctrine of the Manichæans, who maintained that the world is governed by two coeternal and independent principles, or deities, the one benevolent and the other malicious; and that from the perpetual conflict between them arises the mingling of joy with woe in the condition of mankind. This belief, irreconcilable, as it appears, either with sound reason or pure religion, existed even in the bosom of the Christian church in its earlier ages, so renowned a theologian as St. Augustine having once adhered to it; and some traces of it, perhaps, remain to the present day, in the vulgar doctrine respecting devils. It is hardly necessary to say, that, from a warfare which has been going on from all eternity between two equally powerful deities, nothing but confusion could ensue; so that the theory is at once rebuked by the order and harmony that prevail throughout the universe. Their alternate reign might explain recurrent periods of unmingled happiness and unmingled misery, but would not do away with the objection arising from the mixture at the same moment of good with evil. Both could not be almighty, since the unbounded power of one would be a limitation (that is, a negation) of the infinite power of the other. On the other hand, they must be equally mighty, since, otherwise, their purposes always clashing, the stronger would certainly destroy the weaker, or reduce him to inaction. But the existence of two finite beings of equal attributes, the one perfectly good, and the other irredeemably wicked, is just as difficult to be accounted for as the coexistence of good and evil among mankind, to explain which this theory was first invented.* It is but supposing that the class of the virtuous is diminished in number till but one representative of it remains, and that the same thing takes place with regard to the wicked; — a supposition which throws no light upon the main question, why any wickedness is permitted.

Polytheism is the oldest religious belief. — But having already accounted for the presence of evil, we need not concern ourselves about this fable, — for it is a fable, or legend, rather than a doctrine of philosophy or theology, — except to point to it as one of the forms of *polytheism*, or of those religious systems that are not based upon the dogma of the unity of God, the subject which I propose to discuss in the present chapter. If we look only at what Hume calls the natural history of religion,

---

* "The Manichæan doctrine, of two eternal and mutually repugnant principles," says Dr. Crombie, "seems morally impossible. To suppose an eternal and infinite being, possessing unlimited wisdom and power, whose nature is purely malevolent, is to suppose the coëxistence of two irreconcilable contrarieties. *Malignity, implying ignorance and weakness, cannot possibly coexist with the attributes of infinite power and infinite wisdom.* This objection alone appears fatal to the hypothesis.

"Nor is the hypothesis more defensible on the supposition, that the two eternal beings do not possess infinite wisdom and infinite power. If such could without absurdity be supposed to exist, they must either possess these attributes in an equal degree, or one must be superior to the other. If we take the former alternative, the energies of both, engaged in eternal conflict, must be mutually neutralized. Every effort of the one to produce good or evil, must be instantly counteracted by the opposition of the other. Like two equal contending weights, neither could preponderate. Under the conflicting agencies of two such beings, there could exist neither good nor evil. If we take the other alternative, and suppose the superiority of either, it is evident that the inferior must ultimately yield, and the struggle for the mastery terminate in the established ascendency of his more sagacious and powerful opponent." — Crombie's *Nat. Theology*, Vol. II. p. 158.

and put aside the inquiry respecting a primitive revelation to mankind, there is no doubt that polytheism is the most ancient form of religious faith, as it is still the most prevalent one. It is the natural belief of a barbarous or half-civilized nation, who have neither tradition nor philosophy to set them right. The religious sentiment in man is indestructible. Men are inclined to venerate and worship some unseen power or powers, just as strongly as to exercise the benevolent affections, and to seek out some objects, if none happen to be originally near at hand, on which these feelings may expend themselves. The manifestation of *power* is so firmly associated in every one's mind with the presence of *a conscious individual agency*, that striking physical occurrences, such as tempests, earthquakes, inundations, thunder, and the return of the seasons, are unhesitatingly referred, at first, each to its peculiar deity, or conscious cause. The faith of the vulgar is soon systematized, expanded, and recorded in the first rude attempts of a people at poetry, philosophy, and theology, — pursuits which are naturally antecedent to those of the physical sciences, for the same reason that poetry precedes prose; namely, that the imagination works with greater facility and pleasure than the judgment or the logical faculty. When thus partially reduced to order, and enshrined in verse, this faith becomes a system of *mythology*, which, from the variety and interesting character of its materials, will always maintain a strong hold upon uncultivated minds, though the learned and the philosophical will be struck with a view of its incongruities and absurdities, and will strive to fashion for themselves an esoteric doctrine of a single principle, which sustains and governs all things.

The opinion, that polytheism is the first natural product of the religious sentiment among mankind, and that it everywhere preceded a belief in the unity of God, is ably sustained by Hume, a portion of whose argument I borrow the more willingly, as it is sanctioned by the high authority of Dugald Stewart. "It seems certain," says Hume, "that, according to the natural progress of human thought, the ignorant multitude must first entertain some grovelling and familiar notion of

34

superior powers, before they stretch their conception to that perfect Being who bestowed order on the whole frame of nature. We may as reasonably imagine, that men inhabited palaces before huts and cottages, or studied geometry before agriculture, as assert that the Deity appeared to them a pure spirit, omniscient, omnipotent, and omnipresent, before he was apprehended to be a powerful, though limited being, with human passions and appetites, limbs and organs. The mind rises gradually from inferior to superior; by abstracting from what is imperfect, it forms an idea of perfection; and, slowly distinguishing the nobler parts of its own frame from the grosser, it learns to transfer only the former, much elevated and refined, to its divinity. Nothing could disturb this natural progress of thought, but some obvious and invincible argument, which might immediately lead the mind into the pure principles of theism, and make it overleap, at one bound, the vast interval which is interposed between the human and the Divine nature. But though I allow, that the order and frame of the universe, when accurately examined, affords such an argument, yet I can never think that this consideration could have an influence on mankind when they formed their first rude notions of religion."

The progress of science lessens the number of deities. — The number and variety of the operations of nature suggest to the ignorant and uninquiring mind a corresponding number of unknown causes which are active in producing them. The movements and changeable aspects of the clouds, the air, the rivers, the sea, — the growth of plants, and the diurnal and annual revolutions of the starry firmament, are referred each to its hidden cause or separate deity; every volcano has an imprisoned demigod struggling under it, and every thunderstorm suggests an angry deity launching his bolts against his foes. As science advances, objects and events are classified, and causes generalized. Phenomena the most unlike in outward appearance, are found to be explicable through the operation of one and the same power. The law of gravitation alone explains most of the physical changes which were arranged by the ancients under so many distinct heads and sovereigns; many others are traceable to the single law of chemical affinities. Hence, if a mythology were to be constructed now, on the same general principles as of old, Olympus would be less crowded.

If, from purely physical occurrences, we turn to *the vicissitudes of man's condition* and the general course of *human affairs*, we find a similar effect produced on religious belief. In barbarous ages, the lot of individuals seems to be determined by chance, or by the conjunction of an indefinite number of causes. The fortunes of war, the caprices of sovereigns, the ravages (against which ignorance has no shield) of famine and pestilence, the rise and fall of dynasties, and the brief cycles of national prosperity and adversity, introduce so much uncertainty into all calculations respecting the future, that men are tempted to refer all events to the agency of a crowd of independent and often hostile deities, against whose power human strivings produce but little effect. But the study of history and of the laws of the human mind, with a knowledge of the fundamental principles of politics and political economy, brings order into this chaos, and makes the past intelligible, and the future a subject of calculation and foresight. Good and ill fortune are now referred to their true sources, in the characters of men themselves, and the number of special deities who exert any influence over human affairs, is rapidly reduced to one.

Two conclusions may be drawn from this fact of the early growth of polytheism. The *first* is, that the religious *sentiment* alone is no safe guide to the doctrine of the unity of God; it is equally well satisfied by the worship of a crowd of inferior deities. *Reason* alone, or reason aided by Revelation, can enable us to form fit conceptions of the Supreme Being. Natural theology is the product of the understanding and the moral sense; feeling or sentiment only affecting the mode of our perception of its truths, or forming the atmosphere through which we regard them. The *second* inference is, that if, at an early period of civilization, among a people otherwise rude and ignorant, or at any rate, enjoying no special advantages over surrounding nations, a belief in the unity of God is found to be a prominent feature in their religion, the conclusion is unavoidable, that this belief came from immediate revelation. It is not the natural product of the human mind under such circumstances; the unassisted reason could not have attained to it. It is supernatural, then, whether it be a remnant of the knowledge with which man was originally endowed when he was first placed upon the earth, and by which alone he could be fitted for the exigencies of a situation at once novel and perilous, or a special communication from on high, designed as a foundation for a purer faith, and as seed for subsequent diffusion among all tribes, languages, and nations.

Polytheism rejected by educated and thinking minds. — Polytheism being the earliest product of the religious sentiment, and maintaining a strong hold upon the imaginations of the vulgar, we might expect that high mental cultivation would either enable a few minds to detect its absurdities, and to refine it into a system of pure theism, or that these few would themselves fall back into utter skepticism. The enlightened class among the Greeks and Romans really fluctuated between these two extremes. They derided the popular faith, but they had nothing certain to put in its place. Their speculations upon the subject have the air rather of exercises of fancy and rhetoric, than of the argumentative examination of a theme of vital importance to man. Socrates was perhaps the only one among them, of whose opinions and reasonings we have any full statement, who entertained decided notions respecting the character and functions of the Supreme Being; and it was the purity of his ethical system, rather than the soundness of his philosophy in general, which guided him to a right conclusion. His pupil, Plato, mystified his teacher's doctrine with so many strange fancies and untenable conceits, that it is difficult to believe that he was earnest in the inquiry. Of course, I speak only of those who wrote before the promulgation of Christianity, as the silent influence of this faith modified the opinions of many who did not avowedly embrace it. Cicero has little claim to originality in any of his philosophical speculations; and as, at different times, he argued with about equal warmth on both sides of the question respecting the existence of one God, it is not likely that he had formed any decided belief about it.

Polytheism has no evidence or presumption in its favor. — It is matter of history, then, that a system of polytheism has never satisfied the requisitions of the cultivated and inquiring intellect; failing to struggle up from it to clear ideas and firm convictions respecting the unity of the Deity, the best minds, educated under such a system, have fallen back upon a contemptuous estimate of the faith of the common people, and a general distrust of man's capacity to form a purer and better-grounded doctrine. *It is unnecessary*, therefore, *to disprove polytheism*, for there is no evidence or presumption in its favor. *It is a popular prejudice, or a poetical fancy*, — not an opinion resting upon argument, or a system devised after rational inquiry and upon philosophical principles. We have found proof, clear and abundant, of the existence of one God; but we have no testimony, no intimations even, that there are many gods. The presumption is all the other way; the whole course of the reasoning going to show that there is one *Supreme* Being, Creator and Governor of all things. To assert the existence of others, is to deny his supremacy; if polytheism be true, there are beings whom he did not create and does not govern. Indirectly, then, the whole argument that we have thus far considered, is an argument for the unity of the Deity; since the conclusion to which it leads us, is directly opposed to polytheism. I do not say that it disproves the existence of an order of beings superior to the human, but still finite, created, and dependent. There may be such intermediate natures, though the universe to our eyes affords no trace of them, and the question whether they exist or not is one which it does not concern us to answer. By whatever name they may be designated, — angels, demons, or ministering spirits, — *they are not deities;* that is, they are not uncreated, independent, and eternal. "It seems a self-evident proposition, that the First Cause must be one; because, if there were more, they would want some prior cause to assign them their several stations and properties."

Argument for the unity of God. — The argument, if it can be called such, in favor of the unity of God, is usually stated thus: — If one cause is sufficient to account for all the phenomena, it is needless and unphilosophical to suppose that there are several causes. This is the only sort of proof that a negative proposition admits of; and it is admitted to be satisfactory in physical and moral science, the study of which would otherwise be profitless and vain, as it could lead to no definite conclusion. Indirectly, however, we may substantiate the doctrine of the Divine unity, by pointing out the unity of design which prevails throughout the universe. This is a profitable inquiry, though its direct result is rather to establish the wisdom, than the singleness, of the creative and governing Power. As it throws light, however, upon the character of the creation, and upon the nature of the Divine government, I shall devote to it what remains of the present chapter.

What sort of effects imply unity of cause. — Objects and events are considered as simple or complex in more senses than one. If absolutely simple, — as, for instance, a clap of thunder, or the personality of one human being, — the propriety of assigning but one cause to it is sufficiently evident. It is inconceivable, that many causes should coöperate for the production of one effect, which has *no complexity of parts, and does not admit of degrees.* Many arms and levers may act together in turning over a heavy stone; but the effect here is really complex, each lever actually raising some of the weight, in proportion to the power and effort expended upon it. But to call an absolutely indivisible atom or being out of nothingness, necessarily implies unity of cause; for *every exertion of power must produce some effect,* and if two powers were exerted at the same instant, two effects, or an effect in some way complex, must be produced. The indivisible personality of one human being, then, proves to a demonstration, that the beginning of *his* existence is an effect due to one creative Cause. If one man, therefore, formed the whole of creation, the unity of the Creator would be demonstrable. But this is not the case.

Inference from unity of organization. — An object, however, may be considered as single in another sense. If it is not a mere aggregate of parts, but *a system, in which the whole is the result of all the parts* taken and acting together, there is a strong presumption, though not an absolute proof, that it is the effect of one cause. Such is every organism, — a plant, or a human body, for instance, — as distinguished from inorganic masses, like a rock, or a heap of sand. Here the probability is very great, though it does not amount to certainty, that one creative mind presided over the formation of this virtual whole. The organism is complex, indeed, for it is made up of many parts; but as all these parts have an intimate connection with each other and with the whole, we presume that one mind must have planned the whole, and executed it, either directly by its own power, or mediately, through subordinate agents. It is hardly possible to conceive of two minds, or more, perfectly coinciding in their purposes and modes of execution; to our apprehension, at least, two such minds run together and make up one being, when there is no distinction of bodies to keep them apart. Two purely immaterial existences cannot be distinguished from each other, according to human conception, except by *the difference of their purposes and acts;* and any such difference precludes the supposition of their coöperating with perfect equality in the formation of one of these virtual wholes. If their shares in the work were not absolutely equal, then one was superior to the other, and supremacy implies unity. This reasoning, chiefly directed against the hypothesis of two creators, applies *a fortiori* to that of three or more. If to this strong presumption we add the fact, that we have abundant evidence of the being of one God, but not a shadow of proof that there is more than one, the doctrine of the Divine unity is established beyond all question.

Creation everywhere evinces unity of design. — Is the universe, then, one of these virtual wholes? Does it everywhere evince unity of design, and show such a correlation of parts, that the whole may properly be considered as an organism, or as the result of the parts, and not merely as their aggregate? To give all the evidence for the affirmative of this question, would require an enumeration of particulars too copious for your time and patience; but enough may be adduced here to leave no doubt upon the subject.

The universe is composed of *matter* and *mind*, and it is in the close, but, as we believe, temporary, union of these component parts, and in *their present mutual dependence and fitness for each other*, that the more striking part of the proof consists. But we will look first at the material universe alone; and in doing this, I must use, for brevity of speech, the common phraseology of physical science, though with the protest already expressed against the mechanical theory which it implies. Supply the correction in every case, by substituting for supposed *secondary causes*, the *immediate agency* of the Divine mind, and the argument becomes all the stronger.

The general laws of the physical universe evince the unity of their cause. — Consider, first, that the same physical laws, as wonderful for their simplicity as for the vastness of their sphere of operation, govern the motions and determine the state of all the particles and all the aggregations of matter which make up the solar and stellar systems. Through the principles of *inertia* and *the equality of action and reaction*, it is demonstrable, that, if I strike the ground with a hammer, the effect produced, small as it is, is propagated beyond the path of Neptune. It is the same law of gravity which guides the falling of a tear, and governs the revolutions of the planets; which binds the influences of the Pleiades, and loosens the bands of Orion. The simplicity of this law enables us to calculate its effects with so much precision, that, notwithstanding the erratic path, as it appears to direct observation, which the planets describe in our sky, the astronomer turns his telescope with perfect confidence to a mere point in the heavens, where one of these bodies will be found at a given moment a century hence. It has been justly observed, that, but for this marvellous coincidence of observation with the calculated results, we should wholly distrust the assumed precision and minuteness of our knowledge of bodies, which are seemingly so far removed from the sphere of human agency and research. Again, the *light* which streams from these remote orbs, is in all respects identical with that produced by artificial means to illumine our own dwellings; it is diffused in the same manner, travels with the same speed, obeys the same laws of reflection and refraction, and the experiments made in one are repeated with unerring precision in the other. If we extend our view over vast tracts of time, as well as space, the operations of nature still appear uniform, exact, and unchangeable; the same laws hold.* The astronomer calculates and verifies the observations made by the shepherds on the plains of Chaldæa, and the eclipses that were noted in China at the distant period when that empire seems to have excelled all other nations of the earth in physical science.

If we come down to the properties and internal constitution of the various substances with which we are surrounded, to the

---

* The eyes of the Trilobites of the transition rocks, says Dr. Buckland, "give information regarding the condition of the ancient sea and ancient atmosphere, and the relation of both these media to light, at the remote period when the earliest marine animals were furnished with instruments of vision, in which the minute optical adaptations were the same that impart the perception of light to Crustaceans now living at the bottom of the sea.

"With respect to the waters wherein the Trilobites maintained their existence throughout the entire period of the transition formation, we conclude that they could not have been that imaginary turbid and compound chaotic fluid, from the precipitates of which some geologists have supposed the materials of the surface of the earth to be derived; because the structure of the eyes of these animals is such, that any kind of fluid at the bottom of which these eyes could have been sufficient, must have been pure and transparent enough to allow the passage of light to organs of vision, the nature of which is so fully disclosed by the state of perfection in which they are preserved. With regard to the atmosphere, also, we infer that, had it differed materially from its actual condition, it might have so far affected the rays of light, that a corresponding difference from the eyes of existing Crustaceans would have been found in the organs on which the impressions of such rays were then received.

"Regarding light itself, also, we learn, from the resemblance of these most ancient organizations to existing eyes, that the mutual relations of light to the eye, and of the eye to light, were the same at the time when Crustaceans, endowed with the faculty of vision, were first placed at the bottom of the primeval seas, as at the present moment."

rocks, the metals, the salts, and the earths, which form the crust of our globe, we find a similar unity of plan and the same predominance of a few fixed laws. "All things in the universe," says Hume himself, the chief of modern skeptics, "all things are evidently of a piece. Every thing is adjusted to every thing. One design prevails through the whole." Cohesive attraction binds the particles of all bodies together, their chemical elements unite in the same proportions, and the numbers which express these proportions are combined in constant ratios, so that the results of chemical analysis are now recorded by a universally applicable scheme of algebraic notation. It is quite probable, that, before long, chemistry will attain the rank of an exact science. The simple bodies retain their properties all over the globe; one lump of a metal or an earth is always a perfect specimen of the rest, though found in opposite hemispheres. The specific gravity, determined to the thousandth part of a grain, is a perfect test of the purity of gold, whether it is brought from Peru or the Ural Mountains. The elements of pure water, the constituents of the atmosphere, are the same, and are combined in precisely the same proportions, wherever water flows, or the air penetrates.

Unity of plan in the animal kingdom.— The organic kingdoms show a still more marvellous unity of plan, and a nicer adaptation to each other and to the inorganic world. The chemistry here is more intricate, but it is still uniform; and its complexity arises from the great variety of purposes which organism is designed to answer, and from the numberless relations which bind each to each throughout the animal and vegetable creations.* Remembering how the same general type of the skeleton is preserved throughout the vertebrate branch,

* "It was a great discovery in physiology, when it was ascertained that all vertebrata, that fishes, as well as reptiles, as well as birds, as well as mammalia, arose from eggs, which have one and the same uniform structure in the beginning, and proceed to produce animals, as widely different as they are in their full-grown state, simply by successive gradual metamorphoses; and these metamorphoses upon one and the same plan, according to one and the same general process." — *Agassiz.*

amidst numberless modifications of the size and shape of all its parts, so that each animal might be fitted for the exigencies of its peculiar situation and the part it has to play,—believe, if you can, that one mind did not preside over the formation of all the species, and adapt each to its place in one vast system. The laws of birth, growth, and reproduction have the same general character for all, and varieties suited to each; the progressive development of creatures that are so low down in the scale even as the mollusca, throws light upon the embryotic changes of the most perfect animal organism.* If we go back to the extinct races of the oldest geological periods, so far from finding that another general scheme then prevailed, we seem to witness the historical development of one and the same plan; the fossil varieties fill up some gaps that appear in the scale as it exists at present, and the order in which the several new creations appeared, shows with what facility the plan was adapted to the greatest variety of circumstances. Indeed, the whole science of zoölogy, with the light that it has received from recent investigations, is a most instructive commentary upon the doctrine of the unity of God.

Animals and vegetables and the atmosphere work together in one system.—Extending our view to the vegetable creation, and to the relations which connect it with the animal kingdom,

---

* "To study the phenomena manifested by a single individual, would give us an idea of the organic world as imperfect as that which an astronomer would obtain of the sidereal system, by studying the motions and phenomena of a single planet. It is not true that there exists, strictly speaking, a physiology, as of man, peculiar to a single being. Examine any organ, and the processes of which it is the seat, in a given animal; then refer to any other being in the animal series, and you will generally find the organ and its processes repeated. Examine the process of respiration, as it exists in men and in those animals nearly allied to him, and it will be seen, that, so far as regards the essential process, it is one and the same in all, though the manner in which it is carried out may vary to a considerable degree in the different races. By the researches of the comparative physiologist, it has been shown that the animal kingdom is subdivided into certain great groups, and that all the members of those groups are constructed on one and the same plan."—*Jeffries Wyman.*

we obtain fresh and beautiful illustrations of the same great truth. The two kingdoms are essential to each other's existence, both entering into the circuit through which inorganic matter passes, sustaining organic life on its way, and then returning to its primitive or elementary state. "While animals," says the most eminent botanist of this country, Dr. A. Gray, "consume the oxygen of the air, and give back carbonic acid, which is injurious to their life, this carbonic acid is the principal element of the food of vegetables, is consumed and decomposed by them, and its oxygen restored for the use of animals. Hence the perfect adaptation of the two great kingdoms of living beings to each other; — each removing from the atmosphere what would be noxious to the other; — each yielding to the atmosphere what is essential to the continual existence of the other." And further, — "Animals consume what vegetables produce. They themselves produce nothing directly from the mineral world. The herbiverous animals take from vegetables the organized matter which they have produced; — a part of it they consume, and in respiration restore the materials to the atmosphere, from which plants derived them, in the very form in which they were taken, namely, as carbonic acid and water. The portion they accumulate in their tissues constitutes the food of carnivorous animals, who consume and return to the air the greater part during life, and the remainder in decay, after death. The atmosphere, therefore, out of which plants create nourishment, and to which animals, as they consume, return it, forms the necessary link between the animal and vegetable kingdoms, and thus completes the great cycle of organic existence. Organized matter passes through various stages in vegetables, is raised to higher conditions in the herbiverous animals, undergoes its final transformations in the carnivorous animals. Portions are consumed at every stage, and, leaving the ascending current, fall back to the mineral kingdom, to which the whole, having accomplished its revolutions, finally returns."

We are accustomed to consider the unity of organization of a single plant or animal, — to trace the relation, for instance, of digestion to the supply of blood or nutritive fluid, or respiration to the purifying of this fluid, and of its circulation to the nutrition of every part of the body, as well as the fitness of the vessels, conduits, and other means provided for carrying on this round of operations, the growth and continued existence of one particular organism being the combined result. But does not this grand circuit of animate and inanimate nature, this mutual dependence of the atmosphere, in regard to its purity, and of all animal and vegetable life, point out with equal clearness the unity of organization of the universe, and cause us to regard the whole as one vast apparatus, from which no single organ or portion could be taken away without vitiating the result, and reducing the entire fabric to a chaos?

"All are but parts of one stupendous whole,
Whose body nature is, and God the soul."

The progress of science constantly finds new proofs of unity of design. — Consider, also, that the discovery or generalization of these facts, which throw so much light upon the unity of plan in the creation, is among the latest triumphs of science; — and what may we not expect from the future progress of discovery, as tending to reveal to our eyes in full, what as yet we see but imperfectly, that there is not a stone or a clod of earth in the crust of our globe, nor one of the shining points which dot in myriads our nightly sky, that does not play an essential part in the working of the universal organism, the most intimate relations binding it alike to what is nearest and what is most remote? It was on some small, and seemingly irregular and purposeless, features in the arrangement of the planetary orbits around our sun, namely, upon the eccentricities of those orbits, that Laplace founded the sublime calculations which demonstrated the stability of the system. What are now called the "secular variations," because, after a long lapse of years, they begin to retrace their steps, as it were, and thus compensate the disturbance that had gone on increasing during that period, were formerly regarded as disturbing causes that would operate for ever in the same direction, so that they were proceeding slowly, but inevitably, to make shipwreck of the whole plan.

Laplace proved that they were cycles, and therefore that they should be ranked highest among those periodic revolutions which are so frequent in the economy of nature; instead of tending to destroy, they guaranty the permanency of the system. When but a few more such steps have been taken in the career of discovery, we shall see unity of organization in the universe, as clearly as we now do in the human body.

Plants and animals formed on one plan. — Coming back, in some measure, to details, it is remarkable that we can trace similarity of structure and function in cases apparently removed from each other by so wide an interval, that we should not have expected any resemblance whatever, except from the general consideration, that order and harmony must characterize all the works of infinite wisdom. For instance, how unlike, at the first glance, appear plants and animals, and how dissimilar their offices, though each kingdom, as we have seen, is necessary to the other, and the two play an equally important part in the accomplishment of the universal design! Yet it is not more certain, that the rudiments of the human skeleton, as they may be figuratively called, can be traced in the bones of one of the lowest fishes, than that the plant is, so to speak, a rudimentary animal. The functions of digestion, assimilation, circulation, nutrition, and respiration, for example, are common to the two; the distinction of sex belongs to both, and the means of reproduction are strikingly similar. And, generally, the botanist will tell you, between the organs which serve corresponding purposes in the two kingdoms, very obvious resemblances exist. Nature seems for ever at work upon the same general pattern; she is haunted, as it were, by one idea; and in out-of-the-way corners of creation, whither we had wandered in search of novelty, we are startled by the spectral reappearance of the old familiar face.*

---

* "These general views," says Prof. Sedgwick, "help us also to explain and rationalize certain well-known phenomena, such as abortive or rudimentary organs; [the existence of the mammary gland in man, for example. Blumenbach says, there are not wanting instances in which milk has

Mr. Stewart speaks of "the effects which philosophical habits and scientific pursuits have in familiarizing the mind to the order of nature, and in improving its penetration and sagacity in anticipating those parts of it which are yet unknown. A man conversant with the phenomena of physics and chemistry, is much more likely than a stranger to these studies to form probable conjectures concerning those laws of nature which still remain to be examined. There is a certain *style*, (if I may use the expression,) in the operations of the Great Author of all things, — something which everywhere announces, amidst a boundless variety of detail, an inimitable unity and harmony of design, and in the perception of which, what we commonly call *philosophical sagacity* seems chiefly to consist. It is this which bestows an inestimable value on the conjectures and queries of such a philosopher as Sir Isaac Newton."

Exact balance of coöperating agents. — I have but one other remark to make, in this connection, respecting the scheme of the material universe, — which is, that the proportions of the animal and vegetable kingdoms, and the constituents of the atmosphere to each other, were not always the same as they exist at present. There was a time, so geology tells us, when the air was greatly overcharged with carbonic acid, and thus unfitted for the support of animal life. Accordingly, plants were then almost the sole representatives of organic nature, and their continuous operation through many ages gradually purified the atmosphere till animals could live in it. Animals were then introduced, by their consumption of oxygen, and by rendering it back united with carbon, to serve as an offset for the action

been secreted from the breasts of men and other male animals.] These organs may have a muscular use which, in some cases, we do not comprehend. However this may be, they form a part, and an essential part, of a great scheme; and they help us to understand the pattern of nature's workmanship. One use, at least, they have; they tend to complete the order and plan of nature; and this, moreover, we may venture to affirm, that the Author of Nature manifests, in examples without number, a love of order, and harmony, and beauty, which is altogether independent of our conceptions of mere vulgar use."

of vegetables, and to prevent the stock upon which the latter lives from being eventually exhausted. The present exact balance between the wants and the products of the coöperating agents in nature is the result of one great scheme, which has come gradually to perfection, — thus leading us to infer, that one mind not only presides over the system now, but has watched and guided it through the several stages of its growth, the commencement of which dates far back in eternity.

Unity of plan in the relations of mind to matter. — If there remains comparatively little to say on the unity of plan that is evinced in the constitution of mind, and in the adaptation of the intellectual and moral to the material universe, it is because most of the important facts have been already mentioned in connection with other parts of our subject. Thus, I have dwelt at length upon the general laws which uphold and constitute external nature, considered as the necessary means through which reason and freewill are enabled to rival the works of instinct. Looking at the body, also, in its true light, as really external and foreign to the mind which inhabits it for a season, the laws of bodily health and disease, as formerly remarked, are among the strongest safeguards of morals. The organs of sense form the direct avenues of communication between the outer and the inner world, and in their curious and delicate structure are found the most striking tokens of infinite wisdom, adapting the same general plan to a great variety of purposes and circumstances. Man does not find himself a stranger upon the earth, though he is the latest comer; he enters a dwelling fitted and garnished for his reception, and yet taxing his faculties to the utmost, before he can ascertain and apply to use all its accommodations and contrivances. Or rather, to change the figure, he is admitted to a school, where the means and the stimuli of education are furnished in great abundance, together with a bountiful provision for his mere enjoyment.

Coöperation of the eye and the mind in vision. — Even his senses must be educated before they can do their appropriate work. His first and most important step in knowledge, as has been before observed, is to learn to see. The eye is sensible to the impulse of light, and the complex structure of this organ is adapted with the utmost nicety to the laws of refraction. Thus far, however, provision is made only for painting on the retina a very accurate picture, though on a much reduced scale, of external objects. The mind now must do its part in projecting off this picture, as it were, in referring these impressions to their outward cause, and in making the mere bodily sensation to be the type and material of knowledge, — the basis of perception of surrounding things. The sensation alone can teach us nothing as to the distance, magnitude, or even the externality of material objects; nor does instinct, as in the case of animals, supply the deficiency. Slowly the mind learns to refer the sign to the thing signified, and to spell out the world of knowledge which at first lies hidden in the hieroglyphic language of mere visual impressions. And when the organ is fully educated, how quick and various is the information that it gives! The traveller arrives at the crest of a hill, which commands a full prospect of a renowned city that he had never before seen, together with a long reach of the beautiful valley in which it lies. In a moment, his eye takes in the extended and widely diversified scene, — the maze of houses and streets, the projecting spires and towers, the swelling dome of the cathedral, the variegated tints of roofs and walls, the tufted tops of trees rising here and there at irregular intervals, the river winding through the vale; and a tolerably correct estimate of the size, distance, and relative position of these objects is so quickly formed, that it seems a part of the picture. It is marvellous that so great an accession to our knowledge, so large a stock of new and interesting perceptions, should be gained in an instant of time.

The senses proportioned to the wants and occasions of man. — Here, then, in the most familiar of all cases, body and mind coöperate so perfectly, and the adaptation of both to the wants of man, considered as an inhabitant of the material universe, is so complete, that we cannot avoid referring all the parts of the complex contrivance to one Author. Our admiration of the design is enhanced when we reflect, that the organ of sight is entirely formed at a period when no communication exists between it and that element to which every portion of it has so manifest a reference. The scheme of education, of self-improvement, with its obvious moral bearings, which we have seen to be the chief purpose of our being here below, is here visibly kept in view in the earliest physical arrangements that are made for our security and happiness upon earth. In other respects, the adaptation of the organ to man's physical wants, and to the formation of his character, is hardly less remarkable. "If, by the help of microscopical eyes," says Locke, "a man should penetrate further than ordinary into the secret composition and radical texture of bodies, he would not make any great advantage by the change, if such an acute sight would not serve to conduct him to the market and exchange, if he could not see things he was to avoid at a convenient distance, or distinguish things he had to do with, by those sensible qualities others do. He that was sharp-sighted enough to see the configuration of the minute particles of the spring of a clock, and observe on what peculiar structure and impulse its elastic motion depends, would no doubt discover something very admirable; but if eyes so framed could not view at once the hand and the characters of the hour-plate, and thereby discover at a distance what o'clock it was, their owner could not be much benefited by that acuteness, which, whilst it discovered the secret contrivance of the parts of the machine, made him lose its use."

Our mental constitution fitted to the material universe. — It would be easy to follow out this line of argument in regard to the other senses, and the several remaining points in the physical organization of man, and show how he is fitted in all respects to the scale of the world in which he dwells, and to the objects by which he is surrounded. "No other cause," says an eminent naturalist, "can be assigned why a man was not made five or ten times bigger, but his *relation* to the rest of the universe." The law of *the association of ideas*, which is the regulative principle of *memory*, corresponds so exactly with *the uniform succession of cause and effect*, which is *the regulative principle of the universe*, that no one can doubt that the one was specially designed to be the complement of the other. The child associates the idea of burning with that of the fire, and every pleasant or painful feeling reminds him of the occasion when it was first excited; on these connections of thought, the whole value of experience depends. If memory acted disorderly, the effect, for all practical purposes, would be the same as if events succeeded each other at random, and not in an unchangeable sequence. Before the past can be a safe guide as to the future, it is necessary, not only that the same effect should always follow the same cause, but also that the sight of the cause should always and instantly remind us of what is sure to succeed. In this respect, as in many others, the mind is a microcosm; it mirrors to us those aspects of external nature which are most necessary to be presented for the safety of the individual. The law of causation is also the law of memory.*

Uniformity of human nature. — A still more pleasing proof of uniformity of design may be found in the preservation of *the common type of humanity* among all nations, and in all ages of the world. Make out the difference as wide as you can between the savage and the civilized man, yet it is as nothing when compared with the interval which lies between the savage and the brute. This interval is constant. Exhaust all the means and artifices of instruction upon one of the

* The uniformity in the instincts of brutes, moreover, as Dugald Stewart has observed, presupposes a corresponding regularity in the phenomena of the material universe; "insomuch that, if the established order of the material world were to be essentially disturbed, (the instincts of the brutes remaining the same,) all their various tribes would inevitably perish. The uniformity of animal instinct, therefore, bears a reference to the constancy and immutability of physical laws, not less manifest than that of the fin of the fish to the properties of water, or of the wing of the bird to those of the atmosphere." "Through this uniformity in their instincts, also, man can better maintain his empire over them, and employ them to greater advantage as means or instruments for accomplishing his purposes. The instincts, as we have seen, allow some latitude of action, so that the brutes can accommodate themselves, in a small degree, to the ordinary vicissitudes of their condition; and thus they are incomparably more serviceable to man than they would have been, if, like brute matter, they were always subjected to regular and assignable causes."

lower animals, and he never even approaches the boundary line of humanity. On the other hand, all projects for reclaiming the criminal or the savage, go upon the supposition that he is a human being, like ourselves, — that he is moved by the same desires, agitated by the same passions, and has faculties which, though latent now, are capable of as high development. We instinctively recognize this common humanity, and act upon it; the taking of human life is everywhere viewed as a grave and awful deed, to be justified only by pressing necessity; while mere animal existence is sacrificed without a touch of remorse. Persons of delicate feelings, indeed, may shrink from the work; but their repugnance is founded mainly on an amiable illusion, which invests the dumb creature — a favorite domestic animal, perhaps — with some of the attributes of humanity. The individuals who make up the race are constantly changing; one generation succeeds another, and, at the close of a century, hardly one human being survives who was alive at its commencement. But the unchanging characteristics, the type, of the species, survive all mutations, and the subject of history is still the same. In every age and every country, the great features of humanity appear as steadfast as if they were engraved in marble. "It is this," says an eminent writer, "which gives the great charm to what we call *nature* in epic and dramatic compositions; when the poet speaks a language to which every heart is an echo, and which, amidst all the effects of education and fashion in modifying and disguising the principles of our constitution, reminds all the various classes of readers or spectators of the existence of those moral ties which unite us to each other and to our common Parent."

Result of the discussion. — The facts upon which I have dwelt in this chapter are sufficiently familiar; and it is true of all of them, that they *suggest*, rather than *prove*, the great doctrine of the unity of God. The truth of this doctrine is sufficiently established, as was remarked in the outset, by the absence of all evidence to the contrary. We have abundant testimony that one God exists; we have not even an intimation that there is more than one; and this is enough. I have sought to show, however, that this truth, like the other doctrines of natural theology, is continually suggested to us by a study of the universe in which we live, and of which we form a part. In the unity of our own life and consciousness, we find reflected the unity of Him from whom we derived our being. "Every man, a single, active, conscious self, is the image of his Maker. There is in him one undivided animating principle, which, in its perceptions and operations, runs through the whole system of matter that it inhabits; it perceives for the most distant parts of the body; it cares for all and governs all; — thus leading us, by analogy, to form an idea of the one great quickening Spirit which presides over the whole frame of nature, the spring of all motion and operation in it, understanding and active in all parts of the universe, — not as its soul, indeed, but as its Lord, — by whose vital directing influence it is, though so vast a bulk and consisting of so many parts, united into one regular fabric."

CHAPTER IX.

THE IMMORTALITY OF THE SOUL CANNOT BE PROVED WITHOUT THE AID OF REVELATION.

Summary of the last chapter. — Polytheism, it was remarked in the last chapter, is the religion of a barbarous age, and of the uncultivated understanding. It is the natural product of the religious sentiment before the reasoning power is developed, or the mind informed by reflection and careful study of the phenomena of the physical and moral universe. I do not say that polytheism is a natural form of religion, because I do not believe that barbarism and ignorance are natural to man. The great purpose of our being, as I have attempted to show, is self-improvement in the largest sense, — is moral, intellectual, and religious progress achieved by our own efforts; and we are in our natural condition only when we are active in that work. Barbarism is no otherwise natural to the human race than infancy is; it is a point of departure, a commencement of growth. The religious sentiment of an uncivilized people first manifests itself in idolatry, — that is, in a worship of false gods, or a system of polytheism. History and the reports of travellers inform us, that this is the universal faith of savage tribes. A few minds, far in advance of the others in refinement and habits of reflection, may throw off this belief of the populace; but they usually take refuge from it in general skepticism or fanciful speculation, rather than in pure theism. It is of no more use, then, to disprove polytheism than to argue against barbarism; that cannot be disproved which does not rest upon argument or conviction, and which is not so much an opinion or belief, as a popular delusion, the origin or natural history of which is distinctly traceable.

There is no need, then, I remarked, to prove the unity of the Deity, because nothing can be alleged against it; and having found one cause that accounts for all the phenomena, it is a wholly gratuitous hypothesis to suppose that there are other causes. Still, a study of God's works in various ways indicates or suggests the unity of their Author, and I briefly reviewed some of these indications. The universe, I endeavored to show, is an organism, all its parts being *essential* to the perfection of the whole. The same laws prevail throughout its immeasurable extent, governing alike the least events and the greatest. Light, gravitation, electricity, chemical affinity, and the like, are universally operating agents, that bind all the parts of the vast system together. Organized life, whether animal or vegetable, is cast in the same general mould, the great features of one plan being preserved throughout, though with numberless modifications to adapt it to particular cases. The boundary lines of the species are immovable, the type of each race being preserved through countless generations. Plants and animals resemble each other in their organs and functions, and, in connection with the atmosphere, form a great circuit through which matter is continually passing, alternately in an organic and an inorganic state. All these physical laws and agencies can be traced up to their ultimate purpose, in the education of mind and the formation of character; thus the universe of matter and mind constitutes one whole, all the parts working to one great end, so that we are unavoidably guided to the conclusion, that it has but one Author, Designer, and Sovereign.

The proof of the other attributes of God, to the full extent that is needed for religious faith and practice, follows immediately from the doctrines that have already been established. He is *omnipresent* and *omniscient*, who not only designed and created, but directs and governs, all. His power and wisdom are commensurate with his works; and as those works constitute but one system, and are directed to one end, every portion of it, however minute, is essential to its perfection and continuance, and therefore cannot have escaped his oversight and control. The sphere of his existence is certainly coextensive with the sphere of his operation; and this, in our ignorance of the true relation of pure mind to space, is the only conception that we can form of *universal presence*. Whether this *ubiquity*, in the language of the schools, be virtual or essential, those can judge who can best determine whether the human agent, the indivisible unit of personality, is directly or mediately present through the whole of the complex structure of bones and muscles which it inhabits, and with every portion of which it certainly exists in intimate union. The question is one purely of curiosity or mere speculation; the attribute is made known to us as real to the full extent to which we are able to form a conception of it. There is little use in being able to demonstrate the reality of what is inconceivable.

The *duration* of the Deity is *infinite*, since the argument adopted does not stop short of the First Cause, and that which is uncaused must have existed from everlasting. Moreover, that which is ingenerable must also be incorruptible; for there cannot have been originally any cause of dissolution from with out, and any inherent principles of decay and ruin must have manifested themselves during an infinite series of years. If they have not done so in the infinite duration that is past, it is a proof that they do not exist, and that there are none to operate in all future time. Again, as the agency of the Supreme Being throughout his physical creation is immediate, *his moral government is also immediate.* The whole series of arrangements and events by which his law is made known to man, and is upheld by the ordinary course of human affairs, is the direct consequence of his presence and action. The uniformity of this action is a proof of his wisdom and the unchangeable character of his purposes; but it is no proof that his government is exerted through agencies or means which are left to operate of themselves, without his constant supervision and power. The complete recognition of this great truth, *the immediate and universal government of God,* is the vital principle of all religion, the sustaining belief without which true piety cannot exist.

The infinity of the Divine Attributes considered. — I am aware of the common objection to the reasoning which has here been pursued, that human experience, arguing from a limited number of effects, can only establish the existence of a cause proportionate to them, — or that the *infinite* power and wisdom of the Deity cannot be inferred directly from the *finite* evidences, which alone are subject to our observation. The importance of this objection will depend upon the meaning we attach to the word *infinite.* It is commonly said to imply, in regard to the Deity, not merely that his power and wisdom are "beyond all comparison greater than any such qualities possessed by ourselves," but that these attributes exist "in such a degree, that any extent whatever of them being either presented to our observation or conceived by our imagination, the Deity possesses them in a still greater degree, — a degree to which our conception can affix no bounds." Now, of course, we cannot demonstrate a fact which is inconceivable, any more than we can prove a proposition which is unintelligible; so far as the infinity of God cannot be comprehended or understood by the human mind, so far is it removed from the sphere of all argument. Our only *understanding* of an *infinite* quality is that of *one which has no limits or restraint,* — nothing to prevent it from existing to an indefinite extent or perfection. In this sense, the infinity of the Divine attributes does admit of full proof. The universe, indeed, is finite, in respect both to space and time; but it comprehends all that is, its Creator and Ruler alone excepted. The universe, then, being subject to him, as his creature or the work of his hands, there is nothing beyond it to limit his perfections; no restraint, no bound, therefore, is possible. Or the same reasoning may be proposed in another form: — from the unity and infinite duration of the Supreme Being, it follows, that a time must have been when he was literally all in all; every thing that now exists is derived from him, or was made by him, and he must have existed before any thing was made. Then he must have been infinite, as nothing existed to set bounds to his attributes; and what has been created since cannot limit them, as otherwise the creature would be more perfect than the Creator.

What doctrines properly belong to Natural Religion. — I have now finished all that it seems appropriate on the present occasion to say respecting those doctrines of Natural Religion which rest upon full and satisfactory evidence, and so cannot be called in question without impeaching the validity of the ordinary laws of belief, and denying the capacity of man to obtain a knowledge of any facts that lie beyond the immediate cognizance of the senses. Many will think that I have attempted both too much and too little; — too much, because I have tried to prove, from the light of reason and nature alone, that *the moral and physical government of the Deity is immediate and incessant,* every event, even the minutest, being directly caused by him with a view to the moral and religious improvement of man; and too little, because I have omitted all argument for *the immortality of the soul,* and have not considered it necessary, in order to vindicate the justice and goodness of God, to represent our present existence only as a preparation for a life beyond the grave, or to maintain that the scheme of Providence which is now visible to us, is but a faint and imperfect image of a more glorious one, which is to be unfolded in some subsequent stage of our being. As to the former objection, I need not recapitulate the argument that has been laid before you, and which is satisfactory to my own mind, in favor of the immediate agency and perfect moral government of God. As to the latter, I hold that the doctrine of *the immortality of the soul cannot be proved from the light of nature,* — that there is, indeed, *no presumption against it,* but *nothing conclusive or reasonably satisfactory in its favor,* — that men never have attained to a full belief in it except by direct aid from on high, — and that *all proper faith in the doctrine rests upon revelation alone.*

Insufficiency of the argument from the light of nature illustrated. — The only evidence of a future life which the unassisted reason can furnish, is of the same kind, and has about equal force, with the argument that is commonly offered, I will not say to prove, but to show that it is not unlikely, that the other planets and satellites of our system are tenanted by human beings like ourselves. Certainly we cannot *disprove* this hypothesis, and I do not think that there is any strong presumption against it. Why should the third attendant orb, counting from our sun, be fully stocked with animal and vegetable life, while the second and the fourth are left desolate, answering no other purpose known to us but that of preserving the balance of the system, and of appearing as shining points in our firmament? The only rational answer to this question is, that *we do not know.* The subject lies as much beyond the reach of our faculties, as the bodies themselves do beyond the cognizance of our senses. The impossibility of disproving the conjecture that these orbs are inhabited, proceeds from the same cause as the difficulty of substantiating it, — namely, that we have no facts to reason about, no knowledge of the circumstances of the case.

Persons who are fond of pure speculation and hypothesis are very apt to confound *what may be,* for aught we know to the contrary, with *what is,* so far as we are able positively to determine it from our present means of observation and experiment; they mistake the *possibility* that is measured only by human ignorance, for the *probability* that is fairly inferred by the legitimate exercise of the understanding. But we cannot found knowledge upon ignorance; and the theorist who has had no experience under the conditions of his theory, and has no proper knowledge of the subjects to which it relates, necessarily speaks from ignorance and appeals to ignorance, — so that, even if we could not point out a single difficulty, a single false assumption, in his whole scheme and argument, it would still remain a mere hypothesis, alike incapable of proof and disproof. The fallacy to which such speculatists have recourse, is, that the weakness or the absence of any considerations against their theory constitutes a positive argument in its support. No such thing; it affords only a fair presumption of the baseless character of the whole fabric. We cannot *prove* a negative; we can show only the insufficiency of the ground on which an assumption is made to rest. "So far as nature is concerned," says Prof. Sedgwick, "philosophy has nothing to do with *what may be*, but with *what is*."

The argument for more worlds than one compared with the argument for the immortality of the soul. — Coming back for a while to the hypothesis of inhabited planets, it may be remarked, that the common argument in its favor is founded, *first*, upon the impossibility of seeing or proving that they are *not* inhabited; *secondly*, upon the analogy between their situation and circumstances, and those of our own globe; and *thirdly*, upon the assumed fact, that it is inconsistent with what we know of the character and purposes of the Deity, to suppose that he would leave such large orbs tenantless. Change only a few names of things in this description, and it becomes a very exact analysis of the ordinary reasoning, from the light of nature, to prove the immortality of the soul. This argument rests, *first*, upon the impossibility of seeing or proving that what we call death, is the absolute termination of our personal existence; *secondly*, upon the analogy between the transformation which takes place at the close of the embryotic period, (which is a stage in all animal life, our own included,) and the transformation which we may suppose to occur at death; and *thirdly*, upon the assumption, that the course of affairs in this life, the prevalence of sin and suffering, and the promiscuous distribution of happiness, are inconsistent with our notions of the character of the Supreme Being, are irreconcilable with Divine wisdom, justice, and love, — so that we must suppose a future state of existence, to give opportunity for redress, for completion, and for retribution.

The reasoning is both unsound and presumptuous. — I may here remark, that it is the offensive, and, as I think, groundless, nature of this last argument, which makes one feel less scrupulous about exposing the fallacy of the whole reasoning. Those who have labored most earnestly to establish, independently of Revelation, the doctrine of a future life, have unwittingly decried and calumniated the course of Providence in the government of this world's affairs. That there is some danger in pressing such considerations, has been shown by Mr. Hume, who argues with much plausibility, "that the only safe principle, on which we can pretend to judge of those parts of the universe which have not fallen under our examination, is by concluding them to be analogous to what we have observed.

'Of God above or man below,
What can we reason but from what we know?'

Now, the only fact we know with respect to the moral government of God is, that the distribution of happiness and misery in human life is in a great measure promiscuous. Is it not, then, a most extraordinary inference from this fact, to conclude that there must be a future state of existence to correct the inequalities of the present scene? Would it not be more reasonable, and more agreeable to the received rules of philosophizing, to conclude, either that the idea of a future state is a mere chimera, or that, if such an idea shall ever be realized, the distribution of happiness and misery will continue to be as promiscuous as we have experienced it to be?"

The same kind of conclusion obtained in the two cases. — Returning to the comparison, we may observe, that as the reasoning in the two cases is parallel and of the same int insic weight, it might be expected that we should arrive at the same sort of conclusion. All will admit, that *it is not impossible that the planets should be inhabited;* some will think that the balance of probability, on the whole, inclines in favor of the hypothesis. But no one, certainly, will place this hypothesis among the accredited facts of science, and make it a basis of his calculations and reasoning upon cognate subjects. Just so, looking at the matter in the light of nature alone, we must confess, that *it is not impossible that this life should extend beyond the grave;* perhaps there are a few faint indications that it will, — a few gleams that pierce the darkness of that undiscovered bourn from whence no traveller returns; but he who fully accepts and believes the doctrine, allows his wish to be father of the thought, and must be ready, on all occasions, to yield his faith on very slight testimony. I do not say, that, in such a case, he would be justified in disregarding, practically, the least chance of the doctrine proving true; for this, unlike the question respecting the planets, is a practical matter, and *a wise man will always choose the safe side.* It is not likely, perhaps, that one of those who are assembled to hear a sermon, will die within the hour; but it is the part both of prudence and of duty, *so to act* as if the knell were to be sounded for each within that time. In abstract cases, however, in matters of pure science, we argue very differently; nothing can be accepted here which is not *proved.* In examining the other doctrines of natural theology, it has been my aim throughout to show, that they are supported by evidence of the same general character with that on which the whole fabric of inductive science depends, though it is stronger and more abundant than what is often admitted to be conclusive in scientific reasoning. The natural arguments for a future life do not come up to this test; they cannot sustain this comparison; and I therefore discard them, that they may not discredit the reasoning employed to defend the other truths of natural religion.

Continuation of the parallel. — I continue the parallel which has been begun, by showing that virtually *the same answer may be made to the proofs alleged in either case. First,* the impossibility of proving that life is confined to our planet, or that the grave is the limit of human existence, as I have already shown, is no argument at all to prove that the other planets are inhabited, or that the soul cannot die. It simply clears the ground for it, if such an argument should ever be discovered. It leaves the subject entirely open, as one which we know nothing about, and therefore as one that affords no occasion either for belief or disbelief. The well-known principle, that *the burden of proof rests upon him who maintains the affirmative in a discussion,* is a dictate of common sense, no less than of sound logic. I admit this impossibility to the fullest extent, and still maintain, that not one step has been taken towards the solution of the problem.

Secondly, the analogy that is offered, in the one case, appeared just as applicable, a few years ago, to our moon, as to the planets Venus and Mars, — nay, even more applicable, as, owing to the nearness of our satellite, the circumstances are more nearly alike. But the recent discovery that our moon has neither atmosphere nor water, and that its surface is an almost chaotic scene of volcanic action, renders it almost demonstrable that it is not inhabited. If the analogy leads to a false conclusion where it is most nearly perfect, what confidence can we place in it where it is incomplete? In the other case, *the analogy offered is just as conclusive for proving the immortality of an oyster, as that of a man,* the former having also passed through embryotic transformations. He who builds his faith, therefore, upon this analogy between birth and death, must accept the doctrine of the Indian,

> "Who thinks, admitted to that distant sky,
> His faithful dog will bear him company."

To some writers upon the subject, this conclusion has not appeared so revolting as to induce them to give up the argument; but as it is certain that the lower animals have no moral nature whatever, their immortality seems very questionable.

Thirdly, the argument that is based upon our opinion of what is required by the nature of the Divine attributes, in cases which go beyond our experience, our wants, and our powers of observation, appears, as I have already hinted, both unsound and presumptuous. You say, in the one case, that Divine wisdom cannot have created bodies so large as the planets, for no other purpose than that of keeping up the balance of the system, and that no purpose is so worthy as that of making them the abodes of vegetable, animal, and human life. After all, then, the force of your reasoning *depends upon the size* of these bodies; for if they were no larger each than a grain of sand, the supposition that they are inhabited would never have been made. But our ideas of magnitude are wholly relative; or, at any rate, to Omnipotence, the task of creating a planet is no greater than that of fashioning a grain of sand. Is it derogatory to the wisdom of the Almighty to suppose, that any particle of earth or rock upon our own globe does not contribute its part to the support of life? Who will venture to decide in a case presenting so many considerations that are obviously beyond the reach of the human intellect? * Besides, we have no assurance that

* The recent publication in England of an eloquent and ingenious essay on "The Plurality of Worlds," supposed to be written by Dr. Whewell, has revived the discussion of this question, whether there are other orbs in the solar and stellar systems which are inhabited like our earth. The work has been answered with considerable ability and acrimony by Sir David Brewster, at first in the pages of the North British Review, and afterwards in a separate publication, entitled "More Worlds than One." Thus we have elaborate arguments, one on each side of the question, from two of the most eminent men of science in Great Britain. Each conclusively shows the weakness of his opponent's case, and thus indirectly leads the reader's mind to the proper result, that there are no materials for forming an opinion on either side of the question. Dr. Whewell began at a disadvantage, by undertaking to prove a negative; he has very ingeniously brought together the scanty data which astronomical science affords, for judging of the physical condition of other planets, and of the members of other systems, in order to prove that such a being as man could not exist upon any one of them. His antagonist evades such reasoning altogether, by stating that the physical constitution of the inhabitants of other worlds may be very different from ours, and yet be as happily adapted to their abode, as ours is to this earth. This consideration alone, to which no answer is possible, is enough to confute all the positive arguments on the other side; we have only to give the reins to our imaginations, and conceive of the moral and intellectual endowments of human beings lodged

the extension of the plan of organic creation, as it is developed upon the surface of our earth, is *the only object, or the worthiest*

---

in the bodies of fishes, birds, or mythological monsters, in order to find fit inhabitants for tenanting any world under any conceivable circumstances. Sir David Brewster triumphs in this view of the case; but he forgets that it is his duty, as maintaining the affirmative side of the question, to adduce some proof, some shadow of direct argument, that other worlds than our own are inhabited. This he cannot do; the whole positive plea upon his side consists in a very faint analogy, and a very arrogant assumption. The known points of resemblance between this earth and its sister orbs are neither many nor important; the analogy between them, though it may amuse the fancy, cannot direct the judgment. Man cannot so far scan the designs of Omnipotence, as to be able to affirm, that any portion of the universe exists without a purpose, if it be not inhabited by beings like ourselves. From the very nature of the case, the utmost that Sir David Brewster can do, is, to show that, in a certain case, the conditions are fulfilled which render human existence possible. In other words, he can only show, that man *might* live there; but this is not advancing a step towards the proof, that man *does* live there. Man *might* have lived on Pitcairn's Island, before the mutineers of the Bounty went thither; or on Juan Fernandez, before Alexander Selkirk made it his home; but as a matter-of-fact, he *did* not live in either of the places, till these events took place.

Dr. Whewell's best point is his reply to the common assertion of his antagonists, that it would be unworthy of Omnipotence to leave such vast orbs as Mars and Jupiter uninhabited by rational beings. He answers that, as the geologists have satisfactorily proved, this earth did exist, through unnumbered ages, as the abode only of reptiles and still lower orders of being. It was only a few thousand years ago, that the earth seems to have become ripe, so to speak, for the habitation of man. Other planets and other systems may yet be passing through similar ages of preparation — may not yet be ready for this grand consummation of the purpose for which they were created. Here, again, the argument is conclusive against those who dogmatically maintain the opposite side of the question; but it is no answer at all, to those who find as little reason to deny as to affirm, that the planets are inhabited, and who content themselves with saying, that the matter is beyond the reach of the human faculties.

On the whole, the discussion between these two *savans*, brilliant and amusing as it is, leaves the question precisely where it was before, — a matter for fanciful speculation, but not for scientific research or true knowledge.

ne, that can engage the attention of the Deity. Our observation is limited to a speck of earth, and we may not spell out all His designs to whom the universe is indebted for its being. So, in the other case, the assumption, that the existence of evil belies all our notions of the goodness of the Creator, must depend on our ideas of *the nature and magnitude of that evil.* If the presence of misfortune and wrong in any shape, or to any extent, is inconsistent with his perfections, then the permission of them, *even for a limited period, though they should be redressed or removed in a future life,* leaves a stain upon his attributes. It may be consoling for us to believe, that the virtue which does not meet with its desert in this stage of existence, will be rewarded or compensated hereafter; but this does not remove the reproach from the administration of Him who has the government equally of this life and of that which is to come. Besides, *what do you assume to be the only proper reward of purity and virtue?* Is it *happiness?* Then is happiness man's greatest good, and *holiness* is only a means for its attainment. You shrink instinctively from this conclusion, and still demand another life, or the immortality of the soul, not as a means for the improvement of character, an object which is obtainable in this world, with all its imputed defects and evils, but as a sphere or an opportunity for the more perfect enjoyment that you crave. Turn the matter as we may, there is selfishness, as well as presumption, in thus building our hopes of another life on the supposed imperfect justice with which the concerns of this life are administered.

Insufficiency of the metaphysical argument for a future state. — Leaving now this parallel, which I have followed so far only to show, that the reasoning which would not be admitted as legitimate in the ordinary investigations of science, must be rejected also in theology, I pass to a more particular examination of the usual arguments for *the immortality* of the soul, or rather for *a future state,* — inasmuch as hardly one of these arguments has any bearing upon the subject of an *endless* existence. They are properly divided into *the metaphysical and the moral argument,* — the former being derived from the *immaterial* or *indi-*

visible nature of mind or self, while the latter is drawn chiefly from a comparison of the constitution of man with the circumstances in which he is placed at present.* In the former, it is urged that *death* is a very different thing from *annihilation*, and though the course of nature gives us abundant instances of the one, it furnishes not a single example of the other. What we call death, is the cessation of the activity of a complex organism or machine, the various parts of which subsequently decay, or are resolved into their primitive elements; but not an atom of them is lost, not one particle is annihilated. The carcass of an animal is resolved into its constituent gases and earths, which go, for a time, to increase the stock of inorganic matter, perhaps to be again withdrawn from it, to enter into fresh combinations, and contribute to the support of a new life. Here is no absolute destruction, nothing but the resolution of a compound into its elements, and the formation of new compounds. There is no reason to believe that the quantity of matter in the

* Strictly speaking, the metaphysical argument proves only the *possibility* of a future state, and is insufficient, because we can never argue from *what may be*, to *what is*. We know, for instance, that the ichthyosaurus is a possible animal, for we find its remains entombed in the solid rock; but we also know that the ichthyosaurus does not now exist upon this earth. The moral argument is intended to show the *probability* of man's future existence, and is unsatisfactory because it rests upon two groundless assumptions; —*first*, that the presence of apparent evil in this life cannot be explained without impeaching the goodness of the Creator; and *secondly*, that the supposition of a future life, from which evil is excluded, is a satisfactory way, and the only way, of vindicating the Divine benevolence. I deny all these postulates. As we have already seen, the doctrine that *virtue, not happiness, is man's highest interest*, disproves the alleged existence of evil in our present condition, and leaves nothing to be remedied by the prospect of a future life. Again, we have no right to assume that another state of being is the only means whereby an omniscient and omnipotent Creator can vindicate his perfections; he may have provided other compensations that we know not of. Still further, as I have already argued, the supposition of perfect justice and endless happiness hereafter would not account for injustice and misery in our present lot. Why are we not introduced at once to the supposed state of perfection, without the necessity of passing through the evils of this world?

universe is less by one particle than it was at the creation; but there is every reason to believe the contrary. Now we have perfect evidence that the mind, the person, what we call *self*, is an absolute unit; it is even inconceivable that it should be complex, or should consist of parts. What power, then, has death over it? We claim no more for mind than we do for matter, in maintaining that it survives death. Of either it may be said, that it "cannot, but by annihilation, die;" and we have no instance to show that annihilation is possible.

This reasoning is ingenious and plausible; but you perceive that its only effect is to refute the skeptical assumption, that life terminates at the grave. *It opens the way for a proof* from revelation or some other source, *if any such proof can be found*, that life actually continues beyond the grave; it shows the *possibility* of such continuance, but not its *certainty*, not even its *probability*. For there is this capital distinction between the effects of death upon matter and upon mind. We *know* that death is not the annihilation of the particles or elements that make up the material organism, for these remain subject to our observation; we can see and handle them, and trace them into the new compounds of which they go to form a part. But the mind, the man, disappears to mortal vision when the breath has once left the body; we cannot trace *him* after the dissolution of the frail tenement that he once inhabited. Beyond the tomb, to our human perceptions, is a blank, — is nothingness. No voice has ever broken that awful silence, no form has ever returned from that impenetrable shade, save that of Jesus of Nazareth, and those to whom he spake. While we admit, therefore, the possibility that our friends survive, though we see them not, we must admit, also, that we have *no evidence of their existence* but from revelation. A similar remark may be made on the analogy that is often proposed between sleep and death. We know that man awakes out of sleep, as we have repeatedly witnessed the fact; and this shows the *possibility* of such an awakening hereafter. But we do not know, except from God's revealed word, that he awakes after the sleep of death, for such a resurrection we have never witnessed.

Matter is not necessarily indestructible. — The metaphysical argument proves nothing, unless we assume that the elements or primary particles of matter, and, generally, all things which are not compounded or made up of parts, are essentially indestructible; that is, that they exist by a necessity of their own nature. Then the time never could have been when they did not exist; *what is indestructible must also be ingenerable,* as the possibility of its non-existence at any antecedent period, however remote, negatives the supposition of its necessary existence. I adopt, therefore, the conclusion of Mr. Stewart, who says, that "this argument, supposing it were logical, proves too much; for it concludes as strongly against the possibility of the soul's being *created* as *dissolved;* and, accordingly, we find that almost all the ancient philosophers who believed in a future state maintained, also, the doctrine of the soul's preëxistence. Nay, some of them seem to have considered the latter point as still better established than the former. In the Phædon of Plato, in which Socrates is introduced as stating to his friends, immediately before his execution, the proofs of a future state, Cebes, who is one of the speakers in the dialogue, admits that he has been successful in establishing the doctrine of the soul's preëxistence, but insists on further proofs of the possibility of its surviving the body."

The argument by Plato and Cicero examined. — I may add, that in the most remarkable passage of Cicero's writings referring to this subject, — the Dream of Scipio, — the same fact is held to prove both the preëxistence and the immortality of the soul. The argument, indeed, is translated almost literally from the Phædrus of Plato. The shade of Africanus argues thus: — Every thing which derives its motion from something else, may evidently cease to move, and cease to exist; for the cause of its motion may be withdrawn. On the other hand, that which moves itself, as it does not derive its movement from any thing else, but is the source or origin of its own motion and of the motion of other things, never began to be; for that which is itself a source and a primal cause, has no beginning. So, also, as it moves itself, the cause of its motion can never be withdrawn; for it cannot leave or desert itself. It must, therefore, live and move forever. Now the *body* of man is moved by the indwelling soul, which may depart from it, so that the body will cease to move, and will perish; but that *soul* moves itself, and, accordingly, it was not created, and it can never cease to be.*

This is a good specimen of the acute metaphysical reasoning of the ancients; but as it wholly overlooks the consideration, that *a superior being may not only directly move an inferior one, but may give it the power of moving itself for a limited period*, just as man fashions and winds up a watch, which will then, in a certain sense, move itself for twenty-four hours, we need not dwell upon it here. The whole scope of the metaphysical argument, if properly carried out, is to prove the necessary existence both of matter and mind through an antecedent eternity, and through the eternity which is to come.

The limits of human science. — As I had occasion to remark in the former Part, the province of human science in regard to *objects that exist*, is strictly limited to *that which is* and *that which has been*; the former being known to us through observation and experiment, the latter through memory and the testimony of others, or through the permanency of the effects which it has produced. The present and the past constitute our sphere of knowledge; vainly do we attempt to descry the future, except through supernatural illumination. The only exceptions to this rule are, the eternal future duration of the Deity, which we immediately deduce from his antecedent eternity as the First Cause, and that *probability* of certain future events, which is founded upon our knowledge of the uniformity of his modes of operation, and of the fact that infinite wisdom cannot change.

What is called the natural desire for immortality is only the fear of death. — The moral argument for a future state seems to me still more vague and unsatisfactory than that which is metaphysical. Under this head are ranked, first, the presump-

---

* This is a paraphrase, rather than a translation; the original may be found in Plato, *Phædrus*, § 51–53, and in Cicero, *Tus. Disp.* I. 23, and *Somn. Scip.* 8, 9.

tions arising from "the natural *desire* of immortality, and the anticipations of futurity inspired by *hope;*" — the *presumptions*, I say for these feelings surely cannot be considered as affording any positive *proof* of the reality of that state of existence to which they poin. But it is argued, that "whatever desires are evidently implanted in our minds by nature, and are encouraged by the noblest and worthiest principles of our constitution, we may reasonably conclude, will in due time be gratified under the government of a Being infinite both in power and goodness." Now, it is obviously difficult for those who have always lived under the light of the Christian revelation, to know *how strong, or how natural, these desires are,* when they have not been fostered by positive assurances from a source that we cannot distrust. Our minds have been nurtured, our lives guided, by the well-founded hopes which Christianity affords; and certainly it would be a rude and painful shock, to learn that these hopes were vain. But go back to the times antecedent to the birth of our Saviour, and ask how many of the common people, under the Grecian and Roman commonwealths, were accustomed to cherish the desire of an existence beyond the grave. I do not mean to imply, that they had no such hope or expectation. Unquestionably, life is sweet, with all its vexations, sufferings, and cares; and most persons shrink from the termination of it, if for no other reason, from an unwillingness to have the projects of the hour cut short, — to leave the plough in the furrow, the book half read, or the house half finished. *It is not so much that they wish for immortality, as that they fear death;* and it is not because death, if painless, is in itself so terrible, as that at no one time are they just ready for it. Accordingly, with the pagan world, a future state was but a shadowy counterpart, a dream-like continuance, of their earthly life, — a prolongation, in the dusky realms of Pluto, of its exercises, its amusements, and its cares. In the Elysian fields, the warrior still bore his armor and brandished his javelin, the huntsman pursued the flying game, "the hunter and the deer a shade," the poet-priest sang to his harp, and the athletes wrestled in the arena. "Whatever delight, when alive, they had in chariots and arms, whatever pleasure in keeping fine horses, the same tastes continue with them after their bodies have been consigned to the earth." * And still they are vexed with a dim notion of the shadowy and unsubstantial character of these enjoyments of the dead. The shade of the warrior, when questioned on the subject, impatiently declares, that he would rather be a poor slave on the earth, than a monarch over all the spectres of the departed.†

> "The weariest and most loathed worldly life,
> That age, ache, penury, and imprisonment
> Can lay on nature, is a paradise
> To what we fear of death."

In these pictures, which certainly represent the faith of the most refined nations of pagan antiquity, I see *a love of life, or a dread of death, but no proper desire for a future state of endless being.* If a few philosophers and moralists discarded these vain and unworthy conceptions of futurity, they had nothing to substitute for them but some speculations, almost equally paltry, about the preëxistence and the transmigration of souls. It may well be doubted, therefore, whether any such desire as is here made the basis of an argument for immortality, is natural to man; — that is, whether it is a primitive impulse, an original and universal principle in our constitution, so that it would be an impeachment of Divine wisdom to suppose that it was implanted in us without a purpose, or of Divine goodness to believe that it is not to be gratified.

Not all our desires are meant to be gratified. — "If life," says

---

* Quæ gratia currûm
Armorumque fuit vivis, quæ cura nitentes
Pascere equos, eadem sequitur tellure repôstos.
Æneid, VI. 653–655.

† Μὴ δή μοι θάνατόν γε παραύδα, φαίδιμ' 'Οδυσσεῦ·
Βουλοίμην κ' ἐπάρουρος ἐὼν θητευέμεν ἄλλῳ,
'Ανδρὶ παρ' ἀκλήρῳ, ᾧ μὴ βίοτος πολὺς εἴη,
Η πᾶσιν νεκύεσσι καταφθιμένοισιν ἀνάσσειν.
Odyssey, XI. 489–491

Dr Brown, "be pleasing,—and even though there were no existence beyond the grave, life might still, by the benevolence of Him who conferred it, have been rendered a source of pleasure,— it is not wonderful that we should desire futurity, since futurity is only protracted life. The universal desire, then, even if the desire were truly universal, would prove nothing but the goodness of Him who has made the realities—or, if not the realities, the hopes—of life so pleasing, that the mere loss of what is possessed or hoped appears like a positive evil of the most afflictive kind." "This pleasing hope, this fond desire, this longing after immortality" is the sentiment of a Christian poet, though he has put it into the mouth of a Roman Stoic, who is made to find in it a provocation to suicide. Not all the desires which are natural to man are intended to be gratified, as we are continually hankering after a greater measure of happiness than we actually enjoy.* It is enough that this wish, and others of a similar kind, answer a useful purpose, by constantly stimulating us to action, since life itself would otherwise become vapid and sterile.

Insufficiency of the present life to satisfy our aspirations.— Another branch of the moral argument depends on a comparison of our intellectual powers, our impulses and conceptions,

* The desire for health is both natural and universal; but it is not always gratified, and it is not even desirable that we should have an entire exemption from disease. Sickness is both penal and reformatory, and it is useful in both relations. It is one of the most important of the pains and penalties with which transgression is visited, under the moral government of God; and it softens the heart, so as most effectually to prepare the way for repentance. In this instance, and in many others, we can clearly see *why* the gratification of a natural and universal desire is denied; we can discern the moral purpose of the infliction. Reasoning by induction, then, we can easily conclude that such a moral purpose *may* exist, even when, from the imperfection of our faculties, we cannot recognize it. If our present life is so happily constituted that all men desire the continuance of it, and shrink from death, then the goodness of the Deity is sufficiently vindicated already, without having recourse to the violent supposition, that there is to be another state of being, which will be governed on very different principles.

with the condition in which we are placed in this life, where circumstances are for ever impeding our efforts, thwarting our ambition, and baffling our plans. It is urged, that "our faculties are above our condition, and our curiosity is still greater than our faculties can satisfy." The instincts of the lower animals are exactly accommodated to their wants, and to the state in which nature has placed them. They do not appear to be troubled with any desires that they cannot satisfy, or with any fears that extend beyond the safety of their possessions for the moment. But man is restless, curious, and impatient; his conceptions are vague and vast, his ambition unbounded, and his curiosity insatiable. He has the mind of an archangel imprisoned in the carcass of a worm. It is affirmed, that "if he had no intimations of a future existence, it would have been better for him never to have extended his views beyond this globe and the period of human life, instead of embracing, as at present, a stretch of duration and of space which throws a ridicule on the whole history of human affairs." We aspire to know the history, not only of the earlier generations of our own race, but of the mutations which the solid globe underwent in those geological periods, the remoteness of which can harldly be represented by figures, while to our aching conceptions they seem to lie upon the confines of eternity. Not content with the ability to predict the motions and future positions of the heavenly bodies, we torment ourselves with unanswerable questions as to the beings who inhabit them, or the purpose which they serve in the grand scheme of the universe, or the order and law under which they were successively created. The mind returns from these sublime and far-reaching inquiries, to find itself tied to a body which is limited, in comparison, to a speck of earth and a moment of duration. The wants of this body afflict it with a multitude of petty cares, and the ordinary business of life, referring mostly to these wants, seems vexatious and contemptible. It is said that the disproportion here is so vast, that it cannot be reconciled with the notions we have formed of the attributes of the Creator and Governor of the universe, except by regarding it as an intimation of a future and higher state of existence, in which this curiosity and these aspirations shall be fully satisfied.

Proper use of such considerations. — I am far from wishing to lessen the force, or take away the applicability, of such elevated considerations as these. Those whose belief in a future life rests entirely upon the teachings of the author of Christianity, may still dwell upon them with satisfaction and pleasure, as they open new views of the purposes to which the existence beyond the tomb may be subservient. Speculations upon the nature of our employments in another stage of being, and upon the accession to our knowledge that will instantly take place when we are released from the incumbrance of the flesh, though they may not often command our unhesitating assent, will often afford scope for profitable meditation. But *their use is secondary;* they tend to fortify and render inviting the faith which was first conceived upon other grounds. Such a mode of reasoning as is here adopted, if reasoning it can be called, would hardly occur to any one who had not been educated in the Christian belief from infancy, nor to such a one even, if his life had not been devoted chiefly to scientific investigations and speculative pursuits. Vastly the larger portion of the Christian world, even at the present day, can with difficulty be persuaded to use even those means of knowledge which are opened to them; those cannot complain of the barriers which limit the progress of science, who do not know where these barriers are placed, who have not gone over the hundredth part of the field which they circumscribe. There is more danger that men will attach undue importance to the petty cares and transitory interests of this world, than that they will be led to slight and despise them because their intellects can traverse creation, and their curiosity aspires to number the stars in the heavens.

The grand openings which philosophy and science afford into the scheme of God's universe seem intended, not so much to warn us of a future state to which we are destined, as to counteract the influence of those passions and appetites which relate only to the petty objects that are immediately before us, and to the concerns of the moment. *They answer a useful purpose,* *then, in the economy of this life, and have no visible necessary reference to that which is to come.* If the only purpose of reason were to take the place of instinct, in guiding us to the proper mode of satisfying our bodily wants, then, indeed, we might expect that curiosity would be limited to those things which immediately affect our temporal well-being. But if a moral end is superadded, if self-improvement is desirable for its own sake and in any stage of being, then there is an obvious utility in rendering our curiosity boundless, so that the efforts and investigations to which it leads may tend to the unceasing, the indefinite, development of our faculties.* To what other purposes in God's providence this insatiable thirst for knowledge may be subservient, we do not know; it is enough for us to see that it is useful *here*, — that it enlarges the sphere of our enjoyments, sustains our activity, and dignifies our life. Surely we are not driven to the supposition of another, an untried, state of existence, in order to find any benevolent purpose, or any useful result, in causing man to thirst after knowledge as for hidden treasure.

---

* "If the present state is to be the whole of our being," argues Dr. Crombie, "why are not our conceptions confined to the sphere to which our existence is limited? Why are we capable, in imagination and in hope, of rising beyond that sphere? *Why have we a notion of eternity?* The brutes have no such conception. Why is it given to man?"

Surely this argument proves too much. We can form a conception of *infinite power*, just as well as of *endless duration;* but this does not prove that we are to be, not only immortal, but omnipotent.

In fact, our vague longings after indefinitely higher attributes than those which we now possess, are checked by the obvious consideration, that advancement in morals depends upon ourselves alone; that it is our own fault, if we stop short of a perfect compliance with the law of right; and that infinite wisdom and power are incompatible with the existence of moral weakness and imperfection. If we take this reflection along with us, we shall see that these lofty, and even irrational, desires, though they were never to be gratified, still answer a useful purpose, as they stimulate our activity and strengthen our virtuous resolutions. Some disappointment, some vain endeavors, are needed to teach us humility and the duty of self-examination. Here, as elsewhere, we perceive that the great end of life is moral discipline and self-improvement.

The goodness of God needs no vindication from the doctrine of immortality. — I need not dwell long upon the only remaining branch of the moral argument, — *the discordance between our moral judgments and feelings, and the course of human affairs,* — as much of what was necessary to be said upon this point has been anticipated. I do not believe that the moral government of this world stands in need of an apology, or that we must imagine another world in which its errors may be corrected and its imperfections supplied. Do not let us make the same mistake as the Mahometans, and believe in the immortality of the soul, only because we crave a sensual paradise, and cannot find one here below. You say, that the course of human affairs often does not coincide with your ideas of absolute right; that is, the good often seem unhappy, and the wicked triumphant. To remedy these evils, you would create an Elysium in which there should be no temptation, no suffering, — where there would be no call for benevolence, no opportunity for self-sacrifice, — and where, consequently, virtue would be a mere abstract conception, never a reality. If such a state be preferable to the one in which we live, *why were we not placed in it from the beginning?* why not admitted at once to the joys of heaven, without carrying thither any stains from earth? By applying the doctrine of a future life only as a solution of the problem respecting the origin of evil, we do not destroy the difficulty; we only push it a little further off. And, without this doctrine, the presence of apparent evil in this life will not seem inexplicable to those who can see the whole force of our Saviour's allusion to the righteousness which hath its reward, or who can penetrate the meaning of his solemn declaration, — "They shall not say, Lo here! or Lo there! for behold, the kingdom of God is within you."

The doctrine of Revelation respecting a future life. — I do not fear lest these observations should seem opposed even to that belief in the immortality of the soul which is founded wholly upon Revelation. It is certainly conceivable, that the *same* scheme of government, which is begun here, should be continued hereafter, when, though its essential features remain unchanged, its excellence shall be more apparent. We can conceive that the two periods of human existence should stand related to each other as childhood to mature age, the former being a preparation for the latter, and still so justly and benevolently constituted in itself, that, if existence did not extend beyond it, it would yet mirror to our eyes the perfections of the Infinite One. The commands of conscience, though of absolute obligation, are too frequently so weak as to lose their supremacy over the passions. Nothing could tend so effectually to increase their hold upon our attention, and to strengthen their influence, as the assured belief that the consequences of obeying or neglecting them will extend, and will be recognized by us, through an endless futurity. The din and tumult of earthly passions, the force of earthly appetites, which now obscure or drown their utterance, through infinite ages, will be hushed or will have passed away; and as we have formed ourselves here by respecting or contemning their authority, so shall we continue for ever. The incalculable value of a Revelation which should fully establish this great truth, cannot be more impressively set forth than in the few words with which Paley closes his view of the importance of Christianity.

"Had Jesus Christ delivered no other declaration than the following, — 'The hour is coming, in the which all that are in the grave shall hear his voice, and shall come forth; they that have done good unto the resurrection of life, and they that have done evil unto the resurrection of damnation,' — he had pronounced a message of inestimable importance, and well worthy of that splendid apparatus of prophecy and miracles with which his mission was introduced and attested; — a message in which the wisest of mankind would rejoice to find an answer to their doubts, and rest to their inquiries. It is idle to say, that a future state had been discovered already; it had been discovered as the Copernican system was; — it was one *guess* among many. He alone discovers who *proves;* and no man can prove this point, but the preacher who testifies by miracles that his doctrine comes from God."

CHAPTER X.

THE RELATION OF NATURAL TO REVEALED RELIGION.

Summary of the last chapter. — The object of the last chapter was to show, that the doctrine of a future life, and, for yet stronger reasons, that of the absolute immortality of the soul, cannot be made out from the light of nature alone, or by the unassisted intellect of man. Questions of fact come within the range of human investigation only when they relate to the present or the past; the future is for us a sealed book, except so far as we can determine what *may be*, from what *has been*, or can know directly that what *always* has been, always must be. We believe that fire will burn the flesh, and thus cause pain, because we have observed that it has done so; but the fact that man *has* lived, only establishes a presumption that he will continue to live *as he has done*, — that is, in this stage of existence, subject to our powers of observation. When this existence is interrupted by death, and he is wholly removed from our sight and observation, we have no antecedent fact on which to found even a presumption that he continues to live, though in a *different* state of being; for, apart from revelation, we have never known the grave to give up its dead, — we have had no experience of this other state of being. We perceive, then, that a future life is possible, but we have no natural grounds for believing that it is either probable or improbable.

I remarked, therefore, that the doctrine of a future life stands on the same basis with the opinion, that the other planets of our system are inhabited by beings like ourselves; it is a mere conjecture, which never has been, and never can be, either proved or disproved. It lies beyond the sphere of human knowledge; there is no evidence of it in nature, and the only proof of which it is susceptible must be supernatural. If we pass to a particular examination of the several analogies and presumptions which have been offered, from the light of nature, in favor of either of these opinions, we shall find either that they prove too much, or that they are wholly vague and unsatisfactory, answering rather as topics of declamation than as scientific grounds of belief. Thus, the analogy between birth and death affords just as conclusive evidence of the immortality of the whole animate creation as of that of man; since all members, both of the animal and vegetable kingdoms, have equally undergone transformations, or passed from one stage of being to another and quite a different one. The argument from the essential unity of our personal being, and from the fact that death is dissolution, not annihilation, proves the preëxistence, quite as strongly as the future existence, of the soul, — affords not even a presumption that mind is any more immortal than the ultimate particles of matter, — and, in fact, *proves* nothing in regard to either, unless we make the perfectly baseless assumption, that every absolute unit is essentially indestructible and ingenerable. The general desire for immortality, on which so much stress has been laid, I attempted to show, from an examination of the opinions of the ancients upon the subject, was rather a love of this life and a desire for its prolongation, than any natural wish for a state of retribution and endless existence beyond the grave. To assume, as is often done, that another life is necessary in order to make up for the imperfections, and redress the injustice, which are apparent here, is to assert that the Deity does not govern *this* world in righteousness, and therefore to afford very insecure grounds for the hope that he has provided another, which he will administer on different principles. That our curiosity is insatiable, and our aspirations after knowledge are so large, that, in comparison with them, the ordinary business of this life seems vexatious, and the sphere of our present existence contemptible, is a fact of immense importance for the moral education of man, and thus answers so useful a purpose here, that it affords no clear indication of what is to be hereafter.

Revelation teaches something more than the light of nature. — Christianity, then, is not a *mere* republication of the doctrines of Natural Religion. Apart from its precepts, and its communication of abstract truth as to the relations which connect man with the Deity, it has revealed to the world a fact of momentous interest, of which the human intellect alone never could obtain any satisfactory assurance, and which is better calculated than any other, to exert a salutary influence on the life and character. Our conscious being, our hopes, and the consequences of our actions, do not terminate at the grave, but extend onward into a boundless futurity; this is now the assured belief of almost the whole civilized world. Most persons no more think of seriously questioning it, than they do of doubting the fact of their present existence. Whence came this general assent, this unquestioning faith? Contrast it with the dim conceptions and universal uncertainty upon the subject which prevailed before the promulgation of Christianity, and thus recognize the folly of those, who, "upon pretence of the sufficiency of the light of nature, avowedly reject all Revelation, as in its very notion incredible, and what must be fictitious."

How far Revelation must be coincident with Natural Religion. — In passing to a consideration of this topic, — the connection between Natural and Revealed Religion, the importance of the latter, and the nature of the evidence to be required in its support, — our first inquiry must be, What presumptions does the light of nature afford as to the probable character and purport of an immediate Revelation from God, supposing one to be made? As the two schemes come from the same Author, the one being revealed to us through the original constitution of our faculties, and the other by subsequent and special communication, we must expect that they will be coincident in design, or that they will work to the same end by the use of similar means. The law which is directly promulgated, cannot contradict, disprove, or supersede the law which is written on the heart, and indicated by the course of nature; since the purposes of the Almighty cannot change. It may enlarge the scope of the natural law, confirm its claims, and strengthen it by additional sanctions and motives to obedience. It may continue and complete, but cannot abrogate, the system which is founded on human nature itself, and guarded by so many wise arrangements in the outward universe.

Christianity fulfils these conditions. — Taking Christianity as the type of Revelation, inasmuch as its claims are confessedly paramount to all others, we find that all these conditions are fulfilled. Its object is the same, — the moral and religious education of man, the progress of the individual soul, self-attained, in purity and holiness. It reaffirms the moral law, which we have seen embodied in Natural Religion, in its whole extent, and sanctions the severity and absoluteness of its demands. Its precepts have regard, not so much to outward acts, as to the disposition of mind from which such acts proceed, and to the secret purposes of the heart. It declares that the great purpose of creation is a moral one, — that all physical arrangements and events, as we are accustomed to call them, have for their leading object to promote the growth of the religious element in man, and to introduce the reign of justice, purity, and love, of truth and righteousness, upon earth. It distinctly teaches the doctrine of God in nature, and of an ever-watchful Providence, referring all events, even the fall of a sparrow and the clothing of the lilies of the field, to the direct exertion of Almighty power. And lest man, in the infirmity of his vision or the extent of his prejudices, should fail to recognize the high moral purpose to which such events are subservient, their ordinary sequence is interrupted for his instruction. The winds and the sea, the eyes of the blind and the ears of the deaf, the very issues of life and death, are made immediately obedient to the voice of the great Teacher and Exemplar of mercy, holiness, and truth. *A miracle, then, is not so much a suspension of the laws of nature, as a more distinct announcement of the object for which those laws are observed.* It does not evince a change of purpose on the part of their Author, but makes that original purpose more directly evident to man, through a momentary but striking change in the mode of operation. It is a condescension to human infirmity, an opening of the eyes of the blind,

— not an alteration in the laws of sight, or in the purposes of God.

A revelation was to be expected. — This is the only idea that we can form of Revealed Religion, the only conception of it that is possible, since *revelation is itself a miracle.* It is the teaching of Providence, not altered in its purport, but rendered more distinct and obvious to human perception; the law proclaimed on Sinai is but an additional announcement of the law within the breast, though made more clear and impressive, and so more likely to obtain obedience. Knowing the weakness of human nature and the goodness of God, a revelation, a miracle, was precisely what man had reason to expect; and this would be true, though the revealed doctrine neither made any addition to the list of our duties, nor communicated any fact of such priceless value as that of an existence after death. Man had become so hardened, his passions had obtained so much the mastery over him, sluggishness and ignorance had so imbruted his being, that the Divine marks upon his soul were nearly effaced. The law of God, though knowable, was not known by him. What he needed, then, was not the announcement of a new truth, or the promulgation of an additional law, but some startling event to remind him of his origin, the purpose of his being, and his duty. The old law needed to be written in characters of flame, dazzling his outward vision, before it could sufficiently command his attention and subdue his selfishness. Knowledge was not difficult to be had, or unattainable; but obedience was not easy. Ignorance and habit had confirmed the dominion of sin.

What is called Natural Religion is in fact revealed. — But it is true only in one sense, and that not the most obvious one, that Revelation has added but little to the doctrines and precepts of Natural Religion, save the great truth of the immortality of the soul. We are accustomed to speak of Natural Religion as if it were a distinct system of faith, which actually existed and was recognized by men before Christianity was born, while it is still believed and practised by many who do not admit the evidence of any supernatural revelation. But it is not so. What we call Natural Religion, and what I have endeavored to exhibit as such in this work, never did exist before the promulgation of Christianity, or without the aid of a previous revelation,—not even a faint semblance of it; it extends vastly beyond the furthest point which the unassisted intellect of those early ages, or of any subsequent age, ever attained. What we call Natural Religion never obtained, as a distinct system of belief, generally avowed and acted upon by large bodies of men, in any country or in any age. It is not, and it never was, a rival of Christianity, or something which will enable mankind to do without Christianity There is no such thing as a half-way house to heaven. What goes by the name of Natural Religion, is nearly as much the direct gift of revelation to man, as the knowledge of a future life itself. Instead of seeking to eliminate the supernatural element in religion, and to merge Revelation in the natural system, truth requires us to merge the natural system in the revealed, and to look upon the whole as the fruit of immediate communication from heaven. At the time of our Saviour's appearance upon earth, the question for his hearers was not between the doctrine that he taught and Natural Religion, but between that doctrine and Judaism, or polytheism, or some other of the myriad forms of positive religion, or the so-called philosophical unbelief. Just so, at the present day, we have to choose, not between Christianity and Natural Religion,—for it is impossible to rest there,—but between Christianity and utter skepticism, or Mohammedanism, or gross and vulgar idolatry. This is the case so far as opinion, or belief, is concerned; and the conduct of men is a practical confirmation of this view. None but avowed skeptics as to all religion openly reject Christianity, because they cannot resist the testimony in its favor; but they fall back upon an avowal of it in word, and a denial of it in deed. So it must always be.

How far religion and science are natural to man. — But these assertions need explanation and proof, and I proceed to give them. Natural Religion, as I have endeavored to expound it, is a compliance with the moral law in its full extent and purity, *because* it is God's command, or through veneration for the

Divine character; together with a recognition of his presence and constant agency in the universe, and of his immediate government of all events, both physical and moral, with a view to the moral and religious improvement of mankind. Now what is knowable is to be clearly distinguished from what is actually known. The discovery of a truth is not the same thing with finding the evidence of that truth after the discovery has been made; the latter is always much the easier task of the two; it is the work of an inferior understanding. Strictly speaking, all science, both that which is actually possessed by civilized nations in their present state of culture, and all that is attainable by their future efforts, is natural to man; it was originally placed within reach of the human faculties, and was designed to reward study and investigation. What is called Natural Religion is natural to man in no other sense than as a full knowledge of the Principia of Newton is natural to the understanding of every child; that is, when the propositions are placed before him with their evidence, and brought within his comprehension, he immediately recognizes their truth and sufficiency.* Could he, therefore,

* "In one sense, and an obvious sense of the words, religion is a universal want of man. It is required for the development of his moral and spiritual powers. He is suffering, tempted, and imperfect; and he needs it for consolation, for strength to resist, and for encouragement to make progress. It is connected, not with any particular faculty or faculties, but with the whole nature of man, as a moral and immortal being, a creature of God. But religious principle and feeling, however important, are necessarily founded on the belief of certain facts; of the existence and providence of God, and of man's immortality. Now the evidence of these facts is not intuitive; and whatever ground for the belief of them may be afforded by the phenomena of nature, or the ordinary course of events, it is certain that the generality of men have never been able by their unassisted reason to obtain assurance concerning them. Out of the sphere of those unenlightened by Divine revelation, neither the belief nor the imagination of them has operated with any considerable effect to produce the religious character. The belief in these facts, if it exist independently of Christian faith, must either be a mere prejudice, or must be a deduction of reason. But the process of reasoning required to attain the assurance of a Christian, if it might have been successfully pursued by a very wise, enlightened, and virtuous heathen, never was thus pursued; and it

have discovered them for himself, without the aid of a teacher? The Saviour came to make known the will of his Father, and to guide us into all truth; — shall we say that his coming and his instructions were unnecessary, because the truth, when once revealed by him, shines by its own light, and needs not the aid of a miracle for its confirmation?

Even the principles of morals not evolved by reason alone. — These considerations are applicable, not only to the first truths of religion, in the proper sense of that term, but to the first principles of ethics, when viewed abstractly, or without reference to the fact that they are enforced by the Divine command. Because moral laws, when first presented to the reason, are immediately recognized as necessary and absolute truths, binding upon us from their own nature, of intrinsic obligation, and proving themselves, it does not follow that the unassisted reason would have evolved them in our consciousness in all their distinctness and purity. A necessary truth is not necessarily an axiomatic truth, perceived, recognized, and acted upon from the dawn of our intellectual being, before our instruction by others begins. For consider the parallel case of pure mathematics. The whole of mathematical science is necessary truth; all the propositions of the geometer and the algebraist can be reduced, in form at least, to a proposition of identity, or an equation, — to the assertion that $a = a$. Do we say, then, that the child needs no instruction in this branch of knowledge, — that he may be left to complete the task, which even Pascal only commenced, of making all the discoveries of Euclid over again, and working out the whole of a Mécanique Céleste by himself, without instruction or guidance? No; he is abandoned to his own efforts only when he has reached the term of other men's knowl-

is scarcely necessary to say, that, to the generality of the heathen world before Christianity, the facts, that there is a God, in the Christian sense of that name, that man is immortal, and that the present life is a state of preparation for the future, were not matters of religious faith. Nor was there any likelihood that, without Christianity, they would ever become so." — Norton's *Tracts on Christianity*, pp. 373, 374.

edge. And so it is in morals. The human race, in this respect was a dull and froward child, stumbling at the very threshold, spelling out with difficulty the first elements of knowledge, till a Teacher appeared who unclasped the book containing the whole science, and held up the ideal of virtue and holiness to the astonished gaze of the world; — the *ideal*, do I say? — rather the living example, embodied holiness, purity, and truth. But the lesson was too much for the comprehension of that age; and though the civilized world has been studying it ever since, it has not yet climbed to the height of that great argument. "The light shineth in darkness, and the darkness comprehended it not."

What is called Natural Religion, is rather the natural evidence, or the proof from the light of nature, of the greatest part of Revealed Religion. It did not exist before Revelation, nor has it ever existed since, as a separate system of belief. Instead of evincing, by the largeness of its scope and the excellence of its doctrine, that a revelation was unnecessary, it rather shows the breadth and solidity of the foundation on which Christianity rests, in that so large a portion of it, when once revealed, — that is, discovered, or made known, — is found to be in harmony with the other works of God, and so demonstrable by external or internal evidence, without reference to the extraordinary proofs that attended its promulgation. We may admit, then, with Bishop Butler, that "it is certain no Revelation would have been given, had the light of nature been sufficient in such a sense as to render one not wanting and useless. But no man, in seriousness and simplicity of mind, can possibly think it so, who considers the state of religion in the heathen world before Revelation, and its present state in those places which have borrowed no light from it; particularly the doubtfulness of some of the greatest men concerning things of the utmost importance, as well as the natural inattention and ignorance of mankind in general. It is impossible to say who would have been able to reason out that whole system, which we call Natural Religion, in its genuine simplicity, clear of superstition; but there is certainly no ground to affirm that the generality could. If they could, there is no sort of probability that they would. Admitting there were, they would highly want a standing admonition to remind them of it and inculcate it upon them."

What sort of religion existed previous to Christianity. — In arguing, that, in point of fact, we are indebted to Christianity for nearly all that is excellent in Natural Religion, it is not necessary to maintain that the human understanding could not, by any possibility, in any future time, work out a natural system of religious belief as clear and satisfactory as this. It is enough to urge, that the power to recognize and demonstrate a truth, after it has once been made known to us, is wholly different from, and usually much inferior to, the capacity of first discovering that truth; and then to notice the fact, that *the great truths of Natural Religion were not known and acknowledged at the time of the coming of the Saviour.* A tyro in chemistry can test by experiment the law of definite proportions; but the discovery of that law, which had so long escaped the researches of the analyst, was due to the sagacity and penetration of one of the most philosophical minds of the age.* The systems with which Christianity had to contend at its origin, and most of those which have opposed its progress since, were not rationalistic or philosophical in character, — cold and meagre schemes

* "All the truths of philosophy, all those belonging to the higher departments of knowledge, all those connected with the intellectual and moral progress of mankind, all those most important to our worldly comfort and enjoyment, so far as their recognition has depended on man alone, have required strenuous and long-continued efforts of intellect to effect their gradual development, their clear exposition, and their general reception. These efforts have been made by a few individuals, the instructors of their race. The processes of reasoning by which these truths are established, are now gone over and fully comprehended by only a comparatively small portion of men. But the benefit of these truths, the practical result of those investigations, are now a common property and a common blessing. We are wise through the wisdom of others. Human knowledge is the aggregate wealth of civilized man, not the peculiar possession of individuals; and all may share its advantages, whether or not they have contributed to it, or even understand the means of accumulation." — Norton's *Tracts on Christianity*, pp. 378, 379

of pure theism and rigid morality; they were positive, complex, and ceremonial institutions of polytheism and mythology for the multitude, and vague speculation or blank skepticism for the thinking few. Pure doctrine on isolated points of morality and religious belief can be gleaned from the writings of the ancient philosophers; but we find no traces of a system or general theory upon the subject, which does not combine with such doctrine a large proportion of what is puerile, inconsistent, and untrue in opinion, as well as immoral and degrading in practice. Christianity has had scarcely less influence upon the opinions of its avowed opponents, than of its friends. Within a century or two after its origin, a striking change became apparent in the tone of pagan speculation in those countries where the new religion had been preached; the breadth and purity of its doctrine had affected, as it were, the moral atmosphere, and many inhaled some measure of its clearness and truth, who were perhaps ignorant of the source whence they came. It is hardly too much to say, that traces of this silent and indirect influence may be discerned even in the writings of Plutarch and Seneca, who were very nearly contemporary with the founder of Christianity, though they may never have heard his name. Three centuries later, in the works, as well as the character and conduct, of Julian, the apostate emperor, the irresistible directing power of that religion which he repudiated is strikingly manifest. He could not wholly put off the virtues or discard the ideas which he had learned from Christianity, even when his fickle and vainglorious spirit had carried him back to the idolatrous belief of his ancestors. His clemency and moderation, no less than the manner in which he modified and explained away the more extravagant points in the old pagan mythology, showed the effects of the faith which he rejected.

Christianity first revealed the paternal character of God.— Christianity was not a mere republication of Natural Religion, but an early publication of truths which are so far natural to man, that though he could gain but very imperfect glimpses of them without the aid of a teacher, yet, when taught, they appear both evident and familiar, so that we can hardly persuade ourselves that they did not form part of the original furniture of the soul. What doctrine, for instance, appears more evident to reason, or better suited to form the groundwork of a religious system, than that of the paternal character of God? It seems an immediate inference from the belief that he created all things, and that he governs all with constant care and never-failing love. Yet in what religion, or what scheme of philosophical belief, that existed previously to Christianity, — always excepting Judaism, which, for the purposes of this argument, may be considered as merely introductory or preparatory to Christianity, — was the Deity ever distinctly represented under this most intimate and engaging relation? I do not say that the epithet of Father was never applied to any of the deities in the complex scheme of Grecian mythology; Jupiter was called "the father of men and gods." But this was merely one mode of indicating his supremacy, just as a modern prince is called the father of his people; the idea was never made the basis of the worship of Olympian Jove, who was himself represented as the son of Saturn, and as born and nursed in Crete. If ever the lame speculations of a few philosophical minds struggled up to some faint and imperfect conception of the Infinite One, the Creator and Ruler of the heavens and the earth, they dared not add the belief that he watched over his offspring even as an earthly parent careth for his children. The most sublime conception of him which they obtained was the Epicurean one, according to which, he sits apart from creation, eternal, supremely happy, and totally indifferent to the concerns of earth; he was to be worshipped, if at all, on account of the excellence of his nature, and not because he did either good or harm to men. Compare this with the Jewish idea of Jehovah, or with the Christian conception of Our Father in heaven.

The earliest religious doctrines of mankind. — In examining the relation of Natural to Revealed Religion, we must distinguish between what have been called the *logical* and the *chronological* order of our ideas. Of course, we cannot be convinced of the truth of a revelation, until we have proof of the existence of that Being from whom alone a revelation can proceed. We must know, also, that he possesses such attributes as are reconcilable with the idea of his manifestation of himself to men. Bu; this is the order of reason, not of time. Historically speaking, whatever worthy conceptions men possess of the nature of the Supreme Being, and the character of his government, were derived from revelation alone. The word of God first makes known the doctrine, which we then verify from the light of nature. We have already seen that polytheism is the *natural* commencement of man's religious faith, just as infancy is necessarily antecedent to manhood. It is the natural product of the religious sentiment, when not guided by revelation nor disciplined by mental culture, seeking everywhere for a Deity, and finding one in every forest, stream, or star, or in the unknown cause of every stupendous event in the physical universe.

"In proportion," says Hume, "as any man's course of life is governed by accident, we always find that he increases in superstition, as may particularly be observed of gamesters and sailors, who, though of all mankind the least capable of serious reflection, abound most in frivolous and superstitious apprehensions. All human life, especially before the institution of order and good government, being subject to fortuitous accidents, it is natural that superstition should prevail everywhere in barbarous ages, and put men on the most earnest inquiry concerning those invisible powers who dispose of their happiness or misery. Ignorant of astronomy and the anatomy of plants and animals, and too little curious to observe the admirable adjustment of final causes, they remain still unacquainted with a First and Supreme Creator, and with that infinitely Perfect Spirit, who alone, by his almighty will, bestowed order on the whole frame of nature. Such a magnificent idea is too big for their narrow conceptions, which can neither observe the beauty of the work, nor comprehend the grandeur of its Author. They suppose their deities, however potent and invisible, to be nothing but a species of human creatures, perhaps raised from among mankind, and retaining all human passions and appetites, together with corporeal limbs and organs."

Hebrew contrasted with pagan theology. — Accordingly

throughout the night of ages that preceded modern civilization, polytheism was the prevailing faith of mankind, as it is still of those tribes and races upon whom the light of Christianity has not dawned. The classic nations of antiquity erected altars and temples to that crowd of vindictive and obscene gods and goddesses, whom all the glories of Grecian poetry and art could not ennoble, nor all the refinements of modern speculation allegorize into decency. Egypt bowed down before its deified dogs, cats, and bulls. The Magians worshipped fire, or divided their homage between Oromasdes and Arimanes, which are but synonymes for the Good Spirit and the Evil One. In India, the dreamy and meditative spirit of the people forged monstrous and incoherent schemes of theology and cosmogony, which can be fitly characterized only in the language of Hume, as "the playful whimsies of monkeys in human shape." In this long and dreary night, one race alone — and that by no means the one most distinguished for refinement, learning, or acuteness, — upheld the torch of a spiritual faith and a belief in the one true God. The Hebrew theology appears in those remote ages, amid the otherwise universal prevalence of the grossest idolatry, as a miraculous light "streaking the darkness radiantly." I do not need here to insist upon any thing in the literature or the history of this wonderful people, which has been called into doubt by the refinements of modern skepticism. I throw overboard for the present to the infidel the Book of Genesis, and all the contested points in the history of the Jews. I look only to the Psalms, which, as products of the Hebrew mind, of a very high antiquity, whether written by David or not, no unbeliever has ever thought of questioning. Contrast their pure and sublime monotheism with the theogony of Homer and Hesiod, with the popular gods of Egypt and India; and account for it, if you can, consistently with the laws of the human mind, and the history of human progress in civilization, philosophy, and religion, without the aid of immediate inspiration or an antecedent Revelation. We may consider the appearance of these sacred poems — in order to take nothing for granted which is liable to dispute — as a phenomenon in history, with a date as unsettled, if you will, as that of the Iliad and Odyssey, but certainly not more so, — and surely of an antiquity not much inferior to that of these two renowned products of the Greek intellect. Their genuineness, that is, their exclusively Hebrew origin and character, is as unquestionable as the Greek origin of the two epics that record the wrath of Achilles and the wanderings of Ulysses. To make the comparison more particular, take only the nineteenth Psalm, from its sublime exordium, — "The heavens declare the glory of God, and the firmament showeth his handywork," — down to the pure and refined morality of its close, — "Cleanse thou me from *secret* faults; keep back thy servant also from *presumptuous* sins, let them have no dominion over me; but let the words of my mouth and the *meditations of my heart* be acceptable in thy sight, O Lord, my strength and my redeemer." Compare such conceptions of the nature of the Supreme Being, and of the conduct which he requires of his creatures, with the purest and loftiest ideas upon the subject which all pagan antiquity can offer; and then say, if the doctrine of the Psalms can be referred to the *unaided* intellect of the Jews at that early period.

The Jews unfitted to discover moral and religious truth for themselves. — All that we know of the history and character of this strange people is calculated to increase our wonder at the phenomenon. Their intellect was not comparable with that of the Greeks for quickness, sagacity, and refinement; other Oriental nations equalled, if they did not surpass, them in depth and seriousness of thought. They were feeble in war, and not distinguished in commerce or the arts of peace; they were ignorant and perverse, restless and wandering in their inclinations, and prone to idolatry. Whence came their sacred books, their Psalmists and their Prophets? Their existence, unless we admit the reality of a special Revelation, the fruits of which were for a time confined to this people, is the most inexplicable problem in history.

It is certain then, that *the earliest profession upon earth of pure doctrine in religion, was not the fruit of human speculation and research* in the department of what is called Natural Theology. Neither at the period to which their sacred writings belong, nor at any other, was the Jewish intellect capable of proving, from the light of nature alone, the dogmas which it held and taught. There are no traces preserved of any attempts made by them in this direction. Theirs was not an active, curious, and investigating spirit, for ever pondering over the problems presented by God, man, and the universe. They were mere children in matters of speculation, the holders of a doctrine which they always very imperfectly comprehended, but which they held with an implicit and unreasoning faith, or cast aside under the force of temptation, but not from a skeptical turn of mind. The tone adopted by their prophets and religious teachers was mandatory and authoritative, not argumentative or philosophical. They asserted, commanded, or threatened; they did not stop to prove, for the people were incapable of understanding. The refinements of speculation and the subtilties of logic were for a different race or a subsequent age. The Jews appear throughout their history in a condition of tutelage; they were led by the hand like children, and never aspired to take the lead for themselves. They were not an enterprising, not a conquering or a proselyting people; though impatient of foreign dominion, they did not seek to impose their yoke upon others. Who ever heard of a Jew attempting to make converts to Judaism, or even to give a reason for the faith that was in him, other than that it was the patrimony of his nation, and that it came down from heaven? With all their stubbornness and perversity, the law and the doctrine which they professed during so many ages, modified their whole being, and moulded their national character. The religion formed the people, the people were incapable of forming the religion; it was imparted to them, for they could not create it. Hence the fine remark of Pascal: "I find no reason to doubt the truth of the Hebrew Scripture; for there is a great difference between a book which an individual makes and throws among a people, and a book which of itself makes a people. We must acknowledge that the book is at least as old as the nation." And again, — "This race is remarkable not only for its antiquity; it is singular also for its duration, for it has come down even to the present day. While the nations of Greece and Italy, Sparta, Athens, and Rome, which began long afterwards, ended long ago, these alone continue to exist; and in spite of the efforts of so many powerful monarchs, who have a hundred times undertaken to destroy them, as history testifies, and as it is easy to believe from the natural course of events, they have been preserved, a separate and peculiar people, through the long lapse of ages; coming down from the earliest period to the latest, their history comprises within itself all other histories."

The connection of Hebrew with Christian doctrine. — I have dwelt thus long upon the characteristics of this remarkable race, because we find in them the single instance which human history affords, of a people professedly formed and guided from its origin by special Revelation, while all the other nations of the earth have attempted to find their way by the light of nature. Their history, also, is specially interesting to us; for, as Christians, we are the spiritual offspring of the Jews, though Christian nations have been sorely reluctant to acknowledge the fact. Ours, also, are Moses and the prophets, — ours are Samuel and David, Isaiah and Ezekiel. The light in the midst of which we live, is but a rekindling and revivifying of that which appeared to the great Hebrew lawgiver in the burning bush, and which shone from the top of Sinai; and though the brightness of the former is lost in the glory of the latter dispensation, our conduct is still regulated by the decalogue which formed the heart of the Hebrew law. This is striking evidence of the original purity and excellence of that law; *it has stood the test of three thousand years.* Skepticism and wickedness, the rivalry of false religions and the refinements of a vain philosophy, have not prevailed against it. *Of what other scheme of ethical and religious doctrine,* having its origin either in Egypt, India, Greece, or Rome, *can the like be said,* with the addition that it can stand the scrutiny of this skeptical and curious age, with all its advantages of learning and civilization? What other system of popular belief, held and practised for centuries by a whole nation, and thus clearly distinguishable from the speculations of an individual, and even from the dogmas of a sect, has lived so long and triumphs still?

Characteristics of the Jewish race. — We have the Jews among us yet, a distinct race, though they are no longer a separate nation; for the last few centuries of their history, they have been the money-changers and the peddlers of the civilized world. How has the glory departed from Zion, and the sceptre from Judah! But they are the same people still, alike restless in temperament and obstinate in opinion, as of old. We can see in them all the leading characteristics of their ancestors, — a stiffnecked race, who murmured even when the heavens were opened to them, and worshipped the golden calf, even at the foot of the mount whence the God of their fathers was speaking to them in thunder. We can judge how likely it is, that such a people should have invented, or discovered by the exercise of their own reason, the purest system of morality and religion that the world had ever known before the promulgation of Christianity, and have held to it for centuries, amid national distress and subjugation, and the sufferings of exile, while around them the most enlightened nations of the earth were sunk in the grossest idolatry. To the mere student of social and political science, who looks at history without reference to its bearing upon the great topic of God's moral government of mankind, the Jews are a mysterious race, and their fortunes are inexplicable. Their history is the strangest of any in the annals of the world.

How we first obtain our religious belief. — I have said, that the Jews received like children a faith which they imperfectly comprehended, and to which, consequently, in the earlier period, they often faltered in their allegiance. A light from heaven shone about them, and they walked in the midst of it, the figures of their lawgivers and prophets appearing glorified in that supernatural splendor; but the light which should have been *in* them was darkness. They could not have discovered, they could not prove, they could hardly understand, the pure and lofty doctrines which they professed. We are too apt to forget, that even now, the greater part of mankind, including the bulk of civilized nations, receive their religious system in the same manner. Even at the present day, in enlightened and Christian countries, where curiosity is eager and speculation is rife, men do not study out their religion from the light of nature; they are taught it; they receive it from their fathers' hands, and at their mothers' knees. So it must always be, with a system of faith that prevails among a whole people, as distinguished from the speculative dogmas or peculiarities of opinion which are the property of a few studious and inquiring minds. If we except the instances of conversion in mature years from one faith to another, which are so few in number as to be insignificant, it may be said that *religious belief is always received as a revelation,* — a traditional or historical one, it is true, — but *never as a natural science.* Observe, however, that I am now speaking only of those broad features which distinguish one religion from another, and not of the minor points of doctrine which divide sects and individuals; I refer to Christianity as distinguished from Mohammedanism, or Judaism, or gross idolatry.

When we begin to study Natural Religion. — The faith which is thus originally implanted in the soul may be modified, enlarged, confirmed, or shaken off, by the fruits of subsequent inquiry and reflection. But these later studies never begin at the original starting-point of human investigation; we never come to them without bias; we cannot wholly discharge from our minds the results of early instruction. We do not proceed from Natural Religion to Revealed, from deism to Christianity, though this is the order of reason and logic in the abstract consideration of the subject; but in the order of time, or the natural succession, we proceed from Christianity to the study of Natural Religion; — that is, after the spirit of curiosity, and perhaps of doubt, is excited, we endeavor to find what evidence the light of nature affords as to the truth of those doctrines in which we have been instructed from the beginning, "even as they delivered them unto us which from the beginning were eye-witnesses and ministers of the word." This evidence, for the whole of the doctrine to which such a test can be applied, is found to be abundant and satisfactory; the light from God's word. and that which comes from his works and ways in the material and moral universe, are found to harmonize and mingle into one. So sure is the testimony from the latter source, that these doctrines are seen to be capable of standing by themselves, and need not to be corroborated by Revelation. The deist subsequently unites them into what is called the Religion of Nature, and then pretends that Revelation cannot be true because it was not needed, since these doctrines are sufficient for life and practice; in his language, all that is essential in Christianity is as old as the creation. It may be demonstrated, he affirms, by human reason; what need, therefore, is there of a miracle to support it? Just as reasonably might he pretend, because a school-boy can now demonstrate a proposition which it cost a Newton years of anxious and patient thought to discover, that the author of the Principia did nothing for the advancement of science, or to increase our knowledge of the mechanism of the universe. He finds religion in nature, only because Christianity has taught him where to look for it. The proof of this is, that the greatest philosophers and the best men of heathen antiquity anxiously strove to discover these truths, which now seem to us so familiar and so cogent, but were not able. "For I tell you, that many prophets and kings have desired to see those things which ye see, and have not seen them; and to hear those things which ye hear, and have not heard them."

It is just as true, then, in the natural order of our ideas, or as a matter-of-fact, that Natural Religion depends upon Revelation, as it is that, in the order of logic, Revelation depends upon Natural Religion; for the latter, in its full breadth, purity, and excellence, never *has* existed without a Revelation, and we have no good reason to believe that it ever would have arisen independently of such aid, notwithstanding the clearness of its proofs, as they shine to our eyes under the reflected light of Christianity. The one is not so much a complement of the other, or a substitute for it, as a proof and a corroboration of that other. *They are not so much parts of one whole, as different modes of looking at the same truth,* though from one point of view we see more than from the other. Call it sunlight or moonlight, the illumination still comes originally from the same fountain of light in the heavens. The doctrine, that all things are moved directly by the finger of God, who governs all events, both in the material and the moral universe, with a moral purpose, rests, as we have seen, upon sufficient evidence, when examined by the light of nature alone; but will any one say, that your minds were not prepared for the reception of this truth by your previously acquired belief, that the powers and agencies of nature, as they are termed, were subject to the voice of Jesus of Nazareth? And conversely, does not his repeated declaration, that the care of his Father in heaven extends even to the minutest objects and events, for "the very hairs of your head are all numbered," render the natural proofs of this doctrine more cogent and acceptable? Natural and Revealed Religion, then, mutually depend upon and strengthen each other.

But Revelation goes beyond Natural Religion. — But the latter *adds* something to our knowledge; besides clearing up the prospect, it widens the view. It dissipates the darkness which the natural eye cannot penetrate; for it opens the portals of the tomb, and exposes to mortal vision the endless life that lies beyond. *Two things* are necessary for right conduct, — *to know what our duty is, and to be persuaded to act in conformity to it.* The former is fully provided for by the present constitution of things. The law is written upon the heart in characters that we cannot mistake, and its authority is proclaimed in the depths of our consciousness by a voice to which we must listen. Still, obedience is voluntary, temptations abound, and the appetites which stir this mortal frame, with the passions that keep the spirit in activity, wage a fearful war with the requisitions of conscience. *We need helps to obedience;* the inducements to right conduct must be strengthened by a fuller view of the consequences of sin. Transgression, indeed, brings its own bitter fruits along with it, even in this world; but our existence here is but a span, and the soul which has disregarded the authority of the law, may be indifferent also to its terrors, if our life is to terminate at the grave. But open the view beyond it, and let sin be seen bearing its own burden through an endless futurity, and even the most frivolous and the most perverse will be induced to pause and reflect. Nothing is revealed in this respect for the mere gratification of a vain curiosity. We know not how we shall be employed, with what bodies we shall be clothed, or how far the relations in which we stand to each other in this life will be preserved. But we do know, since we have received assurance of it from Him who spake as never man spake, that the same righteous God presides over both states of being, and will administer that which is to come upon the same principles of justice, mercy, and love, which appear in his government of this world's affairs. Then, to our eyes, the scheme of his providence, which is but imperfectly seen and understood here, shall be visible as a whole, and we shall know even as we are known.

CHAPTER XI.

THE NATURE OF THE EVIDENCE OF A REVEALED RELIGION.

Summary of the last chapter.—The relation of Natural to Revealed Religion was the subject of the last chapter. I endeavored to show, that the latter was not a mere republication of the former; for, besides adding to it the certain knowledge of a future life,—a fact of greater interest to human beings than any other truth whatever, the being of a God alone excepted,—it first announced those great doctrines which are now included under the title of Natural Religion, and which human reason is competent to prove, though it was not competent to discover. What now seems to us both obvious and demonstrable, has often baffled the ingenuity and research of enlightened nations for centuries, before it was first made known or generally recognized as a principle in science, or a rule of conduct.

Natural Religion coincides, as far as it goes, with the doctrines of Revelation; it comprises that portion — far the larger portion — of these doctrines, which are susceptible of proof from the light of reason and nature, without appealing to the authority of the Author of the revelation. Instead of Natural Religion, then, it ought to be called the natural evidence, or proof from the light of nature, of the greater part of Revealed Religion. The instance of mathematical science is enough to show, that truths of great comprehensiveness and importance, which are necessary or demonstrable, which, in fact, are reducible to identical propositions, may still be so recondite and difficult of discovery, that the finest minds may be successively employed for ages in laborious study before they can be ascertained and established. And even now, these truths are *taught* to the learner; that is, they are *revealed* to him as antecedent discoveries, and he is not left slowly to grope his own way towards them in the painful path of original investigation. When once revealed, the school-boy can demonstrate them.

Applying these general remarks to our particular subject, I remarked that Polytheism is Natural Religion; that is, Polytheism is the first and natural product of the religious sentiment and the unenlightened intellect. Reason shows that this is the probable result; history proves that it was the actual result. The doctrine of the existence of one God, the Creator and righteous Governor of heaven and earth, first had place in the religious system of the Jews, a people so peculiar in character, so inferior in intellectual power and cultivation to the nations which surrounded them, and which were sunk in polytheism and idolatry, that their belief in monotheism is inexplicable, unless we admit the truth of their history, which declares that it was the fruit of revelation. The contrast between the Decalogue and the Psalms, on the one hand, and the poems of Homer and Hesiod, with the sculptured gods of Egypt and India, on the other, is so glaring and marvellous, that no hypothesis but that of a special interposition of God in the affairs of the Jews will solve the mystery. The Jews were emphatically a God-guided people; their character, their opinions, their history, their present condition, are inexplicable facts, when not viewed in their religious aspect, and with the eye of faith. They are, in some sort, the living witnesses of the miracles that are recorded of their nation. They were always children in matters of faith, — wayward and stubborn children, too, — slow to learn and quick to forget. They discovered nothing for themselves; they were not given to speculation, either in philosophy, theology, or ethics. But the vital features of their religion have stood the test of three thousand years; and they triumph still, for they belong to Christianity. And the bulk of mankind are still, what the Jews were, children in matters of faith. They are not capable of working out for themselves a scheme of Natural Religion; with them, the choice lies between Revealed Religion, skepticism, and idolatry.

Antecedent probability of a Revelation. — There is no antecedent presumption against Christianity, then, on the ground that a Revelation is not needed. Reasoning upon the nature of the case shows, what is also demonstrated by the history of mankind, that without miraculous interposition and special instruction, the human race, even under the most favorable circumstances, gives itself up to false doctrines, false gods, corrupt morals, and a sinful and unhappy life. The antecedent presumption, therefore, runs the other way; it is in favor of a revelation. If the Deity is infinitely benevolent, we must *expect* that he will interpose to rescue man from degradation and sin, — to put him upon the right path, and then leave him to follow it or not, at his own good pleasure. It is no more incredible, that what are called *the laws of nature* should be interrupted for the instruction of man, than that they should be first established and generally maintained for his instruction. The latter we have proved to be the case by irrefragable arguments drawn from the light of nature; we look, then, with equal confidence, for the former supposition to be realized. If the Deity is always present in the material universe, vivifying, guiding, and moving all, we look also for his constant presence in his moral creation, to warn, to teach, and to govern mankind. And as the history of the brute earth, through its geological epochs, shows that the preserving agency, though uniform, is not mechanical or blind in its operation, but that one mode of action is, after long intervals, substituted for another, — the continuance of animal and vegetable species in the natural way being interrupted after a given time, the old species destroyed, and new races, new orders of being, introduced, — so we must expect that the history of man, or the annals of the moral universe, will show similar *periodic* exertions of Divine power and wisdom; the old mode of action, after a certain period, giving place to a new one, and the ancient dispensation being replaced by another, which, for this later time and for the altered circumstances of the case, is a more perfect manifestation of Divine holiness and love.

The creation of man himself, his first establishment upon the earth, *forms one of these transition epochs*, from which dates a new era in the history of God's providence. There is hardly a single fact in all natural science now more conclusively proved, than the comparatively recent introduction of human beings upon this globe, anciently tenanted only by plants and brutes, as it was at a still earlier day by plants alone; the old skeptical objection upon this head, that the human race, for aught we know, has been perpetuated through an endless series of generations, has been entirely refuted by the recent discoveries of geologists. What a signal and momentous interruption was here, of the former course of nature and the old dominion of physical law! What miracle of later times equals in importance that through which the reign of moral law began, and this world, till then a theatre for the display only of the *natural* attributes, was fitted to mirror also the *moral* perfections of the Infinite One?

Antecedent probability of the revelation to the Jews. — From the contemplation of this grand event, we pass, by a natural and easy transition, to the first recorded intervention of the Deity in the affairs of men, or rather to the first striking change in his providence, made for the purpose of showing that he is always with them, — to the revelation to the Jews. In one sense, then, it is no strange and inexplicable occurrence, when our eyes are first greeted by that mysterious light which we have traced shining in the midst of surrounding darkness; we were prepared for it by the antecedent history of the world, and by our ideas of the manner in which God governs the universe that he has made. The law given to Moses is but another step in the series, in which were previously recorded the successive introductions of vegetable, animal, and human life. Vast intervals of time, according to our conceptions, separate these grand epochs from each other; but these are as nothing with Him in whose sight a thousand years are but as one day. During these intervals, what we call the laws of nature hold without break; but if they are rightly considered in the light in which I have attempted to present them, as the constant effects of the Deity's immediate action, these laws themselves prepare our minds for their own interruption whenever an emergency may arise; because they are subservient to the same purpose which such an interruption is designed for, — namely, the education and the moral improvement of the human race.

What is the proper evidence of a revelation. — With this very brief view of the antecedent probability of a revelation, I pass to the only remaining topic, — the nature of the evidence to be required in its support. *First*, then, neither to the contemporaries of the revelation, nor to those who come after it, must the evidence in its favor be of *that direct and overpowering character which would compel assent and enforce obedience.* This rule results from the very nature of moral government, which excludes the idea of compulsion. If the heavens should be rolled together like a scroll, and the earth should give up its dead, all in direct attestation of a call to repentance, and an eternity of reward or punishment should be revealed as the immediate consequence of compliance or neglect, then there would be *no merit in obedience*, and the whole object of the revelation, the moral improvement of man, would be frustrated. Even the near and certain prospect of a future life, it has been well observed, would so far deprive this stage of existence of all value in our eyes, that we should rather be unfitted for its duties than better prepared to meet them. God does not thus deal with his creatures. If an earthly sovereign or master, indeed, should issue commands to his servants, he would take care that their meaning should be obvious, and that the source whence they came should be well known, so that obedience would be sure. But the object in this case, as Butler well observes, is merely *to have the thing done*, as such a master does not trouble himself about *the motive or principle upon which it is done.* But in religion, *the external act is of no importance whatever*, while the motive for doing it, or the frame of mind in which it is performed, is the great end in view. The improvement of character, or the perfection of our moral nature, affords the only reason why a revelation should be made; and in reference to this end, it is plain, that the obedience which is rendered only from awe, fear, or selfishness, is no obedience at all.

Different character of the evidence of Christianity at different epochs. — "The first Christians had higher evidence of the miracles wrought in attestation of Christianity than what we have now." Of course, they had; they had the evidence of their senses, while we have only the evidence of their testimony. But then, they were without that strong testimony in its favor which we now possess, arising from *its conformity with our preexisting views of morality and the light of nature.* It was a hard thing for them to accept the evidences of a spiritual religion, of one which aimed only at the conversion of the heart and the life, instead of a grand ceremonial law, backed by earthly pomp and power. The Jews, for instance, were very reluctant to take a kingdom in heaven in exchange for that kingdom upon the earth which they had expected their Messiah to establish, together with the temporal rule and sovereignty of their own nation over all others. The Sermon on the Mount seemed to them to contain strange, if not incredible, doctrine; for it was at variance with all their preconceived opinions; while, to the modern skeptic, it appears the most obvious and natural doctrine in the world. It is all self-evident, he says, or provable from conscience and the light of nature; there is no need of a revelation to teach us *that.* But was not a revelation necessary to teach such doctrine eighteen hundred years ago?

The first converts to Christianity had the evidence of their senses as to the reality of the miracles, while we have only historical testimony of their occurrence. *We do not expect that a revelation would renew or repeat itself*, through a continued series of miraculous occurrences, so that there should be direct evidence through all time of its truthfulness. Such an arrangement would defeat its own end, inasmuch as *the marvel that is constantly repeated, ceases to be a marvel*, and the miracle which is frequently renewed, becomes to our eyes a law of nature, or an ordinary event. A revelation is a fact in the history of mankind, just as much as the rise or fall of an empire, or the peopling of a newly discovered continent. We can have such proof only that it actually took place, as we have of the reality of all past events. There is a record of it, or there are traces of its occurrence; and we form an opinion of the genuineness and authenticity of that record, we seek to interpret those traces, according to the ordinary rules by which we investigate historical testimony. We do not expect that the validity of such testimony will be enhanced in the eyes of each successive generation by a fresh interruption of the ordinary course of God's providence. No one undertakes to impeach all history; no one pretends that we can be certain of nothing but that of which we have direct sensible evidence. If it were so, human knowledge would indeed be limited to a span. My point is, that the history of a revelation is to be judged precisely like any other history. "The supernatural reaches us in Scripture," says Isaac Taylor, "*not supernaturally*, but precisely in the same way in which all other matters, conveyed by document, reach the parties interested." In the first place, we have to consider the intrinsic credibility of the events narrated; and in the next, to weigh the positive testimony of their actual occurrence.

As much evidence for sacred, as for profane history, and more. — If the principles which I have already sought to establish are well founded, a revelation is intrinsically probable; the way was prepared for it by the antecedent dealings of God with men; mankind had reason to expect one. We come, then, to an examination of the external testimony in relation to it,

40

precisely as if it related to an ordinary fact in profane history Skepticism seldom assails the latter to much purpose, even when it records events that were contemporaneous with those mentioned in the Gospels, or long anterior to them. We ask, therefore, what principle justifies us in rejecting the truth of the Gospels, regarded merely as records of events, which will not also require us to consider the annals of the world as one universal blank, down, at least, to the reign of Tiberius? If we will not believe Matthew and Luke, how can we trust Thucydides and Tacitus? No one will dare to say that these historians show more of honesty, candor, and an apparent disposition to tell the truth, than must be ascribed, on the best internal evidence, to the four Evangelists. Then why is the narrative of the deeds and crucifixion of our Saviour unworthy of credit, if the story of the exploits and the assassination of Julius Cæsar be not also fabulous? The Christian may fearlessly invite the comparison of external testimony that is here indicated; he may challenge the skeptic to separate, if he can, the history of the origin of Christianity from that of the destruction of the Roman republic, or to show sufficient difference in the historical evidence to be a valid reason for rejecting the one and accepting the other.*

Let us look for a moment at the relative weight of proof in the two cases, confining our attention to a few centuries imme-

---

* "What is it then," asks Isaac Taylor, "which the question concerning the truth of Christianity supposes to be doubtful; or what is it which can be regarded as open to argument among those who are at once well informed and candid? Not the actual existence of Christianity as a visible institution, up through the course of time, from the present age to that of the Julian Cæsars. Nothing within the range of history — nothing mathematically demonstrated — is more certain than is the series of facts to which we now refer. Thus far then, we presume, there can be no controversy, or none amongst educated persons. Let church history be what it may in its qualities, assuredly *it is history* — and this, close up to the moment of its alleged origination. The testimony of the Roman historian to this effect, is by none called in question. 'Auctor nominis ejus Christus, qui, Tiberio imperante, per Procuratorem Pontium Pilatum, supplicio affectus erat.'" — *Taciti Annales*, xv.

diately preceding and following the commencement of the Christian era. How many events in the profane history of this period are now universally admitted on the *testimony of a single historian, though he could not have been an eye-witness of a thousandth part of them;* while, in the case of the Gospel narrative, we find *distinct and harmonious records by four individuals,* each marked by striking peculiarities of style and manner, and agreeing as to all essential points, two of the writers appearing to have been direct observers of the facts which they narrate, and the writing and publication of the testimony of all four being brought by irrefragable evidence within a few years, at the utmost, of the time when these events occurred! Is it said, that *incidental allusions in the contemporaneous literature* of the period confirm most of the facts mentioned by the profane historians? But the narratives of the evangelists have also a great amount of collateral testimony, in the shape of numerous epistles, written at the same period, addressed both to individuals and to large societies, making frequent allusions to these facts, even placing particular stress upon them, and betokening, throughout, a state of things which is totally inexplicable, unless these facts did really occur.

Momentous consequences of the establishment of Christianity. — But it may be urged in favor of profane history, that, as it relates to kings, nations, armies, and governments, the facts recorded in it were of universal notoriety, and of such magnitude and importance, that they left a deep imprint, as it were, on the annals of the world, and shaped and colored all subsequent events in the records of nations, so that to question their reality would be an act of silly affectation. Very well; how stands it with the history of our religion in this particular? The establishment of Christianity, viewed merely in the extent and momentous character of its external results, is the great fact in the history of the world, and from the time of Tiberius to the present day, this history is an inexplicable enigma without it. Let it not be said, that the world is still far behind the glorious stage of progress which the establishment of our religion seemed to promise for it, if that religion had been Divine. Christianity has no more been a failure than the primitive creation of the race. Sin, indeed, has continued to stalk the earth, and human misery to track its footsteps, ever since the expulsion from Eden, and even since the resurrection of Jesus Christ. But if we compare pagan Babylon, and Athens, and Rome, in their imperial magnificence and their moral squalor and wretchedness, with the present condition of the civilized and Christian world, with schools in every hamlet, with institutions of beneficence in every city, and with churches on a thousand hills, and still more with the glorious promise of the future, we may well say that the founding of our religion — viewed not only in the purity of its doctrine and its ethics, but in the compass and grandeur of its outward consequences — is a work as worthy of Omnipotence as the first establishment of man upon the earth. The religion itself, with its lessons of redemption and peace, its inculcation of love to God and man, and its revelation of a life beyond the grave, is worthy of "that splendid apparatus of prophecy and miracles," by which it was heralded and accompanied.

Apparently scanty means of accomplishing these great results. — I borrow an eloquent illustration from Julius Hare. "Let us cast our thoughts backward. Of all the works of all the men who were living eighteen hundred years ago, what is remaining now? One man was then lord of half the known earth. In power, none could vie with him; in the wisdom of this world, few. He had sagacious ministers and able generals. Of all his works, of all theirs, of all the works of the other princes and rulers in those ages, what is left now? Here and there a name, and here and there a ruin. Of the works of those who wielded a mightier weapon than the sword, — a weapon that the rust cannot eat away so rapidly, — a weapon drawn from the armory of thought, some still live and act, and are cherished and revered by the learned. The range of their influence, however, is narrow; it is confined to few, and, even in them, mostly to a few of their meditative, not of their active hours. But at the same time, there issued from a nation, among the most despised of the earth, twelve poor men, with no sword in their hands, scantily supplied with the stores of h ıman learning or thought. They went forth east, and west, a ıd north, and south, into all quarters of the world. They were reviled; they were spit upon; they were trampled under foot; every engine of torture, every mode of death, was employed to crush them. And where is their work now? It is set as a diadem on the brows of the nations. Their voice sounds at this day in all parts of the earth. High and low hear it; kings on their thrones bow down to it; senates acknowledge it as their law; the poor and afflicted rejoice in it; and as it has triumphed over all those powers which destroy the works of man, — as, instead of falling before them, it has gone on, age after age, increasing in power and in glory, — so is it the only voice which can triumph over Death, and turn the King of Terrors into an angel of light."

Specification of the historical evidence of Christianity. — We possess in great completeness the history of the early diffusion of the Christian faith, and can show the marvellous and — in all but one view — unaccountable rapidity of its progress, till it became established and coextensive with the Roman dominion. Within the lifetime of the contemporaries of its founder, it had become extensively known throughout the fairest and most civilized provinces of Rome. Besides the incidental evidence of this fact derived from the travels and writings of Paul and the other Apostles, we have the distinct testimony of two of the most trustworthy Roman historians, Pliny and Tacitus, both belonging to the first century, and neither of them being a convert to the new faith, that, in their times, men called Christians were imprisoned and put to death on account of the obstinacy with which they adhered to their religious belief; and this sect was so numerous, that the former writer, in his capacity of governor of a great province, applied to the emperor himself for advice as to the manner in which they should be treated. Of course, many of the persons thus punished had probably received the facts of the Gospel history directly from the Apostles, and it is not unlikely that some of the Apostles themselves were among their number. In the next century, the new religion had spread so widely, that the acts and writings of its adherents and opposers occupy a conspicuous place in the history and literature of the age. But little more than three hundred years after the birth of its founder, the first Christian emperor swayed the sceptre over most of the civilized world.

How closely the history of this progress of the Church is connected with the truth of the personal incidents related of our Saviour, appears from *the institution of the Eucharist*, mention of which is found everywhere in the annals of our religion ever since its birth. We have a vague account of it even from Pliny, — such as we suppose might come by rumor to the ears of a haughty Roman magistrate. Thus a slight and — to a mere worldly view — very insignificant event in the life of Christ, his supping together with his disciples on the night on which he was betrayed, may claim as great an amount of evidence of its authenticity as can be awarded to any event in Greek or Roman history. The fact, that a few poor Jews met together one night at table, in a provincial city, more than eighteen hundred years ago, appears on the page of history in a broader blaze of light than surrounds any one incident in the life of an emperor of the Roman world.

Under what circumstances a system of mythology is created. — The sufficiency of this mass of evidence, especially when compared with the historical proofs of other events that are admitted without question, will be more apparent, if we consider the general character and degree of civilization of the period when the facts to which it relates are supposed to have taken place. Heroic legends and fables belong only to the infancy of society. A system of mythology, properly so called, embodying the religious ideas of a people, can be created only in the faint morning twilight of civilization, and many centuries must elapse before it can acquire form and distinctness. It must be *anterior even to the art of writing;* for its only source is in the imagination of bards and minstrels, in songs and ballads preserved only in the memory, liable to frequent changes and additions, and sung at lofty banquets, or, while wandering about the country, by a class of persons devoted to this profession alone. Men are exalted into heroes and demigods only when there is not light enough to see their true proportions. Hercules and Theseus, Numa and Egeria, Odin and Thor, are proper mythical personages, gigantic forms seen only in the mist of ignorance, fancy, and superstition, when the songs of wandering bards are the highest intellectual entertainment of a barbarous people. When the art of writing is invented or introduced, this process of formation ceases; written copies can be compared with each other, and the additions to the poem or legend by the ever-teeming fancy of the minstrels are detected and thrown out as spurious, not having the sacred stamp of antiquity. The formerly fluid elements of mythology curdle into shape, crystallize into rigid forms, and the religion of the people becomes fixed, though their poetry, recognized as such, may continue to advance. Even Homer and Hesiod did not invent their theogony; the work in great measure was done to their hands. Written copies of their poems contributed to stay the progress of invention in the national religion, and to check and control the imaginations of the bards who came after them. The mythology of the Greeks and Scandinavians, the legendary history of Rome under the kings, may be faintly traced back towards their poetical birthplaces by the light of the traditions embodied in them; but *with the appearance of the first written record, authentic history begins.*

Character of the age in which Christianity had its origin.— But when did the Christian religion have its origin? Just at the close of the Augustan age of Roman literature, when the civilization and refinement of the classic ages, in fact, had passed their culminating point, and were already beginning to decline. The fine arts had begun to give place to the more useful; laborious and faithful annalists were taking the place of the more elegant, but perhaps less truthworthy, historians; diligent observers of nature, like the elder Pliny, critics, like Quintilian, ethical philosophers and dramatic poets combined, like Seneca, writers on law, antiquities, husbandry, military tactics and strategy, showed that an age of analytic and minute labor was succeeding to one of inventive genius and original and daring speculation. It was *not a credulous, but a skeptical period.* Law had become a complex science, and its practice was a distinct and honorable profession. Trials were held and facts investigated by shrewd and wary advocates, in a manner not unlike the sharp practice of our modern courts. The rude sounds of war were heard only on the distant frontiers; for the might of the Roman arms had long been peacefully acknowledged in the provinces and tributary kingdoms near the great heart of the empire. The arts, luxuries, and refinement of Rome were rapidly diffused in Judea, especially by the influence of Herod the Great, and were mingled with the indigenous elements of civilization and learning. The priesthood and the scribes were bodies of learned and intelligent men; the luxurious and skeptical sect of the Sadducees alone opposed a strong barrier to the propagation of marvellous and unfounded stories, or the rise of new superstitions. The people were fanatically attached to their ancient faith, were instructed from infancy in the Hebrew Scriptures, and looked for the august coming of their Messiah, under whom the renewed splendors of a theocratic government should far surpass the majesty even of hated Rome. This was no period, Jerusalem was no place, for the invention of a new scheme of religion, founded upon fable and imposture, — upon deceptions that must have been practised, if at all, before the eyes of acute and jealous magistrates, both Roman and Jewish, and of watchful and hostile religious sects.

In reference, then, to the transmission to our own day of the doctrines and the facts of the Christian Revelation, in its purity and completeness, we have all the evidence that the nature of the case admits, — all that can be required without claiming a continued series of miraculous occurrences, which would enforce conviction only by stunning the intellect, shaking our confidence in the laws of nature, and thereby unfitting us for the duties of this life. The history of Christianity cannot be impugned without giving up the credibility of all history, and maintaining that we can have no satisfactory assurance of the reality of any events but those of which we are eye or ear witnesses, — a degree of skepticism so monstrous, that, although it may be avowed from caprice, it cannot be entertained as a sober judgment, or be allowed to influence our conduct.

Character of the events narrated in the Gospels. — As the mere external evidence, then, vastly preponderates in favor of the sacred record when compared with the profane, it cannot be rejected for an assumed deficiency in this respect, and the only reason which is left for questioning its truthfulness is *the extraordinary character of the events narrated in it.* We are obliged to accept the four Gospels as faithful records of what actually occurred, unless we are prepared to maintain this proposition: — *that a narrative of miraculous occurrences, properly so called, under all circumstances, or whatever may be the weight of testimony in its favor, is intrinsically incredible.* This is the position of Hume, and it is one which every skeptic must assume before he can deny the truth of Christianity. Hume's celebrated argument is intended to show, *not that a miracle in itself is impossible,* — a doctrine which, as he knew, cannot be maintained for a moment,* — but *only that we cannot believe in one,* that an account or record of a miracle is essentially incredible; and on this point the believer joins issue with him.

How far the character of the events narrated affects the credibility of the narrator. — Before taking up the general subject, a preliminary remark is necessary as to the effect which accounts of miraculous events — even supposing that these are impossible to be believed — should have on the general credi-

---

* "The assertion that a miracle is impossible, and consequently, that such a miraculous intervention of the Deity as Christianity supposes is impossible, must rest for support solely on the doctrines, that there is no God; but that the universe has been formed and is controlled by physical powers essential to its elementary principles, which, always remaining the same, must always produce their effects uniformly according to their necessary laws of action. This being so, a miracle, which would be a change in these necessary laws, is, of course, impossible.

"But when we refer the powers operating throughout the universe to one Being, as the source of all power, and ascribe to this Being intelligence, design, and benevolence, that is, when we recognize the truth, that there is a God, it becomes the extravagance of presumptuous folly to pre-

bility of the narrator. If these accounts are interspersed in a record of other occurrences, which in themselves are thoroughly probable, are perfectly consistent with each other, and are supported to a reasonable extent by collateral testimony, and if the reputation of the narrator for veracity in all other respects is free from stain, then we affirm that his reputation is not destroyed by these accounts; this is the almost unanimous judgment of historical critics. There is hardly one of the old Greek and Roman historians who does not occasionally introduce stories which are wholly incredible, so that no person hesitates for a moment in rejecting them. Yet he never thinks of rejecting the whole work along with them; he throws out the part of the narrative which he believes to be fabulous, and retains the rest; and it is from such reservations that nearly our whole knowledge of ancient history is derived.

Eye testimony relates only to the outward events. — But I go much further. If all the conditions just mentioned are fulfilled, and if the account of the miraculous occurrence is by an eyewitness, his narrative of this very event must also be accepted, even if we admit that miracles are inexplicable. The occurrence is complex, embracing several facts. The witness testifies only to the *outward* facts, to what he heard and saw; and these facts are not impossible. *The miracle consists in the connection of cause and effect between these facts, and this connection is not a matter cognizable by the senses, but is an inference of the understanding.* It may be the narrator's inference, —

---

tend, that we may be assured, that this Being can or will act in no other way than according to what we call the laws of nature; that he has no ability, or can have no purpose, to manifest himself to his creatures by any display of his power and goodness which they have not before witnessed, or do not ordinarily witness.

"The assertion, therefore, that a miracle is impossible, can be maintained by no coherent reasoning, which does not assume for its basis, that all religion is false; that its fundamental doctrine, that there is a God, is untrue. The controversy respecting it is not between Christianity and atheism; it is between religion in any form in which it may appear, and atheism." — Norton *on the Genuineness of the Gospels,* vol. i. pp. 254, 255.

that is, he may declare his *belief* in the miracle; but this *belief* forms no proper part of his testimony as to the outward facts, and therefore must not cause the rejection of that testimony. The inference may even appear to all reasonable persons to be quite irresistible; — that is, they cannot see *how* such events should happen, unless they were related to each other as cause and effect; but they can easily believe that the mere events themselves *did* happen.

A few *illustrations* may make this doctrine clearer. If you tell me, for instance, that you cannot see *how* a word, uttered even by Divine power, should open the eyes of the blind, perhaps I may agree with you; but if, when many credible persons seriously declare, that a man blind at one moment had good use of his eyes at the next, and that they were present at the time and saw the change, you say further, that you will not believe them, I shall have no great respect for the soundness of your judgment. Take another case; it is perfectly credible that a violent storm at sea should be suddenly followed by an entire calm, and that one of the passengers on board a ship should be speaking just at the time when the wind lulled. If one of the other passengers, a sober and truthful person, seriously informs us that this actually happened, we admit the possibility of it, and believe him without hesitation. After we have made this admission, he informs us, for the first time, that the words spoken at the critical moment were these: "Peace! be still." Is our knowledge of this additional particular to destroy our belief of the other events, which we have just declared to be perfectly credible? and is it not just as possible, in the nature of things, that the passenger should have uttered these words as any other?

Inability to explain the events does not disprove the fact of their occurrence. — My point is, that the testimony of the witnesses relates only to the outward facts, to what was visible or audible, and is always admitted to be sufficient when it satisfies the ordinary conditions under which evidence is received in a court of justice, or in investigating points of history, whatever may be the inference of the understanding as to the relation of cause and effect which subsists between these facts.* I have somewhere read a narrative, attested by several officers of the highest respectability in the British army, of the feats accom-

---

* Upon this point, it is well to cite the opinion of an eminent jurist. The following is an extract from "An Examination of the Testimony of the Four Evangelists, by the Rules of Evidence administered in Courts of Justice. By Simon Greenleaf, LL. D., Royal Professor of Law in Harvard University," and author of a standard work on "The Law of Evidence."

"In almost every miracle related by the evangelists, the facts, separately taken, were plain, intelligible, transpiring in public, and about which no person of ordinary observation would be likely to mistake. Persons blind or crippled, who applied to Jesus for relief, were known to have been crippled or blind for many years; they came to be cured; he spake to them; they went away whole. Lazarus had been dead and buried four days; Jesus called him to come forth from the grave; he immediately came forth, and was seen alive for a long time afterwards. In every case of healing, the previous condition of the sufferer was known to all; all saw his instantaneous restoration; and all witnessed the act of Jesus in touching him, and heard his words. All these, separately considered, were facts plain and simple in their nature, easily seen and fully comprehended by persons of common capacity and observation. If they were separately testified to, by witnesses of ordinary intelligence and integrity, in any court of justice, the jury would be bound to believe them; and a verdict, rendered contrary to the uncontradicted testimony of credible witnesses to any one of these plain facts, separately taken, would be liable to be set aside, as a verdict against evidence. If one credible witness testified to the fact, that Bartimeus was blind, according to the uniform course of administering justice, this fact would be taken as satisfactorily proved. So, also, if his subsequent restoration to sight were the sole fact in question, this also would be deemed established, by the like evidence. Nor would the rule of evidence be at all different, if the fact to be proved were the declaration of Jesus, immediately preceding his restoration to sight, that his faith had made him whole. In each of these cases, each isolated fact was capable of being accurately observed and certainly known; and the evidence demands our assent, precisely as the like evidence upon any other indifferent subject. The connection of the word or the act of Jesus with the restoration of the blind, lame, and dead, to sight, and health, and life, as cause and effect, is a conclusion which our reason is compelled to admit, from the uniformity of their concurrence, in such a multitude of instances, as well as from the universal conviction of all, whether friends or foes, who beheld the miracles which he wrought." — pp. 61, 62.

plished by a band of jugglers in India. One of the company, much muffled up, was suspended in the air, a few feet above the ground, seemingly without any support either from above or beneath. The officers were allowed to pass on each side of this person, close to him, and to cut the air both above and below him with their swords, so as to satisfy themselves that no cord or wire, however slender, supported the weight. Now if the witnesses on this occasion, highly respectable men, should appear before you and vouch the correctness of this account in every particular, there is not one among you who would be inclined to reject their testimony, and to set down the whole statement as a falsehood. You would accept the whole; you would admit the facts to be as they stated them; and you would then exert your judgment and ingenuity in order to determine, whether the law of gravitation was suspended in this case by a miracle, or whether some combination of this law with other principles of mechanics would allow such an effect to be produced without supposing that gravity ceased to operate, or whether some very artful deception was practised, which eluded the watchfulness of the spectators. Whichever of these conclusions you might adopt, it would be *an inference from the facts* as stated to you, *not a denial of those facts,* nor an impeachment of the veracity of the witnesses. Suppose you could not rest satisfactorily in either of these conclusions; — that neither your mechanical skill, nor your acquaintance with the arts and shifts of jugglers, would enable you to devise any rational explanation of the phenomenon; still, you would believe in that phenomenon, you would trust the veracity of those who told the story. Instances of this sort might be multiplied indefinitely. I cannot tell *how* the grass grows; but I am not therefore to conclude *that it does not grow.*

How we learn that a miracle was wrought. — So it will be in every other case. In one instance, the facts, the external circumstances of the case, considered in all their breadth and variety, may lead me to the conclusion that a miracle was wrought; in another, I infer with equal positiveness that the event was a mere piece of jugglery. You may attack the soundness of my judgment in either case, if you will; you may say that my conclusion is drawn from insufficient premises; but this is not impeaching the credit of the witnesses who furnish the accounts on which both my reasoning and your own are founded. Miracles are distinguished from jugglery, by the judgment of the hearer, not by the credibility of the witness; for we learn from the witness only what the facts were, and then put our own interpretation upon them. To try to limit the confidence reposed in reputable witnesses, or to deny the credibility in certain cases of any amount of testimony, not merely from our narrow views of what is possible, but from our power of devising a satisfactory explanation of the *modus operandi*, or of showing *how* the thing was done, is a foolish and groundless assumption.

I believe that Jesus "cried with a loud voice, Lazarus, come forth! And he that was dead came forth, bound hand and foot with grave-clothes; and his face was bound about with a napkin." It is for you to decide, in view of all the circumstances of the case, of the character and doctrines of Jesus, the life that he led, the men that he had about him, and the enemies who were watching to destroy him, whether this was a miracle or a piece of jugglery. Whichever way you may decide, the fidelity of the narrative, the truth of the account, remains unshaken; for it would be monstrous to say, that you would accept the strangest, the most marvellous statements, when there was even a suspicion that there was jugglery in the case, but would reject them, if the attendant circumstances made it probable that a miracle was wrought. Neither Hume's argument, then, nor any other argument, disproves the authenticity of the Gospels on the ground of the marvellous occurrences that are recorded in them; at the utmost, it affects only our interpretation of these facts, or the doctrines which we seek to establish as inferences from them. His argument, if it be worth any thing, is not a rule of evidence, but a principle of interpretation.

How much is proved from the evidence now adduced. — It is important to mark the breadth of the conclusion at which we have now arrived. The truth of the Gospel narrative being tried by all the tests which are applicable to the history of past events, and being found to answer all the conditions under which we admit the testimony of others as to the reality of occurrences which we have not ourselves witnessed, must be considered as established. The facts that are recorded respecting the origin of our religion the inquirer must believe; he may put what interpretation upon them he chooses. We are to reason upon these facts, therefore, precisely as if they were events of yesterday, which had taken place under our own observation. Jesus of Nazareth lived and taught, as is related; he set forth the doctrines and the claims which are imputed to him. At his command, the blind received their sight, the lame walked, the lepers were cleansed, the deaf heard, the dead were raised up, and the poor had the Gospel preached to them. That he did these works was the answer which he returned to John in prison, who had sent to him to inquire whether he was the promised messenger from God. He appealed to these works in proof of his special commission and Divine authority, and we are to decide, as John did, whether this proof is sufficient, — whether these deeds were truly miraculous; and, if so, whether they afford sufficient evidence that the doctrines which Jesus taught were a revelation from Heaven, — that the words which he spake were not his, but his Father's who sent him.

And here we might fairly leave the subject, having carried the inquiry quite as far as the legitimate boundaries of the human understanding will permit. There is a blindness of the heart, as well as of the intellect; reasoning may cure the latter, but it will have no more effect on the former than on the nether mill-stone. Any one who can believe that the writings of the four Evangelists constitute a faithful and true history in all their parts, and still deny the Divine origin of the Christian religion on the ground of mystical speculations and metaphysical subtilties, labors under an incurable disease in his moral condition and sympathies, and is beyond the reach of argument. But as waiving the discussion of miracles in the abstract might seem like an implied admission that there was an insuperable difficulty in the case, and this might affect the convictions even of those who did not know what the difficulty was, I have attempted to prove generally in this work, not only that there is no valid presumption against the occurrence of miracles, but, when the proper conditions are fulfilled, that there is a strong antecedent probability in their favor.

Why miracles have been deemed incredible. — Practically, the objection to them consists altogether in a shortsighted reference to the assumed invariability of the laws of nature. The improbability of a violation of law, of a break in the continuity of events, is gauged entirely by what would be the measure of one's own surprise, if, on the speck of earth which he calls his home, in his personal experience, which is but a dot in the history of the universe, there should suddenly be a wholly arbitrary and purposeless suspension of the usual sequence of cause and effect, — if the sun should cease to warm, the fire to burn him, or the water to slake his thirst, — if he should lose his eyesight without a cause, and acquire it again without a remedy. A man's sanity would very properly be suspected, who should now actually look for, or fear, such a meaningless subversion of the order of nature and Providence. His expectation would be akin to the folly of a child, who hopes that without industry or thrift some lucky accident will suddenly make him very rich, or some blind chance throw down the huge obstacle that now lies between him and the accomplishment of his wishes. But the silly longings of that child are hardly less philosophical than the narrow self-conceit of the man who errs in the opposite extreme, and would fain weigh the great epochs in the history of a universe in the narrow scales of his own infinitesimal experience. *Events are strange or marvellous, not in themselves considered, but in relation to the means by which they are accomplished, or to the purpose that calls them forth.* If men had talked a century ago of transporting themselves a hundred miles within the hour, or of sending a message in the twinkling of an eye to a place a thousand miles off, the bystanders would have supposed that they were quoting from the Arabian Tales; but railroads and steam have accomplished the one, and the magnetic telegraph has effected the other. And men do not stupidly sit still and marvel that these things are so. *The means are seen to be proportioned to the end;* the purpose and the want have created or founded the sufficient power.

Presumptions in favor of the Christian miracles.—In case of an alleged miracle, it is the part of reason to inquire, *first*, whether the circumstances are such as to render it probable that the Deity would interpose, or alter the usual character of his dealings with men; and, *secondly*, whether the effect to be accomplished by it, supposing it to be real, would be commensurate in dignity and importance with the means employed. We cannot believe that the usual course of God's providence would be changed, except for some grave purpose, or on some striking emergency. Hence we reject almost without hesitation the marvellous stories in which the credulous often seek an excuse for their superstition; while, on occasions of so vast moment to all mankind as the giving of the law at Sinai, or the resurrection of our Lord, to confirm the waning faith of his disciples, a miracle seems not only probable, but almost natural. It is because the purposes of the Almighty are unchangeable, that we believe *a law may be suspended for the same object which has hitherto kept it in operation,*—namely, the moral improvement and guidance of mankind. In the vast extent and beneficial character of the results produced by the Jewish and the Christian revelations—results which are matter of unquestioned history or immediate experience—I find a strong presumption that these revelations were miraculous, or that they came from God; and in the usual character and steadfast purpose of the Divine government, as it appears to the eye of reason alone, in watching the ordinary current of this world's affairs, I find what changes this presumption almost to certainty, even before examining the direct evidence in the case. Before we hear the witnesses, or read the record, we have stronger reason to suspect that there must have been miraculous interposition in founding these religions, than that there was deception in the case, to which I have alluded, of Indian jugglery.

Miracles more probable after the creation of man than before.—For look to the antecedent history of this earth, as it is chronicled in the very stones upon which we tread, and ask if the creation of a reptile, an insect, a worm, is a fit occasion for the special exercise of Almighty power, and not the redemption of all mankind from sin? Remember, that, upon the lowest theory respecting physical causation, the institution, the first establishment, of a new race or species of beings upon the earth, cannot be accounted for by the ordinary operation of the laws of nature, but we are compelled by it to bring in the action of a supernatural cause. Did Omnipotence, then, become weary only after God had created man in his own image, the noblest of his creatures, though unintelligent tribes or a desert earth through countless ages had been visited with frequently recurring tokens of oversight and protection, of a care which never slept?

What the human race would have been without Christianity.— Ask, again, as a means of estimating the benefits produced by these assumed miraculous displays of infinite goodness, what the situation of the world would probably have been, if neither of them had been made. Suppose that the law had not been given to Moses, and that grace and truth had not come by Jesus Christ, so that neither the Jewish nor the Christian religion could be counted among the elements which affect the condition and the hopes of mankind. How different would be the aspect of modern civilization, how faint the light afforded by human reason alone for the pursuit of truth, and how feeble the motives for urging men to the practice of all the virtues! Imagine the human race still hesitating between skepticism and polytheism, the doctrine of the one true God being still, as it was in the days of Plato and Aristotle, a mere speculation of the philosopher in his closet, and the great truth of a future existence and an endless retribution being, as it was then, a vague dream, a blank hypothesis, which can neither be proved nor disproved, like the supposition that the other planets are tenanted by animated beings. Suppose that an oath had no sanction, that the Sabbath had never existed, that there was no known object of prayer, that the practice of morality was not enforced by a Divine command, and that neither the hopes of the innocent nor the remorse of the guilty were quickened by an assured belief that the justice and goodness of the Deity would be amply vindicated beyond the grave. We are accustomed, perhaps, to think of the change that would thus be produced in our own feelings; but let us widen the prospect, and ask how the lot of the whole human race would probably be affected, and what the record of history must have been, if these appalling suppositions were realized. If the consequences would be afflicting in the highest degree, were men to give up the faith which they now possess, and which has already wrought its good work for eighteen hundred years, what would they have been, if this faith had never been established upon the earth? Carry this reflection along with us, and we cannot hesitate to admit that a miracle was highly probable for the establishment of Christianity. We shall open the record of its origin with a full expectation of finding that it was attended by signs and wonders, such as befitted the magnitude of the occasion, and its inestimable importance to the human family. Having vouchsafed a miraculous attestation of it at the beginning, we can believe that the Deity "committed its future progress to the natural means of human communication, and to the influence of those causes by which human conduct and human affairs are governed."

END.

www.ingramcontent.com/pod-product-compliance
Lightning Source LLC
LaVergne TN
LVHW020914110826
845150LV00004B/670

* 9 7 8 1 4 2 5 5 5 5 7 6 4 *